PHARAOH TRIUMPHANT

The Life and Times of

RAMESSES II,

King of Egypt.

K.A.Kitchen

ARIS & PHILLIPS Ltd – WARMINSTER – ENGLAND

BENBEN PUBLICATIONS – MISSISSAUGA – CANADA

MONUMENTA HANNAH SHEEN DEDICATA

II

(Handel, Semele, ii, 18)

To my Egyptian colleagues and friends

wa neb hir ran-ef

'Each one, individually'.

U.K.   ISBN 0 85668 215 2
Canada   ISBN 0 920808 06 9
3rd corrected impression, 1985.

Published in England by Aris & Phillips Ltd, Teddington House, Warminster, Wiltshire.
Published in Canada by Benben Publications, 1483 Carmen Drive, Mississauga, Ontario.
Printed in England by Biddles Ltd, Woodbridge Park, Guildford, Surrey.

CONTENTS

LIST OF ILLUSTRATIONS

MAPS

PREFACE AND ACKNOWLEDGEMENTS

This book attempts to sketch a vista of life against a spectacular backcloth of great monuments and stirring events. The centre of the stage is held by Ramesses II, pharaoh of Egypt, man of boundless energy, by turns stubborn, shrewd, kindly or harsh, and his remarkable family. Around them moves a host of other personalities, high and low. Men of integrity and distinction rub shoulders with rogues and tricksters; all within a wider international world of great powers, crises and wars, romance and the coming of peace.

This present work was born of a suggestion by Mr A.J.V. Cheetham in the 'Year of Tutankhamun', 1972; various unforeseen factors have delayed its appearance (first completed in 1974; revised since), and my thanks go to the present publishers for presenting it to a wider public. This book is offered for enjoyment, not study; those desiring technical detail beyond the brief notes at the end are referred to the writer's forthcoming *The Egyptian Nineteenth Dynasty*; the relevant hieroglyphic texts are mostly to be found in my *Ramesside Inscriptions*, I-VII (Blackwell's, Oxford).

For help in visiting Egypt for this book and other matters in 1973, my thanks go to Dr Gamal Moukhtar and Dr Henri Riad (former Under-Secretary of State and Antiquities Organisation chief); to Mr Samir Raouf (Egyptian Tourist Information Centre, London) and his Cairo colleagues; very specially to Mr Mohamed El-Dorry, Eastmar head office, Cairo; in Luxor, to the former Chief Inspector, Mr Ahmed Taher, and former West Bank Inspector, Mr Mamdouh Abdel-Zaher, besides the tomb-ghaffirs under Sheikh Nagdi Abdel-Ma'boud.

But the writer's personal indebtedness to his Egyptian friends and colleagues far outruns the 1973 visit. The dedication of this book gratefully reflects his appreciation of the immense helpfulness, innumerable kindnesses and warm hospitality of Egyptian colleagues and friends at all levels on repeated visits to Egypt during a decade and a half for my studies of Ramesside monuments on which this book in turn so greatly depends. I trust that each one of them may kindly accept my personal thanks embodied in this book's dedication, and find in it an encouragement in their own lives and labours.

During the decade during which this work has been in preparation, much kind help has been received from many quarters, and both author and publishers wish to thank the individuals and institutions named below for their kind co-operation and permission to use pictorial data in their possession; (apologies are extended for any inadvertent omission):

Alinari Photos (15; 30); Messrs. Aris & Phillips Ltd. (51); American Schools for Oriental Research (9); the Trustees of the British Museum (33; 45); the Brockhampton Press (47; 48; 50); the Brooklyn Museum, New York (69); Centre of Documentation and Study on Ancient Egypt, Cairo (19c; 21; 32; 54); Deutsche Orient-Gesellschaft, Berlin (26; 28); the Egypt Exploration

Society, London (46); Professor H.W. Fairman, Liverpool (49); Professor G.A. Gaballa, Cairo (42; 44); Institut Français d'Archéologie Orientale du Caire (51; 60; 61); Musée du Louvre, Paris (36; 73); the Trustees of the Metropolitan Museum of Art, New York (63); Munich, the Bavarian State Collections (52); the NASA Space Agency, USA (1); the Oriental Institute of the University of Chicago (14; 39; 40; 53; 72); School of Archaeology and Oriental Studies, University of Liverpool (4; 11; 56; 62); the University Museum of Pennsylvania, Philadelphia (16; 65). For preparation of many illustrations for this book, special thanks go to Messrs. Douglas Birch, I. Qualtrough and C. Roberts, Faculty Photographic Service (Arts/SES), University of Liverpool.

Illustrations the property of K.A. Kitchen include: 2; 3; 5; 7; 8; 13; 17; 19a; 19b; 20; 22-24; 27B; 34; 37; 38; 41; 54a; 57; 58; 64B; 71; 74; 75; Maps 1-4.

Kenneth A. Kitchen. Woolton, Liverpool, March 1974; January 1981; March 1982.

1: RAMESSES' EGYPT

First Approaches

Those bony southeast fingers of Europe, the rugged mountains of Greece, descend from barren heights through hard-tilled fields, wreath themselves at the shore in golden sands and plunge into the intense blue waters of the Mediterranean.

These gnarled 'fingers' point southeast, far beyond Crete, across Homer's wine-dark seas, to where the dancing waves finally break gently along the eastern limit of Africa's northern shore — the Delta coast of Egypt, two hundred miles of sand-bars and shoals, lagoons and salt marshes, low, barren and featureless under the burning sun, and interrupted only by the mouths of the sluggish Nile, darkening the blue sea brown with silt suffused into the eastward drifting sea-currents along the coastline.

At all times Egypt has presented this 'low profile' to visitors from the north, whether to merchants and buccaneers in fragile galleys in the thirteenth century B.C., or to the modern traveller by liner or jetplane in the late twentieth century A.D. But so bleak and unpromising a front is merely the modest curtain-raiser to a strikingly-different two-part stage beyond: the broad Delta and narrow valley of the Nile.

The front part of our 'stage' is the broad, level triangle of the Nile Delta — Lower Egypt — carpeted with lush green vegetation wherever the river waters reach. The apex of that great triangle lies a hundred miles south from the coast, near modern Cairo. On either side, the fruitful Delta is flanked by barren, tawny deserts of rock and sand which, near Cairo, hem in the river and its plain within a valley barely twelve miles across — the gateway leading on southward up the long Nile valley, Upper Egypt, the rear part of our 'stage'. There could hardly be a greater contrast in one land than that of the great Delta spreading as far as the eye can see, with the narrow, sinuous valley of the Nile, a ribbon of green only two to twelve miles wide, shut in for hundreds of miles between continuous deserts and cliffs on either hand.

The sole point from which these 'Two Lands' have ever been ruled effectively is at the point where the Valley opens out into the Delta, precisely in the district near whose centre stands modern Cairo. And barely fourteen miles south of Cairo, across the west bank of the river, once lay the populous city of Memphis, Cairo's predecessor and Egypt's effective capital for most of the three thousand years of her ancient history.

North of Memphis on its west bank and past Cairo and Heliopolis on its east bank, the Nile divides into the main branches and canals that water the fields and palm-groves, towns and villages of the Delta. Today, only two river-branches flow to the sea — a western to Rosetta and an east-central to Damietta. But in 1300 B.C., the Nile possessed three great streams and from two to four lesser channels to the Mediterranean. Thus, the 'Western River' of the pharaohs bounded the west edge of the Delta against Libyan sands and tribesmen, reaching the sea not far from the site of the later Alexandria (at Canopus). Here once were many of the most famous vineyards of the pharaohs who delighted in 'good wine of the Western River'. Through the middle of the Del-

1

1. *View of Egypt's broad Delta from a space-satellite.*

ta to Tjeb-nuter (now Samanud) flowed the 'Great River'. Its main branch probably curved west and north past ancient Buto, to the sea, while a secondary branch (today's main stream) flowed as the 'Waters of Amun' north and east past Sma-Behdet (a city of the god Amun) to the sea.

Ramesses' Homeland

But for our story the most important of all was the third, easternmost branch of the Nile, now vanished except for sections now occupied by later canals. This, the 'Waters of Re', left the main Nile opposite Heliopolis, city of the sun-god Re, going north-east. As the main stream approached Bubastis, abode of the cat-goddess Bast, the Sweet Water Canal ran off due east along the Wady Tumilat to the Bitter Lakes, being followed by the main ancient route to central and southern Sinai. But the main 'Waters of Re' went on past Bubastis as the eastern artery of the Delta, watering a region of rich fertility, including the Biblical 'land of Goshen'. Some 20 miles

2

downstream from Bubastis, the stream skirted the west side of the important township of Avaris, home of the unruly god Seth, helper of the sun-god Re against the wicked serpent. By 1300 B.C. this town had already had a long history. Five hundred years before, first known as Rowaty, 'Mouth of the Two Roads', then as Avaris ('Mansion of the Administration'), this town had already become the main focus for traffic coming by the south-eastern road via Tumilat and (more important) by the north-east road along the Mediterranean coast from the province of Canaan (Palestine). By this town, the 'Waters of Re' became locally the 'Waters of Avaris'. As they ran on north and east to the sea, past the border-post of Sile (now, near Qantara) by the Ways of Horus, they became at last the 'Waters of Horus', the Biblical Shihor, entering the sea near Sinu, the Pelusium of the Greeks. In the area between the Nile, Wady Tumilat and the Bitter Lakes extends a triangular wedge of desert, looking out to Sinai.

But it was the rich stretch of fertile lands, the 'Tract of Re' from Heliopolis down to Avaris that formed the pleasant cosmopolitan homeland of the family whose most illustrious son is the principal hero of our account — Ramesses, son of a military family that lived and served here on the eve of the thirteenth century B.C. Past here had marched Egypt's victorious armies, to and from Canaan and North Syria. Past here, too, Syrian merchants sailed up the Nile for Memphis, or came in from Sinai by donkey-caravan. Avaris itself knew from of old a babel of tongues in its streets, markets and offices. And, personifying the unruly elements in nature, Seth was easily assimilated to Baal, Hadad, Teshub or Tarkhuns, the storm and weather-gods of the foreign visitors.

The Southland

The road and river south from Avaris led on inevitably to Memphis, the ancient capital in its palm-groves with, as backcloth, the line of pyramids of olden times rising from the yellow sands against a luminous blue sky. Many and many a time, as prince and as Pharaoh, our man Ramesses was destined to set sail from Memphis or the Delta, ascending the Nile's stream up the narrow valley, to the southern capital, Thebes, or to travel the full six hundred miles to Aswan where the river tumbled down over the granite boulders of the First Cataract. As many a Nile traveller since Ramesses' day has discovered, such a journey discloses an ever-changing panorama of the life of Egypt along the river banks, the real Egypt only a few miles wide between its desert cliffs. Some 50 miles south from Memphis, the valley widens to a rich plain on the west. Here flourished the town of Ninsu (Heracleopolis of the Greeks). It guarded a break in the desert hills through which an ancient canal linked the Nile to the Fayum province and its lake — a garden-province, where the pharaohs from of old had frequently stopped off for brief holidays, fishing and fowling in the fens, rich in wildlife. Near the entry to the Fayum was a harim-palace, a pleasant resort for the pharaoh's sporting visits and otherwise a hive of 'cottage industry'.

But business in hand oftener carried Pharaoh — and now, ourselves — ever onward and southward up the shimmering river. Past Hermopolis (Khmunu, now Eshmunen), abode of Thoth, god of wisdom and writing, and the desert bay where the 'heretic' Akhenaten had mushroomed his new city (now Amarna) which the boy-king Tutankhamun had in turn given back to the sands. On past Siut, onward to holy Abydos, most sacred city of Osiris, god of the afterlife, and past Iunet (now Dendera), abode of the goddess Hathor, patroness of motherhood, love and jollity.

Until at last, after perhaps a fortnight's stately progress, the pharaonic state barge or the modern tourist steamer can drop anchor at the quays of imperial Thebes, marked now by modern Luxor. In this greatest metropolis of the south, Amun or Amen-re was truly King of the Gods in 1300 B.C. On the east bank, his vast temples (at Karnak and Luxor) were the greatest in Egypt. On the west bank, the memorial temples of the kings lay on the desert edge beyond the lush green plain and backed by the desert cliffs, these pock-marked by the doorways of the tomb-chapels of the nobility and screening the hidden Valleys of the Kings and Queens, where pharaohs and their queens slept out eternity, sheathed in imperishable gold. But, if bent on granite for statues and the like, the pharaoh or his emissaries would sail yet further south, on past Edfu, the eyrie of the falcon-god Horus, embodiment of kingship, through the narrows at Khenyt (now Silsila) whose sandstone quarries supplied stone for most of Egypt's greatest temples. And so finally to Aswan and the island of Elephantine, below the great granite outcrops through whose treacherous rapids — the First Cataract — the Nile tumbled into Egypt and out of Nubia. Here, the ever-changing tones of the river-waters reflected the contrasts of golden sands, glistening black granite rocks, blue skies and green plots topped by the greyish, feathery palms — a last oasis before the rigours of Nubia.

2. *Cliffs at Gebel Haridi, hemming in the Nile Valley in Upper Egypt.*

4

The Nubian Province

South from the delights and busy quarries of Aswan and its islets, the empire of the pharaohs ribboned its way for yet another 800 miles along ever-receding reaches of the Nile, between vast deserts, to a point barely more than some 300 miles north from modern Khartum in the Sudan. This incredible thread of a domain was Nubia, ruled in the pharaoh's name by the Viceroy of Nubia, and the lure was gold. The first 200 miles from Aswan to the Second Cataract (some 30 miles of unnavigable rapids) constituted the sub-province of Wawat (Lower Nubia). Most of the way, the river was fringed only by the narrowest strip of green cultivation, at times literally only a yard or two wide. At Baki (now, Quban) a small plain gave room also for a fort, and two temples — jut beyond lay the head of the dry valley of Wady Allaki, whose south-east course led into a parched, howling wilderness whence came 'the gold of Wawat'. Round a double bend in the Nile the traveller would reach a richer plain on the opposite (west) bank, site of Miam (now, Aniba), the capital of Wawat and seat of the Viceroy. At the northern foot of the Second Cataract the large fort and town of Buhen stood guard, matched by other outposts (now Semna and Kumma) at the south end.

The rest of the long course of the Nile in pharaonic control was the sub-province of Kush (Upper Nubia). Half-way on to the Third Cataract along that twisting course, Sai Island boasted the fortress of Shaat, the capital of Kush and a second seat of the Viceroy until Ramesses II established a new residence-town, fort and temple, 'Ramesses the Town' a few miles north at Amara West on another island. Again, gold was the magnet, as these sites adjoined the deserts whence came 'the gold of Kush'. Beyond the Third Cataract lay the agriculturally more fertile region of modern Dongola, neighboured by the wells of Irem to the west. Past this area, the Nile makes a vast double-bend. Halfway along that colossal loop stood Napata below its spectacular flat-topped 'Table mountain', the 'Holy Mountain' of the god Amun. This was the last major Egyptian outpost before the Fourth Cataract, and the Egyptian border-district of Karoy perhaps to be located near Abu Hamed and Kanisa Kurgus on the way to the Fifth Cataract, close to yet another gold-bearing district. Here, too, the exotic products of tropical Africa might enter the Empire from the mysterious lands yet further south.

This enormous realm along the Nile, then, from the distant cataracts all the way to the flat Delta coasts of the Mediterranean — to which were added the provinces of Canaan and South Syria — represented the Greater Egypt that came under the rule of the family of Ramesses II, himself the most spectacular king in pharaonic Egypt's long history. From Simyra and Beirut to Memphis, on to Thebes and along the whole course of the Nubian Nile to the borderlands of Karoy towards the Fifth Cataract, Ramesses' word was law for almost 2000 miles, the distance that any emissary of his would have to travel if he were ever to traverse the entire north-south length of that breathtaking ribbon of Empire.

The Backcloth of History : Egypt before Ramesses

Thirty-three centuries ago, when in 1300 B.C. the future Ramesses II was not more than a boisterous teenager, his native country was for him already a land of great antiquity. It had by then witnessed a pageant of history for almost 2000 years before Ramesses had even been born.

For him, precisely as for us, the line of mighty pyramids behind Memphis already belonged to *ancient* Egypt, and were even then a tourist-attraction for the historically-minded scribes of Memphis on their days-off from their office-desks.

The Egyptians of Ramesses' day were acutely conscious of both the vast span and considerable glories of their great past — glories which had reached a staggeringly brilliant climax and had then been dealt (seemingly) a nearly catastrophic blow within the very lifetime of young Ramesses' own immediate forefathers. They, therefore, had longed in their turn to see the prompt restoration of Egypt's greatness; and when their chance came to do so, they and he grasped it firmly with both hands, as will presently been seen. But, first, a bird's eye view of the tumultuous cavalcade of history peopled by men and events in the centuries before Ramesses. So shall we gain something of the perspective, the backdrop, against which he lived and of which he, too, had a real consciousness.

Beginnings

Far back in the aeons of prehistoric time, a vast stream carved the Nile valley out of the sandstone and limestone rocks of the north-east corner of Africa. With varying flow it cut the valley cliffs into terraces. With its silt and mud, it filled the valley floor with rich earth; and the triangular bay into which this ancient 'super-Nile' once flowed became likewise the broad, flat Delta, simply built of silt.

In time, the Nile's flow lessened to a stream more like that of today, the Sahara steppes desiccated to a desert, punctuated but rarely by oases, fed from underground water. Man descended perforce into the valley, to hunt, and in due time not only to reap but also to cultivate the seed-grasses, whence he could gain flour for bread as regular food. This bounty depended then (as ever since) on the Nile. Each summer, following the monsoon rains on the mountains of distant Ethiopia, the swollen streams of the Atbara and Blue and White Niles, scouring myriad tons of earth and silt, swept northward with their spoils and, during July to September, would flood the lower Nile valley of Nubia and Egypt, laying each year a fresh new carpet of fertile tilth on which the water and warm sun encouraged luxuriant plant-growth. Such was the annual inundation of the Nile.

The early Egyptians learned to expect the annual gift, and to fear its failure: a low Nile meant no water, no crops, starvation. They learned to channel the precious water along their fields, to hold it in basins to store it when the river retreated to its normal levels. In due time, village-communities perhaps came together in virtual 'provinces' under local rulers, and such districts into kingdoms, until by the 32nd century B.C. the long valley from Aswan to the Fayum entry was practically one realm under the Falcon-kings of Upper Egypt, wearers of the tall mitre known as the *White Crown*. In the Delta, a rival kingdom emerged, based on the early settlements in the west, at Sais and the ancient double town of Buto. These princes wore the *Red Crown*, a remarkable flat-topped cap with front spiral and rear projection upward.

3. White, Red, and Double Crowns of Upper, Lower, and all Egypt.

Inevitably a clash came, and in about 3100 B.C. the Falcon-king from the south, Narmer, triumphed over the north, and Egypt became one realm. The reign of the gods, and of the 'Followers of Horus' was now over (as Ramesses would have viewed it), and henceforth the pharaonic monarchy was begun. But the two kingdoms of valley and Delta were never forgotten; every pharaoh was 'Lord of the *Two* Lands'. Narmer perhaps adopted a new title of 'Protegé of the Two Ladies' (Nekhbet and Udjo, vulture and cobra, patron-goddesses of South and North) — and with it the name Meni, 'the Enduring', known to later ages as Menes, traditional founder of the pharaonic monarchy of Egypt, and of its capital Memphis at the junction of the Two Lands.

From this momentous event flowed the whole course of later Egyptian history. Narmer-Menes founded a line or 'Dynasty' of kings, and this was followed by another. These, the First and Second Dynasties of later records, are the Archaic Period of Egyptian history. This was a pioneering age in which the unified realm reached out to maturity in many fields: a full-scale administration to run the country, keeping its records in the pictorial script — the hieroglyphs — first invented just before the union of Egypt. A splendid royal architecture was developed, as shown by massive brick tombs in two series, behind the new capital Memphis and the ancient holy city of Abydos. Development of the fine arts flowered in exquisite jewellery, marvellous vases carved from the hardest stones, and delicate ivory-work from royal furnishings.

First Brilliance of the Old Kingdom

After the centuries of growth and growing-pains, a new line of pharaohs, the Third Dynasty, ushered in Egypt's first age of superlative achievement: the Old Kingdom or 'Pyramid Age' of the 3rd to 6th Dynasties, about 2700 to 2200 B.C. Early in the Third Dynasty, king Djoser and his able minister Imhotep erected the first monumental stone buildings in the world — the Step Pyramid in its vast enclosure of satellite buildings, a tomb and palace for eternity in glistening white stone, the new technology of the age. Good king Snofru, founder of the Fourth Dynasty, built himself two pyramids — this time, with smooth sides, not steps. Henceforth, the pharaoh's soul ascended a ramp like the sun's rays, not a stairway, to heaven. His son Kheops built the Great Pyramid, vastest of all, at Giza to the north-west of Memphis. Of his sons, Hardjedef became a famous sage like Imhotep, and Khephren as king built the Second Pyramid at Giza, carving a rock knoll near his temple into a colossal guardian Sphinx, with the king's head upon a lion's body. And the other arts of civilization matched the pyramids of these giants among kings. Later kings sought security in and for their pyramids not by size but by magic rituals (Pyramid Texts) engraved within the innermost rooms. Egypt's power already reached up the Nile into Nubia to the Second Cataract if not beyond. Expeditions sailed to Byblos on the Syrian coast to fetch the cedars of Lebanon. In Sinai was mined copper and turquoise. As time passed, royal power was increasingly widely shared across an ever more elaborate administration; local provincial governors in Upper Egypt became more independent in attitude. Finally, under a combination of pressures from royal weakness and local ambitions within and would-be settlers from Palestine without, the Egyptian state cracked and crumbled at the end of the 94-year reign of Pepi II (enthroned as a boy of six). Thereafter, shadowy kings reigned rather than ruled from Memphis (7th - 8th Dynasties), low Niles brought famine, Asiatics penetrated the Delta. A new line of kings from Ninsu near the Fayum claimed the sceptre (9th - 10th Dynasties), gained recognition and recovered the east Delta. But in the far south a line of princes broke away as a separate little state based on the town of Thebes which thus entered Egyptian history.

Renewed Vitality in the Middle Kingdom

So, by 2100 BC there were once again (as a thousand years before) two Egypts. And once more, the kings of the south conquered the north, when the Theban king Mentuhotep II restored the unity of Egypt by eliminating the last ruler of the Tenth Dynasty, about 2030 B.C. Later Thebans viewed him as a second founder of Egypt, comparable to Menes. In Thebes, before the west bank cliffs he built his tomb and memorial temple to which the image of Amun was carried by boat and procession each year — the beginnings of the Festival of the Valley, so splendid in later days (Chapter 8).

But soon after the great king's death, more low Niles and troubles over the succession brought the throne to the vizier Amenemhat (I), who thus founded a new line, the able Twelfth Dynasty which restored the unity, prosperity and power of Egypt (absolute rule to the Second Cataract in Nubia), for 200 years, 1991 - 1786 B.C. Thebes was not suited to be capital of a reunited Egypt, so Amenemhat founded a new administrative centre, Itjet-Tawy ('Grasping the Two Lands') just south from Memphis. The new dynasty survived dangerous opposition at first (using literary propaganda as one of its counter-weapons), but gradually replaced the too-powerful local governors of provinces by more pliant royal officials. Sesostris I and III occupied Nubia with fortresses; Amenemhat III developed agriculture and the Fayum. All went so well.

Until the mainspring broke . . . A new royal line, the Thirteenth Dynasty, saw a rapid succession of kings with power passing to a more stable series of viziers. Political power declined, local rulers showed themselves in the Delta. And again, Asiatics penetrated Egypt. At length one of their princes took over not only the east Delta and its vital centre of Avaris but by coup d'état made himself pharaoh at Memphis and Itjet-Tawy, reducing the Thirteenth Dynasty to vassal-rulers at Thebes in the south, about 1650 B.C. This line of six foreign kings was the Fifteenth or 'Hyksos' Dynasty, from the Egyptian term for 'rulers of foreign countries'. They favoured Seth, god of Avaris, so like the Western-Asiatic storm-gods. With Hyksos in the north, Thebans in the south, and local princelings in Nubia, there were three 'Egypts' by 1600 B.C. Once more, tensions between the rival states led to conflict. Again, for the third time, southern princes took the lead. Seqenenre Tao II quarrelled with the north, then his son Kamose struck at the Hyksos ruler Apopi in a brief, brilliant campaign, recovering most of Egypt south of Memphis, and perhaps raiding very briefly to Avaris itself before returning jubilantly to Thebes. But Kamose died before he could follow-up his advantage, and it was through his brother Ahmose I that the reunion of Egypt was achieved for the second time by Theban kings.

The Glories of Empire : The New Kingdom

With Ahmose I began not only a new dynasty, the Eighteenth, but a new era in Egyptian history. But at his accession, it can hardly have seemed so, with the Hyksos still firmly in possession of Avaris and the Delta. Since the Pyramid Age, each pharaoh as King of Upper and Lower Egypt took a 'throne name' compounded with that of the sun-god Re, putting it within an oval or 'cartouche'; in front of his personal name (also enclosed in a 'cartouche') he would prefix the title Son of Re. So did young Ahmose appear as King of Upper and Lower Egypt, *Neb-pehty-re*, 'Lord of Might is Re', the son of Re Ahmose, in about 1550 B.C.

At last, after ten years of inconclusive activity, Ahmose stormed Avaris, chased the remnants of the Hyksos over the border into Palestine, and so reunited Egypt. Lower Nubia had to be reconquered and a revolt or two crushed. But with Egypt firmly secured and its administration renewed, centralized and streamlined, Ahmose in his Year 21 or 22 (1530/29 B.C.) returned to the attack in Western Asia, subduing Palestine (or Canaan, or Khurru, the names used then) and southern Phoenicia. Egypt sought thus to prevent any recurrence of a Hyksos take-over from that quarter, but thereby also became a world power. Ahmose's son Amenophis I (1525 - 1504 B.C.) also probably raided Syria (perhaps to the Euphrates) besides Nubia, but his main energies were devoted to restoring Egypt's internal prosperity and rebuilding temples. Hitherto, kings were buried in pyramids, but Amenophis I broke with this custom, putting his tomb back in the West-Theban cliffs away from his memorial temple. For the work, he founded a special force of Workmen of the Royal Tomb whose 'patron saint' he became during the reigns and centuries that followed.

Then came a century of Syrian conquest under restless warrior-pharaohs. Tuthmosis I (1504-1492 B.C.) established the very furthest limits of Egyptian imperial power, in both the North, at the River Euphrates, and the South, on the approaches to the Fifth Cataract of the Nile (Kenisa Kurgus). At home, he greatly extended Amun's Karnak temple in Thebes, while on the west bank there he established the Royal Tomb workmen in a permanent settlement (Deir el Medina) and had them cut him a rock-tomb in the desolate wady — the first there — that became the Valley of the Kings. His son Tuthmosis II (1492 - 1479 B.C.) died prematurely, leaving the throne of empire to his son in turn, a boy-king, Tuthmosis III. Such a power-vacuum was intolerable. So his step-mother, the dowager-queen Hatshepsut, took over the reins of government for 20 years, proclaiming herself joint-pharaoh. Her time was marked by peaceful expeditions to Phoenicia for timber, Sinai for turquoise and down the Red Sea to distant Punt for frankincense and other exotic products, and by the building of temples such as her superb memorial-temple at Deir el Bahri next to that of old Mentuhotep II in Western Thebes. However, by the time that Hatshepsut died, Egypt's Syrian possessions had evaporated, partly into independence and partly into the orbit of a new power in Western Asia — Mitanni, a kingdom expanding from beyond the River Euphrates. And by then, the boy-king had grown up into a restless young man, bursting with energy, eager to restore his grandfather's wide domains in Syria. Thus, from 1457 B.C., as sole ruler, Tuthomosis III threw himself and his armies into a series of seventeen vigorous campaigns in Syria, repelling Mitanni back over the Euphrates and making Egypt for a spell the greatest power in the ancient world. The kings of Babylon, Assyria and the Hittites hastened to send their emissaries with diplomatic gifts, Egypt's hour of outward glory was forever linked with the names of *Men-kheper-re*, 'Abiding in form is the Sun-god', Son of Re Tuthmosis III, Ruler of Thebes. Within Egypt, the dynamic king maintained a like taut efficiency in administration. Memphis was now the real capital of the country once more, and Thebes the southern centre and imperial home of the Dynasty, visited by the pharaoh for the great festivals of Amun. Two viziers governed the land in south and north, aided by the chiefs of treasury, of granary and other departments and their staffs. The provinces were ruled by civil 'Mayors' of the capital-town of each province in valley or Delta. The Viceroy and his staff maintained the flow of gold from Nubia. Governors of the Northlands oversaw the local princes in Syria, grouped in three provinces, of Canaan (Palestine, centre at Gaza), Upi (inner south Syria, centre at Simyra west from Damascus), and Amurru (coastal Syria, centre at Simyra up the Phoenician coast),plus the Phoenician cities from Tyre to Ugarit. And throughout Egypt in Tuthmosis III's 54 years of rule (1479 - 1425 B.C.), no one hitherto built so many temples as he did, even as far away as Napata near the fourth Cataract in Upper Nubia. He was the classic empire pharaoh, a world conqueror, delegate of the gods, great builder, shepherd of his people, bringing them justice, order and prosperity. The old king's son Amenophis II (1427 - 1396 B.C.) had all of his father's fierce energy, not only as a warrior but as sportsman who outdid his contemporaries — 'superman' whose bow no one else could draw. The briefer reign of his son Tuthmosis IV (1396 - 1386 B.C.) saw a major change in Syrian affairs. Neither Egypt nor Mitanni could really expel each other from north Syria, so at last they made peace, sealing their alliance by marriage of a Mitannian princess to the pharaoh. This alliance could 'outgun' all other powers.

Pinnacle of Splendour : Theological Eclipse

Thus, at his accession, the youthful Amenophis III (1386 - 1349 B.C.) as *Neb-ma-re*, 'Lord of Right is Re', Son of Re Amenophis III, Ruler of Thebes, was heir to domains of vast extent, buttressed by a strong ally in Western Asia, and ruled from the most opulent court in the ancient world. One expedition in Upper Nubia apart, his nearly 40 years as king were marked by prosperity and splendour at home and peace abroad. Superb temples arose by the Nile, elegant as well as immense. Greatest of all was Amun of Thebes, King of the Gods, endowed with a complete new temple at Luxor, a colossal new pylon-gateway fronting his great Karnak temple, and the vast memorial temple of the king over on the west bank before whose pylons sat gigantic twin statues later famed as the 'Colossi of Memnon'. With the temples went widespreading endowments in fields, cattle, a labour-force to cultivate these assets, and gold, gems, timber, slaves, all the booty of successive warrior-kings, beyond that given to any other deity. Thus, Amen-re, King of the Gods, increasingly became in the eyes of his theologians the real king of Egypt, with Pharaoh as his obedient son executing his commands. But this too subservient role, as mere client of Amun, was not acceptable to the pharaohs. Their office was lynch-pin of Egyptian society and the state alike, focus of stability and effective government. Pharaoh was indeed delegate of the gods on earth, but not a mere tool of any one of them, still less of the pretensions of his priesthood (themselves only Pharaoh's deputies) and their economic wealth.

So, tensions had arisen behind the glittering façade of Egypt's imperial splendour and international renown. The pharaohs would not snub too openly Amun, giver of victory, or his priesthood, but they determined to maintain their own proper position by wider distribution of their favours and practical demonstration of their executive powers. Successively, Amenophis II, Tuthmosis IV and Amenophis III appointed a variety of men to be High Priest of Amun in Thebes — either trusted comrades from campaigning days, or else nonentities who owed their all to the king's favour and so were 'king's men', or even men not from Thebes but from Memphis, a far older centre of culture and theology. Amenophis III sought to counterbalance the prominence of Amun by two other devices. First, he gave increased recognition to other great gods of Egypt. He signally honoured Ptah, creator-god of Memphis, by appointing his own eldest son Tuthmosis as High Priest of Ptah there and bestowing upon him the prestige title of 'Superior of the Priesthoods of All Gods of the South and North', or 'Primate of All Egypt' — a kind of honorary super-archbishop, so to speak. More important even than Ptah, he patronized the sun-god Re of Heliopolis as *the* royal god, and at court a special form of the worship of this god developed as the fashion: of the sun-god as shown forth in the visible disc of the sun — *Aten*, in Egyptian. A second counterpoise to Amun was the open proclamation of the divinity of the pharaoh himself — not simply and crudely of the the human being who happened to sit on the golden throne, but of the kingship itself, and chosen facets of the kingship as exemplified by the reigning king. So in Nubia Amenophis III dedicated his great temple at Soleb to 'Neb-ma-re, Lord of Nubia' his kingly genius in the role of master of Nubia. Colossal statues of the pharaoh were given the names of divine forms of the king, and so could serve as foci for popular devotion to the king and the royal cult. Such included Amenophis III as 'Ruler of Rulers', the 'Sun of Rulers', or as 'Montu of Rulers', Montu being the old Theban war-god. Thus, while endowing Amun on an irreproachably magnificent scale, Amenophis III also sought to offset Amun's overweening prominence by the honours done to Re and Ptah and by greater emphasis on the practical and ideological role of the king.

Before his long reign ended, the now ailing king probably appointed as co-regent (or, joint-Pharaoh) his son Amenophis IV. With his long, narrow features, heavy breast and hips, the new pharaoh cut a strange figure in piquant contrast to his ravishingly beautiful wife, Queen Nefertiti. In character, he had little of the tact and practical diplomacy of his forebears in domestic politics, and seemingly little interest at all in foreign affairs. These were serious flaws, and almost fatal at this juncture. Early on, the young king and queen built a great temple east of the Karnak temple of Amun in Thebes — not to Amun but to the sun-god as Aten. By the 5th or 6th year of his reign, the king discarded Thebes completely as southern capital, ceasing to commute between there and Memphis, and instead founded a brand-new capital in Middle-Egypt half-way between the two traditional capitals: Akhet-Aten, 'Horizon of the Sun's Disc'. And henceforth no longer as *Amen*ophis ('Amun-is-content') but as Akhen*aten* ('Effective-for-Aten'), he would rule as partner and sole representative of the sun-god on earth. Thereafter, Amun and the pantheon of gods were abolished at a stroke, their temples closed and priesthoods disbanded, their estates doubtless transferred to the service of the new temples of Aten. In an endeavour to enhance the unique role of the kingship, Akhenaten and Nefertiti were to be the main focus of the people's worship, and they were the principal servitors of the Aten who was, in some measure, embodied in Akhenaten himself.

11

4. *Sethos I and Prince Ramesses offer before the cartouches of their royal ancestors.*
(Temple of Abydos).

Abroad, however, international crises were now developing thick and fast. Egypt's once great ally, Mitanni, suffered two palace-revolutions whereby a 'government-in-exile' disputed the new king's right to his throne. In the south, Egyptian preoccupation with internal affairs and the the long absence of Egyptian armies emboldened the more restless and ambitious spirits among the local city-state rulers of Canaan and South Syria to 'forget' to pay tribute to Egypt and to return to the old strife of each trying to expand his own little realm at his neighbours' expense. A chorus of letters for help from the rivals rained on the Egyptian foreign office in mutual contradiction, each 'defending' the king's realm and opposing his 'enemies' (oftener the writer's than the king's). Then at last, a major war broke out. In Asia Minor (now Turkey), the kingdom of the

12

Hittites or 'Great Hatti' had awoken to new life under an energetic and ambitious new king, Suppiluliuma I. He took the part of the Mitannian exiled prince, and the reigning king of Mitanni — Tushratta — declared war. Suppiluliuma conducted a brilliant campaign, pushing back Mitanni and conquering all of north Syria right down to Qadesh, the key city that had been a bastion of Egypto-Mitannian power (proudly taken by Tuthmosis III, long since). After this reverse, Tushratta was murdered, Assyria seized half the realm for the once-exiled pretender, and Tushratta's son had to call in the Hittites to recapture the remaining half of the once-great realm for himself. In central Syria, the province of Amurru consisted principally of the kingdom of Amurru, subject to Egypt. But its rulers played a double game, swearing loyalty to Egypt in letters sent south, while making show of submission to Suppiluliuma on his great campaign to the north. Meantime, Amurru had enlarged its hold on the Phoenician coast from Byblos up towards the state of Ugarit, and made alliance with Ugarit — which state had already submitted to the Hittite emperor.

By now, in Egypt, a different kind of crisis had come about. Akhenaten had no sons, only daughters. So he made his brother Smenkhkare his co-regent. But probably within a year, even months, of Akhenaten's death, Smenkhkare also died, a youth of hardly more than 20, leaving the empty throne to his baby brother, Tutankhaten, a chubby little boy of nine. At this time of inner crisis in Egypt, Syrian affairs reached a head. Suppiluliuma compelled the kingdom of Amurru with all its gains (as an ally of his vassal, Ugarit) to become a Hittite vassal also. A frantic scribe wrote to Egypt, "all lands from Byblos to Ugarit" have fallen away from their lord, the king of Egypt, and been swallowed up by the Hittite Empire, now the new great power in the Ancient Near East. With this defection by Amurru, Egypt lost an entire Syrian province of her own empire that she was destined never to regain permanently again.

5. Cartouches of Ramesses II : Usimare-Setepenre, Ramesses II, Beloved of Amun

6. Seth as a god in foreign dress.

The Political World of Ramesses' Parents

The boy-king Tutankhaten reigned, but hardly ruled. Real power was wielded by the old family retainer (and in-law?) Ay, and by the general Haremhab. The worship of the old gods was now already reinstated and Aten was simply one of the pantheon. By his 3rd year or so, the young king's name was changed from Tut-ankh-*aten*, 'Pleasant-is-the-life-of-Aten', to Tut-ankh-*amun*, 'Pleasant-is-the-life-of-Amun', and a decree published officially restoring all rights, staff and property to the gods of Egypt, especially Amun. For nine years the young king reigned, growing up to be a promising lad of eighteen or nineteen; perhaps some day he would lead Egypt's armies again to Syrian victories.

Then calamity struck. Tutankhamun suddenly died. He left no heir, the Egyptian throne stood vacant. But his strong-willed widow, Ankhsenamun decided she would marry no commoner with whom to share the throne, and sent word to the Hittite emperor Suppiluliuma, requesting a son of his, that she might marry him and make him king. The wily old emperor was dumbfounded — 'never has anything like this happened in my life!', he justly exclaimed. But too wily . . . He sent not a son but a spy to check the Queen's story, found it true, then sent a son. But too late . . . . In Egypt, Ay had taken in hand Tutankhamun's funeral-arrangements, and proceeded to inter the dead king in a hastily-finished tomb in the Valley of Kings at Thebes. Who buries the pharaoh (as did Horus, Osiris) becomes pharaoh — so Ay reigned. The Hittite prince arrived, in time to be executed. This was a dreadful mistake on Ay's part. Immediately the enraged Hittite emperor swore dire revenge on Egypt, and threw armies against her Syrian possessions, taking many prisoners to be slaves in distant Hatti. Thus was born a distrust and political enmity between Egypt and Hatti that lasted three-quarters of a century — until ended by Ramesses II as we shall see.

Meantime within a few years faces changed. Ay reigned but four years, while in Hatti Suppiluliuma was succeeded by two sons, the younger (Mursil II) speedily becoming a seasoned campaigner like his father. In Egypt, the succession was less clear-cut. The outstanding man of the day was the general Haremhab, already appointed King's Deputy by Ay in his short reign. Haremhab was also married to Mutnodjmet, probably Nefertiti's sister and last heiress of the Eighteenth Dynasty. So with the burial of Ay, Haremhab became legitimate pharaoh in turn. He devoted a long reign to the internal reform and reconsolidation of Egypt above all else. By drastic decrees, he sought to purge corruption from an administration that had grown lax during Akhenaten's obsession with the Aten. His mainly peaceful reign and firm hand gave Egypt the calm she needed to regain internal order, prosperity and poise. The army, too, was set in order; a rebellion crushed in Nubia gave it a trial spin. Inevitably the eyes of Haremhab and his commanders turned to Syria where Egypt had lost so heavily under Akhenaten. Haremhab did not launch upon an exhausting series of campaigns, but at a time of temporary Hittite weakness may have made one brilliant raid along the coast up to north Syria, bringing Ugarit back to his side for the moment, and even striking out to Carchemish and back, where hardly a pharaoh had been seen since Tuthmosis III well over a century before. But it was a flash in the pan, and no occupation was attempted by Egypt; at least, the flag would have been shown and notice served that Egypt did not regard her north-Syrian losses as permanent.

Restorer of just and effective government, builder on a large scale in the temples of Amun and the gods, victor in a brief but brilliant campaign, Haremhab might well appear to have had all that a successful pharaoh might reasonably dream of, at that point in time. Everything, that is, except a son to succeed him. So, once again, as he advanced in years, the succession-question loomed large on Egypt's horizon.

Family Frustrations

During the closing years of the glittering reign of Amenophis III and the years of agonizing crisis under Akhenaten, there grew up a youngster named Sety, 'the man of Seth'. He and his family took their names from the god Seth of Avaris in the east Delta, the old Middle-Kingdom and Hyksos route-centre on the way to Canaan, set in a prosperous province, in the 'Tract of Re'. Young Sety entered the army to make a military career - but under Akhenaten, he could hardly have taken up a more frustrating calling. Apart from the transient 'glory' of conquests, a military life was the path (via the chariotry) to a prestigious career in the foreign service as a Royal Envoy; one saw the world, and visited fascinating foreign courts on business of the king. A glamorous career, with, beyond it, prospects of high civilian adminstrative office in later life. But not under Akhenaten. No campaigns to show one's mettle, merely occasional, inglorious defensive scuffles under local commanders. And the king cared nothing for local disturbances in Syria or elsewhere. While Egypt's armies thus largely kicked their heels idly, Hittites and Mitannians clashed in the far north, the Hittites came south, annexed territory strictly Egyptian in former days, and the Egyptian forces were not allowed to act. Pharaoh was too busy worshipping Aten 300 miles upstream from the Delta and its idle forces. Nevertheless, despite these frustrations and lack of opportunity, Sety rose to attain the respectably high rank of a Commandant of Troops, but not to the coveted ranks of Royal Envoys and the upper echelons of service.

Family Fulfilment

Sety thus witnessed the humiliation of Egypt's losing the entire province of Amurru (to say nothing of the rich state of Ugarit) without a bowshot fired in protest, at about the time of the deaths of Akhenaten and Smenkhkare. And the new king Tutankhaten was a child hardly older than his own little boy Pramesse ('Re has fashioned him'). Meantime, Sety's contemporary Haremhab had become a power in the land, first under Tutankhamun (as the boy-king became) and then as King's Deputy under Ay. And finally, king. Perhaps there was hope for Egypt at last.

By then Sety's son Pramesse was a lad of twenty or so who followed his father's example by going in for an army career — no longer a 'dead end', as under Haremhab the army was the main power in the land. But under Haremhab Pramesse attained a career surely beyond his father Sety's wildest dreams. At first he attained the rank of Commandant of Troops (as Sety had done), but then became a Superintendent of Horse, giving him entry to the elite chariot-corps. As a King's Charioteer he then became a candidate for entry to the ranks of the Royal Envoys who relayed diplomatic messages of Pharaoh and other monarchs between the courts and capitals of the day. This particular career brought contact with the court in Memphis, with chief ministers, and with Pharaoh himself. Men of ability like Pramesse were noticed and got on. He reached the rank of General, became Fortress Commander (probably the border-post of Sile) and Superinten-. dent of the Mouths of the Nile, and so had responsibility for border-security with Canaan and the coasts of the Delta.

Advancing to maturer years, Pramesse rose higher still in the hierarchy of Haremhab's prospering and crisply-governed Egypt. He became Vizier, chief minister of state next to the king himself. As there were normally two viziers, Pramesse may have served with a colleague, perhaps as Theban vizier to keep a loyal eye on affairs in Amun's city. Haremhab had reinstated the policy of Amenophis III, insofar as he made splendid additions to the temples of Amun, but also as 'counterweight' honoured the other great gods, Re (in his orthodox form) and Ptah. Furthermore it was on his northern-born colleague Pramesse the vizier that he bestowed the great religious prestige-title of 'Primate of All Egypt', and not on one of the high priests (and certainly not the high priest of Amun).

Heir of Pharaoh

The office of vizier was the highest station in the state that any commoner might ever aspire to attain, to be right-hand-man of Pharaoh. But Pramesse was destined for higher things yet. As the years passed and he entered his sixties, Haremhab needed to delegate more of his royal duties to others. And, looking to the future, the ageing and childless pharaoh needed an acknowledged successor if Egypt was to be spared yet another crisis over the fate of her throne.

Among his entourage, Haremhab's eye-sought out a man to be his deputy now and successor later. It had not far to wander before it fell upon his well-tried vizier and one-time military colleague Pramesse. So it came about that in due course Pramesse was openly proclaimed both as 'Deputy of His Majesty in the South and North' as pharaoh's representative for the present, and as 'Hereditary Prince in the Entire Land' to announce his future role as intended successor, heir-presumptive, to Haremhab the king.

Prince Sethos and Baby Ramesses

Doubtless it was his integrity, ability and loyalty that won for Pramesse his exalted role as Deputy to Haremhab. Twin statues of himself that Pramesse set up in Thebes, in the Karnak temple of Amun, were a gift, a mark of honour bestowed on him by the king — 'given by favour of

7. *Raia and Ruia, the parents of Tuya, mother of Ramesses II, wife of Sethos I.*

17

the King', their dedications proudly proclaim. But in Haremhab's eyes, Pramesse had yet another qualification that well fitted him to be also the pharaoh's destined successor — a line of heirs. Pramesse had a fine upstanding son, Sety, named after his grandfather. Probably born about the time of Haremhab's accession to the throne, young Sety had grown up knowing no other regime than the firm, mainly peaceful rule of Haremhab. He was in his twenties perhaps, when his father Pramesse was appointed heir-apparent. Knowing from his father and grandfather of the past glories of Egypt and of the losses sustained from Akhenaten's reign, the younger Sety yearned to restore Egypt's former power and glories fully, and to blot out the Akhenaten episode from history. With his own father heir to the throne, such an opportunity seemed beckoningly nearer. Like his forebears, he was brought up in the military life, and saw the path of arms as the eventual means whereby to wrest from the Hittites what in Syria they had purloined from Egypt in the days of her weakness.

The younger Sety married within his social horizon — a girl named Tuya, daughter of Raia a highly-placed Lieutenant of Chariotry and his lady Ruia. The young couple in turn began to found a family. A first-born son probably died early, doubtless in infancy. A daughter arrived next, called Tjia. And then, somewhat later, Sety and Tuya had a second son. This time, following family tradition, the new baby boy was named after his grandfather as Ramesse or Ramesses — our future Ramesses II. A younger daughter Hent-mi-re, born much later, completed the little family.

So, before his death, the aged Haremhab could know that Egypt's farther future was assured, so far as succession to the throne was concerned. His chosen successor was already a father and grandfather, a dynasty already.

The New Kings

Ramesses I (1295 - 1294 B.C.)

Full of years and honour, Haremhab at length died and was interred in his sumptuously-decorated tomb hidden away in the Valley of the Kings. Chief officiant at that rite was, as planned, his faithful deputy Pramesse, who now ascended the throne of the pharaohs as Ramesses I, a vigorous man perhaps in his fifties.

The new pharaoh was deeply conscious that his accession opened a new era. Unlike his former chief, he had no personal link at all with the previous royal family, the Eighteenth Dynasty of history. But the immense achievements of that Dynasty in works of war and peace alike presented a model and so a programme for the new king. For his model, Ramesses I went back to the beginning. Founder of the previous Dynasty and its glory had been Ahmose I, expeller of the Hyksos and inaugurator of empire. So, as symbolic declaration of his chosen role as a 'new' Ahmose founding a dynasty (the Nineteenth of today) to be as glorious as the Eighteenth, Ramesses I modelled his most important formal titles on those of Ahmose I. So, just as Ahmose chose the throne-name *Neb-pehty-re*, 'Lord of Might is Re', now Ramesses I adopted that of *Men-pehty-re*, 'Enduring of Might is Re'. Just as Ahmose had been Son of Re, Ahmose with no fancy epithets, so now Ramesses I had his name written in the same simple way, in stark contrast to the habit of the previous two centuries. And as Horus or Falcon-king, where Ahmose I was 'Great of Kingship', Ramesses I added the similarly-written epithet 'Flourishing in Kingship' to the standard imperial phrase 'Strong Bull'. As protégé of the Two Goddesses of South and North, Ramesses I linked himself with the older form of the sun-god Re, 'Appearing as King like Atum', and as Golden Falcon announced his ideal as 'Establishing Right throughout the Two Lands'.

In Thebes, the new king and his energetic son planned a vast monument to their official regard for Amun, giver of victory. In front of the great pylon-gateway that prefaced the Karnak temple under Amenophis III, there extended a vast open court fronted by a new pylon-gateway erected to Amun's glory by Haremhab. Ramesses I and his son Sety now planned to turn this great open court into a huge hall of columns — the biggest in all Egypt — in honour of Amun. Besides actually building and decorating the new hall, this also meant erasing all the decoration on the rear face of Haremhab's new pylon and redecorating that also, to fit in with the roof-level of the hall. So the masons went to work, building huge columns and enclosure-walls in rough masonry, erasing Haremhab's fine scenes, and filling the new hall with earth (as scaffolding) up to the top, to lay the roof. Then, the decorators worked down the walls and columns, drawing, carving, painting scenes of king and gods on every hand, moving down gradually as the earth fill was progressively removed. Details left over could be done from ordinary wooden scaffolds. The new 'ownership' of the front Pylon was effected by carving the names of Ramesses I over that of Haremhab, whose scheme was now superseded.

Meantime, the king and crown prince sailed back north to Memphis. From there and in the Delta camps, Sety drilled and 'rallied the army and gave it unity of purpose'. In the conduct of affairs, he was his father's willing aide, saying of Ramesses I and himself, 'while he was very Re effulgent, I was with him like a star at his side.' Those activities included a warning raid with the retrained army into Canaan, perhaps even to southern Phoenicia, as try-out and showing the flag. As Sety later put it, 'I subdued for him [Ramesses I] the lands of the Fenkhu, and I repulsed for him the dissidents from the desert land, so that I might protect Egypt for him as he desired'.

At the opposite end of the Empire, in distant Nubia, more peaceful undertakings were a-foot. In the winter of Year 2 while at Memphis, Ramesses I decreed new endowments for the temple at Buhen, at the foot of the Second Cataract: loaves, cakes, beer, vegetables, for Min-Amun and his serving priests, 'filling the workshops with slaves, both men and women, from the plunder of His Majesty' — doubtless from among the hapless Canaanite prisoners brought home by Crown Prince Sety in the summer.

But this decree was virtually the last public act of Ramesses I. His health now failing, he appointed his son as co-regent, to ensure his acceptance publicly as the next king. Intended to be set up in the temple of Montu at Madu (now, Medamud), just north of Thebes, a statue of Ramesses I had around its base the matching titles of both kings — Ramesses I as 'the likeness of Re', and Sety as 'star of the land'. The association of the two men came not a moment too soon. For, Ramesses I died almost immediately afterwards, leaving the throne to his son, now king 'like Re at dawn', as Sethos I. Across the base of the new statue in Madu, the name of the father was swiftly altered to that of the son; it should now represent the new king before the temple's god.

In the traditional seventy days allotted for embalming the dead pharaoh, activity in the Valley of the Kings in Western Thebes was at fever pitch. There, Ramesses I had ordered the excavation of a long corridor-tomb deep into the rock, following his accession. But now, at his premature death only 16 months after his accession, that tomb consisted solely of two steep stairways and a corridor, leading into an unfinished antechamber. All the rest was only on the drawing-board. And there it stayed. Instead, the antechamber now became the burial-hall, and side chambers for funerary provisions were hastily opened-off from it. The walls were quickly smoothed, plastered, drawn and painted with scenes of the King and the gods, and extracts from the funerary books; no time to sculpt them in delicate low relief. As soon as possible, the unfinished outer coffin or sarcophagus of red granite had its inscriptions finished off in yellow paint (not cut), and was installed ready for occupancy in the newly-adapted burial-hall. So in due time, the founder of the new line went to rest in the Theban mountain only a few hundred yards away from his former chief and close friend Haremhab, just across the floor of the royal Valley. In his place, now, the new ruler of Egypt was an eager young man in his early thirties, and the heir to his throne, was little Ramesses, perhaps aged about eight or nine. Following the burial of his father and before leaving Thebes again, Sethos I probably picked the site for his own tomb in the Kings' Valley, just along from his father's, and ordered the continuation of the great works over at Karnak temple. There, in the great columned hall, only a few reliefs had been cut; the rest was in rough, at Sethos's disposal. Henceforth it would be known as 'the Temple 'Effective is Sethos I' in the Domain of Amun'.

Sethos I (1294 - 1279 B.C.)

Master of Egypt, Sethos I could now indulge his twin ambition to be the new Tuthmosis III (greatest conqueror) and a new Amenophis III (finest builder) all in one. As King of Upper and Lower Egypt, he chose a name *Men-ma-re*, 'Enduring of Right is Re', on the same model as his father's throne-name (*Men-pehty-re*), but which was also a subtle hybrid formed from those of Tuthmosis III (*Men*-kheper-re) and Amenophis III (*Neb-ma-re*). To it, he added at will epithets already favoured by Amenophis III, and no king since: 'Heir of Re', 'Image of Re'. To his name Sety or Sethos, he added the epithet Merenptah, 'Beloved of Ptah', reflecting his preference for Memphis and its god over Amun and Thebes. As Horus the Falcon, Sethos was 'Strong Bull Appearing in Thebes', again in imitation of Tuthmosis III, but added 'Nourishing the Two Lands'. As protégé of the two goddesses of South and North, Sethos proclaimed himself as 'Bringer of Renaissance, Strong-armed, Subduing the Foe', and as Golden Horus, 'Repeating Appearances, Mighty of Bows in All Lands'. So, his programme, in a style openly based on the greatest kings of the Eighteenth Dynasty, was to be the renewal of Egypt, not least by deeds of arms.

Safely in the saddle and his father's obsequies over, Sethos hastened to fulfil the first half of his twin ambition: to restore Egypt's Syrian Empire in full. Fickle vassals would not trifle with Egypt's might again. Or so he intended. Within Canaan, the local rulers had still felt free to 'ignore the laws of the Palace', pursuing their own feuds, 'each killing his fellow', regardless of Pharaoh's wishes. Sethos considered that they needed a sharp lesson that would not quickly be forgotten. In his own inscriptions in the war-scenes later sculptured on the walls of his great hall in Karnak at Thebes, he put it thus with startling ferocity:

'Year 1, the 'Renaissance', of King Men-ma-re (Sethos I), endowed with life.
His Majesty was informed as follows: 'The Shosu bedüin-foe are plotting rebellion.

20

Their tribal chiefs are united as one, standing their ground on the hills of Khurru (Palestine). They have instigated confusion and tumult (there), each killing his fellow — they ignore the laws of the Palace.

His Majesty was pleased at it. Now, as for this goodly god (the King), he exults at beginning the battle, he delights to enter into it; his heart is gratified at the sight of blood. He lops off the heads of the dissidents. More than the day of rejoicing he loves the moment of crushing (the foe). His Majesty slays them at one stroke — he leaves them no heirs, and who(ever) escapes his hand is brought prisoner to Egypt'.

The Shosu had picked, unwittingly, a bad moment to rebel, with such a king just spoiling for a showdown and itching for the fray.

So in Year 1, in the summer of 1294 B.C., Sethos led his forces out from the border-fortress of Sile and swept along the Sinai coast-road to Canaan, clearing the wells and minor settlements on the way of any local resistance, until he entered Gaza, administrative centre for the

8. *Sethos I at war in Canaan (N.E. wall, hypostyle Hall, Karnak).*

21

Egyptian province of Canaan, defeating the Shosu nearby. The child Ramesses was perhaps left safe at home. The pharaoh commanded an army deployed in at least three main divisions, named after the gods of empire. As he moved north confirming his hold on Canaan, perhaps bound for Megiddo, further intelligence reports reached the king. In the words of his later inscription:

'On this day, His Majesty was informed as follows: 'The despicable foe who
hails from the town of Hammath has gathered a large force, capturing the town
of Beth-Shan. And in league with the people of Pahil, he has prevented the chief
of Rehob from getting out'.'

Thus had a hostile chief and his cronies taken one Egyptian outpost and besieged another. The king's reaction was swift:

'So His Majesty dispatched the 1st Division of Amun, 'Mighty of Bows',
against the town of Hammath; the 1st Division of Re, 'Abounding in Valour',
against the (captured) town of Beth-Shan; and the 1st Division of Seth, 'Strong
of Bows', against the town of Yenoam. In the space of a single day, they had
fallen to the power of His Majesty!'

The towns of the Esdraelon plain were thus secured, along with the North-Jordan valley, while a pre-emptive strike up to Yenoam precluded any interference from South Galilee. In Beth-Shan was erected a commemorative inscribed block or stela, from which the above quotations are excerpted. After these decisive three-pronged operations, Sethos may have proceeded to occupy Galilee and the south end of the Phoenician coast (perhaps up to Tyre), before returning smartly to Egypt with the pacification of Canaan seemingly well accomplished.

Back at the border-fort of Sile, the proud king rode across the canal-bridge in triumph, to be greeted with bouquets of victory by the high officials of the realm. And this was but the beginning. The next two or three years saw Sethos I back in Canaan, striking further north, both along the Phoenician coast and inland. Thus in north Canaan, Yenoam had to be finished off, and a second triumphal inscription set up at Beth-Shan reports also the quelling of disturbances in Galilee. The bulletin runs:

'His Majesty was informed that the Apiru of Mount Yarmutu, along with
the Tayaru [tribe], had arisen and attacked the Asiatics of Ruhma. Said His
Majesty, 'Who do they think they are, these despicable Asiatics?' . . . So His
Majesty ordered out a detachment of men from his abundant infantry and
chariotry, and they set their faces towards Djahy. After the lapse of (only)
two days, they returned in peace from the district of Yarmutu, bringing
booty . . . and prisoners . . .'

Mission accomplished.

Inland further north, Sethos I secured the south-Syrian province of Upi, reaffirming Egyptian rule both in its administrative centre at Kumidi and east of the Anti-Lebanon hills at Damascus in its jewel of an oasis. On the victorious return from Damascus to Beth-Shan, he left another

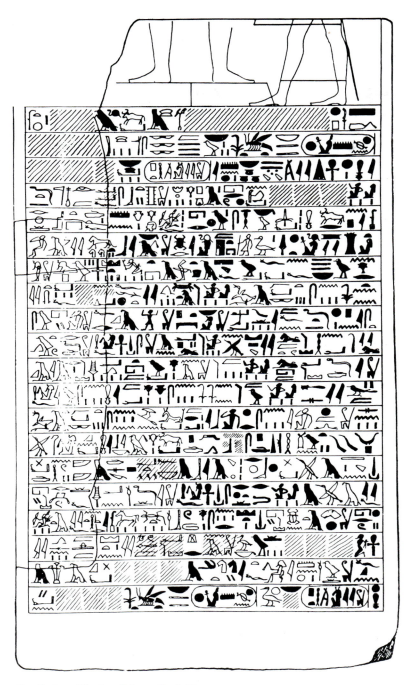

9. *Stela of Sethos I from Beth Shan.*

triumphal stela at Tell es-Shihab, south-west from ancient Ashteroth-Qarnaim. Thereafter, he was free to march up to the coastline of Phoenicia — Tyre, Sidon, Byblos, Simyra, all the old seaports that had long been the preserve of Egypt. Thus in Lebanon he could again have the great cedars felled for shipping to Egypt, 'for the great river-barge of Amun, and likewise for the great flag-staffs of Amun', as the Karnak inscriptions record. Once more, returning through Tyre, he left yet another victory-inscription, boasting of rebels subdued and tribute levied.

So far, Sethos I had plainly and vigorously reaffirmed in these two or three sharp, hard-hitting campaigns Egypt's hold upon her admitted provinces in Canaan and Upi, and upon her formerly-acknowledged claims to at least the southern half of the Phoenician coastline. By taking back this last region, he had cut off the Hittite-controlled state of Amurru from command of that seaboard (except in the far north), and Sethos's territories now ran shoulder-to-shoulder with Hittite-controlled territory. Inevitably, the clash came. In his third or fourth campaign, Sethos I did battle with the Hittites, perhaps for the possession of northern Phoenicia or even for Amurru. This was a tougher proposition. So far, Sethos had faithfully followed out the practical strategy of his great exemplar, Tuthmosis III: a firm hold on Canaan, and then control of the main ports on the Phoenician coast from which in due course to launch an attack into central and north Syria. However, the Hittite Empire which controlled these northern regions in his time was more formidable than even the doughty Mitanni of Tuthmosis III's day. But before further conclusions could be tried between Hatti and Egypt, an interruption arose elsewhere.

Prince Ramesses' First Taste of War

Styled 'Eldest King's Son, Ramesses', as a lad of ten, the, the boy-prince was accorded the titular rank of Commander-in-Chief of the army. Obviously it carried no actual powers; but of that high status he was ever after to be proud, as in later days obsequious courtiers took care to remember. During the fierce reconquest of Canaan and Phoenicia, young prince Ramesses was firmly and prudently kept at home; Sethos probably had no desire to lose his principal son as prey to some foreign disease or other mishap. But as the boy grew up, robust in health, these fears gradually receded. He was openly recognized as heir-presumptive by being given the titles of 'Senior King's Son and Delegate on the Throne of Geb'.

By Year 4 or 5 came an interruption in the Syrian contest. Instead, news came of unrest in Libya, on the western marches of Egypt's own Delta. Not for generations had Egypt had any worry over security there. Unknown to Sethos, new pressures were unsettling his neighbours, and the defence of the Delta - home territory - became suddenly a prime necessity. As a campaign here was near home and Prince Ramesses was nearly fourteen or fifteen years old, he now might be permitted his baptism of war and victory. In the ensuing brief but sufficient campaign, he was probably not allowed too close to the firing-line, but it was a beginning. When the great battle-scenes of the war were engraved at Karnak, young Ramesses' role was so minor that he was simply omitted from the original design. But soon, orders were given to squeeze in his modest figure, as would-be combatant with his father against a Libyan chief.

Freed of the threat from the west, Sethos I could next year (his 5th or 6th) return to the contest in Syria against Hatti. It was well over a century since the key city of Qadesh in central Syria had explicitly been subject to a pharaoh. This must be put right; Sethos was determined 'to vanquish the land of Qadesh and the land of Amurru' The exact course of his campaign is uncertain, but he probably (in best Tuthmoside fashion) sailed his army straight to Phoenicia, overwhelmed Amurru into at least temporary submission, and then struck inland and stormed Qadesh itself. To mark this epochal event, Sethos had set up a victory-stela to Amun, Seth and Montu within Qadesh itself.

Again, Prince Ramesses accompanied his father, and personally shared in these historic and soul-stirring events — brave days in which for a moment the Egyptian Empire seemed poised to regain the full extent of its former dominion. However, the new Hittite emperor, Muwatallis, also young and vigorous, was not prepared to lose territories held by his father and grandfather before him, regardless of how they had been gained in the first place. Thus, Qadesh and Amurru soon relapsed into Hittite overlordship, and the two monarchs probably agreed to a *status quo*: Hatti would recognize Egypt's legitimate interests, including particularly the seaports of southern Phoenicia, while Egypt in turn would desist from further attempts to regain Qadesh and Amurru. A formal compact was probably signed (in accord with Hittite usage), but it was given very little public notice in Egypt.

So, by his 6th year, Sethos I had covered himself with outward glory abroad, had restored some part of Egypt's erstwhile domains in the Levant, and shown the capacity to attempt much more if he so wished. Honour was satisfied, and further conflict with the massive Hittite power seemed pointless. Young Ramesses, however, perhaps did *not* relish the quiet relinquishment of Qadesh and Amurru in whose recapture he had personally shared, enjoying with his father the momentary exhilaration of having restored for a split second in historical time the empire of Tuthmosis III so basely atrophied by Akhenaten's laxity. Perhaps, some day, he might himself do better?

Works of Peace

The almost annual summer campaigns, however, occupied only a few brief weeks each year, two or three months as the most. Otherwise, Sethos was well occupied with routine administration at home, and in celebrating the major festivals of the great gods, such as the magnificent Opet Festival of Amun at Thebes in the winter, warm and sunny then compared with the mists of the Delta. And occupied, too, with the other half of his twin ambition — to equal in size and magnificence the great buildings of his other model, Amenophis III. So at Thebes the decoration of the north half of the great columned hall at Karnak proceeded steadily. The interior was carved with scenes of temple-ritual and the great festival barges of Amun all in beautiful low relief, while the north exterior walls were engraved with six vast series of battle-reliefs illustrating — like the shots in a cine-film — the victories in Canaan, Syria and Libya, converging on towering triumphal reliefs of Sethos before Amun. Across the river on the West bank, his memorial temple was also taking shape and being carved in the same fine style, while the work-force at Deir el Medina operating in the Valley of the Kings tunnelled his great corridor-tomb ever deeper into the bowels of the desert mountain. Meantime at holy Abydos, for Osiris and the gods of Empire, he erected in pure white limestone the noblest shrine of all: a vast and splendid temple arrayed in the most delicately sculptured scenes that his very best artists could produce, brought alive with brilliant colour, and — thanks to the quality of the stone — surpassing even most of the splendid work being done at Thebes. Back in the north, he began new work at the ancient temples of the sun-god Re in Heliopolis and of Ptah in nearby Memphis. Finally, back home in the east Delta, he built himself a glittering summer-palace whose white-plastered rooms were gay with dados and doorways overlaid in brilliantly-glazed tilework in white and blue. Thus, in peace as in war, doing nothing by halves, Sethos I bade fair to rival if not surpass the greatest pharaohs of empire as both champion and patron of the gods that they in turn might correspondingly bless him, Egypt, and its people.

Nor was the King heedless of those who served him so ably. Having come up from among the people, he as Pharaoh did not forget the people. In Year 6, the quarrying-work for the great royal buildings progressed steadily, but Sethos had no hesitation in giving his adjutants and work-staff every encouragement. A Silsila quarry-inscription of that year records how:

'His Majesty was in the Southern City (Thebes), doing the pleasure of his father Amen-re, (even) lying awake devising benefits for all the gods of Egypt. So, next morning, His Majesty brought together a King's Messenger with a body of 1000 men of the army and likewise [ships furnished] with their crews, in order to ferry monuments of fine hard sandstone for his father Amen-re, and for Osiris and his conclave of gods.

Now His Majesty increased what was issued to the army-force, in terms of ointment, beef, fish, and plenty of vegetables without restriction. Every man of them had 4 lbs. of bread daily, daily; and a bundle of vegetables, a portion of roast meat and 2 sacks of grain monthly.

They worked for His Majesty with a loving heart — his ideas were pleasing in the opinion of the people who were with the King's Messenger. He had:- best bread, beef, wine, oils, pomegranate-wine, honey, figs, grapes, fish and vegetables every day, and likewise the great bouquet of His Majesty which was supplied to him from the temple of Sobek, Lord of Silsila, levied (for him) daily — and likewise 6 sacks of grain supplied from the granary for the standard-bearers of his army-force.'

Supplied thus in princely fashion, Sethos's quarrymen and transport-force worked with a will, and the great temples in Thebes steadily rose towards completion as the stream of barges from Silsila poured sandstone blocks into their building-sites.

3:   THE PRINCE REGENT

Ramesses Crowned : the Boy-King

By about Year 7 of the reign of Sethos I, Prince Ramesses as his son and heir, a youth in his mid-teens, was already becoming attuned to the round of royal duties: wars abroad, tours of inspection up and down the Nile to supervise the workings of the administration, progress on temple-buildings, and the rest. This apprenticeship probably consisted of simply accompanying his father, to see what (and how) things were done.

It seems that Sethos I considered that Ramesses now needed a more rigorous training for kingship. With a relatively 'new' dynasty, it was always prudent to leave no public doubt about the succession. So one day, in public audience of the multitude and before the grandees of the realm, the king formally invested his son as Prince-Regent, bestowing upon him also, all the outward trappings of a king. Short of a formal co-regency, this was the highest possible enhancement of the young prince's authority. In an address to the court as sole monarch a few years later, Ramesses recollected this auspicious occasion thus:

> 'When my father appeared to the populace, I being just a youth in his embrace, he spoke (thus) concerning me:
> 'Cause him to appear as King, that I may see his beauty while I yet live!'
> So, he had the Chamberlains summoned, to set the crowns upon my brow. 'Place the Great Crown upon his head!', — so said he of me, while he yet was on earth — 'he shall direct this land, he shall attend to [its affairs], he shall command the populace'. He spoke thus . . . because so great was the love for me within him.
> He furnished me with a household from the Royal Harim, comparable with the 'beauties' of the Palace; he selected for me wives . . . and concubines brought up in the Harim'.

Thus was Ramesses set up as a nominal king, with a full household establishment as understood in the Ancient East. On the model of his father's titles, *Men-ma-re* and 'Sethos Beloved-of -Ptah', he was given the style of *Usi-ma-re*, 'Strong in Right is Re', and 'Ramesses (II) beloved-of- Amun'. Doubtless the proclamation and crowning-ceremony duly brought the plaudits of court and people, and the new household certainly ensured the succession with a large progeny.

The Court of Sethos and the Prince

In the second half of the reign of Sethos I, during the prince-regency of Ramesses, various personalities at Court come into view. Alongside Sethos sat his consort Queen Tuya, a quiet, mature woman now fortyish, not prominent in acts of state, but deeply cherished by her son

Ramesses. Some time before Ramesses I had brought the family to the throne, young Ramesses's elder sister Tjia had married a young man Tia son of Amen-wah-su. These relatives benefited from their royal connection; Tia became a Royal Scribe (a senior rank) in the administration, while his father Amen-wah-su was Table-Scribe of the Lord of the Two Lands and therefore partly responsible for palace food-supplies. The palace-harim at Memphis was in the able care of Hori-Min. Advancing in years, he was honoured with a royal audience in which:

> 'The King said to the officials who were by him, 'Give much gold to
> the Favourite, the Superintendent of the Royal Harim, Hori-Min! His are
> long life, a happy old age, above reproach, without any misdeed in the Royal
> Palace. May his mouth flourish and his steps (continue) their way in goodly
> old age with a happy burial (at the end)!'

In return, laden with gold collars-of-honour, the gratified Hori-Min gave thanks:

> 'O Ruler beloved like Amun! You endure here forever like your
> father Re, attaining his lifespan, O Ruler who creates prosperity among
> men, who has 'made' me with his bounty!'

Of more importance to the running of the country were such eminences as the Vizier Nebamun, and the loyally-efficient Viceroy of Nubia Amen-em-ope, responsible to Pharaoh for the gold-supply from his vast southern domain.

At this well-peopled court, very often domiciled in Memphis the traditional capital, younger men also appear, merely on the threshold of their careers like young Prince Ramesses himself. One of these young hopefuls probably had quite special reason to remember the crowning of the Prince Regent. Son of the High Priest of Amun, Nebneteru and Meryt-re, the young man Paser had entered the service of the Palace, became one of the Chamberlains or personal attendants to Sethos I and, by his crisp efficient conduct, gained promotion in his twenties to the position of Chief Chamberlain at court. He thus acquired the picturesque titles of 'High Priest of the goddess Great-of-Magic' and 'Chief of Secrets of the Two Goddesses' — i.e., he was Keeper of the royal crowns, the great Double Crown of both Egypts, and of the individual crowns of the Two Lands of which it was composed. It was in all likelihood his hands that gently and firmly set the crowns on the brow of the young Ramesses II.

Among the Prince's companions of about his own age was Amen-em-inet. When Ramesses became heir and Regent, Amen-em-inet in turn became his personal retainer and companion — a path to steady promotion later, as it came about. Amen-em-inet already had relatives in important positions, such as his uncles who were High Priest of Min and Isis in Koptos (north of Thebes) and Commandant of Troops in Nubia, right-hand-man to the Viceroy there. Of a lad Bakenkhons in the Training-stable of Sethos I who went on to enter the full-time priesthood of Amun in Thebes, we shall hear more rather later on.

Close in service to both Sethos and Prince Ramesses was one of Paser's contemporaries, Asha-hebsed. A Commandant of Troops quite early in life, this dynamic young man was rapidly promoted to that elite group whose members boasted the title 'Royal Envoy to All Foreign Lands'. However, his royal masters liked his service at home as well as on roving commissions, so he be-

10.   *Figure of Sethos I carved in low relief (Abydos)*

came also a King's Cupbearer — in his case, perhaps a marshal in attendance on king and prince rather than merely a servant handing them the wine-cup. His duties took him to Sinai in Year 8 and later, perhaps to oversee the production of the turquoise mines. At the ancient temple of the goddess Hathor, 'Lady of Turquoise', he left his 'visiting cards' in the form of inscriptions:

> 'Praise to you, O Ruler rich in troops and chariots, *Men-ma-re* Sethos I —
> and to his royal son, *Usi-ma-re* . . . beloved of Hathor, Ramesses II!',

exclaims the loyal Ashahebsed in one of these, honouring king and prince-regent in one breath.

Asha-hebsed's 'loyalist' name, 'Rich in Jubilees' — a good wish to the king, may have concealed a non-Egyptian origin. Many an intelligent young foreigner from Canaan or Syria got on in the cosmopolitan society of imperial Egypt of the New Kingdom, and it was fashionable for them to adopt names loyal to the Crown. One such man who simply kept his own outlandish name was Urhiya, who served as a general under Sethos I. In the alien Hurrian language of North Syria, his name signified 'True', short for Urhi-Teshub, 'True is the Storm-god'; his eldest son was a boy Yupa, bearing a good Canaanite name. But Urhiya's loyalties were to the land of his adoption rather than to his distant and less stable homeland, and his personal monuments were in rigorously Egyptian taste and style.

Revolt in the Deep South

In Year 8, in the winter of 1287 B.C., whispers of imminent revolt far up the Nile in Kush were relayed back north to Sethos I, who was then enjoying the warm, mild climate of Thebes. The territory affected lay beyond the Third Cataract, west from the river in the land of Irem. This part of the Nile valley was better watered, cultivated and populated than most of Nubia (marked even today by the towns of Kerma and Dongola). Beyond the desert hills westward, the dry steppe was relieved by wells both permanent and seasonal. From here, the roving populace of Irem perhaps meditated seizure of land, people or cattle and crops in the richer valley.

However, 'someone blabbed', the Viceroy's agents heard, and the plot got to the ears of the pharaoh. His record, as set up later in the Viceroy's southern capitals, tells the story thus:

> 'Year 8, Season of Winter . . . (under) the Lord of the Two Lands,
> *Men-ma-re* Ruler of Thebes, Son of Re, Sethos I, Beloved of Ptah . . .
> Now His Majesty was in the City of Thebes, doing what was pleasing
> to his father Amen-re. His Majesty was informed as follows:
>
> 'The enemies in the land of Irem are plotting rebellion!'
>
> So His Majesty bided his time for them, to learn of their plans in detail.
> Then said His Majesty to the high officers, courtiers and retinue, 'What are the
> despicable Irem, that they should dare trangress in My Majesty's time? It is
> my father Amen-re who shall cause them to fall to My Majesty's sword. I
> can cause any land to retreat, and (this) land likewise before My Majesty!'

So His Majesty drew up battle-plans against them and he decreed slaughter
for them, that he might strike down their chiefs wherever they were. Then
His Majesty dispatched the infantry and also much chariotry. His Majesty's
army arrived at the Fortress 'Pacifier of the Two Lands' in the 3rd month of
Winter, Day 13 [late January, 1287 B.C.]. They went up (onto the desert)
against the foe. The strong arm of Pharaoh was before them like a blast of
fire, trampling the mountains.

Came the dawn, 7 days (later), the strong arm of *Men-ma-re* brought
the (foe) in, without missing even one of them, men and women alike. It
plundered 6 wells all in one victory; here are their names:- Tipaw, Tabnuta,
Tairosu; a Well; Kurokasa, Tusarsu. So, the population of their wells was
brought back to the river-bank as captives, and all their cattle likewise,
going before them as [the booty of Pharaoh's strong arm].'

The list of booty appended originally included well over 600 captives.

So, in a week's swift raid through the wells (or minor oases) beyond the Nile, the intended
secession of Irem from Egyptian power was nipped in the bud, and any designs on the river-val-
ley extinguished. Conducted by the Commandant of Troops with the Viceroy on the King's
account, this was the last of the wars of Sethos I, a very modest affair and quickly over. In commemoration, the Viceroy Amen-em-ope set up two stelae, one each in his southern seat at Shaat
on Sai Island, and one in a new centre he was building on an island a little further north (now
Amara West, attached to the west bank), to be his new southern capital. In Thebes, it sufficed
the royal vanity merely to alter a few names from Canaanite to Nubian on the place-name lists of
the great triumph-scenes at Karnak, and not even using those of the the trifling wells concerned.

Deserts and Quarries

Soon after the Irem incident, the attention of Sethos I and Prince Ramesses was focussed
on more peaceful enterprises. The barren, sun-scorched, inhospitable deserts between the Red Sea
and the Nile held one overriding lure for the pharaohs — gold. Some 70 miles upstream from
Thebes, opposite Edfu, began part of the 'gold-country' that extended far south into Nubia. In
Year 9 the indefatigable Sethos determined to take in hand personally the question of a better
gold-supply from the Edfu desert. So, in the heat of June, 1286 B.C., he penetrated almost 40
miles into the sun-seared wilderness to see conditions for himself. The urgent need for a good
well and a stopping-place in the desert soon imposed itself on the dusty, thirsty monarch, and so
Sethos promptly organized the digging of a well and construction of a small temple and compound
to serve the needs of his gold-miners. In that same temple (at Kanais) he caused to be engraved
a vivid account of the royal explorations for water for the gold-diggers:

'Year 9, 3rd month of Summer, Day 20 [early June, 1286 B.C.] . . .
Now this day, His Majesty traversed the deserts right up to the mountains.
In his mind he wished to see the mines from which gold is obtained. When
His Majesty had gone many miles, he stopped for a rest on the way to

31

Drawing by Coleman

11. A.   *Ramesses II (followed by Princes Amen-hir-wonmef and Khaemwaset) puts to flight rebel Nubians. At left an injured man is helped homewards, while a boy runs to announce the Egyptian attack as a woman cooks a meal.*

B.   *Ramesses II sits in state to receive the spoils of war and Nubian tribute. This includes gold rings, bags of gold dust, bows, animal pelts, shields, chairs, fans, ostrich-eggs and plumes, tusks, and both domestic and wild animals. Top centre, the Viceroy of Nubia is rewarded with gold collars. (Beit el-Wali temple, outer hall)*

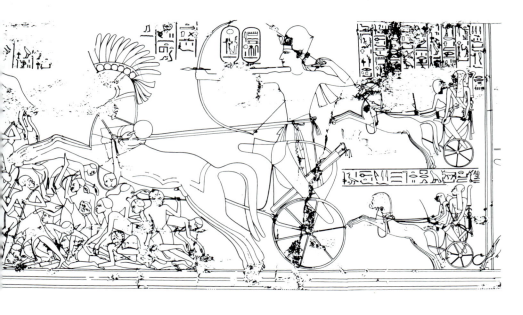

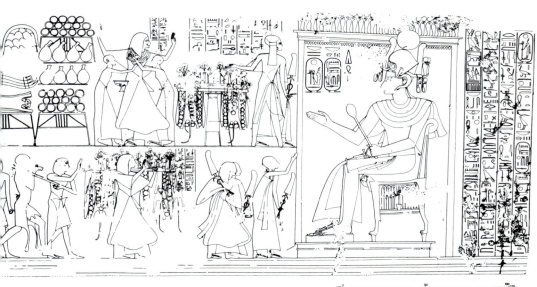

cm 0   50   100 cm.

12. Figures of Ramesses II and his son in incised relief

think things over. Then he said, 'How difficult is this waterless road! What happens to the travellers to relieve their parched throats? Who shall quench their thirst? The (watered) land is far away and the desert is wide — woe is the man who thirsts in the wilderness! How can I care for them, so that I can provide a lifeline for them? . . .'

After His Majesty had weighed these things up in his mind, he reconnoitred the desert, seeking out a spot for making a well; God guided him, so as to fulfil the wishes of those whom he loves. Stonemasons were charged to excavate a well among the mountains to pick up the weary and cool the hearts of those parched by the summer heat. Then this place was built in the great name of *Men-ma-re* (Sethos I) — and it welled up with

34

water in great quantity, like the Nile-flood at Aswan. . . . Then His Majesty gave command to the Director of Royal Works. . . . So there was excavated in this mountain the temple of these gods: Amun, Re, Ptah, Osiris, . . . After the monument was finished, and its inscriptions engraved, His Majesty returned to praise his fathers, all the gods.'

But of course, Sethos's ultimate concern was for the gold, intended for the treasury of his superb temple at Abydos, the finest work of his reign. So in a further inscription, he warned future generations not to interfere with the miners and gold-supply of his great temple, calling down blessings on those who might respect his arrangements and hearty curses on any who dared upset them:

> 'As for any future kings who shall confirm my arrangements, . . .
> Amun, Re-Harakhte, Ptah-Tatonen, Osiris [and the other gods] shall make them flourish, they shall rule the lands in happiness . . .
> As for any future kings who shall overthrow my plans . . . , this will be bad in the eyes of the gods, he will be accused in Heliopolis, the Divine Tribunal will be red as firebrands to burn up whoever does not heed me. They will destroy whoever upsets my plans, to cast him (down) on the slaughter-block of the Netherworld.
> As for any official who shall encourage his lord to remove the personnel for other service . . . , he shall be doomed to the fire — it shall burn up his body, it shall devour his limbs! . . .
> As for anyone (at all) who shall be deaf to this decree, Osiris shall pursue him, Isis will be after his wife, and Horus chase his children — all the great ones of the Necropolis shall execute judgement against him!'

Here, indeed, with a blessing, is a really hefty 'curse of the pharaohs' — but directed (as almost always) at those who, long ago, might upset the king's economic concerns, many worlds away from the archaeologists and tourists of millennia later who come only to preserve or to admire!

So much for father — what about son? During his father's desert ventures, Prince Ramesses was also active at the south end of Egypt. Year 9 saw the two combing the quarries at Aswan for granite suitable for great statues and other monoliths. Two rock-inscriptions attest their surveys. The lesser one records:

> 'Year 9 . . . His Majesty caused that great statues of black granite be made. Then His Majesty discovered a new quarry for statues of black granite whose crowns (would be) of red quartzite from the Red Mountain. Never had their like been seen since the time of Re. The name of the quarry which His Majesty discovered is 'the Quarry of *Men-ma-re* Ruler of the Two Lands'.'

The larger inscription reveals that Prince Ramesses was charged with the general oversight of these major works at Aswan (doubtless seconded by experienced aides), while his father went hunting gold mines:

> 'Year 9 . . . His Majesty commissioned a multitude of works, to make very great obelisks, and great and marvellous statues in the name of His Majesty. He fashioned great barges to transport them, from the quarry, with officials and transport-men hastening (the work along)' And his Senior Son [i.e., Ramesses] was before them, doing (real) service for His Majesty.'

Prince Ramesses the Builder

The next six years passed mainly in peace, but certainly not in idleness. Now in his forties and less physically energetic (especially after his gruelling trip in the desert's summer heat), Sethos I was increasingly content to regulate the country's administration from the comfortable palaces of ancient Memphis, summering in his own palace at Avaris in the east Delta (receiving Asian tribute), and wintering in warmer Thebes to attend there the great Opet-Festival of Amun.

The more so, as over the years he had picked a series of mainly able men to conduct the major departments of state. It was about this time (Year 10 or soon after) that the highest office in the land fell vacant, that of southern or Theban vizier. And Sethos I now made an appointment, which, even for those days, raised a few eyebrows and sent a suitably-discreet ripple of comment through the Court. His Chief Chamberlain Paser was to be the next vizier. At hardly more than thirty, Paser was young — and as Keeper of Crowns, surely a strange choice? But not so; Sethos I evidently considered he knew ability when he saw it, and events were to prove him right in the sequel.

Paser was immensely proud of his meteoric rise to the heights, but was duly mindful of his duty to 'deliver the goods'. As he later put it in an inscription in his splendid tomb-chapel (No. 106) in Western Thebes:

> 'My Lord commanded that this humble servant should be promoted to be First Companion of the Palace, and he advanced me to be Chief Chamberlain . . . Then he appointed me to be Vizier . . . , charged to receive the revenues of the southern and northern foreign lands for the Treasury of the Victorious King. Because of my efficiency, I was sent forth . . . to compute the revenues of the Two Lands throughout the provinces of Egypt, South and North.'

Also by this time, his elderly father Nebneteru was appointed as High Priest of Amun in Thebes, a signal honour and a 'golden handshake'; this office he held until almost the end of the reign.

Meantime the great building-projects went steadily on. At Abydos, the physical structure of the great temple neared completion in rough: two vast open forecourts, two broad columned halls, seven sanctuaries for the state gods, Osiris and family, and the king, then the Osiris suite

13. The Great Hypostyle Hall, Karnak — cross-section

proper, and various service-rooms to one side. But the exquisitely delicate sculpturing of the scenes on the temple walls necessarily went much more slowly, beginning with the most sacred parts of the temple towards the rear. Behind the great temple, Sethos had constructed a special underground structure — the Osireion, a kind of cenotaph for him and Osiris.

Here, Prince Ramesses kept an intermittent eye on the progress of the work. From the beginning of his appointment as Prince-Regent, 'in the first year of my appearing' as he said, he was busy there; '(I) fashioned my father in gold anew', thus superintending a new gold statue of Sethos I for the temple sanctuaries. Eventually Ramesses got from his father permission to build his own temple to Osiris at Abydos. This, as befitted the junior partner, was on a smaller scale than his father's huge edifice, but executed in the same beautiful creamy limestone by the same corps of accomplished craftsmen, in the finest style. But, significantly, most of its decoration was no longer in the low relief preferred by Sethos. The less-patient Ramesses had his temple-scenes carved more quickly, with the figures and inscriptions incised into the stone

At Thebes, the great Hall of Columns rose structurally complete in Amun's Karnak temple. The decoration of the north half of the hall was fast nearing completion; the south half in the names of Sethos and Ramesses had a great deal of decoration yet to be done. The Hall comprised a vast forest of columns in a huge expanse, 170 feet long by about 340 feet wide. The central nave of twelve great columns carried the central roof almost 80 feet over the head of the visitor. On either side, a grove of 61 columns a mere 40 feet high gave vast lateral depth to the hall, as in the dim light it seemed to stretch out into infinite darkness through vistas of painted

37

columns. As in a cathedral, light filtered down through tall window-gratings that joined the upper and lower roof-levels on either side of the central nave, illuminating the coloured reliefs that glowed jewel-like from walls and columns in the half-light that dissipated into the mysterious darkness of the wings of the hall.

Across the Nile on the West bank, the memorial temple of Sethos I included by now a special chapel for Ramesses I, while other reliefs commemorated the crowning of young Ramesses II. It thus was almost a chapel royal of the new dynasty. Here too, as at Abydos, the building-work had long outstripped the patient work of decoration in low relief. Still further out to the west, in the lonely Valley of the Kings, the workmen of the Royal Tomb had by now tunnelled a magnificent tomb for the king, corridor upon corridor, hall after hall, for over three hundred feet, down and down into the western mountain. While the veteran foremen Baki and Neferhotep the Elder supervised generally, the draughtsmen Pay and Pashedu drew the outlines of texts and scenes with an incredibly sure hand, afterwards painting the completed work so delicately sculptured by Piay and his colleagues in the interim. Rarely is it possible to give credit to specific men who have produced works that still compel wonder and admiration (and justly so)

14. Facade of the memorial temple of Sethos I, Qurna.

millennia afterwards, but with this particular community their overall record makes it pleasantly feasible. Nor was this massive tomb their sole care. Perhaps even while his father still lived, Ramesses was allowed to order work to begin on his tomb in the royal valley, as his father's neared completion.

While Ramesses might visit various work-sites, whether at Aswan, Abydos, Thebes or elsewhere, much of the work in Thebes was the direct concern of the southern vizier Paser, not least the workmen of the Royal Tomb, who, through their foremen and scribes, were responsible directly to him. Some of them may even have worked on his fine new tomb-chapel in among the tombs of the nobles in Western Thebes.

Back across at Karnak, east of the river, Paser's concerns were less with Amun's buildings than with his furnishings. In temple workshops, sphinxes, fine vases, statues of the king, in gold or valuable stone, came steadily from the craftsmen's skilled hands, to be inspected for quality by the vizier. In his chapel, Paser had himself shown at such an inspection, where he remarks to a sculptor, 'May Ptah favour you, sculptor! Very good indeed is this statue of my Master that you've made. 'Let it be fashioned like the ancient model', — so Pharaoh says.' Paser had good reason to be proud of the work of his artists, when at a subsequent royal audience he was rewarded with gold collars-of-honour by the king; an event likewise commemorated in his tomb-chapel.

Among the skilled men that served Paser and Prince Ramesses in Thebes was Dedia, Chief of Draughtsmen-painters in Karnak, who came of a long family tradition. For six generations before him his forebears had served Amun thus, beginning with Pethu-Baal, who had settled in Egypt from Canaan or Syria, and whose descendants speedily had become assimilated by marriage and in culture to Egypt. Through such men as Dedia and his colleagues throughout Egypt (including those of the Royal Tomb), Sethos I came very close indeed to fulfilling his ambition to rival even Amenophis III in the splendour and scale of his buildings.

Enter the Family

Productivity in Ramesses' case was by no means confined to tombs and temples. When crowned, he had been presented with a full-scale royal household. During the years of the regency, the young 'king' early began to rear quite a family. Of principal wives he had two: Nefertari and Istnofret. On the family background of these two girls, history so far has preserved a discreet silence. Nefertari at all events was certainly a personable young lady, more than 'comparable with the Palace beauties' to use Ramesses' wording. But Istnofret remains a shadowy figure as we shall see.

Both girls bore a series of sons and daughters to their husband. In ten years up to the death of Sethos I, they each presented Ramesses with at least five sons and a couple of daughters, while the lesser ladies of the harim (discreetly veiled from us) may have accounted for another five or ten sons and as many more daughters. So, in the closing decade of Sethos's reign, the Palace nurseries must fairly have resounded with the gurgles, yelps and whimpers of each year's crop of bouncing royal babies, taking no account of such as may have passed away in extreme infancy. Sethos was a grandfather many times over.

Nefertari produced Ramesses' first-born son, Amen-hir-wonmef, 'Amun is at his right hand', and Istnofret the second son, named Ramesses after both father and great-grandfather. Next time round, Nefertari bore Pre-hir-wonmef, and Istnofret the fourth son Khaemwaset, 'Appearing in Thebes', and then the eldest daughter, given the pure Canaanite name of Bint-Anath, 'Daughter of Anath'. The passing years added many more. Thus, Nefertari's later children included the fourth daughter Meryetamun and other sons down to the sixteenth, Mery-Atum. Istnofret's off-spring included the thirteenth son, Merenptah. All of these children were destined to play their part in the years that followed.

Scuffles in South and North

By about the thirteenth year of his father's reign, and now aged about 22, Prince Ramesses was now deemed old enough to tackle modest wars on his own. A minor revolt in Lower Nubia saw Ramesses heading south accompanied by two little sons, Amen-hir-wonmef the eldest (aged five), and Khaemwaset (aged four). The 'campaign' was a trifle, militarily speaking: a chariot-charge, the Nubian ranks broke and fled back to their villages, carrying news of the Egyptians in hot pursuit, and all was over in an hour or two. Ramesses led the charge: his little sons, each in the care of a charioteer, 'charged' too, probably at a safe interval behind the main front! In the military tradition of Ramesses' forebears, this was their initiation into war. In celebration of victory, and in relation to a strategic point on the Nile, Ramesses ordered the cutting of a small rock temple (Beit el Wali), near Kalabsha which guarded a narrow point on the river. In its front hall, the north wall showed merely symbolic reliefs of northern victory, against Canaan and Libya; Ramesses had warred in both theatres but merely in accompanying his father. But on the south wall were placed vivid scenes of his own, personal Nubian victory: the pursuit, and the receipt of loot and tribute presented by the two princes and the Viceroy, Amen-em-ope. Soon after this, with the little temple largely complete, this viceroy disappears from view, perhaps dying 'in harness' or retiring in old age. At all events, Sethos and Ramesses now chose a new man for the post — Iuny from Ninsu near the Fayum, who (on a first trip out to the Edfu desert) left a scene of his respect for Sethos I close to the latter's temple for the gold-miners.

This little Nubian war had been 'kids' stuff', even for young Ramesses II. On the north coast of the Delta, a more serious threat had developed: Mediterranean pirates. In the Aegean and the East Mediterranean, unrest was slowly growing, and groups of shipborn marauders had long been a nuisance to the Hittites and other states in Western Asia Minor. And by the early thirteenth century B.C., these buccaneers had begun to harry the Delta, raiding up the Nile mouths, probably looting and destroying the villages and small townships that were caught un-awares.

That such victors in Asia and Nubia as Sethos I and his son should allow free rein to looting and terrorism of this sort on their very doorstep was unthinkable. Prince Ramesses, therefore, prepared troops by land and ships near the river-mouths. Next time the Sherden pirates came, the trap was sprung, they were overwhelmed, captured in good numbers, and press-ganged into the Egyptian army. If fight they must, it might as well be with Pharaoh and for Egypt rather than against them. Ramesses II took pride in his 'clean-up' operation years afterwards, on later stelae:

'(one) who vanquished the warriors of the sea, the Delta now lying
(safe) asleep', and 'whose renown crossed the sea . . .the unruly Sherden

whom no one had ever known how to combat, they came boldly [sailing] in their warships from the midst of the sea, none being able to withstand them. [But he plundered them by the strength of his valiant arm, being brought into Egypt] — Ramesses II'.

Death of Sethos I

So matters stood by the sixteenth year of Sethos I. Firmly and well ruled, Egypt was prosperous at home and respected abroad, holding a considerable empire. Minor eruptions were quickly put down. Splendid new buildings, unequalled in scale since Amenophis III, had been built to the great gods, and decorated with a delicacy (if not always the taut vigour) rivalling the superb works of the Eighteenth Dynasty.

In that sixteenth year, Sethos I would have been approximately fifty, and perhaps hoped for at least another decade of life and reign. But it was not to be. In the summer of 1279 B.C., perhaps in his new palace hard by Avaris, the king suddenly died, leaving the throne and empire to Ramesses II, now no longer an 'apprentice-king' but absolute monarch of virtually all he surveyed.

15. *Statue of the youthful pharaoh Ramesses II, Turin*

4: WARS AND RUMOURS OF WAR

Calm before the Storm

Ramesses II, Sole Pharaoh

Soon after dawn, in early June of the summer of 1279 B.C., 3rd month of Summer, Day 27 in official terminology, the formal accession was announced (probably at the Avaris summer-palace) of:

> '*Falcon King*, Strong Bull, Beloved of Right, Truth.
> *He of the Two Goddesses*, Protector of Egypt who curbs the foreign lands.
> *Horus of Gold*, Rich in Years, Great in Victories.
> *King of Upper and Lower Egypt*, *Usi-ma-re*, 'Strong in Right is Re', (to which *Setepenre*,
>   'Chosen of Re' was later added).
> *Son of Re*, Ramesses II, Beloved of Amun.'

Aged about twenty-five, already schooled in kingship and bursting with energy and optimism, Ramesses II now took up the reins of empire in full. With a vast peaceful, prosperous domain at his command, the possibilities of the day must have seemed — to him — limitless.

However, the young king's immediate concern was the burial of his father in approved fashion. The traditional seventy days for mummification began, while messengers carried the news quickly to Thebes for the vast royal tomb to be made ready for the burial; all the funerary furnishings must also be completed. In the meantime also, Ramesses announced that, henceforth, the Avaris summer-palace with its satellite buildings and military installations were to be the nucleus of a new city, and were now to be known by a new name — *Pi-Ramesse A-nakhtu*, or 'Domain of Ramesses-Great-of-Victories'. But the grandiose plans he had in mind must await the completion of his father's burial for their due fulfilment.

At last, by about mid-August of 1279 B.C. (early in the 2nd month of Inundation), the great cortège of ships set sail for the South, carrying the mummy of Sethos I for burial. A short stop at Heliopolis, then on to Memphis for ceremonies of recognition of the new king, then southward. With favourable winds (and laborious towing when these failed), the flotilla probably docked at Thebes about a fortnight later. In due course, after more ceremonial in Sethos's memorial temple, Ramesses II and the immediate family escorted the golden coffin of the dead king and its long procession of bearers with furnishings, headed by the ritual priests, up the desert route into the Valley of Kings. The last rites over and the huge tomb closed, sealed and buried, Ramesses may have spent a few moments inspecting work on his own great underground mausoleum across the valley-floor before returning to Thebes of the living. By virtue of burying his father as the god Horus did for his father Osiris, Ramesses II in his turn was now legally king in the fullest sense, one with all the kings who had ever preceded him, down to his own father. As full pharaoh, he now led the celebration of the great Festival of Opet for Amun during September, accompanying Amun's golden barge on its two-mile journey upstream from Karnak to Luxor temple to the plaudits of the populace, and then back again twenty-three days later at the festival's end — 'corresponding to Regnal Year 1 on his first royal progress to Thebes' as a later account has it.

Council of State in Thebes

During the time of this festival of Opet, important political decisions were often taken, and thus gained an especially auspicious and impressive setting. On this occasion, the new pharaoh had to appoint a new High Priest of Amun, besides making promotions within the ranks of the hierarchy of Amun's priesthood in Karnak.

Since the recent death of old Nebneteru, father of the vizier Paser, the pontifical throne of the high-priesthood of Amun had remained vacant. Now, Ramesses II, his councillors and the portable image of the god Amun assembled in conclave to appoint his successor, doubtless after due preliminary deliberation. Various names were submitted to the god. Finally, after several refusals, his oracle approved the name of Nebwenenef, high priest at nearby Thinis and Dendera. But the fortunate candidate was not to learn of this until Ramesses reached Abydos. Lower down the Theban hierarchy, other appointments were made. Near the bottom Bakenkhons (already a junior priest) now joined the college of Divine Fathers of Amun, his first step on the ladder to eminence. In an entirely different career, Ramesses' boyhood companion Amen-em-inet became a royal Charioteer and Superintendent of Horse.

Other men of consequence were confirmed in office for the present. Paser continued as Theban vizier. In Nubia, Iuny remained viceroy, and his job was much concerned with buildings. At his new vice-regal seat (Amara West) begun by Amenemope, Iuny reversed the orientation of the new temple from south to north; the new settlement became 'Ramesses the Town'. At Aksha near the Second Cataract, plans for a new temple were ready, and the building of the precinct had already been begun under Sethos I. But the chief deity of the temple as now built was to be none other than a form of Ramesses II himself, '*Usima-re* . . . , the great god, Lord of Nubia', following the example of Amenophis III at Soleb and Tutankhamun at Faras. Thus was modestly begun a re-emphasis on the importance of the kingship on the lines already marked out in the preceding dynasty.

Promotions and Restorations at Abydos

So, the days of festival passed busily for the new king. They included orders to push ahead with the great Hall of Columns at Karnak, now to be known as the temple 'Effective is Ramesses II' in Amun's domain, and to complete his father's memorial temple on the West bank. Even more important was the ceremony at which Ramesses II 'stretched the cord' for the founding of his own vast memorial temple, the Ramesseum — a structure of courts and halls to be some 600 feet long inside its great precinct. Back on the east bank at Luxor temple, plans had earlier been laid for a great new pylon and forecourt, fronted by obelisks and statues. This, Ramesses II now pushed forward in his own name with every energy.

But at last in mid-October of Year 1, 3rd month of Inundation, Day 23, the day of departure dawned. The great golden barges of the King and the royal family, attended by a flotilla of lesser vessels, stood out into the river, their gleaming sides shimmering reflections over the ripples of the sunlit waters. Against a backdrop of black earth-banks, crowned by vivid green vegetation, beyond which rose the pink-flushed Theban mountain of the West against a pearly-blue morning sky, the great fleet turned north, rowed downstream by ranks of practised mariners whose oars swung in unison like the legs of great gold water-beetles upon the green and bluish waters. The destination hundreds of miles north was the newly-proclaimed Delta Residence; but only a day or so's journey out, Ramesses had other business to settle at Abydos:

> 'Regnal Year 1 . . . Beginning the journey, setting sail, the royal ships
> illuminating the waters, turning northwards towards the Seat of Valour,
> the Domain of Ramesses II Great-of-Victories. His Majesty turned aside
> to see his Father (Osiris), traversing the waters of the Abydos canal to
> make offering to Wennufer (Osiris) with every good thing that his spirit
> loves.'

Once landed there, the king found a rather unsatisfactory state of affairs among the tombs and temples of Abydos:

> 'He found the buildings in the cemetery belonging to former kings,
> their tombs in Abydos, falling gradually into ruins, and part(s) still under
> construction . . . walls lying [unfinished], one brick not even touching
> the next. What was barely begun had already mouldered back to dust.
> No one continued the building work, . . . after the owners had departed
> to heaven. No son renewed a father's monument in the Necropolis.
> Indeed, the Temple of *Men-ma-re* (Sethos I) had its front and rear
> still under construction when he went to heaven. Its monuments were
> unfinished, its pillars not set up on the terracing, its statue lay on the
> ground, without being fashioned in accord with the regulations of the
> Sacred Workshop. The divine offerings had ceased to function, likewise
> the priestly service. The products of its fields were taken away, as their
> boundaries were not marked out on the land.'

Ramesses could hardly brook quite so blatant a breakdown of work and service at his father's temple so indecently soon after Sethos's burial. No word is spoken of any slackness in the work on his *own* temple nearby — could it be that, with mistaken zeal, the local officials responsible for the work in both temples (and the area generally) had pushed work on the son's temple so hard that the father's edifice had been unduly neglected? Sethos had not perhaps visited the South for some years, and Ramesses as regent had been more preoccupied with Thebes, until now.

Therefore, he summoned the court and, after their obeisance and praises, announced his intentions:

'See, I have had you summoned concerning the matter that is before me. . . . I have considered that it is a worthy deed, to benefit those who have passed away. Compassion is a blessing; it is good that a son should be concerned to care about his father. I am determined to confer benefits on Merenptah (Sethos I), such that it will be said forever after, 'It is his son who perpetuated his name!' So may my Father Osiris favour me with the long lifespan of his son Horus, according as I am one who does what he did . . .'

This said, along with reflections on his former regency already cited (and rhetoric besides), the king got down to detail:

'His Majesty decreed that orders be given to the Chiefs of Works. He assigned soldiers, workmen, sculptors, . . . every grade of craftsman to build his father's temple, and to restore what was ruined in the cemetery.'

Likewise, the offerings and services were resumed, statues carved, the temple-estates and endowments set down in writing, and the administration set to rights, all in the care of a High Steward of the foundation.

Meanwhile, Ramesses had not overlooked the appointment of the new High Priest of Amun, which he had decided on in Thebes. Nebwenenef of Thinis and Dendera was summoned and duly invested with his new dignity by the King in the presence of Queen Nefertari and the court. Years later, he had the scene carved in his spacious tomb-chapel (No. 157) in Western Thebes, suitably inscribing the event thus:

'Year 1, 3rd month of Inundation, — when His Majesty sailed north from Thebes, having done the pleasure of Amen-re, . . . Mut, . . . and Khons . . . in the beautiful Festival of Opet. Returning thence . . . and landing at Abydos.
The (prospective) High Priest of Amun Nebwenenef was ushered into the the presence of His Majesty. Now, he was (then) High Priest of Anhur and of Hathor Lady of Dendera, and local Primate of all Gods in the south from north of Thebes to Thinis in the north (near Abydos).
Then said His Majesty to him, 'You are now High Priest of Amun! His treasury and his granary are under your seal. You are chief over his domain, all his foundations are under your authority. The domain of Hathor Lady of Dendera shall now be under the authority of your son [who shall inherit] the functions of your ancestors, the position you have occupied (until now). (I swear) as Re lives for me and loves me, and my Father Amun favours me, I set before (Amun) the (names of) the whole 'Establishment' . . . (and of) the priests of the god, the great men of Amun's domain who were in his presence. *He* was not satisfied with any of them, until I mentioned your name to him. So, serve him well, according as he has desired you! I know that you are efficient; do even more, and then his spirit will favour you, and

mine also. He will cause you to abide at the head of his domains, he will grant you old age therein, and he will bring you to port in the sacred soil of his City (at death)........

Then His Majesty gave him his two gold signet-rings and his electrum staff-of-office on being promoted to be High Priest of Amun, and Superintendent of (his) Treasury, Granary, workforce and all craftsmen in Thebes. A Royal Envoy was dispatched [to announce throughout the land] that the domains of Amun, all his property and all his staff were assigned to his (Nebwenenef's) authority, by the favour of Amun's Ruler (Ramesses II), enduring forever!'

So, the new pontiff travelled south to his new diocese, while the king tidied up affairs in Abydos and sailed on northwards to plan out his new Delta Residence to rival Memphis and Thebes in splendour.

6. *Ramesses II and Queen Nefertari in the Window of Appearance, at Abydos, when appointing Nebwenenef as High Priest of Amun.*

Research in Theology!

Year 2 passed quietly and swiftly. But by then, Ramesses had decided to change his royal style a little. As King of Upper and Lower Egypt, the simple form *Usi-ma-re* (with occasional epithets) modelled on his father's equally simple *Men-ma-re* no longer satisfied him. He now added the epithet Setepenre, 'Chosen of Re', to the *Usi-ma-re*, giving the final form *Usi-ma-re Setepenre*, 'Strong in Right is Re;(king) Chosen by Re'. This marked a trend that was later to be given great impetus — Ramesses II's 'special relationship'with the sun-god Re of Heliopolis, in the early days as his 'son' and then especial representative, and later as a very form of that god on earth. A pompous stela at Aswan merely reflects continued quarrying-works done there, and commemorates the former regent's successes in Nubia and in the Delta against the pirates.

By Year 3, in 1277 B.C., the great forecourt, pylon and obelisks at the front of Luxor temple had been finished, and their decoration — always a more leisurely process — well begun. In his dedicatory text, Ramesses claimed to have 'done his homework', tracing up in the sacred archives the mysterious theology of Amun as ultimate deity, so that he might build worthily for him. On the mundane level, he took care also for his workmen, quite in his father's style:

> 'As for this goodly god (the king), he is a scribe, accomplished in
> learning and in knowledge like Thoth (god of wisdom), — one who knows
> the (proper) procedures, skilled in precepts . . . Now His Majesty did re-
> search in the office of archives, and he opened the writings of the House-
> of-Life. He thus knew the secrets of heaven and all the mysteries of earth.
> He found Thebes, the very Eye of Re, as being the original plot of earth
> which arose in the beginning, since this land has existed, and Amen-re
> [functioned] as king — he illumined heaven and shone upon the sun's cir-
> cuit, seeing where his Eye's rays might alight. His Right Eye, in the Theban
> province (and) in its City, is 'Southern Heliopolis' (Thebes itself); and his
> Left Eye, in the Heliopolitan province, is 'Northern Heliopolis' (Heliopolis
> proper) — even, the King of Upper and Lower Egypt, *Amen-re* : Eternity
> in his Name, Everlasting is his Nature, and his substance is all that exists.'

Theological research duly done, came the practical application:

> 'Said King *Usi-ma-re* Chosen-by-Re (Ramesses II) to his nobles
> attending on him, 'I am one who proclaims effective deeds . . . See now, my
> mind is set on executing works for [Amun . . .], erecting constructions
> in his temple within Southern Opet' (Luxor). The King spoke, giving instruc-
> tions to conduct the work . . . the activity of the soldiery, . . . [with ships]
> as many as their crews, sailing both north and south, . . .[bringing] . . . their
> allowances in grain, [and all the needs of] their limbs, and none said, 'Oh
> that I had (this or that)!' The work was completed in Year 3, 4th month of
> Inundation, Day 10 . . . in all its work, being the (best) craftsmanship, of
> granite, . . . hard white stone, and all kinds of genuine and beautiful stones
> . . .'

So arose the new forecourt, its pylon, monuments and colonnades gleaming fresh and bright in the strong sun.

'Gold in those far Hills'

Meantime, far north in Memphis, the restless young pharaoh's thoughts turned to visions of gold. For so many splendid projects he had in mind, generous quantities of the yellow metal were needful. That meant, again, the eastern deserts, particularly in Nubia. Here, tantalisingly, rich deposits were reported — but in a region cursed with a chronic water-shortage that killed off prospectors like flies. Ramesses, however, pressed home his efforts to the point of success where water was concerned, as his subsequent inscriptions jubilantly were to record:

'Year 3, 1st month of Winter, Day 4 [December, 1277 B.C.] . . . under the Majesty of Ramesses II. . . . Now, one of those days, it so happened that His Majesty was sitting on the electrum throne, wearing the head-fillet and tall plumes. (He was) thinking about the desert lands where gold could be got, and meditating on plans for digging wells along the routes made difficult by (lack of) water, in accord with a report made as follows: There is much gold in the desert of Akuyati, but the road to it is extremely difficult because of the water (problem). If a few of the gold prospectors went there, it was only half of them that ever arrived there, for they died of thirst on the way along with the donkeys that went before them. There could not be found for them their needs for drinking, either going up or coming back, in terms of water in skins. So it was that no gold was brought from this land at all, through the lack of water.'

Then said His Majesty to the seal-bearer who was by his side, 'Now summon the grandees of the Court, so that My Majesty may deliberate with them about this land. I shall take the matter in hand!' They were immediately ushered into the presence of the goodly god, . . . jubilating and doing him homage . . . The King spoke to them about the nature of this country, discussing it with them, and about how to open up a well on its road.

Then they said to His Majesty, 'You are like Re in all that you have done — whatever your heart desires comes to pass. If you desire something overnight, comes the dawn and it happens immediately! If you say to the water, 'Come from the mountain!', then the waterflood shall come forth promptly after your word, inasmuch as you are Re in person, the dawning sun in his true form. . . . As for the country of Akuyati, this is what has been said about it — *Report by the Viceroy of Nubia to Your Majesty*: 'It has been in this difficult state regarding water since the time of God; people die of thirst there. Every previous king has wanted to open up a well there, but they had no success. King Sethos I tried likewise. In his day, he had them dig a well 120 cubits [180 feet] deep. It was abandoned unfinished, because no water appeared in it. But of course, if *you* were to say to your father the Nile god . . . 'Let water

49

flow from the mountain!', then he would do it in accord with all that you asked . . .'.

Said His Majesty to these nobles, 'True, true indeed is all that you have said, my friends! Water has never been struck in this territory since the time of the God, as you say. But *I* shall open up a well there yielding water daily [just like in Egypt] at the command of Father Amun . . . and the Falcon-gods, the Lords of Nubia . . .'. Then the grandees praised their lord, making obeisance, exclaiming to the highest degree.

Then said His Majesty to the Chief Royal Scribe, . . .' [Send a letter to the Viceroy of Nubia as follows:- 'You shall send a survey-party] halfway to Akuyati, and allow a full month to elapse, then you shall send (instructions) to these [workmen, so: *instructions now lost* . . .]. [So, the Chief Scribe sent the letter and the Viceroy] did according as he had been ordered.

Now when he set the men to [go digging, the] Nubians [and others said], 'What's all this that the Viceroy is doing? Is the water [really there? Shall] His Majesty's [word] really happen, commanding it to appear on the route to Akuyati? Never has anything like this been done since the times of former kings!' . . .

Then, someone came with a letter from the Viceroy of Nubia, as [follows:- . . .] 'O Sovereign my Lord, every [thing has happened just] as Your Majesty said with his own mouth! Water appeared in it (the well) at 12 cubits [18 feet], there being 4 cubits deep in them, [of water . . .]. It (spurted) out, just as a god would do it, through being satisfied by your devotion! Never has anything like it happened [before . . .]. The chief of Akuyati rejoiced immensely. Those who were far-off [marvelled . . . , they came to] see the well created by the Ruler — the very waters of the Netherworld heed him, when *he* digs for water in the [mountain!. . .]'. This, the Chief Scribe read out, just as communicated by the Viceroy.

Then the Court was delighted . . . [They said, 'You are very Thoth himself], effective in plans good at instructing; all that you say [certainly comes to pass! . . .]'.

[Now, the name of] this well shall be 'The Well, Ramesses II is valiant of [deeds(?)].'

So, at the stroke of a pick — and perhaps a stroke of luck — Ramesses' agents got their water in the barren wastes of Wady Allaki, and the precious gold could be mined. Whatever he did, the young pharaoh seemed to have the magic touch.

War in Syria

Triumphant builder and restorer, water-diviner for the gold-mines, dispenser of high office to able aspirants, dismissing minor revolts in lofty fashion, Ramesses at last decided to apply his magic touch in a disputed realm that had lain dormant now for a whole decade — the Syrian question, patched up by his father with the Hittites after the victory at Qadesh. Qadesh and the neighbouring state of Amurru had belonged to Egypt ever since Tuthmosis III, and were only lost through the neglect of Akhenaten, 'that criminal of Akhet-Aten' and his fellows. That his father Sethos had reconquered Qadesh only to give it up by treaty evidently rankled deeply in Ramesses' mind. Young and optimistic, he determined to recapture all of Egypt's former territories, step by step. First, confirm his hold on the coastline, and retake Amurru. Then Qadesh, then inner North Syria to Aleppo or beyond . . . let the Hittites try to stop him!

So in Year 4, possibly in the summer of 1275 B.C., Ramesses II set out for Syria. Canaan was docilely his, and he soon reached the coastland of southern Phoenicia, touching at Tyre and Byblos, firm Egyptian possessions. Further along the coast, he may at this time have taken Irqata by seige; the main part of Phoenicia was his. But from that convenient base-line he then struck inland and eastward through the mountains, to attack Amurru. No details are known of what ensued, but within a couple of months or so, Ramesses was master of Amurru and in a position to threaten Qadesh, further inland, when he wished. After a decade of peace, Benteshina king of Amurru was caught entirely by surprise, and was in all probability soon overwhelmed by the sudden Egyptian attack from the coast. There was no time to summon aid from his overlord, the Hittite emperor in distant Asia Minor. Benteshina could only submit and agree to become a tribute-paying vassal of Egypt. However, he had no intention of allowing the Hittites to write him off and condemn him as a perfidious rebel; so, he sent a message to his former suzerain that he could be his vassal no longer.

With his 'First Victorious Campaign' of the new reign seemingly crowned with success, Ramesses II travelled back south at leisure via Phoenicia. Various mementoes marked his passage — a stela at Byblos of Year 4, another at the Dog River headland (Nahr el-Kalb) of that year, and another may have been set up in Tyre then. Amurru was once again Egyptian, and doubtless during his triumphal return to Pi-Ramesse, the king's aim was 'Qadesh, next year!' The Empire could be restored fully, after all.

But in the far-distant North, from the lofty vantage-point of the palace at Hattusas on the high Anatolian plateau, matters looked radically different. The Hittite emperor Muwatallis duly received Benteshina's formal announcement of his involuntary switch of alliegance from Hatti to Egypt. But hardly with indifference. There quickly formed in Muwatallis's mind a threefold resolve — to recover Amurru, to prevent the loss of Qadesh (or any other district), and to deal the truculent young pharaoh such a devastating blow that the Egyptian forces would never threaten the Hittite domains in Syria again.

As was proper, Muwatallis turned first to the gods of Hatti. To them he made a vow, promising rich gifts if they granted him the reconquest of Amurru:

'On which campaign My Majesty shall march, then if you O Gods, support me and I conquer the land of Amurru — whether I overcome it by force of arms, or whether it makes peace with me — and I seize the King of Amurru, then . . . I will richly reward you, O Gods . . . !'

His vows made, Muwatallis turned to the practical means for their fulfilment. Throughout that winter and the early spring of 1274 B.C., he took in hand elaborate preparations, arranging with vassals and allies from all points of the compass to assemble a massive army, perhaps one of

51

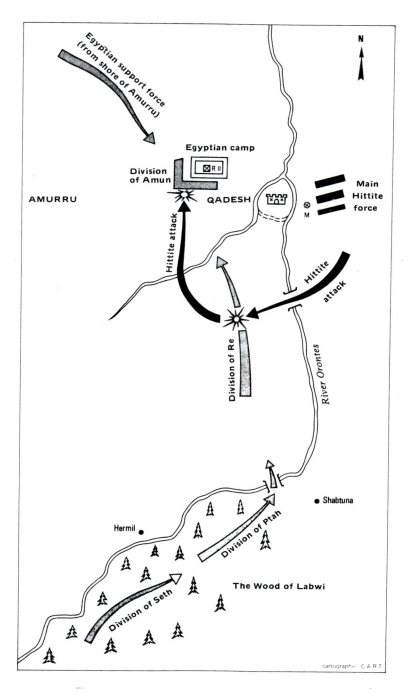

17. *Battle of Qadesh – the crucial moment.*

the largest ever levied in the history of the Hittite Empire. The later Egyptian reports list his forces as deriving from 16 different provinces and allies besides Hatti itself, with figures of 2,500 chariots and two groups of warriors numbering 18,000 and 19,000 men respectively. Whether this be exact or exaggerated, a massive force was undoubtedly assembled to deliver what Muwatallis fondly hoped would be a crushing blow, a knock-out.

Triumph in Disaster at Qadesh

Swift Journey

In the warm spring sunshine at the end of April in 1274 B.C., all was hustle and bustle at Pi-Ramesse in the east Delta. Battalions of infantry were marshalled, squads of chariotry wheeled round in the dust as their captains tried the mettle of their prancing steeds. An endless flow of bows, arrows, spears, swords, poured out of the arsenals and stores, checked off by harrassed scribes harangued by gesticulating platoon-commanders intent on getting *their* group's quota of kit. Away from the barracks, in the ever-growing royal palace, the king finalized his campaign-plans with his generals. While he led the main army overland through Canaan and South Syria up to Qadesh, a support-force would go directly along the Phoenician coast and then cut inland, eastward to link up (via the Eleutherus valley) with Ramesses at Qadesh the day of his arrival. At last:

> 'When His Majesty had got ready his troops and chariotry and the Sherden whom he had captured victoriously, (all) equipped with their weapons, and the battle-plans given to them, — then His Majesty set off northwards with his forces. He began the march well, in Year 5, 2nd month of Summer, Day 9. His Majesty passed the border-fortress of Sile, being powerful like Montu when he appears; all the foreign lands trembled before him, their chiefs bringing their tribute and all the rebels coming in homage through dread of His Majesty's might.'

Riding in his glittering chariot at the head of the army in its four main divisions — named for the gods Amun, Re, Ptah and Seth — Ramesses was attended by one of the viziers, some of his young sons (with other members of the royal family), and by his household-staff and bodyguard. Passing through Gaza, the great force passed swiftly through Canaan. Up through Galilee past Lake Huleh and the sources of the Jordan, up through the passes into the broad upland vale — the Biqa — between the Lebanon and Anti-Lebanon ranges, the Egyptian forces steadily marched:

> 'his troops went on through the narrow defiles, just like being on the roads of Egypt.'

In the broad Biqa vale, the king reached the township of 'Ramesses the Settlement which is in the Valley of the Cedar', probably Kumidi, the Egyptian administrative centre for the province of Upi close by.

Thus, exactly one month after his departure from Egypt, by late May of 1274 B.C., ('Year 5, 3rd month of Summer, Day 9'), on his 'Second Victorious Campaign', young Ramesses II 'awoke hale and hearty in His Majesty's tent upon the ridge [Kemuat Hermil] south of Qadesh . . . he appeared splendidly like the brilliance of the sun, when he had donned the panoply of Montu.' All seemed well early that bright morning, only a few miles south of Qadesh itself.

Therefore the young king hastened to reach Qadesh as soon as possible. He and his immediate staff and bodyguard set out northwards, followed by the 1st Division of Amun. Behind them, the other three divisions gradually came into line, stretching many miles back along the route. As he went through the woods of Labwi to reach the ford across the Orontes River near Shabtuna, two Shosu tribesmen of the semi-desert borderlands fell in with the royal party, professing to offer to Egypt the allegiance of their brethren the tribal chiefs, in preference to the Hittite yoke. Immediately, Ramesses had them interrogated — where were these chiefs? At once, they answered, 'They are where the Ruler of Hatti is, for the Hittite foe is in the land of Aleppo to the north of Tunip — he is too afraid of Pharaoh to come south since he heard that Pharaoh was coming north!'

Safe Arrival

Such wonderful news — that the Hittite emperor was skulking in North Syria, 120 miles away, and declining to show fight — seemed too good to be true. As, in fact, it was. Elated by this flattering report Ramesses and his intelligence-corps cross-questioned these ready witnesses no further, but pressed on gaily through the river-ford and across the plain towards Qadesh, the army of Amun following close behind them. Easy victory last year, rapid progress and no hint of serious trouble this time — the Egyptian king and commanders were now lulled into a light-hearted complacency bordering on outright carelessness, as they drove north over the plain to establish themselves on a suitable camp-site out on the north-west from Qadesh. That township stood on its mound — shroud of earlier settlements — upon a tongue of ground between the Orontes flowing north past the east side of the town, and a stream from the west that flowed into the Orontes on the north-west of the town. By cutting a channel across from the stream to the river to the south of their town, the inhabitants of Qadesh had turned their city into virtually an island, that much safer against attack.

The Illusion Shattered

After crossing the western stream in the early afternoon, Ramesses with his staff and the army of Amun began to pitch camp opposite the town which (they fondly imagined) they would besiege next day. But even as the pharaoh settled himself on his golden throne to await the rest of his forces, there fell a bolt from the blue. The intelligence-corps had sent out scouts on security-patrol — and one of their squads stumbled on two Hittite counter-spies, overcame them and beat the truth out of them, and brought them post-haste before the astonished Ramesses:

'Then said His Majesty, 'What are you?' They replied, 'We belong to the Ruler of Hatti! He sent us out to see where Your Majesty was.' Said His Majesty to them, 'Where is *he*, the Ruler of Hatti? See, I heard it said that he

18. *Scene of the Battle of Qadesh. In centre, the Egyptian camp attacked by the Hittite chariots (at top), as the king (left) learns of the Hittite presence (beaten out of captured Hittite spies, below him). At far right, sudden arrival of the Egyptian support-force. (Luxor Temple).*

was in the land of Aleppo, north of Tunip.' They replied, 'Behold, the Ruler of Hatti has (already) come, together with the many foreign lands that he brought as allies . . . See, they are poised armed and ready to fight behind Old-Qadesh!'

Thunderstruck at this shock disclosure that his foe was hardly two miles away rather than 120, and furious at the slackness of his intelligence-service, Ramesses summoned his chief officers, broke the appalling news and upbraided them roundly — 'See what state my provincial governors and high officers are in, that they go on saying daily, 'Oh, the Hittite ruler is in Aleppo, away north north of Tunip !. . . . But now, this very hour, have I heard from these two Hittite spies, that the Hittite ruler has (already) come with his allies, with innumerable troops. Even now they are poised hidden behind Old Qadesh - and my generals and officers in charge of my territories here could not tell us that they had come !'

Ramesses then began energetic counter-measures against sudden attack. The division of Re was already crossing the plain towards the camp, but the other divisions had yet to cross the Orontes. Followed by a cup-bearer and a scout, the vizier was immediately sent off to speed up at least the division of Ptah still in the woods of Labwi, with the urgent message, 'Hurry forward! Pharaoh your lord stands in battle all alone!' The royal family was to flee quickly westward out of immediate danger, led by Prince Pre-hir-wonmef. Then the blow fell.

In cold fact, the captured spies had spoken only too truly. Having gathered his huge forces — perhaps twice the size of the Egyptian army — Muwatallis had quietly marched them down into south Syria, assembling his host behind groves of trees or other features, on the east bank of Orontes, opposite Qadesh. His scouts had observed the Egyptian march from the south, the Shosu had been sent as decoys to fool the conceited king, and meanwhile the massive striking-force of chariotry was made ready to dash west across the lower fords of Orontes, just south of Qadesh, at the crucial moment, led by several Hittite princes.

Disaster

That moment came even as Ramesses and his generals were discussing emergency tactics. Suddenly, rank upon rank of Hittite chariots appeared from the river and charged west across the Qadesh plain, smashing into the columns of the division of Re caught totally unprepared as they marched, cutting them in two, and then turning and doubtless cutting them to pieces. Re's ranks broke up and, with Hittite chariotry in hot pursuit, fled north to the camp. still being set up by Amun's division with the king. Seeing first the distraught fugitives and then a dustcloud of enemy chariots bearing down fast upon them, the men of Amun's division panicked hither and thither. The Hittite chariotry swept around the camp and swooped where they pleased — all was uproar and confusion. A torrent of fighting-men, horses and chariots burst through the palisade of shields along the west side of the camp. All now seemed lost — in a moment, the pharaoh and his attendants would be overwhelmed, all of Ramesses' dreams would perish with him forever, and the Hittite emperor Muwatallis would have crushed his opponent finally and for good.

But Ramesses was no idle spectator of this headlong rush of events. Even as the confusion

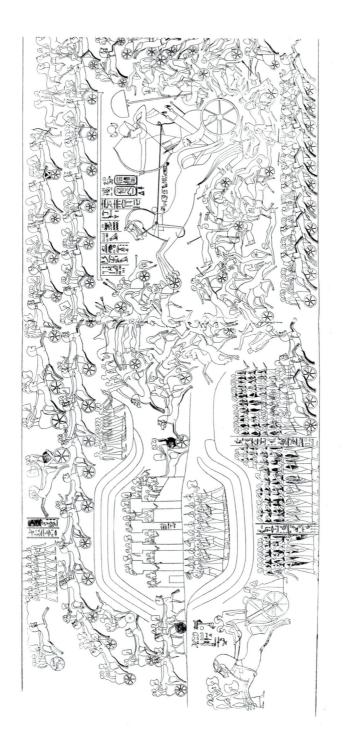

19. Scene of the Battle of Qadesh. At right, Ramesses II charges into a mass of Hittite chariots, driving them back into the river which (at left) loops round Qadesh. Above the town and river, Hittites pull their fellows out of its stream. At base (on the opposite bank to the battle), the Hittite king and infantry watch helplessly. (Luxor temple).

20a. *Ramesses II learns of the Hittite attack (Ramesseum, pylon)*

20b. *City of Qadesh, encircled by rivers and channel (Abu Simbel).*

20c.   Egyptian counter-attack across the Orontes river at Qadesh (Ramesseum).

began, he threw on his kit, shouted to his charioteer and leapt into his chariot. Vainly he summoned his panicking troops to support him, ready to fight to the death and preparing to take on the Hittites single-handed. In the king's words later,

> 'When Menna my shield-bearer saw the vast number of (enemy) chariots hemming me in, he blanched and fear gripped him. He cried out to My Majesty, 'My good Lord, Mighty Prince, . . . we stand alone amidst the foe. See, the infantry and chariotry have deserted us! Why do you stay to save them? Let's get clear, save us, Usi-ma-re!' Then said His Majesty to his shield-bearer, 'Stand firm, steady yourself, my shield-bearer! I shall go for them like the pounce of a falcon, killing, slaughtering and felling them to the ground!'

So, able to rally only his immediate attendants, the king attacked the assailants with the fury of near desperation, a thousand thoughts racing through his mind — the perversity of his panicking troops, a prayer that Amun whom he had so fervently served would spare him now. Six times he savagely charged into the fray, creating at least local confusion among the incoming enemy ranks.

At this very juncture, help came from a quarter all but forgotten in the melée. The support-force from the coast of Amurru — the Nearin — suddenly arrived from the west in impeccable formation, and smartly went over to the attack. Caught between the support-force on their west flank and the furious counter-charges by Ramesses and his immediate followers on their east flank, the Hittite chariotry found itself in danger, in its turn, of being surrounded and cut to pieces. Wisely, its canny commanders drew back their ranks southward from the battered Egyptian camp, to regroup and (hopefully) crush the embryo Egyptian counter-attack before it could develop any further. But it was not to be. Given that minute breathing-space, Ramesses could now quickly rally his motley of support-force and retainers, and moved in with truly a falcon's speed to the offensive. Thus he and they charged and charged again, halting, and then driving back, the discomfited Hittite chariotry southward and then eastward, pressing them back to the river bank whence they had come. Even when a new wave of Hittite chariots was thrown in as reinforcements, they too became entangled in the grand confusion.

Across the river, with his main infantry-force marshalled but stood at ease, the canny Muwatallis heard the din of battle with a smile of satisfaction, as a mile or two away his massive chariot-force supposedly did its work. But then, suddenly, his satisfaction must have turned to stupefaction. For now, Hittite chariots came into view — but fleeing headlong to the river bank, followed by Egyptian forces in hot pursuit, the pharaoh in their forefront. Before the Hittite king's horrified gaze, the Egyptians pressed the Hittites pell-mell back into the river, prince and plebs alike threshing the water, swimming for dear life back to the east bank and to the safety of their own lines, dragging each other out, exhausted, onto the mud. The prince of Aleppo swallowed so much of the river on his way back across it, that his retainers had to hold him upside-down by the ankles to empty him out!

Victory and Reproaches

So, as the last Hittite stragglers crawled out on the far side and the Egyptian chariotry wheeled to a halt on the west bank, Ramesses was left in possession of the field. At the close of the action, the 1st Division of Ptah finally appeared, led by the vizier. They were quickly occupied in rounding up prisoners, collecting booty and taking tally of the enemy dead — readily computed in grisly fashion by taking one hand per corpse. Meanwhile the abashed survivors of the 'shell-shocked' division of Re and the panicky division of Amun gradually drifted back to the main body of support-troops, Ptah division and retainers. As Ramesses had it later,

'My army then came to praise me, [amazed] at seeing what I had done
. . .' And he was quick to reprove their indiscipline and cowardice: "What will people say, when it is heard of: your deserting me, I being left all alone? And not an officer, captain or soldier came to give me a hand as I fought!

60

I took on *millions* of foreign lands, alone with Victory-in-Thebes and Mut-is-Content, my great chariot horses! They it was, I found to help me when alone, fighting the foreign armies. I shall personally stoop to providing their feed in my presence every day when I am in my palace — they it was whom I found (of help) amidst the battle, together with the charioteer Menna my shield-bearer and my palace cupbearers beside me, witnesses of mine as regards the fight. I *did* find them (by me)."

By sunset, and with the belated arrival of the division of Seth, the Egyptians finally camped down for the night. Across the river, the Hittites too had probably been taking stock and holding an inquest on 'what went wrong'. In fact, the Egyptians had two divisions badly mauled (Amun, Re), two divisions intact (Ptah, Seth), plus the support-force. The Hittites had two massive infantry-formations intact, but must have lost heavily on chariotry. Even more poignant for Muwatallis and his war-council was the loss of leaders, even if the Prince of Aleppo did survive his surplus intake of Orontes water. Losses included two of Muwatallis's own brothers, two of his shield-bearers, his secretary, his chief of bodyguard, four leading charioteers and six army-chiefs of some rank, besides the general casualties. As for their failure to crush Ramesses, the young pharaoh's outstanding physical courage, arrival of the support-force (overlooked by the Hittites ?), and capture of their scouts were the root causes.

21. *Battle of Qadesh. The Hittite Prince of Aleppo is up-ended to empty him of all the water that he swallowed in swimming back over the Orontes! (Ramesseum)*

End of the Battle

Early next morning, Ramesses judged that it was his turn to take the main initiative. He rapidly marshalled his forces for battle and attacked the Hittites with all the fury that he could command. Such an attack, by surprise and with more chariotry than the foe, would have caught the Hittites on the wrong foot and have initially driven them back. But their main forces were perhaps twice the size of the Egyptian army, and, well-disciplined, they stolidly held their ground after the first shock. With inadequate chariotry, the Hittites could not properly repulse the Egyptians, while the Egyptians could not rout the solid Hittite masses commanded by Muwatallis. So came stalemate, and the armies disengaged.

At this point, true to his dynasty's policies, Muwatallis sought to end the impasse by diplomatic means. Some fifteen years before, he had made peace with Sethos I by which both parties had agreed to accept the *status quo* — including the retention of Amurru and Qadesh by the Hittites. Seeing no point in further fighting for its own sake, and expecting that Ramesses might by now feel that honour had been satisfied (if not also somewhat chastened) and be ready to consider ending hostilities, Muwatallis sent an envoy to the Egyptian camp, bearing a letter with peace-proposals. The details remain unknown; doubtless Muwatallis complimented the pharaoh on his bravery and then suggested an agreement for a territorial *status quo* as before.

Ramesses summoned his commanders and informed them of the Hittite proposals, to test their reaction:

> 'Then said they with one accord, 'Peace is good above all, O Sovereign
> our Lord! There is no blame in reconciliation when you make it — for who
> can withstand you on the day of your wrath?'.

Thus it was evident that his forces had no stomach for any further immediate clash with the Hittites or attempt on Qadesh itself. On the other hand, the ambitious pharaoh could not bring himself to make peace, and so soon, on the same objectionable terms — no Qadesh or Amurru for Egypt — that had rankled with him ever since his youth when his father had acquiesced in them. Therefore (with notable lack of foresight) Ramesses boldly resolved the dilemma temporarily by pushing it firmly into the future. He disdained any treaty that compromised his claims to Qadesh and Amurru, but agreed to desist from any further conflict this time. So he was able to order his army to pack and begin the long march home — but reserved his fancied right to lay forceful claim to Syria whenever he might choose to do so. Thus, Muwatallis had gained a brief respite for all his trouble, but had neither banished his mercurial foe nor pinned him down to any real peace-settlement.

Homecoming under the Stormclouds

During the latter part of the 3rd month of Summer, the Egyptian host moved off southward — over the Orontes at Shabtuna, back to Canaan, and early in Year 6 and the 4th month back through the Sile frontier of Egypt proper to the Delta Residence; doubtless, Ramesses put on a brave triumphal display of prisoners and booty in his train as he rode his gleaming chariot into the palace-square of Pi-Ramesse in the enervating heat of June/July, 1274 B.C.

Meantime, back up north, sinister moves were afoot. With the Egyptian departure, Muwatallis was left in sole possession of the field. On the epic day of crucial conflict, young Ramesses II had snatched out of crushing disaster a victory of narrow personal brilliance. The second day of battle was a stalemate, and Ramesses found it expedient not to push his dispirited forces further, but to leave the field for home. Now, in the weeks that followed, came the final bitter truth of essentially a political defeat. Muwatallis speedily reaffirmed his hold on Qadesh nearby, then moved west to bring the erring state of Amurru smartly back to heel. Its unhappy king, Benteshina, was arraigned by the irate Muwatallis, peremptorily dethroned, and replaced by a new man, Shapili. Benteshina at least escaped with his life, but was sent into exile to Hattusas where later on the emperor's brother Hattusil claimed him as a servant.

Muwatallis thus had achieved his first basic aim of restoring Amurru and Qadesh to Hittite rule, even if the other aim of crushing Ramesses had badly misfired. Now he, in turn, saw his opportunity to exploit his position and push the Egyptians still further back. Even as Ramesses neared home, Muwatallis led his forces, not back north but *south*, along the Biqa valley, overwhelmed the Egyptian centre of Kumidi, and wheeled east through the Anti-Lebanon range to occupy Damascus and the whole Egyptian province of Upi. Egypt would have more to think about than aiming at Amurru and Qadesh, and the Hittites thus gained a prosperous addition and 'buffer-territory' for their realm. If Ramesses refused a 'reasonable' treaty, he must pay the price.

By now, even Muwatallis had to attend to pressing affairs back home in the Hatti-land, as Hittite kings had always a regular round of religious festivals to attend, and there were victory-vows to pay . . . So he marched off north to Hatti, leaving his forceful brother and right-hand man, Hattusil, to organise their 'new' province of Upi.

But for their military and tactical success the Hittites in turn had to pay a price. In the wake of the Egypto-Hittite blood-bath at Qadesh, the bold king of Assyria, Adad-nirari I, saw his chance. The land of Hanigalbat (remnant of the great Mitanni-realm of Akhenaten's day) had long been the object of dispute between Hatti and Assyria. Hanigalbat had aided Muwatallis at Qadesh, and doubtless suffered its share of the losses. So now, when Hatti and Hanigalbat were least expecting it, the Assyrian swept westward, overcoming king Wasashatta and adding Hanigalbat to the Assyrian domains, extending them right up to the west bend of the River Euphrates. In consequence of his exploit, cock-a-hoop with his success, and with singular lack of tact, Adad-nirari I wrote to Muwatallis, claiming by his exploit the status of a 'Great King' ('great power' status), and proposing 'brotherhood' (or, alliance) with the Hittite; otherwise, he might be inclined to come over into Syria and visit the Amanus mountains — even deeper into Hittite territory!

To this cheeky missive, in apoplectic rage, the infuriated Hittite emperor slammed in a stinging reply:

> 'You brag [about your victory] over Wasashatta and the Hurrian land.
> By force you indeed conquered. You also have vanquished my [ally] and
> become a 'Great King'. But what do you keep saying about 'brotherhood'?
> . . . You and I, were we born of one and the same mother?! (On the con-
> trary), even as my father and grandfather were not accustomed to write

about 'brotherhood' to the King of Assyria, so you shall stop writing to me about ['brotherhood'] and great-kingship. I have no wish for it!'.

So, even for the Hittites, the consequences of Qadesh were not all gain. Added territory in the south (Upi) was little comfort when the entire Syrian province was more closely threatened from the east by the loss of the buffer-state there, of Hanigalbat. Eventually, it is true, a new ruler of Hanigalbat, Shattuara II, was destined to arise and side with the Hittites against Assyria, but this future event could not yet console Muwatallis when Wasashatta fell to the Assyrian wolf so soon after Qadesh.

The Struggle for Syria

Celebration, Promotions, Work at Abu Simbel

Safely settled back in his rapidly-expanding new Delta Residence, Ramesses II decided to immortalise for all time his personal exploit in retrieving transient victory from the jaws of total disaster at Qadesh. If *he* had not led the way, rallied his attendants and capitalised on the sudden arrival of the support-force, where would Egypt be now? Probably leaderless, and her entire empire lost. But valour had carried the day. True, Qadesh was not taken, and the Hittite had truculently annexed Upi as well as Amurru once more — but (in Ramesses' optimistic view) this could all be put right in a year or two, with better military intelligence and a fully refurbished army. In that light, his heroics at Qadesh would be not the end of a dream, but the herald of greater achievements to come.

So, Ramesses commissioned his scribes and artists to produce an 'epic' composition of great scenes and major inscriptions to celebrate his high deeds, which could then be engraved on a vast scale on the walls and pylon-façades of the greatest temples in Egypt. They duly came up with a splendid 'two-dimensional' record of the whole — two major scenes and an 'epic' account. The first tableau should show the Egyptian camp, the King seated by it, the beating of the bad news out of the two Hittite scouts, the attack of the Hittite chariotry on the camp, and the arrival of the support-force, all with appropriate 'label'-inscriptions. The second tableau was designed to show the King in his chariot, charging bravely against the enemy, driving them back into the Orontes, beyond which stood the Hittite king, impotent, with his columns of uncommitted troops; above, as background, was set the moated citadel of Qadesh. As a humorous touch, spotted by keen-eyed Egyptian observers, there was included the unfortunate Prince of Aleppo being emptied of water. When the temple wall-surfaces permitted it, supplementary tableaux could be added, showing presentation of prisoners to the King, and then the King and his sons leading prisoners and offering booty to the gods. To accompany the whole, a splendidly florid and poetical narrative was composed, to tell of the start of the campaign, the Hittite onset, the pharaoh's bravery and prayer to Amun, his army's panic, the repulse of the Hittites, and the next day's battle and Hittite 'plea' for peace.

22A. Abu Simbel, facade of the Great Temple of Ramesses II, showing the four colossi of the King, hewn in the sandstone cliff.

This remarkable composition, then, of word and picture (like snapshot and soundtrack) was duly engraved on the north and west exterior walls of Ramesses' new temple at Abydos, along the entire south exterior wall of the great Hall of Columns at Karnak (later to be partly replaced by scenes of other wars), along the South Approach at Karnak (west side), thrice over at Luxor temple (pylon-facade, exterior of courts), and then twice over in the Ramesseum's fore-courts across the river. As we shall see, yet another example was given monumental setting in distant Nubia.

In the wake of his army's failure in 'intelligence' and combat at Qadesh, Ramesses doubtless undertook a drastic reshuffling of his military 'top brass'; but history so far draws a discreet veil over details. But promotions follow demotions. Here at least, one may perhaps place the advance-ment of Ramesses' longstanding companion Amen-em-inet to be henceforth a Royal Envoy to All Foreign Lands. In this new capacity, Amen-em-inet says, "I reported back to him (the King) on the foreign lands in all their aspects" — a sample of Rameses' new 'intelligence-network'?

But the tireless Ramesses found time for other plans besides wars. His eyes again turned southward, to Nubia. A few miles north of Aksha, on the west bank of the Nile, sloping steeply up from the narrow river-plain, there arose two great bluffs of pinkish sandstone — the rock of Abshek, today's Abu Simbel. Here, two great sanctuaries were to be carved from the living rock. In the south bluff, a great façade — proportioned like a towering pylon — with four colossal seat-ed figures of the king (over 65 feet high) was to be the prelude to a temple whose halls were to be cut entirely in the living rock, 160 feet into the mountain. On the north interior wall of the first, great pillared hall, was to be placed a great representation of the Battle of Qadesh filling the entire wall. This gigantic edifice was to be Ramesses II's own memorial temple in the province of Nubia, under the patronage of Amun and Re. Meantime, in the northern bluff a few hundred yards away, a second splendid façade was to mark the entry to another rock-temple (going some 80 feet into the mountain), this time dedicated to the goddess Hathor, for Queen Nefertari. Its 'family' character was marked by the six colossal standing statues of the King and Queen adorning the façade, together with lesser figures of their children. So, two temples, 'His and Hers' in effect.

Moreover, the men charged with inaugurating the work on these huge twin-projects were able to leave their 'signatures' there for posterity. The man on the spot, the Viceroy Iuny, placed a scene of himself before the king, exactly aligned with the north edge of the façade of the Queen's temple, on the rock-face, linking himself publicly with the work. However, it was his last major act; soon thereafter, a new Viceroy took over these tasks with the rule of Nubia — Heqanakht. But the other man particularly concerned with starting-off Abu Simbel was a trusted retainer — Ramesses' principal cupbearer Asha-hebsed, now promoted to First King's Cupbearer of His Majesty, and bearing the full loyalist name of Ramesses-Asha-hebsed, "Ramesses-rich-in-Jubilees', a pious wish for long life for his master. Once he had arrived 'on site' in Nubia, this ever-active man got busy with the arrangements for the great temple. Like Iuny, he left his 'card', a deeply-cut rock inscription (with himself before the King) in which he declares:

*22B. Abu Simbel, facade of the Temple of Queen Nefertari, framing statues of
the king and queen cut in the living rock.*

'Behold, His Majesty's mind was alert to discover every good opportunity for conferring benefits on his father, the god Horus of Meha - in fact, making his Temple of Millions of Years, it being executed in the mountain of Meha . . . He brought many workmen, the captures of his strong arm from every foreign land, he filled the estates of the gods with the children of Syria as bounty. The King's Cupbearer was charged to set in order the land of Kush anew, in the great name of His Majesty . . .'

So, Asha-hebsed had sweeping powers, to regulate affairs in Nubia (perhaps Iuny was failing in vigour) and to expedite work on the great new temple. Meha was the name given to the south bluff, sacred to the local Horus-god, as Ibshek, the north bluff was to Hathor. But Horus of Meha was not destined to enjoy any great prominence in the king's temple thereafter.

Recuperation and Rebellion

For a twelvemonth, during his regnal Years 6 to 7, including the summer of 1273 B.C., Ramesses II undertook no major campaign, but concentrated on rebuilding his battered army. Naturally, the restored war-machine would benefit from a trial spin; so, perhaps it was that summer that Ramesses gave his refurbished forces an easy try-out on the stamping-ground of his youth, the coastland of Libya, to preclude any movement there as his eye turned to Syria.

Meantime, trouble was erupting in that very quarter. The retreat of Ramesses after Qadesh, the loss of Upi without counter-action, and the absence of an Egyptian army and king the season after — all this was taken in Canaan as a sign of Egyptian weakness, and Egyptian tax-collectors found the local rulers very unforthcoming with tribute. Across the Jordan in Eastern Palestine, new kingdoms had been forming, such as Moab beyond the Dead Sea, and Edom-Seir south of it. These now refused to recognise Egyptian rule, while the semi-nomads from Seir (the Shosu) went raiding into Canaan. There had been no trouble like this for twenty years past, since the beginning of Sethos's reign.

Nothing more could be done that season, but next spring for Years 7/8 (summer of 1272 B.C.), Ramesses took things in hand. In no time he reached Gaza, and showed Canaan that there would be no change in its vassal status. A flying-column swept the Shosu back east, out of Canaan entirely. Then Ramesses dealt with East Palestine. Led by the senior prince Amen-hir-khopshef (formerly Amen-hir-wonmef), the flying-column struck down through the Negev hills, across the rift valley south of the Dead Sea, and up into Edom-Seir, conquering their settlements. Then the Prince's forces swung north across the deep ravine of the Zered into the heartland of Moab and along the traditional 'King's Highway' to conquer Butartu (Raba Batora). At the same time, Ramesses himself swept round in a clockwise arc to complete the pincer movement — across the hilly central ridge of Canaan past Jerusalem, over the Jordan, past Jericho and the north end of the Dead Sea, and south into Moab, striking at Dibon. That settlement taken, he then came on south across the Arnon valley and stream, to link up with Prince Amen-hir-khopshef.

With Canaan quietened and East Palestine subdued, Ramesses could look north once more. He could now at will continue up the 'King's Highway' by Heshbon, Ammon, past Ashteroth-

Qarnaim and so to Damascus and over to Kumidi, restoring the lost province of Upi to Egypt. With his own possessions thus firmly restored, Ramesses could return confidently to Egypt.

The New Syrian Offensive

At last Ramesses felt ready to resume his Syrian ventures. The summer of Years 8/9 (1271 B.C.) saw him crushing the last flickers of resistance in the north of Canaan, dissidents in the Galilean hills (Marom, Beth-Anath), and occupying the port of Accho. From here, Ramesses could advance north along the south-Phoenician coast, affirming his rights in the ports of Tyre and Sidon, Beirut and Byblos, Ullaza, Irqata and Simyra. A rock-inscription may have been engraved at the Dog River headland.

So far, not even the Hittites could take umbrage. But Ramesses did not stop here. Wasting no time on either Amurru or Qadesh, he out-flanked them by marching east and inland through the Eleutherus valley and then north down that of the Orontes, advancing deep into Hittite-held territory where no Egyptian army had been seen for 120 years. He thus overcame Dapur in the northern fringe of Amurrite territory — 'a city which His Majesty vanquished in the land of Amurru', as stated in a text of Year 8. Further north, Ramesses then took over the territory of the city-state of Tunip. In Dapur itself, the pharaoh openly proclaimed his sovereignty by erecting a statue of himself in that city, perhaps in its principal temple. By thus occupying the middle course of the Orontes, Ramesses sought to establish a possible stranglehold on Hittite-held southern Syria — Amurru was bisected, and it and Qadesh were isolated from ready communication with their Hittite overlords up north in Aleppo, Carchemish and Hatti proper. This bridgehead could bring Ramesses eventual victory over Amurru and Qadesh which had been thus isolated and afforded him the opportunity to expand in north Syria.

Early in Year 9, therefore, Ramesses II probably arrived back in Pi-Ramesse with a considerable sense of achievement — so far. And without much Hittite reaction, this time. For this, there was probably good reason. After possibly a quarter-century on the Hittite throne, Muwatallis had by now probably died, precipitating a crisis in the royal succession. He left no son by his principal queen, only a stripling, Urhi-Teshub, by a concubine. This young man now became emperor as Mursil III. But he felt over-shadowed by the strong man of the day, his uncle Hattusil. Distrustful of Hattusil, the young king kept his ambitious uncle out on the northern marches of Hatti, with inadequate forces, to stand guard against the unruly Kaskean tribesmen. Mursil III probably did not feel able to leave the Hittite homeland (and Hattusil) behind him to deal with Syria personally, and so left to his Syrian viceroy, the King of Carchemish, the problem of opposing the new Egyptian attacks in Syria.

Syrian Stalemate

Once Ramesses had gone back to Egypt, the emissaries from Hatti and Carchemish probably had little difficulty in persuading such towns as Tunip and Dapur to eject their new Egyptian commissioners and return to Hittite allegiance Egypt was very far distant, while the armies of Carchemish, Aleppo and Nuhasse were quite near — such a practical threat to their self-preserva-

23. *Ramesses II receives Moabite prisoners flanked by two of his sons at the fort of Batora in Moab. (Luxor temple).*

tion probably induced the briefly-occupied centres to resume their usual relationship with Hatti.

Ramesses II was still not deterred. Year 10 (1270/1269 B.C.) found him on campaign once more. A third stela at Dog River attested his passage through Phoenicia. Again east and north, to subdue Dapur once more. Now in his mid-thirties, Ramesses still boasted of his physical prowess. Reliefs of him in the Luxor and Ramesseum temples firing off flights of arrows at Dapur were thus inscribed:

> 'As for this way of standing and attacking this Hittite city in which Pharaoh's statue is, His Majesty actually did it twice in the presence of his troops and chariotry, while leading them, attacking this Hittite enemy city which is in the region of the city of Tunip in the land of Naharin. His Majesty took up his coat-of-mail to wear it, [only after] he had (already) spent 2 hours standing and attacking the city of the Hittite foe, in front of his troops and chariotry, [without] a coat-of-mail on him. Only then did His Majesty come back to pick up his coat-of-mail again, to put it on. Now, he had spent 2 hours attacking the hostile Hittite city, . . . without wearing his coat-of-mail'

69

As this rather prolix little bulletin makes clear, Ramesses was out in front again, setting a brave lead for his troops. Luckily, no marksman on the Dapur battlements drew a bead on him with a fatal shot. Doubtless the king again forced Dapur to submit . . . until he returned to Egypt. Then the Syrians simply went back to their Hittite masters. How many years this inconclusive Punch-and-Judy contest continued is not clear now, at this distance in time. Stubborn and persistent as he was, even Ramesses must gradually have realised that, short of reducing all of North Syria as far as the Euphrates and the Taurus, he simply could not hold down central Syria in piecemeal fashion. So, in Years 11 to 17, his northern campaigns perhaps quietly ceased, and he was at last more content to hold his traditional territories, and to turn his attentions to other fronts. Meanwhile, in distant Hatti itself, the ever more tense relations between young Mursil III (Urhi-Teshub) and his uncle had steadily approached breaking-point.

The Exodus of the Hebrews

In the Egyptian East Delta, from of old were to be found a medley of tongues and peoples. At the end of the Old Kingdom, and particularly in the later Middle Kingdom, culminating in Hyksos rule, Semitic-speaking groups had entered and made their home in the east Delta, had become servants in, and members of, Egyptian households even far up the Nile Valley. Joseph (Genesis 37, 39-50) was one picturesque example of the current flowing into Egypt then. Under the great pharaohs of the Eighteenth Dynasty, stricter control over whoever passed by Sile probably obtained. But to the foreigners already domiciled in Egypt were now added many thousands more, Canaanites, Amorites, Hurrians, as prisoners-of-war, to be employed on the great estates of major temples and state departments. With the building of stores and *entrepots* for tribute, an increasing number not only of prisoners but of other groups living in the Delta came in for compulsory labour on brickfields and other public works. Nor were foreigners restricted at all to the lower levels of society. Besides merchants and visiting envoys at court, such people were free, like general Urhiya, to gain high positions in society, even (as cupbearers and councillors) by the side of Pharaoh himself. On the lower level, Haremhab may have given impetus to new building-work in the east Delta, adding to the Temple of Seth in Avaris. Among the motley array of people 'press-ganged' on such works, were those termed Apiru (Habiru, in cuneiform sources), mainly displaced, rootless people who drifted or were drafted into various callings — including hard labour on building-projects. In Ramesses II's middle years, we read of 'the soldiers and the Apiru who are dragging stone for the great pylon-gateway of . . . Ramesses II'.

Lumped in with the Apiru generally were doubtless those who in the Bible appear as the Hebrews, and specifically the clan-groups of Israel, resident in the east Delta since the distant days when their forefathers Joseph and Jacob had first come to Egypt to escape famine. They, too, were fair game for Pharaoh's press-gangs, 'Making their lives bitter with . . . all manner of service in the field' (Exodus 1:13-14). The biblical tradition speaks of how one child in particular escaped a pharaoh's drastic mode of birth-control, by being brought up in a royal harim by a princess, until in due time he sided with his people and fled Egypt on a murder-charge, namely Moses (Exodus 2). In due time, also, the Hebrews had to share in brickmaking for Avaris and Pi-Ramesse for Sethos I and into the early years of Ramesses II — 'they built for Pharaoh, store-cities, Pithom and Raamses' (Exodus 1:11), the latter being (Pi-)Ramesse. Until Moses returned to claim his people from the pharaoh to deliver them from servitude. Only after repeated interviews would the stubborn king concede that they should leave, under the pressure of signs in nature from an unduly swollen Nile, ruined crops, disease and plague, and finally death of the firstborn (Amen-hir-khopshef?). So Moses led his people away from the environs of Pi-Ramesse, south and east to Succoth, and then north again by the Bitter Lakes. Trapped! Ramesses saw his chance, sent out a substantial chariot-force to round up this considerable body of disappearing slave-labour (Exodus 14:7). But on the lakes or Sea of Reeds, strong winds drove aside the shifting waters long enough to let the fleeing Hebrews through — and veered round in time to bring the water back with a rush, swamping the chariot-squadron with heavy losses. On the far bank, the triumph-hymn was not by pharaoh's bards but from the Hebrews (Exodus 15). Thereafter, the Hebrews were taken *not* along the main coast-route to Canaan ('the way of the Philistines'), too easily subject to Egyptian military control, but off south and east into Sinai. There before the mountain, they became a nation under their own 'Great King', by covenant with the God of their forefathers who delivered them from Egypt, and (Exodus 20) constituted them a people on stabler, saner bases for life and society than subjection to an ideology of deified power.

That event, the biblical 'exodus', finds no echo in Ramesses' proud inscriptions; one did not celebrate the loss of a chariot-squadron and other unfortunates would have to replace the lost labour in the brickfields and workshops. The plagues and losses of the year quickly became just an unpleasant memory to be pushed out of mind, and any lesson they taught was soon lost. For imperial Egypt, the exodus was a fleeting, if unpleasant incident; for the Hebrews, it was epochal, and for the spiritual history of the world, of incommensurable effect. In the narratives (Exodus 1-20), much is reminiscent of New Kingdom Egypt, such as the close oversight of workmen (especially foreign labour), visible also at Deir el Medina; the question of quotas of bricks, use of straw, as in contemporary papyri, the issue of holidays off work (again, as at Deir el Medina), and the pharaoh's harshness to foreign labour-forces (to be seen again in Nubia with the Viceroy Setau) in contrast to care for Egyptian workpeople, and the characteristic stubborn persistence of the proud Ramesside king. The 'unpleasant incidents' may well have fallen inside the first three decades of Ramesses II's long reign, perhaps sometime after Year 15; Hebrew tradition is on the whole reconcilable with some such date.

African Ventures

The North-West Frontier

On the opposite side of the Delta, Ramesses II had other pre-occupations. As a young prince, he had shared in his father's Libyan campaign. Now, sometime in his own reign, perhaps in the involuntary lull after Qadesh, Ramesses II decided on a more far-reaching method of controlling the Libyan coastal strip, to keep its population under observation. Along the western desert edge of the Delta, between Memphis and the sea, he strengthened a series of settlements, sometimes building new temples in them to the local gods of the west, ancient towns that are now mere mounds (the Koms, 'mounds', of Abu Billo, Hisn, Firin, Abqain, and El-Barnugi). Then, from the edge of the Delta near the Mediterranean, the pharaoh set up a chain of fortresses stretching far out to the west, along behind the Libyan coastline. These extended west from today's Gharbaniyet and El-Alamein (of later fame!) right out to Zawiyet Umm el Rakham, over 200 miles away from the mouth of the 'Western River'. The three known forts were probably only a few out of a whole chain, never more than two days' quick march (or one day's chariot-ride) apart. The series of garrisons could thus keep watch on movements by Libyan tribesmen (including new groups from further west), and could swiftly report back to Egypt any significant news, and call up an expeditionary force to counter any invasion-threat the moment it began to materialise. Thus did Ramesses plan to safeguard Egypt from any interference from that quarter. It worked well, so long as he lived, and so long as ordinary vigilance was maintained. A 'legionary' fortress of this kind could be quite substantial. At Zawiyet Umm el Rakham, 200 miles from home territory, the Royal Scribe, Army-commander and Governor Neb-re ruled a large fort whose precinct contained three major buildings, at least one a temple.

Back to Irem in Upper Nubia

For a generation or more, Nubia had remained quiet. Irem had been well chastized in Year 8 of Sethos I, and Ramesses as Prince-Regent had quickly snuffed-out a minor affair in Lower Nubia. By Years 15 to 20 of Ramesses II, memories of both escapades had probably already grown dim among the Nubians. The regular rule of the Viceroys, their persistent exploitation of gold — and of locals to mine it — and levying of taxes on the otherwise very limited Nubian economy were all very well, for Pharaoh, but every so often a local chief weary of such impositions would (from boldness or desperation) try to revolt in hope of throwing off Egyptian rule.

So now in Irem, with the campaign under Sethos I long forgotten, Ramesses II duly sent out his forces to assist the Viceroy. Four princes took part, including Set-em-wia and Merenptah, his eighth and thirteenth sons, youths perhaps in their early twenties. With less doing on the Syrian front they could get their military experience in Nubia. The campaign, inevitably, was soon over; more than 7,000 captives were taken, and Irem sank again into enforced quietude, never again to challenge Egyptian rule. At the new provincial capital of 'Ramesses the Town' at Amara West, the temple-walls had no suitable space left to display this local triumph, so the scenes of combat and spoils were engraved along the thickness-walls of the main town gate, the West Gate, that all going in or out might remember the might of Ramesses in the South and think of rebellion no more. At Abydos, a lesser record was to be added to the second pylon of Ramesses' temple there, but some interruption came and the inscriptions were never finished.

5: THE PEACE

Storm before the Calm

Crisis! Palace Revolution in Hatti

For seven years, as Mursil III, young Urhi-Teshub had reigned as Hittite Great King. Totally distrustful of his uncle Hattusil in the far north, who (while defending that border) was collecting various dissidents into his own service, the suspicious ruler progressively cut down the size of Hattusil's province, finally limiting him to one principal centre, Hakpis, where Hattusil had long been local king and high priest, installed there by his brother, the now dead Muwatallis.

Then came breaking-point: Urhi-Teshub sought to remove even Hakpis from Hattusil's rule. Arrest and eclipse seemed imminent — Hattusil could take no more. He accused Urhi-Teshub of opening hostilities, and publicly put their dispute to the judgement of his patron the goddess Ishtar of Samuha and the Weather-god of Nerik. Urhi-Teshub and his forces advanced to apprehend Hattusil. But the latter trapped his attacker in Samuha itself, taking him captive. Hattusil thus emerged triumphant. The Hittites now had a new 'Great King', the strong man of the day, now to reign as Hattusil III, with his wife, now Queen, Pudukhepa at his side. The new emperor did not execute Urhi-Teshub, but instead exiled him to the principality of Nuhasse in North Syria.

This all transpired by about the Year 16 of Ramesses II, whose envoys doubtless kept him well posted on these dramatic developments within the very heart of the great rival empire. But suddenly he himself was to become directly involved in the rush of events.

Crisis! New Threat of War

For, young Urhi-Teshub was *not* content to sit meekly in exile in Nuhasse. Perhaps within months, he began intrigues with the court of the king of distant Babylon. But the plot was discovered, so Hattusil III banished his erring nephew to the seacoast (perhaps even across to Cyprus). Hattusil III himself now opened up an intensive diplomatic campaign abroad, to obtain fullest recognition as legitimate Hittite ruler from the kings of other major states. He at length made alliance with Kadashman-Turgu, king of Babylon. In Assyria, he sought rapprochment with its new king, Shalmaneser I, who had come to power quite soon after Hattusil himself. Only with Egypt did hostilities persist. Despite the success of his eastern diplomacy, Hattusil's troubles were far from over. For now, the ever-contrary Urhi-Teshub had slipped away again and finally landed in Egypt. So, in about Year 18, Ramesses II found himself welcoming in the audience-halls of Pi-Ramesse, a deposed Hittite emperor, the son of his old sparring-partner, Muwatallis of Qadesh fame.

At once, Hattusil III perceived here the most appalling threat to his own throne — what would happen if so longstanding and formidable a foe as Ramesses II chose to back Urhi-Teshub as legitimate claimant of the Hittite throne? So Hattusil promptly demanded the extradition of the young emigré by Ramesses — and Ramesses refused.

This meant war! Hattusil III prepared to mobilise his forces. When informed of this, Kadashman-Turgu of Babylon promptly severed diplomatic relations with Egypt and offered to send — even to lead — his troops against Egypt alongside Hattusil. This help was courteously refused by the Hittite king (preferring to fight his own battles), but never had the international storm-clouds thickened more darkly in the world of the Ancient Near East than now, even at Qadesh. For his part, Ramesses II probably also had marshalled his armies and may have taken up position in the north of Canaan province, at Megiddo and Beth-Shan, ready to strike north in defence of his empire, if the Hittite-Babylonian threat materialised. While awaiting intelligence, he doubtless assured himself of the adherence of his own vassals. A formal stela of Ramesses II at Beth-Shan, dated to year 18, 4th month of Winter, Day 1 (February,1261 B.C.), may mirror by its presence the flurry of activity in Year 18.

Crisis! Hanigalbat Liquidated

Then, in about Year 18 or 19, came a further dramatic twist to the succession of crises. For some time, Shattuara II, the new prince of Hanigalbat, had survived by acknowledging the overlordship of Assyria (whose king had removed his predecessor, Wasashatta). But Shattuara II felt no compelling loyalty to the new Assyrian king, Shalmaneser I, and returned to the Hittite fold. Knowing that an Assyrian counter-attack was only a matter of time, Shattuara and his Hittite neighbour the king of Carchemish made what preparations they could to fend off the blow, occupying passes, routes and watering-places.

At last, Shalmaneser I struck westward against Shattuara II and his Hittite support, with maximum force, overwhelming their defences, and vanquished the whole of Hanigalbat, right up to the gates of Carchemish just across the Euphrates river. Some 14,400 prisoners were taken, the capital and nine main towns overcome, and 180 settlements sacked. Of far greater import was the fact that, *this* time, the Assyrian was here to stay — the entire realm of Hanigalbat was incorporated within the body of Assyria proper, and was never to be a distinct state again. So now, the actual frontier of Assyria ran along the Euphrates, marching with that of the Hittite Empire itself, and directly adjoining (and potentially threatening!) the Syrian province of that empire. The centuries-old tradition of an intervening Mitanni or Hanigalbat had gone brutally and forever. This sudden and catastrophic blow was like a cold douche for Hattusil III. He must now have realised that, despite the alliance with distant Babylon, he was now faced with foes on two fronts — east and south — directly on his own wider borders. To fight both was impossible — but how to escape the dilemma?

Peace at Last

Volte-Face by Hattusil

For Hattusil III to offer peace-overtures to a victorious Assyria in these humiliating circumstances was impossible — neither he nor his counsellors could stomach such a climb-down. What about Egypt? Perhaps the imagined threat from Ramesses II on Urhi-Teshub's behalf was more terrifying than real. After all, Egypt had not actually attacked the Hatti lands, despite accepting Urhi-Teshub into the Egyptian court. So a reversal of Hittite policy here seemed possible, with some pretence of honour being satisfied.

So in due course the Hittite king began discreetly to sound out the possibilities for peace with Egypt, doubtless after a clear interval of ostentatiously taking no hostile action in Syria. Of the quiet negotiations that moved from tentative soundings through earnest discussion to eventual agreement during the next couple of years, we know nothing. But agreement did come and draft documents could be exchanged. Ironing out details, envoys scurried back and forth for months between the two capitals — palm-groved Pi-Ramesse in the flat, warm Delta, and rugged Hattusas high on the bracing Anatolian plateau. By fast messenger, the journey took a month each way, but it was at least twice as long for any larger cavalcade.

The Treaty — Peace Agreed

At last, in Year 21 of Ramesses II, in November/December, 1259 B.C., there travelled down from Hattusas through Syria to Egypt a distinguished posse of charioteers, heading for Pi-Ramesse:

> 'Year 21, 1st month of Winter, Day 21, under the Majesty of . . .
> Ramesses II. This day, behold, His Majesty was at the City of Pi-Ramesse,
> doing the pleasure (of the gods. . .). There came the (three Royal Envoys
> of Egypt . . .) together with the 1st and 2nd Royal Envoys of Hatti, Tili-
> Teshub and Ramose, and the Envoy of Carchemish, Yapusili, bearing the
> silver tablet which the Great Ruler of Hatti, Hattusil (III) sent to Pharaoh,
> to request peace from the Majesty of Ramesses II'.

It must have been a poignant moment of very mixed feelings for Ramesses as he sat enthroned amid the splendours of the great Delta palace, when he bade the six men advance towards him and unveil before his eyes the great glittering silver tablet, engraved with long lines of close-set wedges of the cuneiform script and bearing in its centre (both front and back) a roundel engraved with kings, gods and strange hieroglyphs the like of which he and his court had rarely if ever seen. This outlandish glittering object was to be the final seal on all his valour in Syria for Egypt against Hatti. Like kings of old, including his father, he too was now to be bound by formal peace to the distant power of Hatti. No more wars and victories — Qadesh and Amurru would never be his.

But to set against any such regrets, there were ample compensations. From now on suspicion and uncertainty about Syria could cease; what was Egyptian would stay Egyptian. And Egypt's rights in the Phoenician ports would be guaranteed. Better still, Hattusil III was willing to concede this right of access all the way north to Ugarit, where Egypt's emissaries had not had free access since the palmier days of Amenophis III a century before. So, as the rigours of the battlefield also had possibly become less attractive to the now middle-aged pharaoh, the opportunity to have done with inconclusive conflicts and to turn his energies to quite other fields must have seemed increasingly attractive. This, then, was what flowed from the silver tablet, and its humbler copies in clay

75

24. *Egypto-Hittite Peace treaty. The Egyptian version on a great wall-stela, temple of Karnak, with Ramesses II worshipping the gods in scenes at the top.*

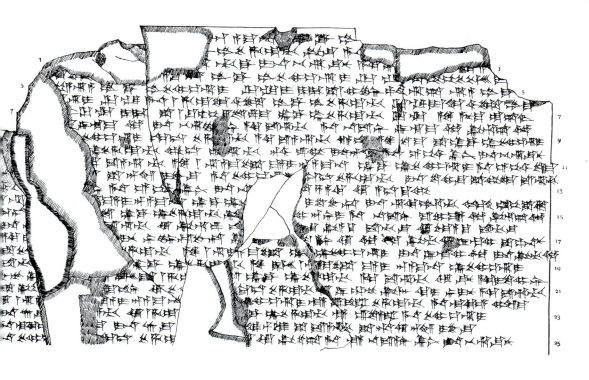

*25. Egypto-Hittite Peace treaty.   The Hittite version, inscribed in Babylonian cuneiform
(then the international language of diplomacy), on clay tablet from the Hittite capital*

in the Hattusas archives and Egyptian version on papyrus in the foreign office at Pi-Ramesse —
the latter in Egyptian, but the former not in Hittite but in Babylonian, the international diplomatic language of the day.

As befitted a major instrument of international law, drawn up between two equal Great
Powers, the Treaty was set out in two complementary versions — one as from Hattusil to Ramesses
and one *vice-versa*. Paragraph by paragraph, the document set out the ending of hostilities, the
establishment of a friendly alliance ('brotherhood'), adherence to a mutual non-aggression pact,
a mutual defensive alliance against attack by any third party ('another enemy', i.e., not Egyptian
or Hittite), on safeguarding the royal succession in both states, on mutual extradition of fugitives, and the humane treatment of those extradited. Finally, the great document closed with
the ultimate sanction for its authority — the two rulers invoked as witnesses to their pact, the
thousand gods of Hatti and the thousand gods of Egypt, who should bring down curses on whoever broke the treaty, and blessings on those who kept it. Great formal documents of this type
were perhaps less usual in Egypt (where Pharaoh's word was law) than throughout the Hittite
empire where such treaties were standard practice between overlord and vassal, and needed only
slight adaptation for use between equals. The Egyptian text of the Treaty, translated from a
cuneiform draft, and subsequently set out in Egyptian hieroglyphs on the walls of Karnak and

the Ramesseum in Thebes, shows well the dignified legal style of the day. In this version Hattusil addresses Ramesses:

'Now as regards the time of Muwatallis the Great Ruler of Hatti, my brother, he fought with [Ramesses II], the Great Ruler of Egypt. But now, as from today, behold Hattusil . . . [makes] a treaty to establish the relationship which Re made and which Seth made — the land of Egypt with the land of Hatti — to prevent hostilities arising between them, forever.

Behold, Hattusil III . . . binds himself by treaty to Ramesses II . . . beginning from today, in order to create peace and good brotherhood between us forever — he being friendly and at peace with me, and I being friendly and at peace with him, forever . . .

The Great Ruler of Hatti shall never trespass against the land of Egypt, to take anything from it. Ramesses II . . . shall never trespass against the land of Hatti, to take anything from it.

As for the standing treaty which was current in the time of Suppiluliuma (I), . . . , likewise the standing treaty which existed in the time of Muwatallis, . . . I now adhere to it.

Behold, Ramesses II . . . (also) adheres to it. The peace which has become ours together, beginning from today, we adhere to it and we shall act in accord with this regular relationship.

If some other foe should come against the territories of Ramesses II . . . , and he sends word to the Great Ruler of Hatti, saying, 'Come with me as ally against him!', — then the Great Ruler of Hatti shall act [with him, and] shall slay his foes. But if the Great Ruler of Hatti is not disposed to go (personally), then he shall send his troops and chariotry and they shall slay his foes . . .' And so reciprocally, Ramesses II for Hattusil.

'If an Egyptian, or two, or three, shall flee, and they come to the Great Ruler of Hatti, then the Great Ruler of Hatti shall seize them and have them brought back to Ramesses II, Great Ruler of Egypt. As for the person handed back to Ramesses II, Great Ruler of Egypt, let not his error be charged against him, let not his house, his wives or his children be destroyed, and let him not be killed. Let there be no injury (done) to his eyes or his ears, his mouth or his legs. (In fact), let no crime be charged against him.'

And similarly in the other direction, in the paragraph that followed.

'Now as for these terms of the treaty which the Great Ruler of Hatti has made with Ramesses II, the Great Ruler of Egypt, they are written upon this silver tablet.

As for these terms, a thousand gods of the deities male and female
who belong to Hatti, together with a thousand gods of the deities male and
female who belong to Egypt — they are with me as witnesses, and they have
heard these terms. (Namely):-

The Sun-god, Lord of Heaven, the Sun-god(dess) of the city Arinna;
the Storm-god, Lord of Heaven, the Storm-god of Hatti, . . . of Arinna; the
Storm-gods of Zippalanda, Pittiyarik, Hissaspa, Saressa, Aleppo, . . .; Astarte
of the Hatti-land, . . . the Lady of Karahna, the Lady of the Battlefield, the
Lady of Nineveh; . . . the Queen of Heaven; the gods, the Lords of the Oath;
. . . the Rivers of Hatti-land; the gods of Kizzuwatna.

Amun, Re and Seth; the gods male and female; the streams and mountains of the land of Egypt. Heaven; Earth; the Great Sea; the Wind; the
Storm-clouds.

Concerning these terms on this silver tablet for Hatti and for Egypt:-

As for him who does not keep them, the thousand gods of Hatti together with the thousand gods of Egypt shall destroy his house, his land and
his servants.

As for him who shall keep these terms (written) on this silver tablet,
Hittites or Egyptians, . . . , the thousand gods of Hatti and the thousand gods
of Egypt will cause him to flourish, will make him to live, together with his
household, his land and his servants.'

The Egyptians were evidently fascinated by the motifs engraved within the roundels on
both sides of the silver tablet. When the royal command went forth to inscribe the Treaty at
Thebes, the scribes included at the end a verbal description of what was visible in those roundels. These were, in fact, reproductions in the silver of the impressions (usually stamped on clay,
of course) of the great state seals of the Hittite kingdom and its rulers:

'What is in the middle of the silver tablet, on its obverse:-
Inlaid figure of the Storm-god embracing the figure of the Great Ruler of
Hatti, surrounded by a border-inscription as follows: Seal of the Storm-
god, Ruler of Heaven; seal of the treaty made by Hattusil (III), Great
Ruler of Hatti, the Valiant, son of Mursil (II), Great Ruler of Hatti, the
Valiant.' What is within the surround of the outline-figure: 'Seal of the
Storm-god, Ruler of Heaven.'

There follows a closely similar description of the seal on the reverse, figuring the Sun-god-
dess of Arinna with Queen Pudukhepa and appropriate label-texts. As original documents from
the Hittite archives actually show, Ramesses' scribes here gave an almost archaeologically precise
description of the state seals on the silver tablet — precisely similar seals are known, showing the
Storm-god embracing a Hittite king, usually with a ring of cuneiform text around the circular
field of the seal, and a label-text in Hittite hieroglyphs within the field of the seal.

Mutual Congratulations!

The occasion of the signing of the Treaty was one of official rejoicing, and messages of congratulation and good wishes passed between the two royal courts of Egypt and Hatti. And not merely between the two kings as signatories to the Treaty. In Hatti, Hattusil III customarily associated with himself his Queen, Pudukhepa, in all major acts of state. So when her husband sent greetings to Ramesses, Queen Pudukhepa wrote a parallel letter of greeting to Queen Nefertari, still Ramesses II's principal consort in Year 21. The Egyptian court quite entered into the spirit of the whole occasion. From Egypt, alongside Ramesses II himself, his mother the dowager-queen-mother Tuya sent a letter of greetings to Hatti, as did the current Crown Prince, Set-hir-khopshef and the Vizier Paser. In appropriate response to Pudukhepa, Queen Nefertari sent official letters of reciprocal greeting to her Hittite 'Sister', rendered into cuneiform on clay tablets by the Foreign Office scribes at Pi-Ramesse, thus:

> 'Thus says *Naptera* [Nefertari], the Great Queen of Egypt:- 'To Pudukhepa, the Great Queen of Hatti, my Sister, speak thus:
> 'With me your sister, all goes well; with my country all goes well.
> With you my Sister, may all go well; with your country may all go well! See now, I have (duly) noted that you, my Sister, have written to me, to enquire after my well-being. And (that) you have written to me about the (new) relationship of good peace and brotherhood in which the Great King, the King of Egypt (now stands) with his brother, the Great King, the King of Hatti.
> May the Sun-god (of Egypt) and the Storm-god (of Hatti) bring you joy; and may the Sun-god cause the peace to be good, and give good brotherhood to the Great King, the King of Egypt, with his brother the Great King, the King of Hatti, for ever. And (now) I am in friendship and sisterly relations with my Sister, the Great Queen (of Hatti), now and forever.'

International relations was a new and unfamiliar field for Nefertari, as her rather stilted letter betrays.

By way of practical and visible evidence of the new cordiality the two courts exchanged presents — Nefertari sent jewels, dyed stuffs and royal garments to her 'Sister', and Crown Prince Set-hir-khopshef reports, 'Now I have sent gifts to my Father (the Hittite King) through (the Envoy) Parikhnawa.'

So the new relationship got underway to a promising start. Egyptian envoys did go as far as Ugarit, where vases in the name of Ramesses II reached the local palace. Hattusil III could now face up to Assyria or local foes on the north or west of his homeland secure in the knowledge that Egypt was now bound legally to aid, not hinder, him. Which was just as well. Within a few years only, Kadashman-Turgu of Babylon died, leaving his throne to a young man (Kadashman-Enlil II) who came under the influence of an anti-Hittite (and pro-Assyrian) faction at the Babylonian court, headed by the formidable vizier Itti-Marduk-balatu. So no comfort would reach Hattusil III from that quarter.

26. A. *Hittite state seal, showing the Hittite storm-god with king Muwatallis in his embrace.*
   Hittite hieroglyphs at left read 'Great King Muwatallis', and at right 'Storm-god' and
   'Great King'. Royal titles in cuneiform encircle the whole seal.
   B. *Hittite state seal, naming in Hittite hieroglyphs 'Great King Hattusil (III)' at left and*
   'Great Queen Pudukhepa' at right, under the winged sun-disc(Hittite version).

In Egypt, Ramesses II could now bend his energies to other projects, such as the completion of his great rock-temples at Abu Simbel. But the new beginning was not without its shadows, as in Year 22 or early 23 his mother Tuya passed away, a quiet, gracious lady in her sixties. For her, her doting son had prepared a splendid tomb in the Valley of the Queens at Thebes, where now he laid her.

A Hangover — Post-Treaty Tensions

But so radical a re-alignment had its growing-pains, where friendship must replace two decades of warfare and nearly a century of intermittent hostilities. The king of the little state of Mira in Asia Minor was foolish enough to ask Ramesses II about Urhi-Teshub, political exile at the Egyptian court. However, Ramesses gave him a blunt reply — 'as for the Urhi-Teshub affair, it is not as you present it . . . Take note of the good relations that (I) the Great King, the King of Egypt, have established with the King of Hatti, my brother. . .'
Despite the closing of the ranks, the Urhi-Teshub question nevertheless remained a sore point; possibly Hattusil had wished to apply the terms of the treaty retrospectively, to obtain his

81

extradition. But if so, then Ramesses certainly refused — for Urhi-Teshub was still resident at the Egyptian court well over a decade later. Likewise, Ramesses II may have hinted at seeking border-adjustments in Syria in his own favour, but equally got no change from Hattusil. While both monarchs were touchy at first over the fate of Urhi-Teshub, Hattusil was equally so over what he judged to be the overbearing tone of Ramesses II's letters, treating him (Hattusil) more as an inferior than an equal. Ramesses II in turn abruptly denied the charge and sought to re-assure his 'brother':

> 'I have just heard all the words that my Brother has written to me, saying:- 'Why did you, my brother, write to me as if I were a (mere) subject of yours?' Now, what you wrote saying, 'as if I were a (mere) subject of yours' — this word my Brother wrote me, I resent! . . . You have accomplished great things in all lands; you are indeed Great King in the Hatti lands; the Sun-god and the Storm-god have granted you to sit (enthroned) in the Hatti land in the place of your grandfather. Why should *I* write to you as though to a subject? You must remember that I am your brother. You should speak a gladdening word, 'May you feel good daily!' And instead, you utter these meaningless words, not fit to be a message!'

Having made his point, including tactfully recognising the usurper Hattusil as a true successor of his redoubtable grandfather, the great Suppiluliuma I (whose Syrian success Ramesses had in vain tried to undo!), Ramesses II than passed on to other topics — envoys; mutual gifts (Hattusil sent only one slave, and he a cripple!); the sending of Egyptian doctors to the Hittite land, and special herbs, both of which the Hittites were to value greatly in the years ahead.

27. *Hittite capital of Hattusas, reconstruction of the north facade of the royal citadel. The throne-room was in the big windowed building in the middle.*

However, the frictions gradually eased off as the two partners learned to live with each other's foibles, limitations and different cultural outlooks. Hattusil III's peevish complaints were now addressed instead to Babylon, whose new young king Kadashman-Enlil II had accused him of trying to interefere in the renewal of relations between Babylon and Egypt. This, Hattusil denied — he and Egypt were now allies, why should he object if Babylon resumed her former relations with Egypt? Eventually, Babylonian relations with Egypt were to become so good that Ramesses II even accepted a Babylonian princess into his harim. However, under his show of unconcern, Hattusil III was probably rather anxious about the Egypto-Babylonian rapprochment. After all, the new Babylonian king was friendly towards Assyria, and an Assyria-Babylon-Egypt axis could be a very dangerous threat to the Hittite king, isolating him completely in the great-power diplomacy of the day. 'If you can't beat 'em, join 'em!' Not exactly a Hittite proverb, but in due course it was the line that Hattusil took. A decent interval having elapsed since the liquidation of Hanigalbat, Hattusil III now felt able to resume overtures and then firm relations with Shalmaneser I of Assyria. The circle of relationships was now complete — Hatti-Assyria-Babylon-Egypt-Hatti — and on all sides, sea-pirates and northern tribesfolk apart, the world of the Ancient Near East looked more stable and reassuringly peaceful than it had for a long time past.

An International Royal Wedding

Haggling over the Bride!

As the years passed, so stable did the Egypto-Hittite alliance become that Hattusil III proposed to Ramesses that the latter should accept the hand of his daughter in marriage, to set the seal upon their alliance. To this proposal Ramesses duly agreed, at which Hattusil expressed his pleasure, which was then reciprocated by Ramesses.

So matters probably stood, early in Ramesses II's 33rd regnal year in the autumn of 1246 B.C., as the royal envoys sped between the two capitals. At this juncture in a rather foolish gesture of ostentation, the elated Hattusil promised a magnificent dowry with his daughter's hand:- 'greater will be her dowry than that of the daughter of the King of Babylon, and that of the daughter of the King of B[arga?] . . . . This year, I will send my daughter, who will bring (also) servants, cattle, sheep and horses, to the land of Aya — may my brother send a man to take over these in Aya . . .!'

Ramesses gladly complied, and outlined his arrangements for receiving the princess and her dowry at the Hittite border-post of Aya in south Syria, near the Egyptian province of Upi:

'Now I have written to the governor Suta, in 'Ramesses the Settlement' (Kumidi) which is in Upi, to receive these Kaskean slaves, these droves of horses, these flocks and herds which she will bring, and he will conduct them until the bride reaches Egypt.

[Furthermore, I have] written to the governor Ptah-[. . .] in the Ramesses-town (Gaza?) which is in Canaan . . . (likewise). And what my Brother has written, 'Look after the needs of the bride's escort', — thus you wrote — now I will command that it be done according as my Brother has written!'

However, at this point of the negotiations, some delay seems to have occurred on the Hittite side, which probably drew forth reproaches from Ramesses — first promised a princess and splendid dowry, now all delays. But Ramesses' reproach did not immediately reach Hattusil at his capital — the emperor was doubtless 'out of town' attending to one of the innumerable local feasts or rituals that kept Hittite rulers on the move around their homeland. Instead it fell to Queen Pudukhepa to send, not a mere parallel to a letter by her husband (as usually happened), but a full-scale reply and riposte in her turn. Ramesses had taken up Hattusil's boast about the dowry (especially with the delays) all too enthusiastically, and now claimed he did need a really 'golden handshake'! Scandalised by what *she* evidently considered to be Ramesses' outright cheek, the doughty Queen did not spare his blushes in writing thus to her 'brother' monarch, Ramesses II:

> 'Now you, my brother, wrote me as follows:- 'My Sister wrote me, 'I will send you a daughter' — yet you hold back from me unkindly, still. Why have you not yet given her to me?'
> — You should not distrust but believe (us). I would have sent you the daughter by now, but [. . . *various difficulties* . . .] ; [. . .] burnt is the Palace. What was left over, Urhi-Teshub gave to the great god(s). As Urhi-Teshub is there (with you), ask him, now, whether this is so or not! What daughter in heaven or earth shall I give to my Brother? . . . Shall I marry him off to a daughter of Babylon, or Zulabi or Assyria? . . .
> — My Brother possesses nothing?? If the son of the Sun-goddess or the son of the Storm-god has nothing . . . (only then) have *you* nothing (also)! That *you*, my Brother, should wish to enrich yourself from me . . . is neither friendly nor honourable !!. . . .'

This picture of the great Ramesses, builder of mighty temples and developer of gold-mines, pleading poverty and roguishly demanding the massive dowry is a grotesquely comic role in which to find the hero of Qadesh! However, to the prim and stalwart Hittite Queen, it was less amusing than outrageous.

In this same very long letter she chided the pharaoh for criticising delays in sending the princess and much else. Amusingly, she ends on a juicy piece of international gossip going the rounds of the courts of the Ancient Near East at that moment. Long since, Ramesses II had taken a Babylonian princess into his harim, but (like Amenophis III a century earlier) he did *not* allow her father's envoys to visit the girl in Egypt. Queen Pudukhepa had earlier commented on this cagey attitude, and Ramesses had picked her up on the point in his letter which was now under fire. So, quoting these facts, she goes on to reveal her 'sources':

> 'This story was told me by Enlil-bel-nishe, envoy of the King of Babylon. But just because I'd heard this tale, should I have ceased writing to my Brother? But as my Brother now distrusts me, I'll do so no more. What pains my Brother, I really will not inflict on him!

However, the irrepressible pharaoh was not deterred by Queen Pudukhepa's scoldings, and did not hesitate to continue the debate. But the matters outstanding were at last cleared up,the Hittites finally declared themselves ready to send the princess, and asked that a special Egyptian delegation might come to Hatti, with finest oil to anoint the young lady as she prepared for the journey of her lifetime. To this, Ramesses promptly responded in letters to the Hittite royal couple. In that to Pudukhepa, he announced:

> 'I have seen the tablet that my Sister sent me, and I have noted all
> the matters on which the Great Queen of Hatti, my Sister, has so very,
> very graciously written me . . . The Great King, the King of Hatti, my
> Brother, has written to me saying, 'Let people come, to pour fine oil
> upon my Daughter's head, and may she be brought into the house of
> the Great King, the King of Egypt!' . . . Excellent, excellent is this
> decision about which my Brother has written to me . . . (our) two great
> countries will become as one land, forever!'

The special delegation made its journey and did its job, probably in the early summer of 1246 B.C., as Queen Pudukhepa proudly wrote:

> 'When fine oil was poured upon (my) Daughter's head, the gods
> of the Netherworld were banished . . . ; on that day, the two great
> countries became one land, and you the two Great Kings found real
> brotherhood . . .'

All formalities being now completed, Ramesses doubtless welcomed this news and prepared to welcome the princess herself.

The Wedding March

So at last, in Year 34 of Ramesses II, in the late autumn of 1246 B.C., the Hittite princess left her upland home for the last time, surrounded by a glittering escort of soldiers, dignitaries and the envoys of both lands. Before her went her dowry — droves of animals; slaves, and a rich caravan of precious jewels and stuffs, the wealth of the Ancient Near East. Down through the passes of the Taurus Mountains, into Kizzuwatna (now Cilicia), east over the Amanus to the plain of Aleppo in North Syria. Then south to the river Orontes, on to Qadesh by the borders of Amurru, and so to the frontier of Egyptian-held Syria. Here, Queen Pudukhepa bade her daughter farewell. Welcomed by the Egyptian escort, the princess and her cavalcade were now conveyed on to Canaan, then along the Sinai coast-road, and so at last to Egypt. The great throng at length arrived in Pi-Ramesse, the rich dowry being presented before the king — and at last, in February of 1245 B.C., Ramesses II received his long-awaited Hittite princess in the great palace of Pi-Ramesse. She, we hope, was charming as Hittite princesses go; he in his fifties was still a handsome man, even if incurably proud of his past achievements, and treated as deity upon earth. However, general rejoicing attended the great event, and throughout the major temples of Egypt, copies were engraved of a huge inscription composed specially for the occasion. Such was done in Thebes (Karnak), Elephantine, Aksha, Abu Simbel and Amara West. For the goddess Mut in Karnak, a special briefer version was set up. Loyal officials who had played their part in bringing the princess to Egypt were duly rewarded — the senior royal envoy Huy was promoted to be the next Viceroy of Nubia.

In colourful contrast to the dozen or more earnest diplomatic exchanges in cuneiform that had taken the preceding two years of haggling and negotiation, the great poetical compositions from Ramesses' bards were florid and rhetorical in the extreme, especially the major Marriage inscription, vaunting Ramesses' might in a manner that would have jarred horribly on Hattusil III's feeling about great power equality:

> "Year 34, under the Majesty of . . . Ramesses II.
> Beginning of the splendid commemoration,
>> to magnify the power of the Lord of Strength,
> exalting the valour and boasting of the victory,
> the great and mysterious wonders that have happened with the
>> Lord of the Two Lands,
> very Re embodied, more than any previous king ('god') who has
>> ever been born,
> for whom valour was decreed . . . Ramesses II".

After 30 lines of rhetorical praise of the king, and how the Hittite king besought in vain the favours of Ramesses II, deciding finally to send his daughter, the text continues:

'Then he (the Hittite King) caused his eldest daughter to be brought, with splendid tribute (set) before her, of gold, silver, much bronze, slaves, spans of horses without limit, and cattle, goats, rams by the myriad, limitless — (such were) the dues they brought for Ramesses II.

One came to give pleasure to His Majesty, saying, 'Behold, the Great Ruler of Hatti has sent his eldest daughter with rich tribute, they (fairly) cover the roads(?), the Princess together with the grandees of Hatti-land, bringing it. They have traversed remote mountains and difficult passes, and have now reached the (Syrian) boundary of Your Majesty. Let the army and officials go forth to welcome them!'

So His Majesty rejoiced, (entering) the Palace happily, when he had heard about this marvellous event, utterly unknown (before) in Egypt. He then dispatched the army and officials to receive them speedily.

Now His Majesty had pondered in his mind, saying, 'How will they manage, those whom I have now sent to Syria, in these days of rain and snow that happen in winter?' So, he offered a great oblation to his father (the god) Seth, . . . saying, 'The sky is in your hands, the earth is under your feet, whatever happens is what you command — so, may you not send rain, icy blast or snow, until the marvel you have decreed for me shall reach me!'

Then his father Seth heeded all that he said, and so the sky was calm and summer days occurred in the winter season. So it was that, with light step and happy heart, his army and officials set out joyfully.

Behold, as the daughter of the Great Ruler of Hatti entered Egypt, the troops, chariotry and officials of His Majesty escorted her, mingling with the troops, chariotry and officials of Hatti . . . They ate and drank together, in unity like brothers — none spurned his fellow, having peace and friendship between them, in the manner of the god himself, Ramesses II.

Thus, the ruling chiefs of every land that (the cavalcade) passed by, they cringed, turning away faint, when they saw all the people of Hatti united with the army of the King of Egypt . . (as for Ramesses II), . . . the land of Hatti is with him just like the land of Egypt. Why, even the sky is under his thumb and it does whatever he wishes!

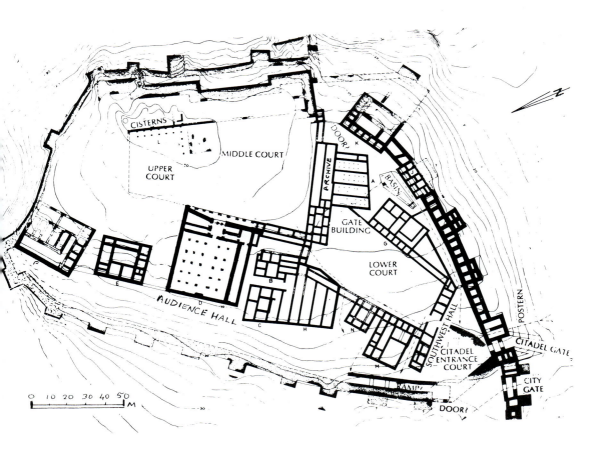

28. *Hattusas, restored plan of the royal citadel. The whole citadel was surrounded by massive ramparts and bastions, and overlooked the walled city of Hattusas (now, Boghaz-koy).*

87

Now when the cavalcade(?) reached Pi-Ramesse, it came(?) as celebration for them, a great marvel of valour . . . in Year 34, 3rd month of Winter, of Ramesses II.

Then the daughter of the Great Ruler of Hatti was ushered in . . . before His Majesty, with great and rich tribute in her train, limitless, all manner of things. Then His Majesty beheld her, as one fair of features, first among women — the grandees [honoured her as?] a very goddess! Behold, it was a great and mysterious event, a precious wonder, never known or heard of in popular tradition, never recalled in writing, since the time of the (fore)fathers — the daughter of the Great Ruler of Hatti coming, proceeding into Egypt, to Ramesses II.

Now, she was beautiful in the opinion of His Majesty and he loved her more than anything, as a momentous event for him, a triumph which his father Ptah-Tatonen decreed for him.

Her (Egyptian) name was proclaimed as:-
'Queen *Maat-Hor-Neferure,* may she live. daughter of the Great Ruler of Hatti, and daughter of the Great Queen of Hatti'.

She was installed in the Royal Palace, accompanying the Sovereign daily, her name radiant in the [entire?] land . . ."

Beside the outward glory of this magnificent state occasion, the rejoicing crowds in the streets, squares and taverns of Pi-Ramesse, the dazzling splendour of the dowry, the slim figure of the princess by the side of the proud pharaoh in his brilliantly-tiled and columned throne-halls, there was also the practical spin-off from the strengthened alliance as recorded by the royal scribes:

"Thereafter, if a man or woman went out on business to Syria, they could (even) reach the Hatti-land without fear haunting their hearts, because of the victories of His Majesty" — including matrimonial conquests!

The New Queen

Almost a year later, in the winter of Year 35 (early December, 1245 B.C.), the glittering occasion still echoed through Egypt. That year, the god Ptah of Memphis conferred his blessings on Ramesses II, in a great inscription which was composed for engraving in the major temples throughout Egypt and Nubia, making a pair with the great Marriage Stela of the previous year. Here, referring to the recent royal marriage, Ptah is made to remark, "never has it been heard since (there began) the secret Annals of the Gods in the House of Books, from the time of Re until Your Majesty — unknown hitherto had been the relationship of Hatti in one mind with Egypt".

At first, Ramesses II's Hittite Queen was given a full share in the honours of the palace with her Egyptian compeers, the princess-queens Bint-Anath, Meryet-amun or Nebttawy. Her name — "She who beholds the Falcon (King) that is the visible splendour of Re" — appeared on the monuments of Pi-Ramesse, as a full queen on royal statuary and on glazed plaques used as amulets or laid in foundation-deposits. But, as we shall see, in rather later years, as a matron in her forties or fifties she was sent to live at the great Harim by the Fayum garden-province, some 120 miles away from Pi-Ramesse and its visiting Hittite envoys.

International Royal Visits

The Hittite Crown Prince in Egypt

As the 'wedding decade' passed by (Years 33 to 42) and Egypt and Hatti settled down into a firm friendship, old suspicions dropped away and a greater sense of relaxation gradually came into play.

Not only did the customary royal envoys of both nations incessantly pass to and fro, but more exalted personages made the over-800-miles' journey between rocky Hattusas and palm-fringed Pi-Ramesse. One such was no less a personage than Prince Hishmi-Sharruma, son of Hattusil III and Crown Prince of the Hittite realm, who was one day destined to succeed his father as Tudkhalia IV.

Like his sister (now a Queen of Egypt), Prince Hishmi-Sharruma chose to travel from Hatti to Egypt during the winter months, a point remarked on by Ramesses II in a letter to the prince's father, King Hattusil:

"See now, when Hishmi-Sharruma came, he came in the months of (winter) cold!" When, after his visit to Egypt during the equable winter climate of that favoured land — the 'tourist season', indeed! — the prince eventually returned to Hatti (perhaps in the spring), he then went "with the envoys who accompanied him", with presents for the Hittite court. One may well wonder what impression life at the colourful court of Ramesses II made on the future Hittite king. Was he impressed by the sculptured and painted reliefs that adorned the huge stone temples of Egypt's gods? Did he ever, through interpreters, engage in discussion of the nature, forms and organization of Egyptian religion and Egyptian political usage and administration with such notable men as the princes Khaemwaset and Merenptah, then leading sons of Ramesses II? He can hardly have spent his months in Egypt in mute isolation, but we shall probably never know the answers to these or many other intriguing questions. Suffice it to notice in passing that it was Tudkhalia IV who in particular wrought the series of reliefs of the Hurrian-Hittite pantheon of gods in the main part of the great open-air rock-temple of Yazilikaya close by the Hittite capital of Hattusas. He too used Hittite hieroglyphs on a monumental scale oftener than his predecessors. And it was Tudkhalia IV who carried out a survey and inventory of the religious cults of his great realm, setting the archives back in order, recopied and re-checked. One may wonder if his memory of Egypt did not encourage him later to make use of more monumental art and script in Hittite religion and to carry out the kind of inventorising beloved of Egyptian kings and by no means foreign to tidy Hittite usage.

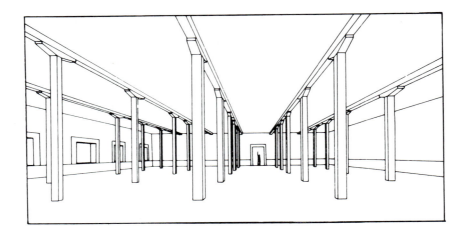

29. *Hattusas, royal citadel, throne room of the audience hall – reconstruction looking to north door, as seen from the Hittite throne.*

Hattusil III Visits Egypt?

Such less formal visits as that of Hishmi-Sharruma, by their success, paved the way for something much bigger: a visit by the Great King Hattusil III himself to Ramesses II in Egypt. The ever-optimistic Ramesses sent a warm invitation to Hattusil, to come and visit Egypt for himself. so that they could get to know each other personally. But, grumpy as ever, Hattusil gave the invitation a rather cool and frosty reception – "let my Brother write and tell me just what we would do there!" By return and quite undaunted, Ramesses wrote back cheerfully:

> "What now has my Brother said?", and repeated his invitation still more pressingly: "The Sun-god (of Egypt) and the Storm-god (of Hatti) will cause my Brother to see his brother; – and may my Brother carry out this good suggestion to come and see me. And then (we) may see each other face to face at the place where the King (Ramesses) sits enthroned. So, I shall go (ahead) into Canaan, to meet my Brother and see him face (to face), and to receive him into the midst of my land!"

Thus Ramesses offered to meet his intended guest in Canaan, perhaps first at a residency (at Gaza?), and then to escort him personally to Egypt and most likely to the nearby Pi-Ramesse.

Perhaps the cautious Hittite monarch was eventually convinced of the sincerity and good-will of Ramesses' invitation. But then (if it were so), a new hitch occurred. Hattusil III got hot feet! More precisely, not a Hittite equivalent of 'cold feet', but some inflammation of his feet that, temporarily at least, prevented his going to Egypt. But at any rate the Egyptians were pro-mised 'a reliable report' on the progress of the Hittite king back to full health – evidently with the intention of then making his Egyptian visit. In fact, Queen Pudukhepa even had a dream about it all, in which she was told by a divine messenger to:

> "Make a vow to the goddess Ningal, of this kind:- 'If that disease of
> His Majesty (called) *Burning of the Feet* will pass quickly away, then I shall
> make for Ningal ten golden flasks set with (blue) lapis gems!"

In due course, Hattusil's feet did heal, and he was ready to be off, to judge from one letter written to say he was 'out of town' and on the road to Egypt. So it may well be that Hattusil III and Ramesses II — perhaps the two most powerful men in the world of their day — did meet personally in Canaan and Pi-Ramesse. Of so prestigious an event, we so far have no certain record — some great stela may have perished in the wreck of Pi-Ramesse long since, of which no trace has survived or can be recognised. But in the 'school' papyri from Memphis, one passage rather playfully has the Great Ruler of Hatti writing to the Ruler of Qode (North Syria), urging him to prepare to hurry down to Egypt and make fulsome greeting to Ramesses II. And a fragmentary jotting from Thebes presents the beginning of a model letter as if written by Ini-Teshub I, King of Carchemish. So, there is a real probability that the historic personal 'summit-meeting' did take place, despite the very fleeting traces so little discernible in later history.

A Royal Wedding Encore

Is there a Doctor in the House?

The Hittite court came increasingly to value Egyptian 'know-how', particularly in the realm of medicine. From the main court at Hattusas, the repute of Egyptian physicians and remedies spread to those of their satellites. Thus, to the forties of Ramesses II's reign (about 1240 - 1230 B.C.) belongs a group of letters exchanged with the Hittite court and employing Ramesses II's new royal style, 'Ramesses II Beloved of Amun' plus 'God, Ruler of Heliopolis' (expressed as *ilum, Sharru Ana*, in official Babylonian). So, when one of Hattusil's vassals, a local kinglet Kurunta, sought Egyptian medical help through his overlord the Great King, Ramesses II was able to oblige:

> "Now I have summoned a learned physician. (Dr.) Pariamakhu will
> now be sent to prepare herbs for Kurunta, King of the land of Tarhuntas;
> he requested (a selection) from all the herbs, in accord with what you
> wrote to me."

On other occasions too, Dr. Pariamakhu was able to oblige. The cuneiform for 'learned physician' is literally 'scribe (and) physician', and equivalent to the Egyptian '(Royal) Scribe and (Chief) Physician'. This man's special skill seems to have lain in his ability to prepare herbal medications. One time as he went out to Hatti, two other Egyptian doctors returned to Egypt. Such comings and goings had long been customary between Egyptian and other Near-Eastern courts, when Syrians came to Egypt to consult Egyptian physicians, or Egyptian doctors were sought by the kings of wealthy Ugarit, far up the coast of North Syria.

91

Hittite faith in Egyptian medical skills knew no bounds, rather to the embarrassment of Ramesses. When Hattusil wrote to the pharaoh requesting a doctor to prepare drugs to help his married sister to have children, the irrepressible Ramesses replied with candour and an ungallant lack of chivalry:

> 'Now see (here), as for Matanazi, my Brother's sister, (I) the king your brother knows her. Fifty is she? Never! She's sixty for sure! . . . No-one can produce medicine for her to have children. But of course, if the Sun-God and the Storm-god should will it. . . But I will send a good magician and an able physician, and they can prepare some birth drugs for her (anyway).'

A New Princess

So cordial did relations become, it seems, that Hattusil III offered a second daughter in marriage to Ramesses II, again with a rich dowry. 'Never say no to a lady' (especially when well-endowed) seems to have been the pharaoh's motto in such matters, and so in due time a second Hittite princess was on her way to Egypt. The vassal rulers, too, contributed their part to the wealth and splendour of this royal encore. Of the diplomatic correspondence and negotiations attending this new marriage, we so far know nothing. But once more pharaoh's court poets went to work for the occasion, stressing this event as a gift from the gods, in a very poetic text set up on stelae in various temples:

> 'His Majesty decreed that [record] be made on [a stela], of the great
> marvels granted by Ptah-Tatonen, . . . (and other gods . . .) to Ramesses II,
> their goodly son, concerning how the Gods of Egypt caused the ruling chiefs
> of every foreign land to bring their tribute to Ramesses II their goodly son,
> even much gold and silver and every kind of noble gemstone.

> The Great Ruler of Hatti sent the rich and massive spoils of Hatti,
>   the rich and massive spoils of Kaska,
>   the rich and massive spoils of Arzàwa,
>   the rich and massive spoils of Qode,

> which were (of scope) unknown in writing, to Ramesses II.

> And likewise, many droves of horses,
>   many herds of cattle,
>   many flocks of goats,
>   many droves of game,

> before his other Daughter whom he sent to Ramesses II, to Egypt, on what was the second (such) occasion.

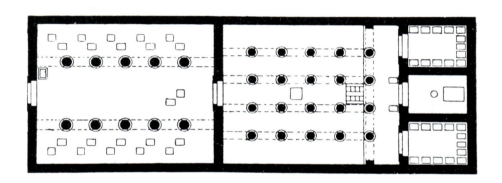

30. *Pharaoh's Foreign Office. Above, in centre, the pharaoh's secretary Tjay makes offerings to Thoth (god of scribes and learning), whose baboon-images guard and occupy a shrine at right. In the outer hall, Tjay in the ministerial chair signs documents brought by minions while in the outer aisles, office clerks produce still more paperwork. Below, a reconstructed plan of the building*

It was not the troops who brought them, nor the chariotry who brought them,
but the might of the Gods of Egypt and of the Gods of every country — *they*
caused the ruling chiefs of every land to carry [their tribute on] their shoulders,
to Ramesses II.
They (the gods) caused the ruling chiefs to carry their gold,
    to carry their silver,
        to carry their vessels of greenstone, to Ramesses II;
    to bring their droves of horses,
        to bring their herds of [cattle],
            to bring their flocks of goats,
                to bring their droves of game,
  it was the children of the ruling chiefs of the Hatti-lands,
    who presented their dues, of themselves, as far as the bounds
      of the territories of Ramesses II.
They (truly) came of themselves, there was no official who went to bring them,
  no troops who went to bring them,
    no chariotry who went to bring them,
      no standard-bearers who went to bring them,
  it was Ptah-Tatonen, Father of the Gods, who places all lands and all
countries under the feet of this goodly god (Ramesses II) forever and ever!'

31. *Abu Simbel, scene from Marriage Stela. Enthroned between the gods Seth and Ptah-Tatonen
Ramesses II receives the Hittite princess, escorted by her father, king Hattusil III.*

So, in an aura of concord and courtly splendour, closed the vision of close Egyptian-Hittite relations under Ramesses II. Of the name and fate of the young lady who followed her sister into Ramesses II's harim, we know no more, nor of subsequent relations between the two courts. Not even the date of this second Hittite marriage of Ramesses II is known for certain, but it probably occurred not any later than the forties of the reign, when he adopted the titles 'God, Ruler of Heliopolis' (reflected also in cuneiform texts), and while Hattusil III still lived. Perhaps at length, when Hattusil III 'went to his fate and became god' as the Hittites would put it, and his son Tudkhalia IV reigned in his stead, relations grew less close and gradually relaxed further. Nevertheless, Egypt and Hatti were to remain allies for quite some time to come, and probably for as long as the two powers co-existed.

For another 20 years or so, to his sixty-seventh regnal year (1213 B.C.), the gradually-ageing Ramesses II reigned on in outward splendour, and Egypt enjoyed not only profound peace but considerable prosperity at most levels of her cosmopolitan society.

Echoes through the Centuries

Though no one could know it at the time, these great and splendid 'royal events' between the two major powers of Egypt and Hatti were to be the last of their kind for centuries to come. Political marriage-alliances continued to be made both in that epoch and in later ages, but were never again celebrated with such pomp, poetry and pageantry. But in Egypt at least, the tradition of these glittering events lingered on in the national memory, and was engraved forever on Ramesses' monuments. Thus, a thousand years later, the traditions of a foreign princess becoming queen in Egypt and of Egyptian physicians abroad were sufficiently known to the priesthoods of Thebes for them to hitch such wondrous tales to the repute of one of the lesser gods of Thebes in the third century B.C., and even to erect an impressive stela spuriously 'commemorating' Khons the Planmaker's part as healer, set away back in the distant golden days of Ramesses II and queen 'Neferure'.

32. Statue of Queen Tuya, mother of Ramesses II. (Vatican Museum)

"The Beauties of the Palace"

The Senior Lady : Queen-Mother Tuya

Peace and war, buildings and battles, took up much of the time and activity of Ramesses II, but by no means all of it. He was patron, too, of family life, and on a grandiose scale comparable with his buildings and his wars. Having had a harim ever since his appointment as regent, and in the course of his reign at least half-a-dozen principal queens, Ramesses II populated the palaces and harims with nearly a hundred sons and daughters in his time.

But for the first twenty years or so of the reign, one lady (other than the chief queen) stood out above the crowd: the Queen-mother. During the reign of Sethos I, Queen Tuya had doubtless been his faithful companion and consort, but she played no prominent role in political and public affairs, and is hardly to be found on monuments from her husband's reign.

Ramesses II, however, was devoted to his mother, and as pharaoh gave her considerable recognition. Statues of Tuya as Queen-mother were erected in the Ramesseum at Thebes, and in Pi-Ramesse; the Vatican Museum possesses one fine formal statue of her. Almost a thousand miles south from the Delta, her image was included with those of Ramesses II and Queen Nefertari and her children along the façades of the Abu Simbel rock-temples. Moreover, in Thebes, along the north side of the Ramesseum, Ramesses II rebuilt a small temple, renewing its dedication to Tuya. Of sandstone, it had a columned portico, court and halls, the pillars being crowned with capitals in the form of the head of the goddess Hathor. Arranged in two parallel suites, the temple may have served both Tuya and Nefertari as a memorial temple. Perhaps from here came reliefs showing Queen-mother Tuya's own parents, the Lieutenant of Chariotry Raia and his wife Ruia. Another major feature of the decoration was probably the legend of the *Divine Birth of Pharaoh*, taken over in his turn by Ramesses II to emphasise the god-given nature of his kingship. By this theological dogma, Amun incarnated himself in the king's father when the queen conceived a son (the king - Ramesses II, in this case). Thus, the young king-to-be was from birth the son both of Amun of Thebes and of his earthly royal father. In the previous Dynasty, both Queen Hatshepsut and Amenophis III had applied the legend to themselves in their west bank and Luxor temples respectively.

So, during her later years the Queen-mother enjoyed signal honours. She lived through the twenty years of conflict in Syria, and lived to share in the official celebration of the Hittite peace-treaty in Year 21, even sending one of the several official messages of greeting to the Hittite court. Meantime in Western Thebes, Ramesses II had prepared for her a splendid tomb in the Valley of the Queens; its stairs led down into three rock-cut halls, ending in a pillared hall. It was finely decorated, lavishly furnished, and a pink granite sacophagus installed to hold her coffins. It was sometime in Year 22 (1258/57 B.C.), so soon after the coming of peace that Tuya — probably in her sixties or so — passed away and so came to rest in her 'house of eternity'.

Sisters of the King

Two other senior ladies at court were Ramesses' sisters, one older, one younger. Even before Ramesses' grandfather had brought the family to the throne, Tjia had married a man Tia. After his accession as sole ruler, Ramesses had appointed his brother-in-law to be Superintendent of the Treasury and Cattle of the Ramesseum, a responsible post in which Tia could keep a family eye on the running of that great temple. Tjia herself was 'Chantress of Amun, of Great-of-Victories', attached to the cult of Amun in the Delta Residence; she had links also with Memphis and Heliopolis.

The younger sister, Hentmire, Ramesses took as one of his consorts, as, being born in the purple to Sethos I, she was in a way an heiress of the kingdom. Therefore, following Eighteenth-Dynasty precedent, she took her place among the official wives of the king. However, Hentmire's role was modest; she rarely appears on public occasions or monuments, except once on her mother's Vatican statue and again on a quite late statue of Ramesses II. It was perhaps in the forties of the reign that she had need of her sarcophagus, which was found at Thebes and is now in Cairo Museum.

The Rival Queens : Nefertari and Istnofret

Among the galaxy of young ladies that peopled the 'household' bestowed by Sethos I upon his Prince-Regent son, two stand head and shoulders above the rest. These were the Chief Queen, Nefertari, and her principal colleague Istnofret. Nothing whatever is yet known of the background and origins of these girls, henceforth the closest companions of Ramesses II into the twenties of his reign. That Nefertari was beautiful, gracious and charming as her husband was handsome and dynamic is perhaps hinted more than proven by the beauty of execution of her monuments, as if it were wished to do her justice. She certainly stood highest in the affections of Ramesses II from the very first. As chief consort, it was she who appeared alongside the king in public, on state occasions and in great religious ceremonials alike, and she whose slim, shapely figure was included by the side of her husband on his great statues set up in the temples in the first two decades of the reign.

Alongside Nefertari, the associate chief queen, Istnofret, appears (to us) as almost an 'also-ran' for that period. No public occasion is yet known to have been graced by her presence then, no colossus shows her by Ramesses' side, no temple was built for her. Was there any ill-feeling or jealousy in the royal harim between the 'First Lady' and 'second string'? No hint of any conflict suffices to prove any such tension behind the scenes. Perhaps Istnofret envied her colleague — perhaps she knew her station and was well content to leave any outward prominence till it should come — as it later did. Certainly Ramesses II esteemed his second consort; a gold bead, from some splendid jewel, bears his name with hers. Nefertari bore the eldest son, Istnofret the second son and eldest daughter; and both bore many more. Moreover, it was Istnofret's gifted sons who ultimately made the greatest mark and attained the succession.

Career and Monuments of Queen Nefertari

Right from the start, Nefertari's prominence was undoubted. She accompanied Ramesses to Thebes in Year 1, gracing the royal audience at Abydos when Nebwenenef was appointed High Priest of Amun. In Year 3, her figure accompanies the king in the scenes carved on the rear of the great new pylon of Luxor Temple (as in other scenes there), likewise carved gracefully in granite with the statues placed by the king's orders around the new forecourt. In Karnak she appears, and across the river may have shared the little temple along the north side of the Ramesseum with Queen-mother Tuya. In the Valley of the Queens, the workmen of the Royal Tomb quarried out and decorated a most splendid tomb — entry-halls, stairway, pillared hall, recess and side-rooms — adorned with the finest quality of scenes carved in low relief and brilliantly painted. It was quite the finest 'eternal home' ever made in the Queens' Valley.

But still greater honours awaited Nefertari in distant Nubia. Of the two great temples at Abu Simbel, one was for Ramesses II and the state gods — the other, for the goddess Hathor, dedicated to Queen Nefertari. Its façade had on either hand a colossal figure of the queen flanked by statues of the king, while smaller figures of their children nestled close to the great royal figures. All around these six giant figures, as they seemed to stride out from the very mountain, was a framing of boldly-cut hieroglyphic inscriptions, to say that:

'Ramesses II, he has made a Temple, excavated in the Mountain, of eternal workmanship . . . for the Chief Queen Nefertari Beloved of Mut, in Nubia, forever and ever, . . . Nefertari . . . for whose sake the very sun does shine!'

Throughout the temple the queen appears as often as her husband; only on the very rear wall of the inner sanctuary does Ramesses II finally take precedence, making an offering to Hathor, shown emerging as a cow to protect him. But at least Nefertari had the privilege of a temple dedicated to her in the Nubian empire, paralleled only by that of Amenophis III for his queen, Tiyi, at Sedeinga in the southlands.

In the king's own great temple nearby, Nefertari was again the companion of Ramesses, together with their children and Tuya. Only in the very last stages of work in the temple does another queen appear — the Princess-Queen Bint-Anath on the rear of a pillar, here just the *once* as a real queen, instead of solely as a king's daughter as elsewhere at Abu Simbel.

In Year 21, at the Hittite peace, Nefertari sent reciprocal greetings to her Hittite opposite number, Pudukhepa, as we have seen. By then she was probably of middle age, in her early forties, having borne her fair share of sons and daughters, at least seven or eight.

Then about Year 24 there came perhaps the last great event of Nefertari's life and career. The two mighty temples at Abu Simbel were at last virtually complete. The time had come to inaugurate these splendid shrines. So, maybe that winter (perhaps February of 1255 B.C.), the royal flotilla sailed on and on ever further south, past Thebes, through Lower Nubia and on to Abu Simbel. The king and queen were accompanied on this occasion by Princess Meryetamun (their eldest daughter), and escorted by the Viceroy Heqanakht and a retinue of dignitaries and servants. At dawn, the sun crept up over the eastern hills, struck across the river to illumine the façade of the Great Temple, suffusing the sandstone with a brilliant orange glow wherever unpainted. Within, the great doors opened, hall by hall, until at last the sun's long rays penetrated finger-like deep within, resting at last upon the statues of Ramesses II and his fellow-gods — Re, Amun, Ptah — carved in the rock at the back of the inner sanctuary nearly 200 feet inside the mountain — 'union with the sun's disc', as the Egyptian priests would express it, the life-giving rays of the sun enduing the images with life. On the rock-surface nearby, the Viceroy Heqanakht left his own memento of the great occasion, a rock-stela. Here, Ramesses II and Princess Meryetamun worship the gods of the Great Temple — Amun, Re, and Ramesses II himself. Below this scene, the Viceroy Heqanakht salutes the enthroned Queen Nefertari with offerings.

Did the gracious Queen survive the nearly 2000-mile round trip into the heart of Nubia and back? Perhaps it is significant that on the stela just mentioned, it is the Princess Meryetamun who actually accompanies Ramesses II in worshipping the gods, while the Viceroy honours Queen Nefertari. Perhaps – a mere speculation, this – the Queen was too ill or fatigued to play her role in the long, complex religious rituals that would attend the dedication of the new temples, and had to rest on the royal barge under the care of her doctors and the guard of the Viceroy while Meryetamun deputed for her mother by the king's side in the temple-rites. However this may be, after the return north to Thebes, Memphis and Pi-Ramesses, we see Queen Nefertari no more . . . Her final cortège to that marvellous tomb in the Queens' Valley may well have found its way there in Year 24 or very soon after.

Queen Istnofret and Daughter

Now at last, for a brief span, Istnofret the 'also-ran' became Chief Queen. Furthermore, as senior king's daughter of them all, her own first daughter Bint-Anath (in Canaanite, 'Daughter of the goddess Anath') became associate chief queen in her mother's place. By about this time too, most of Nefertari's brood of sons had already died in their young years. It was Istnofret's sons who lived on and won advancement in the offices of state.

As last, too, Istnofret appeared fleetingly on the monuments. On a rock-stela at Aswan (about Year 24/30 ?) she is shown with Bint-Anath already entitled Chief Queen and with her principal sons, Ramesses, Khaemwaset and young Merenptah. A few years later, on a splendid rock-stela at Silsila quarries, the two ladies attend Ramesses II with Khaemwaset before him. Here, Istnofret's eldest son Prince Ramesses was now Heir-Apparent —'Senior King's Son' — while Merenptah was by now a 'Royal Scribe, skilled (?) of fingers'. But Istnofret's prominence did not last long. Probably about Year 34 she too was dead and laid to rest in her tomb in the Valley of Queens, a tomb never yet identified but attested in records stemming from the workmen of the Royal Tomb. The role of Chief Queen now devolved fully upon her daughter Bint-Anath, with Nefertari's eldest daughter Maryetamun as her associate-queen.

The First Batch of Sons

Right from his early days as Prince-Regent, Ramesses II produced a growing army of children. Some, no doubt, died in infancy, but a considerable number lived at least to early manhood

33. Queen Nefertari, chief wife of Ramesses II. (Abu Simbel)

or womanhood, and others saw out their father's extraordinarily long reign.

Nefertari produced the eldest son, Amen-hir-wonmef, and the third son, Pre-hir-wonmef ('Amun, Re, is on his right hand'). Istnofret mothered the second son, Ramesses, the fourth son Khaemwaset ('Appearing in Thebes'), besides the eldest daughter Bint-Anath. Near the end of the regency and Sethos I's reign, the two little boys Amen-hir-wonmef and Khaemwaset accompanied their father (at least, ceremonially) on a minor campaign in Lower Nubia, immortalised in the Beit el Wali temple.

At his accession as sole pharaoh, Ramesses II appears to have changed his eldest son's name to Amen-hir-khopshef (Amun is with his strong arm'), and certainly appointed that prince as 'Senior King's Son' or Heir-Apparent, his own real rank until his own accession. Increasing numbers of young princes probably accompanied Ramesses II on his Syrian campaigns, if the great temple-scenes are to be believed. Certainly Pre-hir-wonmef was at the cataclysm of Qadesh, going like the vizier to fetch help. He could hardly have been more than a lad in his early teens at the time of this baptism of fire.

The Army Life for Some

Among those sons shown in the war-scenes, Amen-hir-khopshef quickly became a 'General-in-Chief', and his half-brother Ramesses also, the latter much later becoming 'First General-in-Chief'. For his part, Pre-hir-wonmef was specially entitled 'First Brave of the Army' (to commemorate his modest role at Qadesh?), went into the chariotry as Superintendent of Horse, and finally became First Charioteer of His Majesty — perhaps successor to Menna of Qadesh? This role, he came to share with the fifth son, Montu-hir-khopshef. All of the king's first fourteen sons seemed to have participated in the Syrian campaigns — the heir, Amen-hir-khopshef, acted in the Moabite campaign (about Year 7 ?). The thirteenth son, Merenptah, had a minor share in the wars but Nefertari's youngest sons — Mery-Atum, Set-hir-khopshef — seemingly did not.

Changes in the Succession

The rigours of the military life and hazards of accident or illness doubtless took their toll of Ramesses' prolific brood as the years passed. By Year 20, Amen-hir-khopshef was no longer Heir-Apparent (or, not by that name), and was probably dead. His younger full brothers Pre-hir-wonmef, Sethy and Meryre the Elder had also passed on, all in their mid or late twenties at most. Among Nefertari's younger offspring, there remained Mery-Atum (sixteenth son) and Set-hir-khopshef, probably slightly his junior. While Mery-Atum now held the title of Eldest (living) King's son by Nefertari, the pharaoh's favour passed over him to rest on Set-hir-khopshef, who became heir and 'priest' of his father's official divinity, and a special minister of state relating to northern affairs. As Heir-Apparent, Set-hir-khopshef therefore shared in the official greetings exchanged following on the Hittite Treaty in Year 21. But long before Year 53 (1227/26 B.C.), when his burial at Thebes received some attention, young Set-hir-khopshef had passed prematurely from the scene.

Thus, at last, in the early twenties of Ramesses II's reign, the leading role in the state passed forever from the sons of Nefertari to those of Istnofret. The new Heir-Apparent was General, Prince Ramesses, Istnofret's eldest. He may well have retained this exalted status for up to 20 years, possibly longer, from about Year 25 to Year 50 or so (1254/1229 B.C.). But even a prince with such long service was not destined to succeed to the throne. From the early fifties of the reign, the fourth son (Istnofret's second), the learned Khaemwaset, was briefly heir to the kingdom. But then Khaemwaset himself — of whom much more is yet to be told — died about Year 55 (1224 B.C.). So it was that his younger brother Prince Merenptah finally became the fifth Heir-Apparent of the reign during its closing years. The lad who half a century earlier had been merely thirteenth son, by the second queen, among a crowd of brethren, was at the last the eventual pharaoh, succeeding the longest reign in Egypt for centuries.

Khaemwaset — the Egyptologist Prince

Early Career

Fourth son of his father, second born of Istnofret, Prince Khaemwaset was destined for a fame that far outstripped in time that of any of his contemporaries other than that of Ramesses II himself. Born very early in his father's prince-regency, he was but a boy of five or so when taken on the Lower-Nubian 'campaign'. In later wars in his father's sole reign, Khaemwaset had his share, as shown in temple-scenes.

But war and the army were not Khaemwaset's chosen career. Perhaps quite early, the lad had given evidence of other tendencies — intellectual quality, avid mastery of reading and writing, a penchant for religion, theology, magic, and the scribal arts. As the court resided principally in the north, he entered into the service of Ptah of Memphis — the venerable shaven-headed, mummiform god of arts and craftsmanship, served by a learned priesthood.

Care of the Sacred Bulls

In his twenties, the precocious Khaemwaset was installed as a Sem-priest of Ptah, as right-hand-man to Huy, 'Chief of Artificers' or High Priest of Ptah. This was probably shortly before the death of the Apis Bull (sacred animal of Ptah) in Year 16 (1264/63 B.C.). For burial of the very small mummified residue of the dead bull, a sloping ramp and burial chamber were cut in the desert rock out in the Saqqara cemeteries of Memphis, in traditional fashion, not far from the buried tombs of earlier bulls, each crowned by its little chapel. Such was the 'Serapeum' or burial-ground of the sacred bulls until Khaemwaset's day. On the walls of the new burial chamber, Ramesses II and Khaemwaset were shown in worship before the god Apis. At the burial of Apis, many a notable contributed gifts (shabti-figures, potent amulets, etc.) to the burial-goods of the departed bull. In Year 16, such distinguished donors included (besides the High Priest Huy and Khaemwaset himself) the latter's elder brother, General Ramesses, and the vizier Paser. On the death of a bull, a new bull with the right markings had to be found in the land, and then installed as next

34.   Prince Khaemwaset. (British Museum)

Apis. A new Apis was duly found, and in turn died fourteen years later, in Year 30. This time, Prince Khaemwaset interred the deceased bull in the same tomb as its predecessor, and gifts came from the Chief of the Treasury, Suty, and perhaps another Huy, Mayor of Memphis. Other dignitaries and lesser ranks left stelae outside the tomb door - the learned scribe and lector, chief of embalmers, Piay, the Steward Ptahmose, the Chief of the Harim in Memphis, Amenmose, among others. With the passing of the years, other bulls also 'went West'; one, possibly in a side-room cut in the descent to the double tomb of Years 16 and 30.

Secret Vaults and an Apis Temple

For the later Apis bulls, Khaemwaset hit upon a new plan — a special underground gallery from each side of whose walls would open off not one isolated burial-chamber, but a series, keeping the burials of successive bulls in safety together, and requiring the cutting only of a modest side-room each time. So, in his later years, Khaemwaset had a stairway cut down into the rock, turning through three right-angles into a gallery running north under the desert plateau. Well along its length, a chamber was prepared for the next bull.

The new arrangement also did away with individual chapels built over the tombs. Instead, Khaemwaset built a Temple of Apis, as resting-place for the bull's mummy on the day of the last rites before burial, and as focus for the cult of the dead ('eternally-living') Apis. In a special inscription, the Prince addressed future generations on the nature of his works, appealing finally to Apis himself:

'The Osiris, the Sem-priest, Prince Khaemwaset; he says:- . . . 'O you Sem-priests, High Priests, dignitaries of the Temple of Ptah, . . . , and every scribe proficient in knowledge, who shall enter this Temple which I have made for the living Apis, and who shall behold these things that I have done, engraved on the stone walls, as great and effective benefactions!

Never has the like been done, set down in writing in the Great Festival Court before this Temple. The gods who are in (Apis's) Temple . . . [their images are wrought] in the Mansions of Gold, with every splendid precious stone. I have endowed divine offerings for him; regular daily offerings, (lunar) feasts whose days come on their appointed dates, and (annual) calendar-feasts throughout the year, over and above the food-offerings which are forthcoming in the (divine) presence, at the head of the offerings for Ptah.

I have assigned to him lay priests, lectors who recite the glorifications, . . . temple personnel . . . I have built for him a great stone shrine before his Temple, in which to rest in spending the day when preparing (for) the burial. I have made for him a great offering-table opposite his Great Shrine, of fine white Tura limestone, engraved . . . [with?] the divine offerings, (and) every good thing that is provided at the (Ceremony of) 'Opening the Mouth' . . .

It will indeed (seem) to you a benefaction, when (in contrast) you behold what the ancestors have done, in poor and ignorant works; there is none who should act (against) what is made for the peace of another . . . ; [he who respects such?], he is rewarded, he flourishes!

Remember my name, when decreeing [future such works ?], reward a (good) deed with its like — and may you make yourselves likewise!

O Apis-Sokar-Osiris, great god, Lord of the Shetayet-shrine, I am the Sem-priest, Prince [Khaemwaset]!'

Thus did the enterprising and learned prince set a pattern for the care and burials of Apis-bulls that outlasted him for thirteen centuries — future generations continued to bury their sacred bulls off his gallery, then opened new galleries; and a thousand years after Khaemwaset, the Nectanebo kings built a new Apis Temple before the vaults of the Serapeum. During those long ages, many a dignitary must have seen and read Khaemwaset's inscriptions, and his repute remained and grew during a millennium and more of later history.

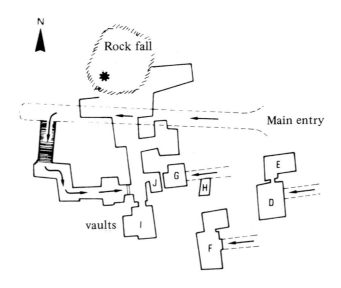

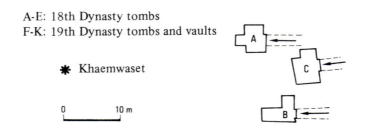

35. *Plan of the Serapeum at Saqqara under Ramesses II and Prince Khaemwaset, showing the earlier separate tombs, and the Prince's underground gallery for the burials of sacred bulls (and perhaps himself too).*

Khaemwaset the Egyptologist

Memphis was steeped in history, reaching back to the days of the Pyramids that peopled with their squat, triangular forms the yellow desert horizon westward. They were the eternal abodes of ancient kings. Thus, as perhaps the world's first Egyptologist, the inquisitive prince visited and investigated the Pyramids at nearby Saqqara and north to Giza. He was no doubt impressed by the superb workmanship of the splendid monuments of a thousand years before — and perhaps also depressed by their state of neglect, mounded up in drifts of sand, temples fallen into ruin.

Deeply affected by all that he had seen, Khaemwaset resolved to clear these glories of antiquity of the encumbering sand, tidy their temples, and renew the memory (and perhaps the cults) of the ancient kings. He probably laid his plans before his father; Ramesses II would thereby appear as protector of the memory of the 'royal ancestors' — and as patron-restorer of the greatest monuments in all Egypt, and of the greatest kings of her antiquity; their glory would be reflected on his reign and epoch also. So Khaemwaset probably got royal assent for his plans quite readily. Khaemwaset then superintended the learned commission, checking off the names of the kings, and having engraved on one face of each pyramid or sun-temple a standard inscription giving in each case the name of the ancient king whose it was, the name of Ramesses II as benefactor, and his decree through Khaemwaset as restorer. Carved in bold hieroglyphs, these inscriptions are not only among the earliest but also surely the biggest 'museum labels' in all history! At Saqqara, the Step Pyramid of Djoser (3rd Dynasty), the great rectangular tomb of Shepseskaf (4th Dynasty) and the lesser pyramid of Unas (5th Dynasty) all benefited. Further north, these attentions were bestowed upon the pyramid of Sahure and a sun-temple of Neuserre (both, 5th Dynasty); up at Giza, the Great Pyramid of Kheops was perhaps similarly labelled, the inscription being 'read' to Herodotus by his guides eight centuries later. Beneath the royal titles of Ramesses II and the appropriate king in each case, the decree and 'museum-label' of Prince Khaemwaset and his father ran as follows (so far as preserved):

> 'His Majesty decreed an announcement (thus):-
> 'It is the High Priest (of Ptah), the Sem-priest, Prince Khaemwaset, who has perpetuated the name of King . . . (So-and-so). Now his name was not found upon the face of his pyramid. Very greatly did the Sem-priest, Prince Khaemwaset, desire to restore the monuments of the Kings of Upper and Lower Egypt, because of what they had done, the strength of which (monuments) was falling into decay. He (i.e. Khaemwaset) set forth a decree for its (the pyramid's) sacred offerings, . . . its water . . . [endowed] with a grant of land, together with its personnel . . . '

At Djoser's great precinct, these works were perhaps undertaken in Year 36, 3rd month of summer, Day 10 (summer, 1243 B.C.), the date of a stonemason's scribble there, noting 'the first day of work by the quarrymen . . .'

Khaemwaset, Administrator

But neither archaeology nor Apis bulls were allowed to monopolise Khaemwaset's time. During his long tenure of high offices in Memphis, he also gradually assumed various responsibilities in local administration, especially relating to the temple and estates of Ptah. A steady stream of official correspondence passed to and from the palace at Pi-Ramesse and Khaemwaset at Memphis. So, in a ship's log of Year 52 (December, 1228 B.C.), a series of letters were sent off 'to the Sem-priest' in the 2nd month of Winter, Days, 26, 28, 29, and in the 3rd month, Days 1 and 4. This ship had 'sailors of the Sem', and received from Memphis a list (?) of people attached to 'the Sem-priest of Ptah, Khaemwaset'. This log and other documents permit a glimpse of Khaemwaset's family and senior staff in Memphis. His eldest son, called Ramesses, was accorded the courtesy title of 'Prince'; by Year 52, Khaemwaset himself was Heir-Apparent and aged almost 60, so his son would be the Heir's heir and be a man of 40. This prince, aide to his father, had his own estate and his personal scribe or secretary, Huy, by whose hand the palace-servant Meryotef in Pi-Ramesse could pass messages to his lady-friend the Chantress Rennut, who probably lived in Memphis.

Khaemwaset's responsibilities radiated from Memphis not only north toward Pi-Ramesse but also up to 60 miles south to Ninsu at the mouth of the Fayum. Thus, Khaemwaset sent an order to his agent Sunero there, saying: 'Let search be made for these messengers of Prince Iotamun who are in the district of Ninsu; let them be made to state their business, and let the shield-bearer Neferhor be ordered to bring them (back)!' Apparently his younger brother's servants had taken French leave. Sunero duly found them, some already in custody at Ninsu; so he duly wrote back for further instructions, taking care not to offend protocol as between Khaemwaset and his other powerful brother, Merenptah.

While Khaemwaset's elder son Ramesses shared in his father's administrative duties, his second son Hori followed his father into the priesthood of Ptah, where many years afterward he became high priest likewise. Hori in turn had a like-named son Hori who — a generation after Ramesses II — capped a civil career by becoming northern, then Theban vizier.

Khaemwaset and Royal Jubilees

Traditionally, the 'jubilee' rites for the renewal of a pharaoh's kingship in his 30th and later years were proclaimed from Memphis under the patronage of Ptah-Tatonen. Ramesses II elected to celebrate his jubilees not at Memphis but in Pi-Ramesse. However, by way of regard for the older capital, he at least had the jubilees proclaimed first of all at and from Memphis, and by Prince Khaemwaset as Sem-priest. So, for each of the first five jubilees (Years 30 to 42), the news was announced on each occasion there, and then Prince Khaemwaset in person carried the glad tidings and proclamation throughout the length of Egypt right to Aswan. In this, he was seconded by a full staff, including the new Theban vizier Khay, a successor of Paser. Record of their passage was left here and there — at Nekheb in the temple of the vulture-goddess, at Silsila in Haremhab's old rock-chapel, and around Aswan. Later jubilees from the sixth (Year 45) onwards, Khaemwaset left to the vizier Khay and others to announce — he was getting too old for such trips, and in fact was not destined to witness many more.

36. *The biggest museum label in the world. Inscription on the Pyramid of king Unas.*

Tomb and Burial of Khaemwaset

As the years passed Prince Khaemwaset — like many another Egyptian — became concerned about his own proper burial and afterlife. True to form, this extraordinary prince had his own special solution in his case. He decided on having a tomb inside the Serapeum itself, the gallery-vaults of the sacred bulls for which he had done so much in his lifetime. So, on the desert above his new gallery, he built a regular tomb-chapel, decorated with splendid relief-scenes by the best craftsmen of Memphis as befitted his rank. But far more revolutionary, he prepared below not only a new chamber off the gallery for another Apis bull — but also a space for himself. When in about Year 55 of Ramesses II, Prince Khaemwaset at length died, after forty years, in the service of Ptah of Memphis, he must have seemed as much a fixture there as did his father on the throne of Egypt. So the conclave of the priesthood of Ptah of Memphis did honour to the venerable prince who had perhaps brought their cults greater royal patronage and prominence than had obtained from the days of the Pyramids themselves, or was to be for most of history to come. Provided with a gold mask, rich jewels in his own name, abundant funerary equipment, and placed in a stout wooden coffin, the deceased prince was finally laid to rest in his chamber in the vaults of the sacred bulls, under the protection of the god Apis himself. Apis guarded his strange secret well . . . over the succeeding centuries, many an Apis-bull was buried in vault upon vault along Khaemwaset's corridor. Then, the ceiling collapsed, smothering the burial of Khaemwaset completely, while by the end of paganism in Egypt, the bull-galleries proper were looted of their other treasures — but Khaemwaset slumbered on in peace until 1852 A.D., when Mariette exhumed his remaining relics, but (bent on Apis bulls) could hardly believe what he had found. So passed Khaemwaset, leaving the heirship and the care of Memphis to his brethren and successors.

109

The Princess — Queens

Bint-Anath and Meryetamun

During the middle and later years of Ramesses II's reign, a younger generation of royal ladies took over the queenship of Egypt. Following the death of Istnofret, her daughter Bint-Anath became Chief Queen, as we have seen. Nor was this role of consort merely formal, as in fact Bint-Anath bore a daughter to her father-husband, the girl being depicted in the scenes of Bint-Anath's tomb in the Valley of Queens. The length of time that Bint-Anath served as principal consort (before retiring to the harim) is unknown, although she survived his death to appear later as one of Merenptah's official consorts. She would certainly have served as chief consort for several jubilees of Ramesses II. Bint-Anath's associate in the queenship initally was her half-sister Meryetamun, daughter of Nefertari. But in Year 34, both ladies had to welcome a third party to that rank —Maat-Hor-nefurere, the Hittite princess. For a time, she doubtless fully enjoyed the royal favour that her high status demanded, but eventually came to spend much of her time in the royal harims, especially the one near Ninsu and the entry to the Fayum. There she probably came to rank as a senior person, perhaps by the time that her younger sister came to Egypt in about the forties of the reign.

In the Harim

Life in the harim at Mi-wer near Ninsu was no mere humdrum existence of bored idleness between occasional royal visits. Rather, the royal ladies were in effective charge of what amounted to 'home industry' and training youngsters, including foreign children, in the arts of spinning and weaving, producing fine linen cloth for the use of themselves, the pharaoh, and other royalty at court — 'royal linen', indeed. Supplies of linen for clothing were regularly drawn from the accumulating 'stores' at Mi-wer, and dispatched to Pi-Ramesse. Garments were, of course, issued handsomely to the royal ladies themselves — rolls of cloth, '28 cubits, 4 palms' long and '4 cubits wide' or '14 cubits, 2 palms' long and same width (two pieces), i.e., either more than 40 feet or more than 20 feet in length by 2 yards wide, were issued to that august lady, 'Queen Maat-Hor-neferure, may she live, Daughter of the Great Ruler of Hatti'. Needless to say, the royal ladies were throughout well provided-for, with generous quantities of fresh fish from the Nile or the Fayum lake, supporting estates yielding grain for their bread, grazing for their cattle (milk; roast beef . . .), and all else besides.

Nor were food and clothing the sole provision. At least one later account reflects the love of jewellery and flowers among the beauties of Pharaoh's harim — quantities of deep blue lapis-lazuli and of green malachite, valued in silver, and of safflower or cardamum by the bushel measure. Thus in both daily needs and personal and house-display, the harim at Mi-wer (as others elsewhere) was well-supplied, while itself a hive of busy activity. Pharaoh's visits to its bright buildings by the garden-province must have been occasions of excitement, pleasure, and vivid display.

Other Queens

Eventually, Meryetamun vanishes from view, and perhaps it was Nebttawy, last of the princess-queens, who took her place in the closing decades of Ramesses' reign. Of this new royal lady, little is known, except that — just like Nefertari, Istnofret, Bint-Anath and Meryetamun — she too had a sumptuous tomb prepared in the Queens' Valley. Over the years many of Ramesses II's other daughters perhaps died quite early in life, like not a few of their brothers; but some at least lived on into the reign of Merenptah, their father's successor.

And as with so many of the princes, little is known of most of the princesses. Here and there, a glimpse may be caught of them. Princess Istnofret II had her own estate with its herds of cattle — we see supplies of milk, bread and herbs being issued to her retainers. Two of her subordinates, the palace singers Pentaweret and Pawekhed, wrote most anxiously to her, to learn of her wellbeing, perhaps while they were away in Memphis:

> 'The Singer Pentaweret and the Singer Pawekhed (each) greet [their lady],
> the Princess Istnofret.
> Greetings! A message to say that I say to all the gods and goddesses of Pi-Ramesse, 'May you (the princess) be healthy, [prosperous], and alive!' May you enjoy the favour of my god Ptah.
> *Further*:- We're alive today, but don't know how we'll be [tomorrow!] ... May Ptah have us brought (safely) back, so we may see you! ... We're very, very concerned about you!'

Merenptah and the Younger Sons

The Younger Sons of Ramesses II

Few of the crowd of the king's younger sons seem to have distinguished themselves. Sixteenth in the standard lists, a later son of Queen Nefertari, Prince Mery-Atum had a career that only modestly compared with that of Khaemwaset. As a youth, Mery-Atum had paid one visit to Sinai, in the care of Asha-hebsed, probably in the second decade of the reign. By the time of the Hittite peace, and in about Year 23, Mery-Atum had outlived his five known elder full-brothers, becoming 'First King's Son' of Ramesses II by Queen Nefertari, with the high honorific rank of Fanbearer. Later still, after his mother's death (by about Year 26 ?), Mery-Atum was given an appointment of some prestige — High Priest of the Sun-god Re in Heliopolis, only a few miles downstream and across the river from Khaemwaset in Memphis. Perhaps the burial of a Mnevis bull (sacred to Re) in Year 26 came at the very beginning of his term of office, perhaps just before it. The twenty years or so of Mery-Atum's tenure were not marked by any special distinction, after which viziers held this high post.

Of other sons, the glimpses are even more fleeting. The twenty-third, Si-Montu, had married Iryet, the daughter of Ben-Anath, a Syrian ship's captain. Si-Montu was at one time in charge of (or attached to) 'the Vineyard of the Estate of Usi-ma-re Chosen-of-Re (Ramesses II) in Memphis'. Perhaps, therefore, it was in this highly cosmopolitan capital that he met his Syrian wife — who knows what 'seaport romance' lies hidden there? But the docket written for her in Year 42 (February, 1237 B.C.) tells us nothing more — as a (Theban ?) jotting, it may imply her burial in a tomb of her husband's at Thebes.

A still younger prince, unknown from existing lists, was Prince Ramesses-Maat-Ptah, to whom at Memphis the palace-servant Meryotef sent greeting. After the customary polite forms of address, his note ran:

> 'How comes it, indeed, that from you I receive no letter? What's the
> meaning of my sending you a series of letters without your answering
> even one of them?'

From this little missive, it transpires that the young prince's subordinates felt able to rebuke him quite freely — obviously, he was a shockingly bad correspondent!

But another young prince speaks to us only from the tomb. Prince Ramesses-Neb-weben was hunch-back and he died at barely thirty years old. Perhaps he died at the great harim of Mi-wer, and it was intended that he should be buried at Thebes. His death was perhaps unexpectedly sudden, for the only great stone sarcophagi that were immediately available for his burial were two fine old pieces originally prepared for the young man's great-grandfather, Ramesses I, when the latter was still only the vizier Pramesse, and discarded as 'surplus to requirements' when he became king. One of these was sent ahead up to Thebes, while the prince's mummification was carried out in the north; but, finally, the decision was made to bury him in the remaining sarcophagus near Mi-wer itself — so the one sent to Thebes *was* buried, but empty!

Merenptah, the Ultimate Heir

After the death of Prince Khaemwaset about Year 55, it was his younger full-brother Merenptah who towered head and shoulders above the crowd of lesser offspring at the courts of Pi-Ramesse and Memphis. Already, Merenptah had in later years been the king's right-hand-man in helping to manage affairs in Pi-Ramesse and the East Delta. Following Khaemwaset's death, he extended his responsibilities as far as Memphis, including taking care of the burial of further Apis bulls, attended by his personal secretary Tjay.

At that time Merenptah also became Heir-Apparent, 'Senior King's Son', as he had it proudly inscribed on ancient royal statues already re-erected in Pi-Ramesse on his father's account, is-suing special scarab-seals to commemorate his exalted rank. For the final twelve years of his aged father's reign, Merenptah was the real ruler of the kingdom, virtually pharaoh in all but name. Being himself in his sixties, he wisely delegated various duties to others — such as sending the High Steward Yupa (son of old General Urhiya) and the vizier Neferronpet to proclaim the later jubilees (ninth to fourteenth, Years 54 to 66) throughout Egypt, while he concentrated on the central administration. So, at last, when Ramesses II did finally go to his rest, it was the patient Merenptah who took up the heritage.

37. Stela of Prince Merenptah and his secretary Tjay, from the Serapeum honouring the Apis bull. (Louvre Museum)

113

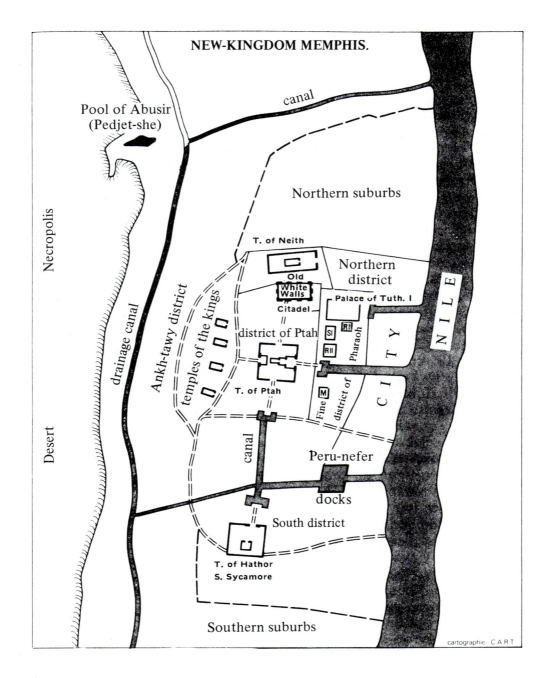

NEW-KINGDOM MEMPHIS.

Pool of Abusir
(Pedjet-she)

canal

Necropolis

Desert

drainage canal

Northern suburbs

T. of Neith

Old
White
Walls

Citadel

Ankh-tawy district

temples of the kings

district of Ptah

T. of Ptah

Northern
district

Palace of Tuth. I

RII

SI

RII

district of Pharaoh

Fine district of

M

C I T Y

N I L E

canal

Peru-nefer

docks

South district

T. of Hathor
S. Sycamore

Southern suburbs

cartographie C A R T

38.   *Imaginative reconstruction of Ramesside Memphis.*

114

A Tale of Three Cities

Ancient Memphis

Here was the real capital of Egypt, set amid the smiling green of the richly-cultivated plain between the west bank of the Nile and the tawny desert-edge, lined with the pyramids that symbolised her proud antiquity, touched with pink and gold in the rising and setting sun. Along the river-bank, particularly towards the south quarter, were the busy wharves and the shipyards of Peru-nefer, 'Bon Voyage'. From here, ships sailed down the Nile to the open sea and the ports of the Mediterranean, and here returned. Nearby lay the foreign quarter, a heady babble of Canaanites, Hurrians, Aegean islanders, and many more besides; Baal and Astarte had their shrines there. Not too far away, perhaps, was the military and 'industrial' area, including the Arsenal — workshops and stores, for chariots, shields, spears and the rest of the 'hardware' for ancient warfare. Amun had his shrine in Peru-nefer, but the major patron of the south quarter was the popular Hathor, Lady of the Southern Sycamore.

Further north from here probably lay the administrative hub of the venerable capital, and behind these 'office-blocks' of low mud-brick, a north-south line of more spacious precincts, beginning in the north with the great, comfortable, rambling old palace, 'the Domain of Akheper-kare' (Tuthmosis I), used by so many kings, down to the garden-girdled royal lodges and harims of Sethos I and Ramesses II himself. But at the very heart of the ancient city lay the original royal citadel, White Walls, from which the city was first named. South of this in the centre lay the great precinct of the venerable Temple of Ptah with its courts, pylons and sanctuaries leading from their east façade inward and westwards. On the west side of the main temple, Ramesses II and Khaemwaset added a superb new Jubilee Hall with a forest of great columns on basalt footings behind a pylon-gateway and colossal statues — the West Hall of the Temple of Ptah. Here, ceremonies were probably enacted in parallel with those in Pi-Ramesse. Out to the west in the Ankh-tawy district, stretched a line of memorial-temples of the kings, from at least Amenophis III to Ramesses II. And in the quarter north of the ancient citadel, was the domain of the goddess Neith, 'North of the Walls'.

Outside the central quarters of the city proper, and extending to north and south of it, there were probably suburbs with the villas and gardens of the great. Like other gods, Ptah, Hathor and the rest had their major festivals, as when the sacred ship of Ptah navigated the canal south to the temple of Hathor of the Southern Sycamore. On such holidays, as contemporary papyri relate:

> 'The like of Memphis has never been seen . . . her granaries are full of
> barley and emmer, her lakes are full of lotus-buds . . . and with lotus-blossoms;
> oil is sweet and fat abundant. . . The Asiatics of Memphis sit at ease, confi-
> dent, . . . lotus-buds about their necks. . . . The lady-wrestler of the South is
> come; she overcomes the northerner, has put her feet on her neck, and her
> hand upon the ground. The noble ladies of Memphis sit at leisure, hands bowed
> down with (festive) foliage and greenery . . .'

The young bloods returning to Memphis from wars or other turns of duty at home or abroad looked forward to reunion with their lady-loves. In one lyric poem, reflecting dawn when the city and its gardens swim into view by morning light,

> 'I fare downstream . . . ,
>> My reed bundle on my shoulder.
> I'm bound for Ankh-tawy,
>> I'll say to Ptah, Lord of Right:
> 'Grant me my Beloved tonight!'
> The River is as wine,
>> Ptah its reed-thicket, Sekhmet its bouquet,
> Dew-goddess its lotus-buds, Nefertum its lotus-blossoms.
> 'Tis the Golden Goddess who rejoices,
>> As the land grows bright with her beauty.
> Memphis is a chalice of fruits,
>> Set before (Ptah) of the pleasant face.'

Imperial Thebes

Several hundred miles south, along the cliff-closed valley of the Nile, the voyager reached Thebes, a city of temperament and setting entirely different from Memphis. With almost 2000 years of accustomed predominance, behind her, Memphis was self-confidently easy-going in tone. With most of 1000 years of royal tradition behind her since the early Middle Kingdom, Thebes was no newcomer. But in her local plain bisected by the Nile against the spectacular outlines of the Western Mountain, this home of the great Eighteenth-Dynasty conquering kings who ejected the Hyksos and subdued Western Asia breathed a more martial air — 'Victorious Thebes', of the great triumphal inscriptions on her temples of Amun, the most monumental in all Egypt. The wealth of Empire reached the quays of Thebes under that Dynasty until Akhenaten banished Amun and his city from favour. But restoration under Haremhab and the family of Ramesses II brought splendour to Thebes once more — although now, she began to take on more the tinge of a 'holy city' of Amun, while remaining the 'Southern City' par excellence, and local seat of a vizier

Along the east bank of the Nile, the main city extended behind its quays as a 'garden-city' of palace, villas, and residential areas the two miles or so from the old town in the north behind the vast precinct of Amun at Karnak, south to Luxor, his other temple in 'Southern Opet'. Somewhere near Karnak was the traditional palace of Thebes proper. Behind the line of Nile and town, a broad plain ran out eastward to the hills and distant triple peaks of the 'Arabian' desert that stretched out to the Red Sea. At Karnak, from the river-canal and quay, a sphinx-lined avenue ran east to the huge pylon-gateway of the Hall of Columns of Sethos I and Ramesses II. Beyond that hall and a narrow court, obelisks and a pylon fronted the dim halls, pylons, corridors and sanctuaries of the old temple of Amun, mainly of the Eighteenth Dynasty around a nucleus

116

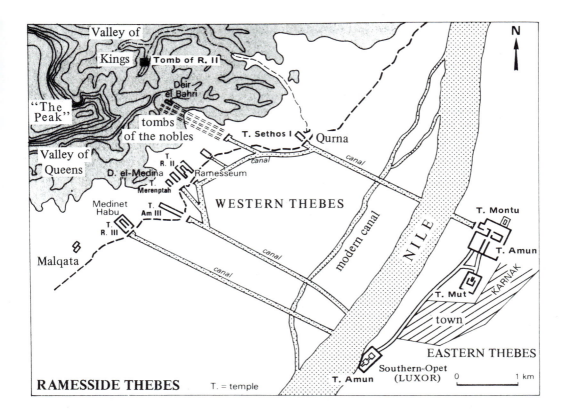

The map contains the following labels:

Valley of Kings
Tomb of R. II
Deir el Bahri
"The Peak"
tombs of the nobles
T. Sethos I
Qurna
Valley of Queens
T. R. II
D. el-Medina
Ramesseum
T. Merenptah
WESTERN THEBES
Medinet Habu
T. Am III
T. R. III
Malqata
modern canal
NILE
T. Montu
T. Amun
KARNAK
T. Mut
town
canal
EASTERN THEBES
Southern Opet (LUXOR)
T. Amun
N
0   1 km

RAMESSIDE THEBES   T. = temple

39. *Layout of Imperial Thebes.*

shrine of the Twelfth Dynasty of seven centuries before Ramesses' time. South from the narrow court (passing the Sacred Lake) ran a processional way through four mighty pylon-gateways (by-passing the Temple of Khons to the west), out along another sphinx-avenue to the Temple of Mut, consort of Amun, half-surrounded by a 'horseshoe' sacred lake within its own precinct. To the north of Amun's great temple, lesser fanes to Ptah and the old war-god Montu completed the Karnak precinct. Two miles south, the Luxor Temple of Amun was now fronted by the py-lon and forecourt of Ramesses II (with obelisks and colossi) before one trod the great colonnades and stately sanctuaries built by Amenophis III. Once a year, on his famous Festival of Opet, Amun travelled from Karnak to Luxor on his great golden state barge amid festivities, and came back in similar state some three weeks later. As we have seen, Ramesses II followed custom in attending the Festival of Opet in person in Year 1 — and probably quite often thereafter.

117

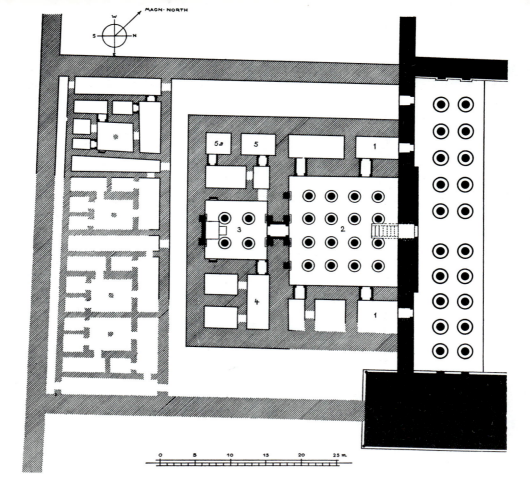

40. *Plan of the palace of Ramesses II attached to the forecourt of the Ramesseum, his great memorial temple in Western Thebes. From its central pillared hall, steps led to a balcony for state appearances shaded by the temple's south portico. Opposite lay a four-columned throne-room and domestic quarters, with a set of suites for members of the royal family across the rear corridor.*

The West Bank was — and is — dominated by the desert cliffs of 'the Western Mountain'. Along the sandy edge before it stretched a line of memorial temples of all the greatest kings of the Empire, that of Ramesses II (the Ramesseum) standing out in the very middle, with its pylons, courts, colonnades and halls, and its towering colossus of a thousand tons. The tomb-chapels of the nobles pock-marked by their dark doorways the front faces of the Western Mountain, but within each was a room or suite decorated in brilliant colour with paintings of the owner and family, with religious compositions needful for the afterlife, and sometimes with scenes from their career and inscriptions of special interest. Once a year also, Amun crossed the Nile in his golden barge to celebrate the 'beautiful Festival of the Valley' in the memorial temple of Ramesses (or in one of the

118

others), while the families of Thebes held overnight feast in the tomb-chapels, the living and the dead united in one celebration. Great ceremonies took place in the temples, with torchlight processions and the gift of bouquets to leading officials — the two-day feast was a traditional favourite in Thebes. Finally, behind the desert cliffs lay the secret Valleys of the Kings and Queens to north and south of the great rock-curtain. And in a fold of the hill just south-west from the Ramesseum was the discreetly-sited village (Deir el Medina) of the special community of workmen of the Royal Tomb, of whom we shall see more later.

Homer later sang of 'hundred-gated Thebes, where the golden ingots gleam', but proud Theban poets sang their own songs of 'Victorious Thebes', model for other cities:

> "Stronger is Thebes than any other city,
>> She has given the land one master by her victories.
> She who took the bow and grasped the arrow,
>> None can fight near her, through the greatness of her power.

> Thebes is the model for every city,
>> Both land and river were hers from earliest times.
> The sand came to delimit her fields,
>> To create her soil upon the primal mound when earth appeared.
> Men arose within her to found every city after her true name,
>> As they (all) are called 'City',
> After the model of Thebes, the 'Eye of Re'.'

Dazzling Pi-Ramesse

To Memphis and Thebes, hitherto the twin foci of life in Egypt, Ramesses II had the ambition to add a brand-new centre, virtually of his own creation, using as nucleus the old family seat of Avaris in the East Delta where his father had established a summer palace. The new capital was ambitiously planned to rival, even to eclipse, the glories of Memphis and Thebes, as the scribes sang of the new Residence:

> 'His Majesty has built himself a Residence whose name is
>> 'Great-of-Victories',
> It lies between Syria and Egypt, full of food and provisions.
> It follows the model of Upper-Egyptian Thebes, its duration
>> like that of Memphis,
> The Sun arises in its horizon, and (even) sets within it.
> Everyone has left his own town and settles in its neighbourhood.'

The energetic Ramesses took a close personal interest in the adornment of his new city, and was ever on the look-out for new resources to that end. Thus, walking in the desert near Heliopolis in Year 8 (December, 1272 B.C.), the keen-eyed pharaoh spotted several outcrops of stone highly suitable for turning into royal statues for the temples of Pi-Ramesse, Memphis and Heliopolis. Eagerly, he admonished the work-crews and their leaders, giving them an early 'productivity-deal'! He addressed them so:

> 'You chosen workmen, valiant men of proven skill . . . , craftsmen in valuable stone, experienced in granite, familiar with quartzite, . . . , good fellows, tireless and vigilant at work all day, who execute their tasks with energy and ability! . . . Abundant provision is before you, and no 'Oh for more!' . . . I am your constant provider — the supplies (assigned) for you are weightier than the work, in my desire to nourish and foster you! I know your labours to be eager and able — and that work is (only) a pleasure with a full stomach. The granaries groan with grain for you . . . I have filled the stores for you with everything — with bread, meat, cakes, to sustain you; sandals, clothing, enough unguent for anointing your heads (issued) every ten days, your clothing annually, that you may persevere daily. None of you (need) pass the night moaning about poverty. I have assigned many people to supply you:- fishermen to bring you fish, others in the gardens to provide vegetables (?), a potter to produce vessels to cool the water for you in the summer heat . . . '

As the centrepiece, the new city had the former summer-palace of Sethos I, with its dependent glaze-factory and military barracks. That palace, Ramesses II greatly enriched and extended. Within the prim whitened walls painted pavements probably led between royal apartments and the more public halls of audience and approach which glittered with splendid glazed tiles. These glowed with warm, rich colours — yellows and browns, a touch of blue, red and black, with grey backgrounds. Thus adorned, the steps and dais for the royal throne had figures of subject foreigners over a dado of marsh-plants in blue; the royal lion devoured a hapless foeman, as terminal-post of the stairway — all in light green and blue glaze. Doorways, walls and balconies had the titles of Ramesses in bold hieroglyphs, white-on-blue and blue-on-white, and triumphal scenes vivid in red, blue, brown, yellow and black. Within the more intimate royal apartments, this official bombast gave way to happier scenes — of birds and animals in the marshes, ladies of the harim, and Bes the comic little god of hearth and home. Thus, in contrast to the white-plastered walls above and around, the main parts of the palace, public and private alike, gleamed with vivid scenes and motifs in rich colours. No wonder that the lyrical scribes praised Pi-Ramesse as 'beauteous of balconies, dazzling with halls of lapis and turquoise'. Strategically near, still, was perhaps one army-establishment, with others in different quarters. For Pi-Ramesse was also the 'marshalling-place of your chariotry, the mustering-place of your infantry, the mooring for your marines'.

Around the royal nucleus arose other public buildings, both administrative and religious. Not far from the palace were the offices and the residences of the highest officials of government — including the northern HQ of the Theban vizier Paser, for example. But the abodes of the gods dominated all. South lay the original town of Avaris, with the temple of Seth, partner to Horus, helper of Re. North of the palace-quarter, the great temple of Re on the east side (facing west) lay opposite that of Amun to the west (facing east). Before the temple of Re stood at least four,

41. *View from pillared hall into the throne-room. Reconstruction of the West-Theban palace of Ramesses III, identical in layout to that of Ramesses II.*

perhaps six, pairs of obelisks; there and in its courts, also two sandstone shrines and a series of royal statues, plus four to six great granite stelae poetically commemorating the might of the king. At the north end of the new city, the temples of Ptah and Sekhmet-Udjo were more modest structures. But perhaps it was close by that, in the thirties of his reign, Ramesses II erected the vast Halls of Jubilee for the rites of the Sed-feast, the renewal of kingship. This edifice was under the joint patronage of Ptah-Tatonen, giver of jubilees, and of Re-Atum, the sun-god, with whom Ramesses claimed a special relationship. A massive granite gateway, perhaps forty feet high, led into a hall of columns, the central four about 35 feet high and ten surrounding columns 22 feet high, allowing clerestory lighting between the two roof-levels, as at Karnak and the West Hall of Memphis. Beyond lay a second hall with six columns 20 feet high, leading to other rooms again. Before these mighty Halls of Jubilee, three major pairs of tall granite obelisks once stood, and perhaps three or four other pairs at other gateways. Huge colossi of pink and grey granite also adorned the approaches. As Ramesses II was impatient to have this massive building ready for his jubilees without delay, the columns had to be obtained quickly, so they re-used some from some derelict older temples elsewhere — but this was nearer and quicker than working the Aswan quarries.

Along the west and north sides of the main city flowed the "Waters of Re", the main east branch of the Nile that then ran on to the north-east. Along the south and east of the city ran a subsidiary channel, probably the "Waters of Avaris" and perhaps connected with the 'Lake of the Residence'. Thus, the city had a defence-work of natural and part-artificial waterways. It was also a first-class inland port, readily reached from the Mediterranean, and in control of all shipping going south upstream to Memphis and beyond. Besides the lesser homes of the ordinary working populace, and the docks and wharves, Pi-Ramesse developed warehousing for storage in kind of tribute and taxes — in effect, a 'store-city', in the classic biblical phrase (cf. Exodus 1:11): "its granaries are full of barley and emmer, they reach up to the sky . . . its ships sail forth and moor (again), so that food and provisions are in it daily — joy dwells here, and no-one says, 'Oh for more!'"

Pi-Ramesse lay close not only to desert on its east but also to a rich agricultural hinterland, with backwaters full of fish and fowl. On high days of festival, when Pharaoh went in state from the Palace to the temples of Seth or Re, the populace came to acclaim him:

> 'The young folk of 'Great-of-Victories' are in festival-dress daily, oil on
> their heads, hair freshly set. They stand by their doors, hands bowed down
> with foliage and greenery of the House of Hathor . . . on the day of the cere-
> monial entry of Ramesses II, Montu of the Two Lands, on the morning of the
> Khoiak festival, vying with each other in calling out their petitions. Sweet
> songstresses from the Memphite school (attend) . . .'

The coming and goings of the king, whether campaigning in Syria or on tours of inspection in Egypt or to Thebes and back, were a major feature of life in the capitals, entailing a flurry of elaborate preparations. A scribal exercise of the day gives some idea of the scale of these grand affairs; orders are given thus:

> 'Get on with having everything ready for Pharaoh's (arrival) . . . Have
> made (ready) 100 ring-stands for bouquets of flowers, 500 food-baskets. Food-
> stuff, list, to be prepared:- 1000 loaves of fine flour; . . . 10,000 *ibshet*-biscuits;
> 2,000 *tjet*-loaves; . . . Cakes, 100 baskets, . . . 70 dishes, . . . 2,000 measures.
> . . . Dried meat, 100 baskets at 300 cuts . . . Milk, 60 measures; cream, 90 mea-
> sures; carob beans, 30 bowls. Grapes, 50 sacks; pomegranates, 60 sacks; figs,
> 300 strings and 20 baskets. . . '

And so it went on — herbs, baked geese, honey, cucumbers, leeks, incense, sweet oils, all manner of fish and fowl, beans, assorted drinks. And a full array of servants in attendance, with brilliantly-decorated chariots and weaponry for the military escort. So, all was ready for a royal appearance in the splendid life-style of Pi-Ramesse. Here reigned Ramesses II by choice, "curber of foreign lands, strong bull beloved of Right".

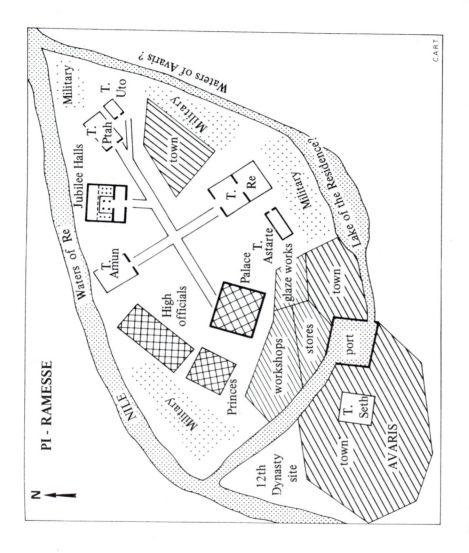

42. *Imaginative reconstruction of Pi-Ramesse, the East-Delta residence created by Ramesses II around his father's summer palace to the north of the town of Avaris.*

43. Block statue of the Vizier Paser (Cairo Museum, J. 38062)

7 : THE CORRIDORS OF POWER AND LIFE AND LETTERS

Viziers and the Law

Paser, the Paragon Vizier

Pharaoh was not only the focus of his capitals' splendour but also the fount of all authority and power. In turn, even he could never rule his vast domains single-handed, however richly endowed by the gods. Delegation of authority was, as always, the answer. So, like every pharaoh, Ramesses II had a body of chief ministers of state, headed by the southern and northern viziers (of Thebes and Memphis, traditionally).

Veteran of Sethos I's reign, Paser continued to flourish as Theban vizier for perhaps another quarter-century into Ramesses II's reign. By his energies, those years passed in relatively smooth and efficient administration; Ramesses evidently found nothing to complain of, in the loyal and long service of his devoted chief minister. Although of northern (Memphite) origin on his mother's side, Paser was much attracted to Thebes, with its great monuments, pageantry and splendid setting, and chose to have his fine tomb-chapel (No. 106) there. His father had ended his days there as High Priest of Amun. Paser's wide responsibilities kept him in the north with the king much of his time. But in Thebes, he was an assiduous watchdog both for efficiency and over others' needs in that context. He was, of course, immediate superior of the community of workmen of the Royal Tomb. He certainly got results, as the beautifully wrought sepulchres of Sethos I and Ramesses II and their relatives still testify to this day – but did so by caring punctiliously for his workmen. He and the Tomb-Scribe Ramose got on well together, and were both quite popular with the workmen, being commemorated in tombs and on stelae there. Paser's taut efficiency and considerate care alike shimmer through a contemporary letter from the Mayor of Western Thebes (another Ramose) to the workmen and their two foremen:

'The Mayor of Western Thebes, Ramose, greets the Chief Workmen and the [whole?] gang, (namely) the Chief Workmen Nebnufer and Qaha with the entire gang, as follows:-
'See now, the Governor and Vizier Paser has sent to me, saying: "Let the dues be brought for the workmen of the Royal Tomb, namely vegetables, fish, firewood, jars of beer (?), victuals and milk. Do not let a scrap of it remain outstanding . . . [Do not] let me find anything of their dues (held back as) balance. [And even] *you* take care [over this]" . . . '

Paser did not intend that any of his workpeople should be cheated of their due rewards, and the message was duly passed on. What they got would in fact be the lot!

However, the care of the workmen, and even for the furnishings and sometimes the festivals of Amun's temples were but two facets of Paser's many duties. With a proud sense of historic tradition, Paser early on had carved in his tomb-chapel a copy of the centuries-old traditional 'Royal Address to the Vizier', associated with his appointment. In many details this 'Address' was already antique in Paser's day. But its two parts — royal advice on appointment, survey of duties — enshrined high ideals of strict impartiality, of public justice, seen to be done as well as actually done. The range of duties and responsibilities of the vizier remained breathtakingly all-embracing: the departments of justice, treasury, armed forces, home affairs, agriculture, government communications (local and central liaison), and others. While in the capital, he had to make report to Pharaoh daily, and cross check with the Chief of the Treasury. He held court as chief magistrate in all kinds of cases, and had final responsibility for all tribute and taxes. So, visits to Thebes (even in the line of duty) must often have been a welcome diversion from the non-stop ebb and flow of affairs in the bustling northern capital-cities.

But at last a day came when Paser felt his years and doubtless looked for release. Long since, when Nebwenenef, High Priest of Amun, had died in Year 12, Ramesses II had appointed as successor one Wennofer, father of his boyhood companion Amen-em-inet. Amen-em-inet himself had passed from a military and diplomatic career to become Chief of Works of all royal monuments, and then specifically in the Ramesseum — just across the river from his father, the High Priest in Karnak. But by about Year 27 Wennofer died, so again the high-priesthood stood vacant. This time, the faithful Paser was richly rewarded by appointment as Amun's new pontiff — a post held a generation earlier by his own father. Perhaps for a decade (to about Year 38?) until he died in his seventies, Paser fulfilled the less frequent roles of the High Priest on occasions of high ceremonial, while (as customary) the details of the daily cult and lesser feasts were carried on by the regular priesthood, headed by the 2nd and 3rd prophets of Amun, such as Bakenkhons and Roma, skilled in the rituals, and Amun's great estates were administered by officials such as Setau.

Law in Action : A Domestic Flare-up

Many cases, of course, were settled locally and never reached the vizier's high court. But records of them often can vividly illustrate details of the life-style of that day, as in the following scenario in Western Thebes. About Year 9 of Ramesses II, the District Officer Simut took to wife the lady Irynofret. For seven years this busy housewife did all her own work (apart from a manservant for heavy outside jobs), made all her own clothes, and so on. Then one day in Year 15, the golden opportunity came for her to invest in a personal labour-saving gadget, to take some of the drudgery out of her housework. The merchant Raia passed her door, offering for sale the very thing — a Syrian slave-girl, just a little lass. So, Irynofret and Raia haggled, settled a price (4 deben, 1 kite, on the silver standard), and the deal was clinched. Triumphantly, Irynofret dubbed her new purchase Gemni-hir-amenti, "I got her in the West", and doubtless found plenty to keep the girl busy with. Of course, in a society where coined money did not exist, and barter in goods against a gold/silver/copper standard by weight was the rule, our worthy housewife Irynofret did not simply hand over actual silver to the weight of 4 deben and 1 kite (373 grams, or about 13 ounces). Instead, she raked together the equivalent of 'ready cash'. There were linen dresses, a shroud and blanket of her own making which (at 2 deben, 2 1/3 kite) met about half the cost. The other half she met by selling to the merchant a miscellaneous lot of copper and bronze vessels — spares and kitchenware acquired for known prices (in deben and kite) from various of her neighbours, then or more likely earlier, to keep on hand as 'ready cash' for just such unforeseen 'best buys' as this one. As any housewife knows, 'you never know when it'll come in handy!'

So, Irynofret, husband, little Gemni-hir-amenti all settled in to their accustomed roles as ever. But not for long . . . One of her jealous neighbours, madame Bakmut, claimed that really Irynofret had paid for the labour-saver with some of *her* property — so *she* had some claim on the girl! Her man, the soldier Nakhy, was prepared to back her claims. The dispute escalated, neither party would give way.

Thus, in due course, probably in Year 16, our lady Irynofret had to defend herself in the local West-Theban court against charges laid by Nakhy on Bakmut's behalf. Then the magistrates ordered her to make her statement, which she pertly did:

'[I am the wife of the District Officer Simut]; we set up home, I worked
. . . and (even) provided my (own) clothes. Now in Year 15, seven years after
. . . , the merchant Raia approached me with the Syrian slave . . . , just a girl,
and said to me, 'Buy this girl, at a price for her!' . . . So now I state the price
I paid for her, before (you) magistrates:- (*Follows the list of linen, metalware
and whence obtained, and their prices*) — total, 4 *deben*, 1 *kite* (worth) of
silver from all sources; . . . it included no article of the lady Bakmut . . .'

At this point, the magistrates invited Irynofret to go on oath: "Said the bench of magistrates to the lady Irynofret:-

'Swear an oath by the Sovereign, saying thus: "If witnesses establish
against me that any property of the lady Bakmut was included in the silver
I paid for this slave-girl, and I have concealed (the fact), then I shall be liable
for 100 strokes, having (also) forfeited her (the girl)." Which Irynofret duly
did.

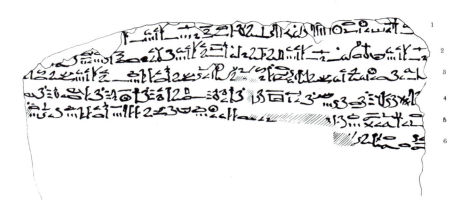

44. *Copy of a letter in Egyptian longhand script('hieratic'), in which Ramose, Mayor of Western Thebes, acknowledges the command of the Vizier Paser to forward all necessary supplies to the royal workmen at Deir el-Medina.*

In turn, Nakhy was called to produce witnesses to substantiate Bakmut's allegations. These are an interesting group. First was Min-inwy, veteran police-serjeant of the Royal Tomb; then, the Mayor of Western Thebes, Ramose (whom we met earlier); Simut's elder brother, Bakmut's elder sister, and three other ladies. Each in turn said their piece.

And . . . there, our piece of papyrus breaks off! The next exciting instalment is lost, perhaps still in Egypt's sands, perhaps destroyed by the hand of time or man. Did Irynofret win her case? If this document was a record from her household files, then perhaps it did once constitute her final, triumphant title-deed to ownership of her labour-saving girl-helper.

Law in Action : the Hundred Years' Wrangle

But Irynofret's little brush with the law was small beer indeed, compared with an epic case then currently running up north in the supreme and local courts at Heliopolis, Memphis and Pi-Ramesse.

Four centuries before, in the heroic days when Ahmose I expelled the Hyksos regime and reunited Egypt, he had rewarded his principal supporters with grants of land. The Superintendent of the Seal and Admiral, Neshi, was given an estate near Memphis, henceforth dubbed 'the settlement of Neshi'. As the centuries rolled by, Neshi's heirs clung firmly to this real-estate legacy, all benefiting from it in common, as the property itself remained legally an indivisible unit. So things went on until the 'time of the Enemy in Akhet-Aten' (as the Ramessides called Akhenaten) and of the lady Sheritre. With her offspring came trouble in Haremhab's ample reign — jealousy between brothers and sisters caused a *first* lawsuit: "A division of property was made for Wernuro and her brothers and sisters in the Great Lawcourt . . . A division was duly made . . . , and Wernuro was made administrator on behalf of her brothers and sisters." Thus the elder sister Wernuro managed to uphold the legal unity of the estate, while her co-heirs' shares were clearly set out; she won Round One.

But not for long. Her sister Takhuru was highly dissatisfied, wanted her pound of flesh (or, acre of land), and opened a *second* lawsuit. A court officer was dispatched, " and each person was given to know his share" once more. But perhaps Wernuro's authority was curbed. At any rate, she and her son the scribe Huy quickly launched a *third* lawsuit, to win back their administrative rights over the estate as a unit. As a result of proceedings that rambled on after his mother's death, Huy was able "to cultivate his lands year by year as he wished . . (and) received the harvest of his fields year by year." So life went along until Huy died, leaving a widow, the lady Nubnofret, and a son, the little boy Mose. The other side of the family saw its chance; egged on by them, the land-shark Khay expelled the widow and her son. But, true to the family's insatiable appetite for litigation, she took the matter straight to court in the *fourth* lawsuit of the series, appearing before the vizier in Heliopolis in Year 18 (?) of Ramesses II. She appealed to official documents: "Let there be brought for me the (tax-)registers from the Treasury, likewise from the office of the Granary of Pharaoh. For, I declare confidently that I am the descendant of Neshi . . . the agent Khay does not know my rights . . . !" Surely, her late husband's tax-returns would prove her right to his inheritance. So, an official was sent on to Pi-Ramesse, but accompanied by Khay, to bring the registers to court. In court, the great scrolls were unrolled, scanned page by page by the practised eyes of the vizier and his clerks. Finally, "the Vizier said

128

to Nubnofret, 'Who is your heir among the heirs in the two registers before us?" And, after an awkward silence in the hushed court, Nubnofret had to confess: "There is no heir of mine in them!" "Then you are in the wrong!", said the vizier. A gleam of hope came as another official intervened, offering to re-check the records for her — but this hope, too, faded when he reported "You are not recorded in them." So, the jubilant Khay accompanied the official with whom he had visited Pi-Ramesse, to claim his share at the (technically illegal) parcelling-out of the estate at the 'Settlement of Neshi" among the heirs. For, these two men had colluded en route to Pi-Ramesse . . . if the official could 'fix' those tax-registers so that Huy disappeared from them they both stood to gain. Leaving the stunned Nubnofret wondering what became of all those tax-returns filed year after year by her husband and then by herself . . .

Mose, for his part, grew to maturity in the middle years of Ramesses II, becoming (as his father had been) a treasury-scribe of the Temple of Ptah in Memphis. All those years, his embittered mother no doubt dinned into him the injustice of their loss, the perfidy of Khay and his crony, and the imperious necessity — some day — of winning back their rights. So at last Mose himself lodged a complaint with the Great Lawcourt, thus initiating the *fifth* lawsuit of the whole series that now had punctuated the legal record for a century. In this re-trial, he and Khay were plaintiff and defendant. Mose rehearsed briefly the history of the whole case, and then laid his double charge: (i) he was (like his parents) truly the descendant of Neshi, and so a true heir to the ancestral holding, and (ii) Khay and crony had falsified the registers in which his parents' names had failed to appear. Khay for his part simply asserted his claim, on registers and *fait accompli*. There arose the crucial question of evidence. Bypassing the falsified registers, Mose appealed to his local folk as living witnesses of his descent. After Khay's reply, each went on oath: "As Amun endures and as the Prince endures, it is the truth that I shall speak, not falsehood! And if I speak falsehood, then let my nose and ears be cut off and I be transported to Nubia." Then, subject to this oath, each witness gave his statement, and each in turn admitted that Mose's father Huy was the son of Wernuro, who had indeed cultivated those same lands regularly, and that Wernuro was the descendant of Neshi. One after another reiterated the same basic testimony. Even Khay admitted the hard fact of Mose's descent. With that point established, Mose could then bring in sundry older written documents as corroborative evidence; the court then had the full facts of Mose's real descent, valid claims, and Khay's sharp practice.

So at last, the court reached its verdict, to be announced by the vizier in traditional manner: "Mose is right, Khay is wrong!" Mose threw his arms aloft in triumph, before the court-officer and seated judges. A damaged scene from Mose's tomb-chapel still preserves that delirious moment of success. Mose had no intention of letting this *cause celèbre* go any further, now that he had won back his family rights. His increased wealth enabled him to afford a decorated tomb-chapel at Memphis. On the north interior wall of its little court, he had engraved the account of the century's litigation just outlined, with (on another wall) a record of some of the principal documents adduced in evidence. And, of course, that scene of final triumph. With so monumental a record as this, Mose intended that no more doubts would be raised to harrass his descendants. So ended one of the longest-running legal disputes ever, certainly in Egyptian history, from its origins under Haremhab to the later years of Ramesses II.

45. *Mose triumphs in the law-court. At top left, the 'bench' of judges seated; a scribe reads out their verdict. Top right, the guilty party bows under the officer's baton while Mose lifts his hand to greet the verdict in his favour. Bottom right, Mose leaves the court, arms flung aloft in triumph, as his cowed opponent bows out. (Cairo Museum, from Saqqara)*

Treasury Chiefs and Financial Tricksters

The Roots of Prosperity

The wealth of Ramesses II's great kingdom was measured basically by the products of the land and the persons of the producers; and those products could be valued against the varying gold/silver/copper standard-by-weight. Arable and pasture lands were in theory all at the disposition of the King as regent of the gods on earth. But in practice, by Ramesses' time, the facts of life were much more complex. Thus there were extensive Crown (i.e., state) lands, whose crops and livestock provided both the food-supply, 'salaries', and general upkeep of the pharaonic administration and its departments. Through such land-domains and estates, worked by cultivators and herdsmen (who thereby earned their own livings), various institutions operated as economic units, such as the royal harims at Memphis or Miwer. Purely 'private' estates were insignificant, other than those of individual kings and some members of the royal family — but these, of course, had to support households and 'expenses' not incumbent upon commoners.

Alongside the state departments and royal holdings, the other principal landholders were the temples of the gods. By this period, Amun of Thebes was by far the richest, his huge estates throughout Egypt yielding vast revenues (in grain, cattle, etc.) that in turn supported his extensive personnel — temple-priests, specialised workmen, general servants — and a cult of splendour befitting his role of god of Empire. These great revenues, of course, had also to feed the land-workers themselves (thus assured of a modest but steady living) — and both they and Amun (with the rest of the gods and their estates) also paid their taxes in kind to the central treasury. For as long as Egypt was fairly and reasonably efficiently governed by officials of integrity at the various levels of government and society, and the land was properly irrigated, drained and cultivated, her wealth and prosperity were assured. The sole factor that annually posed the question, 'riches or ruin?' was the inundation of the Nile, on whose water all else depended. Too little meant starvation; too much meant devastation; a golden mean meant golden harvests.

Panehsy and Suty, Lords of the Treasury

The successive Chiefs of the Treasury stood closest to the Viziers in Egypt's government hierarchy; traditionally, this official and the senior vizier would exchange daily reports on the state of the country and their departments when seeing the pharaoh when they all were in the capital. The Chief of the Treasury naturally had considerable responsibility for taxation and checking on revenues both real and prospective. Several men served Ramesses II in this office during his long reign. Early on it was Neb-iot, and near the end, Pay-ten-hab; but neither of these have left much mark. In the middle years, Panehsy and Suty do allow us some tantalizing glimpses of temple and state finances. The possible copy of a letter written from Memphis by Panehsy to Hori, a priest of Amun in Thebes, opens a remarkable vista of the huge wealth of Amun of Thebes in the middle years of Ramesses II:

'The Royal Scribe and Chief of the Treasury . . . in the northern Region

131

Panehsy [greets the prophet] of Amun in the Southern City, Hori:-

Greetings! This letter is to inform you of the [state of the Domains] of
Amun which are here in the Northern Region under my authority, ... reaching
to the extremities of the Delta, on the three Nile branches, namely the Great
River, the Western River, and the Waters of Avaris.

... [I] hereby forward the lists of them, every man of them [with
his wife] and their children .. I have assessed [them] for their tax-dues, ...
in Year 24, 1st month of Summer, Day 21 (April, 1256 B.C.) under the Majesty of the King, [Ramesses II] ...

Informing the prophet Hori of them, of each man according to his occupation (?). *Summary* ... : Cultivators, 8,760 men, each producing 200 sacks
of barley by the bushel. Cowherds, [...] men, with cattle by herds, each
man having 500 beasts (in care). Goatherds, 13,080 men, ... [Keepers of]
fowl, 22,530 men, each having 34,230 birds. Fishermen, ... their [produce]
valued at 3 *deben* of silver per year. The donkey-drovers, 3,920 men, [each
having ?2,] 870 beasts. The mule (?) -herds, 13, 227 men, each having 551
beasts ...

This is how I have dealt with them. Now, I took men from among them,
and I caused them to build a large granary for the labour-camp (?) of Memphis,
which is assigned 10 *arourae* (about 7 acres). [I have made] corn-bins in it on
all four sides of it, totalling 160 corn-bins. [I have collected?] the goods (due to)
the treasury, a wealth of silver, gold, copper, cloth[ing. ...] ."

Amun's grain-supplies and holdings of livestock were awesome indeed: a revenue of 1¾
million sacks of barley annually, possibly holdings of up to six million or more each of cattle and
goats, and teeming millions of wildfowl on the extensive Delta and valley backwater-marshes and
lagoons; and perhaps 11¼ million donkeys and 7¼ million mules (?). Nor are all these figures
necessarily mere fantasy. Thus, the grain-revenue at 1¾ million sacks (Delta and northern Middle
Egypt) for the *whole* of Amun's Theban temples compares sensibly with as much as one-fifth of
that amount that Ramesses III bestowed solely upon his own memorial temple and four very
small temples only a century later. And 200 sacks per cultivator is very modest compared with
the far larger quantities sometimes turned in by other farmers in other revenue papyri (even up
to 1,600 sacks per man). Likewise, 500 kine or 551 mules (?) in the care of one person compares
closely with the average of 634 beasts per person for five temple-herds of Amun under Ramesses
III. Hence, at least some of the figures in this document do closely reflect reality, and are not
derived solely from the imagination of some student-scribe.

About ten years later, in the thirties of the reign, the next Chief Treasurer was Suty. We
find him reporting to Ramesses II on the annual food-allowances for the community of workmen
of the Royal Tomb:

"The Royal Scribe and Chief of the Treasury, Suty, salutes Pharaoh:
Greetings! This letter is to inform my good Lord of his flourishing affairs
within the Place of Truth, namely of his workforce, and about their annual
expenditure, by account (thus):-
Pot-baked loaves, 31,270; *kyllestis*-loaves, 22,763; beans by the bushel,

132

250 sacks; (other grains), assorted, by the bushel, 132 sacks; assorted fish, 32,700; . . . fresh vegetables, 43,150 (bundles); *tapy*-fish of the store-tanks (??), 50 sacks; pickled, dried meat (cf. corned beef), 60 lots; . . . assorted cattle, 33 beasts; meat-cuts, flank, (?2)18; meat-cuts, loin, 200; entrails (cf. haggis ??), 10 handfuls; . . .

It is the greatly-favoured one . . . greatly loved in the Palace, . . . the Vizier of South and North Khay [who has brought this report for you] . . .

Divided over a year among a workforce of 40 to 50 men (plus their wives and children), these seemingly impressive amounts are by no means out of proportion: an approximate average of 3 loaves per day for the ordinary workman (double, for each chief workman and tomb-scribe); some 500 assorted fish delivered to each of the two gangs for two ten-day periods, and less on the third; 2 to 3 bundles of fresh vegetables daily per workman. Meat was more of an extra on special occasions rather than a daily food; but 5 lots of "corned" meat, 2 or 3 beeves, and 16 to 18 'sides' and 'loins' of meat, per month, was probably good provision for 'weekends', holidays and festivals throughout the year.

Income-Tax and Financial Scandals

Probably in all times and climes, tax-demands have been challenged as often as made; officials make estimates 'upon figures', while worthy citizens quickly point out that figures are not always what they seem. As in the 20th century A.D., so in the 13th century B.C. Only a decade or so after the end of Ramesses II's reign, one irate taxpayer made his protest thus:

'One of my subordinates came and reported to me that you have reckoned for me an excessive amount of barley as (tax-)assessment on my field in the district of Village-of-Re. What's the meaning of wronging me thus? *I* am the one you've picked on to penalise, out of the whole body of taxpayers! That's just fine! I am an attendant of Pharaoh, close to his presence. I shall not be approaching you, to make my complaint to you. I shall approach one . . . (in far higher authority!)'

Nor was this influential courtier's voice alone in the taxpayers' chorus, either in Ramesses II's time or to the end of the Empire period.

But human nature ran true to form in other financial frolics of far shadier hue, motivated by greed and achieved by guile.

In the 30th year of his reign, Ramesses II held the first of his long series of jubilees for renewal of kingship, attended by great preparations beforehand, and by much ceremony in the North. Nothing quite like it had been seen since the palmy days of Amenophis III, a century before. But while so much official attention was thus focussed away on the great ceremonials and their organisation, some less dutiful minds lightly turned to thoughts of loot. In Thebes then, and probably on the West bank, a prominent official had charge of magazines and storehouses of various temples — and found it all too easy to 'transfer' goods from *their* stores to his, or his father's place. When, about Year 29 or 30, he was transferred to another responsible appointment (inspecting herds in the rich North-Delta pastures), he left his wife and daughter behind in Thebes. Then they acted in his name, coolly continuing to enter at least two storehouses (one, of the temple of old Tuthmosis I), having goods 'transferred' to the husband's private store! Evidently the husband had said nothing specific locally about his going north, so leaving his wife and daughter to carry on in his absence, but the lady's cool brashness in invading temple-magazines was her undoing:

> 'The scribe Hatiay lodged a complaint, saying, 'What's the meaning of
> her frequenting the storehouse of Pharaoh, without the controllers' know-
> ledge?' As a result, and in view of the huge 'transfers' of property,
> 'She was taken to the Great Lawcourt, before the Hereditary Prince and
> the chief dignitaries. She was asked, 'What is the meaning of (your) opening
> two storerooms of the (royal) Domain without the controller's knowing of it?
> She said, 'These places (were those) of which my husband was controller, these
> where I was.' The Lawcourt judges said to her, 'Your husband was (earlier) in
> the Domain, [administering] it. But he was removed from there, and appointed
> to another high office of Pharaoh, in inspecting cattle in the north of his land.
> It is not good at all, this deed of yours! — So it was alleged.'

Two lists of 'loot' indicate the scale of the couple's 'fraudulent conversions' of state property — various wines; a whole variety of linen garments, 424 in one lot; 440 leather sandals; 1,300 blocks of copper ore; livestock including 30 bulls, 10 goats, 30 geese; 30 chariots(!) with harnesses to match; and 20,000 bushels of grain.

Naturally, the official himself was produced in court to face charges alongside his erring wife and daughter. The charge read out to him included mention of the arrest of the womenfolk that indicated how Hatiay's complaint had ultimately reached the highest levels in the land:

> 'See now, Pharaoh dispatched a transport-officer . . . and two men, after
> your wife and your daughter likewise. [They were brought in by a Chief of]
> the Great Stable of Ramesses II, [at the time of ?] the Jubilee, in accord with
> the copy of the document which [had been sent ?] to Pharaoh. See now, your
> wife had opened | the stores of the temple] of King Tuthmosis I . . . [She] took
> 200 *deben* weight of copper; 300 reels of yarn; 5 jars of pomegranate-wine; 10
> copper flasks, 4 copper picks, 3 copper cauldrons . . . She put them in your
> storeroom. People are on her trail; she will not be let off again!'

A later passage in this indictment is even more graphic:

> '[It is now known?] according to your documents, which are in your
> (filing-) cabinet ('box') which was found[. . . in your] house. What was found,
> list of it:- Grain, 20,000 sacks; . . . (etc.); salt, 1,200 sacks likewise . . . (etc.).'

But our property-peculator was not perturbed — he denied all, on oath, and launched a counter-accusation against Pharaoh's minions!

'[He took an oath] by the Lord before the great dignitaries, saying:- 'If anything be found [in the possession of] my father in a storehouse [at this time of?] festival, I shall repay it double! If the deficit is found in his keeping, then the goods shall be brought into the 4 Broad Halls (of Judgement) this very day! Now, the janitors of Pharaoh's estate took it, each one of them all! When Pharaoh my good Lord shall appear in his Jubilee Festival, I will inform him of them, because they acted against me last year also! And I had them, (then).' They seized on his statement and are (cross-) examining the janitors.'

At that exciting point in this titillating case, our source suddenly fails . . . The truth was no doubt duly elicited, and the particular scandals laid, and the various miscreants duly brought to book. That Ramesses II was himself determined to get to the bottom of so serious a case is indicated by the fact that the senior man on the judges' bench was, for once, not even the vizier but the Heir Apparent himself who (at this time) would be Prince Ramesses son of Queen Istnofret. The whole case is at once an eloquent testimony to the boldness by which an unscrupulous official could (almost) get away with massive fraud within a complex administration when official attention was largely diverted elsewhere, and also to the integrity of loyal middle-rank officials such as Hatiay and the vigour with which Ramesses II and his courts unmasked and unfrocked the perpetrators of such acts.

Viceroys, Gold and Earthquakes

Earthquake at Abu Simbel

In the first ten years of Ramesses II's reign, the viceroy Iuny had seen the beginning of the great twin temples at Abu Simbel in Nubia. Thereafter, Heqanakht had watched over their completion and probably their inauguration in about Year 24. Soon thereafter, he was perhaps followed in office by a new viceroy, Paser — namesake, but *not* a relative, of the famous vizier Paser of an earlier generation. After Paser (Years 25-34, possibly), the envoy Huy of Hittite Marriage fame was briefly Viceroy (about Years 34-38), and finally Setau served for a quarter of a century (Years 38-63 at least). The regimes of Iuny and Heqanakht were on the whole peaceful. But the tenures of Paser, Huy and Setau were enlivened by very varied happenings.

Paser may conceivably have owed his promotion as Viceroy in part to his membership of the remarkable family of Amen-em-inet, the boyhood companion of Ramesses II, and his own cousin. His own uncle, Pen-nest-tawy, had already been Commandant of Troops in Nubia, and was followed by his son, Nakht-Min, a cousin of Paser. At first, all probably went well enough; Year 30 may have seen commemorative ceremonies for the First Jubilee at Abu Simbel, as at other temples. But very soon after (Year 31 ?), catastrophe struck at Abu Simbel. A sudden, sharp earth-tremor sent a momentary shudder through the sandstone deserts of Lower Nubia, and rocked the proud structures of Abu Simbel to their foundations. The effect was cataclysmic — inside the Great Temple, the mighty pillars cracked and crumbled; the second pillar and royal figure on the north aisle collapsed in ruin, as did the north jamb of the main entrance-doorway. Outside, the south arm of the colossus just north of the entryway came crashing down, while (worst of all) with a thunderous roar, the entire upper half of the opposite colossus just south of the doorway — head, shoulders torso — bit the dust in the forecourt with an impact that must have echoed miles into the hazy distance.

At first sight, Ramesses' greatest Nubian fane must have seemed an unsightly wreck, with shattered lumps of painted sandstone strewn in all directions. However, the dismayed Paser could not afford to linger over the scene of devastation. He immediately took in hand repairs with all speed, probably sending word to the King (a thousand miles to the north) as soon as his efforts seemed to have some chance of succeeding. Thus, the pillars of the great hall were shored up with masonry (later affording a convenient surface for inscribing the Blessing of Ptah in Year 33), and the collapsed pillar rebuilt and restored. The doorjamb was rebuilt but left plain, while the fallen south arm of the colossus north of the entryway was restored with supporting blocking, inscribed with titles of Ramesses II. Alone remained the fallen colossus. Here, all Paser could do was to tidy up, leaving the major parts where they had fallen (nor has anyone done any better since). In commemoration of his works, he set up two statuettes (one, his own) in the repaired Great Temple. The other temple, it seems, escaped much damage.

By Year 34 Ramesses may have felt it better to instal a new man. On the occasion of her marriage to Ramesses that year, the Hittite princess had been escorted to Egypt by (among others) a senior military and diplomatic officer: sometime Lieutenant of Chariotry and Commander of Sile border-fort, now Royal Envoy to All Lands, Huy. Proud of his role as escort, he later described himself "one who came from Hatti-land, who brought its Great Lady — one who (so) reported its whereabouts has never existed! — the Royal Scribe, Huy". Impressed by Huy's conduct, Ramesses promptly appointed him Viceroy of Nubia, but even Huy could do no more for Abu Simbel than had already been done. And, being a senior man, his retirement followed a few years after.

Viceroy Setau — Go-Getter and Gold-Getter

By contrast, the next Viceroy was a younger man entirely, dynamic and forceful, more of a 'whizz-kid'. This was Setau, promoted by Year 38 when he promptly had an impressive double stela engraved at Abu Simbel. In the succeeeding twenty-five years, he fairly cluttered his province with monuments — like his royal master! But prior to this appointment, Setau already had a record of royal intimacy and energetic service at a high level. On his great autobiographical stela, he says:

'I was one whom his Lord caused to be instructed . . . as a ward of the Palace. I grew up in the royal abode when I was a youth . . . I was provided-for, with bread and beer from all the royal meals. I (?), indeed (?), came forth (as) a scribe from the school . . . While I was a youth, I was appointed to be Chief Scribe of the Vizier; I assessed the entire land with a great scroll, being equal to the task (?). I was scrutinised (?), one taking (note) of all that I had done. With all (these) good deeds, one acted for the Lord-of-All (the King). He noticed me, (as) I made offerings to all the gods. I gave increase . . . in doing good. Their treasuries were crammed (?), filled with goods . . . My

46. *Granite Sarcophagus of Setau, Viceroy of*
Nubia. (British Museum)

Lord noticed me, that I was effective, . . . (prospering) the endowments, the fields by the myriad. I caused the granaries to be bulging with revenues . . . I did not act for a father against a child; I caused their (?) children to praise His Majesty.

[His Majesty promoted me] to be High Steward of Amun. I [served Amun] as Superintendent of the Treasury and Festival-Leader of Amun, a pair of golden braziers in my hands, offering them before him . . .'

When appointed viceroy, Setau threw his energies into raising both labour-forces and revenues there, extending Egyptian rule and building temples:

> 'My Lord again found my worth . . . So, I was appointed as Viceroy of
> Nubia . . . I directed serfs in thousands and ten-thousands, and Nubians in
> hundred-thousands, without limit. I brought all the dues of the land of Kush
> in double measure, I caused [peoples] to come (in submission), which no
> Viceroy had done since the year dot. Irem offered tribute, . . . and the chief
> of Akuyata, with his wife, children, and all his company . . .
> Then [I was charged to build the Temple] of Ramesses II in the Domain
> of Amun, it being executed in the Western Mountain in work of eternity, filled
> with numerous people from the captures of His Majesty, his stores being full
> of goods piled up [to heaven . . .]. I (re)built entirely the temples of the lords
> of this land of Kush that had previously fallen into ruin, they being made anew
> in the Great Name of His Majesty, inscribed on them forever.'

On these last undertakings — the building of Ramesses II's temple at Wady es-Sebua and its endowment with captives — Setau's stela is vividly supplemented by another, of the army-officer Ramose, which pins down some of these activities to the Year 44 (about November/December, 1236 B.C.):

> 'Year 44:- His Majesty commanded the confidant, the Viceroy of Nubia,
> Setau, together with army personnel of the company of Ramesses II, 'Amun
> protects (his) son', that he should take captives from the land of the Libyans,
> in order to build in the Temple of Ramesses II in the Domain of Amun, and
> (the King) also ordered the officer Ramose to raise (?) a force from the com-
> pany — so, Ramose.'

Eager to have his temples built with maximum dispatch and minimal cost, Ramesses II thus authorised a raid on the south-Libyan oases of the Western Desert, perhaps Kurkur and Dunkul, or even Selima, oases. He impressed these luckless south-Libyans into his service for building in sandstone and brick with the same *insouciance* for mere aliens that he had shown for the Hebrews labouring in brickfields a generation earlier in the Delta (Exodus 5). All in sharp contrast, of course, to his very different concern for indigenous Egyptian workmen, as illustrated on his Year 8 stela, or at Deir el-Medina (Workmen of the Royal Tomb).

Setau capped the long series of viceroys of Ramesses II. The quality of the temples he built— Wady es-Sebua and Gerf Hussein — leaves much to be desired. Nor can all be blamed on the soft sandstone in which these semi-rock-temples had to be hewn out. Once Abu Simbel was finished, the best artisans were probably drafted back to Egypt for the king's continuing great works there, leaving Setau to rely increasingly on much poorer local skills — and even, on lesser scribes, to judge from the appalling style and poor spellings on Setau's own great stela.

Courtiers in Action

Besides the viziers, treasury-chiefs, viceroys of Nubia, and various others such as chiefs of state granaries and other departments, there were at the court of any empire pharaoh a variety of people with limited official functions but sometimes much real power. Such included the royal cupbearers (compare the 'butler of Pharaoh' in Genesis 40f.) who, by original function, merely served the king his wine, became his trusted confidants, and hence were entrusted with major matters of state: they could thus be used to 'short-circuit' the red tape of ordinary administration, or be charged with the king's direct authority for a specific task (a limited 'supremo'). One such, we have already met; Ramesses Asha-hebsed, who supervised work in Sinai for Sethos I and the Prince-Regent Ramesses (II), who was entrusted with inaugurating work on the Abu Simbel temples alongside the viceroy Iuny, and who acted as aide to Prince Mery-Atum. It was from the ranks of those in the personal service of Sethos I and Ramesses II, that Paser and Khay rose to become successive viziers for Thebes, then High Priests of Amun and of Ptah, respectively, in their later years.

Another position of trust was that of High Steward of the King; that is, administrator of the pharaoh's personal estates, his own wealth in terms of land and the income-in-kind obtained from it. The separate high-stewardship of the Ramesseum's property sometimes was combined with this post. Such a double function perhaps fell to General Urhiya, (after active field-service with Sethos I) under Ramesses II. At the time of the Battle of Qadesh, his son Yupa was just a lad in the training-stables. But half a century later, Yupa himself had risen to be High Steward of both King and Ramesseum, and had the honour of proclaiming his sovereign's ninth jubilee in Year 54 (1226/25 B.C.). In turn, Yupa's son Hatiay became (as Amen-em-inet had been) a Chief of Medjay-Militia, and assisted the High Priest of Amun, Bakenkhons, in building the Eastern Temple at Karnak. But Yupa's brothers, nephew, and second son all entered the priesthood and became learned lector-priests in the service of the great gods.

Learned Scholars

Others, too, became learned scribes and physicians, or served as 'experts' in the royal administration. In the north, Tjunuroy of Memphis was sometime 'Director of All Monuments of the King', with an office, also, in Pi-Ramesse, the Delta Residence. Back in Memphis he proclaimed his devotion to the royal line and his historical learning, by inscribing in his tomb-chapel a list of nearly 60 kings of Egypt from earliest times down to Ramesses II himself, comparable with the royal ritual king-lists in the two temples at Abydos (not to mention the once comprehensive list now known as the Turin Canon of Kings). Tjunuroy's brother Nakht belonged to a practical branch of royal service: he was Table-Scribe of the King, and Superintendent of the Queen's Harim.

In Thebes, the Chief Draughtsman Simut had a clever son, Amen-wah-su, who became Scribe of Sacred Writings in the Temple of Amun, and a grandson Khaemopet who in turn became 'Scribe of Sacred Writings of the King, who inscribes the Annals of All the Gods in the House of Life'. The 'House of Life' was the 'university department' of temple or palace, where learned scribes worked on the recopying of valuable papyri, composing new works on theology and other topics, and training further staff for the more special and difficult tasks of the scribal art.

Still more remarkable was the family of the Lector and administrator Iuny (*not* related to the viceroy Iuny). Hailing from Siut in Middle Egypt, he (like his father Amenhotep) became a Lector and Royal Scribe and entered the royal administration under Sethos I. But Iuny's offspring all became doctors — son Huy, a Chief Physician, and grandson Khay a Chief Physician to the Queen's Residence. Meanwhile, life in the state administration did not always run smoothly. Iuny had trouble with demands by army-officers upon his personnel — perhaps trying to conscript the peasantry for military service. In the event, Iuny vigorously protested; so, the regimental commander, the Standard-bearer Mai-Sutekh, sent out an official circular to the Delta garrison-commanders as follows:

'I have heard that you are interfering with the personnel of the god in the Isle-of-Amun (who are) under the authority of the Royal Scribe, Iuny. What is the meaning of your doing such a thing? By Amun and the Ruler, if (I) hear that you interfere any more with the god's personnel who are in your districts, then I will make real trouble for you, for *your* sakes! The notables of Pharaoh are making real trouble for *me*!

Thus, you shall perform your duties properly. Do not be slack about this letter which I have put in your hands. As for everything in this letter, do not neglect it! . . . When this missive reaches you, you shall not allow work for the god to lie dormant, that you should be jailed! So take note of it!'

The Army : Defence and Training-ground

Egypt's armed forces could field three and four full divisions of perhaps 5,000 troops each (with others on home reserve), and a formidable array of chariotry. The infantry were organised in 'regiments' of 200 men each, led by Standard-bearers; such regiments contained four 'companies' of fifty men, each led by a 'Chief of Fifty'. But the elite corps were the chariotry; those who distinguished themselves could attain to the ranks of the Royal Envoys, and thereafter to the highest administrative posts in the land. Within Egypt, major forces were stationed in both Upper and Lower Egypt. The high command included lieutenant-commanders of chariotry and superintendents of horse, the very highest echelons being those of Commandant of Troops, General and ultimately Generalissimo.

Ramesses' full-time generals and military men (outside Nubia) have left surprisingly little mark either on the monuments or in history. After the debacle at Qadesh, not a few 'top brass' were probably summarily dismissed, and probably the king showed much less favour to the military unless they could prove their worth. But quite a number of dignitaries found army-service a training-ground for developing proficiencies that afterwards gained them promotion in promising civilian careers. Among these, we have already met the treasury-chief Suty and high steward Urhiya (both, former generals); Huy, Viceroy of Nubia after being Royal Envoy at the first Hittite

Marriage; Amen-em-inet, Chief of Works, after being charioteer and Chief of Medjay-Militia, and others. Thus, other than in actual wars, the army played quite a subordinate role in national life, except as a training-ground for the display of some abilities, principally administrative. While doubtless many did pursue a regular army career, the most glamorous service was undoubtedly that of Royal Envoy (promoted from the chariotry), travelling between the courts and capitals of the world powers of the day — a magnet that did attract the young bloods, to the despair of their scribal educators.

Schooldays and Student Life

The Bottom of the Ladder

The viziers, viceroys, treasurers, scholars and generals — these captains of state did not spring full-grown as from nowhere. They all were young once — children cosseted and cuffed, loved and cared-for, by their parents, then as now.

Writing was the gateway to eventual 'success', as scribal educators never tired of pointing out. Doting parents therefore sought to send their little boys to school (from the age of five or so), whenever they could. In the great capitals, scribal schools were attached to major temples, the palace (or, to its administration), and possibly to some state departments. In main provincial towns, schooling was likewise probably attached to temple and local administration; elsewhere, the village scribe probably taught a few lads as occasion allowed.

For four or five years, the boys attended class to learn the long-hand script ('hieratic') — separate hieroglyphs came later on. But, astonishingly enough, their earlier exercises in the script were based *not* on copying from contemporary works, but on scribing short extracts daily from the ancient classics, all written in the dead classical idiom of Middle-Egyptian. They first practised works 700 years old, beginning with *Kemyt*, a manual of 'useful phrases' of about 2000 B.C., set out in vertical columns and divided into word-groups. Then they proceeded to other Twelfth-Dynasty works — the so-called 'Satire of the Trades', an Instruction that extolled the scribe's profession over all other callings, the Instruction of Amenemhat I, and the Hymn to the Nile — all perhaps connected with one author/editor, Khety son of Duauf. Then, on to the famous Story of Sinuhe, 'Prophecy' of Neferty, and the 'loyalist' Instructions in support of the Crown. Other classics such as the Instruction of Hardjedef might be added. As the boys at this stage barely understood anything of what they copied from these venerable works, their errors were gross; but at this stage, mastery of script was the aim — comprehension of content came later. Discipline was firmly set on the adage of 'spare the rod and spoil the child'; as one teacher expressed it:

'Write with your hand, read with your mouth, take advice from those
who know more than you . . . Spend no day in idleness, or you will be beaten.
A boy's ear is indeed on his back, and he (only) pays heed when he's given a
hiding. Pay heed, listen to what I have said; the benefit will be yours!'

Student Life and Letters

Lads in their early teens went on to learn to write the Late-Egyptian script and language of their own day. From 'school' classes they moved on to be attached (perhaps in smaller groups) to training-stables, and to various administrative departments in state, temple or palace offices. Eventually, as students in their later teens and early twenties, they were often 'apprenticed' to full-time officials who were already experienced scribes and could instruct them to higher levels. As students, these lads were commonly set as a practice-test, the Satirical Letter — a lively composition in which one scribe, Hori, mercilessly taunts his colleague Amen-em-ope with ignorance and incompetence. (This work was probably introduced into the curriculum early in the reign of Ramesses II, by which time the general curriculum had been enlarged by the use of contemporary compositions.) With rare relish Hori paints the imagined misfortunes of his colleage as cast in the role of charioteer or envoy abroad:

'You are a warrior, skilled in heroic deeds! . . . The narrow ravine is infested with Beduin, hiding in the undergrowth, (men) six and eight feet tall from head to toe, fierce-looking. They are not gentle and pay no heed to pleas. You're all alone, no helper with you, no armed host behind you . . . You decide to press on, even though not knowing the road. The shivers seize you, your (hair) stands on end, (you taking) your life in your hand. Your path is filled with boulders and pebbles, without touching free passage, and overgrown with tall grasses, thorns, brambles (?), and 'wolf's pad'. The abyss (yawns) on one side of you, and the mountain towers up on the other. You go jolting on, your chariot (falling) on its side . . . Then you imagine the enemy is after you, and you take fright! You reach Joppa and find the meadows at their season's best. You push through (into one) and find the pretty girl tending the gardens. She inveigles you into being her companion, and gets you to sample her embrace. But you are detected, confess, and are judged as a warrior; your fine linen shirt, you must sell (to pay the fine). . . . You sleep, worn out. Some wretch steals your bow, sheath-knife and quiver. Your (chariot-) reins are slashed in the darkness, so your horse goes off (as) a runaway over the slippery ground, the road stretching out before him. He smashes up your chariot . . . your weapons fall to the ground and get lost in the sand.'

Such is the mocking picture that Hori cartoons of his supposedly bungling colleague. This impish caricature crowns and concludes a series of word-pictures: Amenemope's incompetence at arguing by letter; Amenemope is hopeless at organising the building of ramps, moving obelisks, setting up colossal statues, provisioning an army-force; he is harangued over the geography of towns and roads in Syria and Palestine. By this 'cheeky' form of entertaining instruction, budding scribes could be instructed in literary usage, the essential geography of Syrian provinces and states (and spellings of foreign names), and be given glimpses of practical organisation.

However, such specially-designed works of malicious wit neither filled the student's time nor were deemed sufficient to keep him at his studies. The officials of the administration gave their apprentice-scribes at least three varieties of written matter to fill the gaps in both their curriculum and their motivation. Deadly dullest of all were the word-lists, giving practice in writing scores of terms for the natural world, geographical names, human occupations, etc. Much more varied was the miscellany of old correspondence and the like, which the busy official-cum-teacher would root out of his office-files and give to his young hopefuls for practice, either by dictation or to copy out at perhaps three or four pages a day. At least such material did reflect real-life needs and situations. Finally, there were the 'Instructions' by which the administrators sought to encourage their pupils to stick to a 'white collar' career, along which path they might aspire to the highest seats of power in the land. On the model of the old 'Satire of the Trades', they emphasised the advantages of the scribe over others:

'Be a scribe! It saves you from toil and protects you from all kinds of work. It spares you from using hoe and mattock, that you need not carry a basket. It keeps you from wielding the oar and spares you torment, so that you are not subject to many masters and endless bosses . . . Now the scribe, he directs all the work in this land.'
Or: 'Look out for yourself: the professions are set before you. The washerman spends all day going to and fro; all his limbs are weak (with) whitening his neighbours' garments daily . . . The potter is smeared with earth as if a relative had died; his hands and feet are smothered in clay. The sandal-maker mixes tan (?); his odour stands out!'.
And: 'See now, I'm training you . . . to handle the (scribal) palette deftly, to make of you a King's Counsellor, to cause you to open treasuries and granaries and receive (deliveries) from the ships, at the entry to the granary, and to cause you to issue sacred offerings on festival days, being clad in fine linen, horses at hand, your (own) ship (waiting) on the river, you being attended by subordinates who run around inspecting (all). A villa has been built in your city, seeing that you hold an office of power by the King's appointment. Slaves . . . hover round you; people on the estates, in fields that you developed, shall grasp your hand . . . Set your heart on the scribal art, to protect yourself from all manner of hard toil, and be a worthy notable.' Such were the incentives and 'career-prospects' held out.

Negatively, the scribes tried to warn their students against throwing their studies aside in pursuit of a mad whirl of short-lived and short-sighted pleasures, and to offset the attractions of a military career with its call to a life of adventure abroad. In sorrow and disgust, an oft-copied rebuke to a wayward student runs thus:

'I am told that you have abandoned your studies and whirl around in pleasures, that you go from street to street and (the place) stinks of beer every time you leave. Beer undoes a man, it sends your mind wandering; you are (then) like a bent rudder on a ship, failing to respond in any direction . . . You have been found scrambling over the walls after breaking the stocks, men scattering before you when you have injured them. If only you would realise that wine is a curse, you would abjure pomegranate brew, and put beer out of your mind . . . You have been taught to sing to the double pipe, to chant to the flute, to warble to the lyre . . . you sit in the house, call-girls around you . . . , you sit before the girl, soaked in ointments, your festal garment round your neck, drumming on your belly. You stagger, fall flat on your stomach, and get covered in filth.'

Leaving such individualistic lapses aside, the official class was altogether more concerned over losing promising recruits to the glamour of military service abroad, and ever reiterated the trials of army life:

'What's this I'm told that you say, 'the soldier is better off than the scribe'? Come now, let me tell you how it is for the soldier, plunged in torment. He is taken away, just a boy, to be shut up in the barracks. He is dealt a stinging blow to the body, a cutting blow to the eyebrows, and his head split with a wound. He is laid out and hammered like papyrus . . . Here for you is his trip to Syria, his tramping over the hills! His bread and water are across his shoulder like a donkey's load, his neck being ridged like a donkey's.'
'He drinks water (only) every three days, foul and brackish; his body is racked (by) dysentery. The enemy are come, they hem him in with (flights of) arrows — (hope of) life seems far from him! . . . He succeeds in getting back to Egypt, but he's like a worm-eaten stick, ill, seized with prostration, brought in on a donkey-back. His clothes are taken by theft, and his attendant has fled. Scribe, give up the idea that the soldier is better-off than the scribe!'

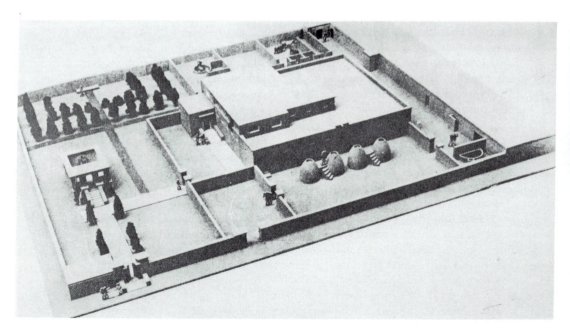

47. *Model of Egyptian villa, Amarna period. The bungalow with entry-hall, living rooms, bedrooms and facilities stands in its own plot, with gardens, grain bins, stabling and chariot-house.*

And much else besides; even the keen young charioteer is deemed no luckier — he trots his horses and 'they throw him into the thorn-bushes, his legs get out by the harness, his side bitten by stings . . . ' Needless to say, the army life (for all its perils) cannot have been so uniformly hopeless, or it would never have posed the temptation that required such counterblasts.

Finally, to whom did the gateway of writing and education open the brilliant careers promised by the educator-scribes, and in fact exemplified by the viziers, viceroys and others whom we have already met in the service of Pharaoh? While tradition theoretically favoured a father being succeeded in office by his son (as Horus followed Osiris), yet in the Empire period — including in Ramesses II's reign — ability not status could be the key to the door of opportunity, regardless of whether a youngster's family was rich or poor. Just following on the end of Ramesses II's reign, the later High Priest in Thinis, Anhurmose, boasted: 'I was worthy as a child, clever as a lad, intelligent as a boy, able as a poor man. I was a poor person, accepted into school without trouble (?), one who was noticed and whom they marked out (for promotion)'. He was, in fact, the son of an official of middle rank; but in the Empire period, the new tradition of advancement by personal ability (especially in royal service, like the vizier Paser) was fairly widespread, being reflected also in the greater number of 'provincials' (as opposed to Theban and Memphite families) who attained the highest offices. So, Ramesside Egypt offered opportunity at several social levels to those prepared to work their way through the rival disciplines of the schools and offices or the ranks of the army, and by ability and integrity — and sometimes, 'influence' — to rise to the top in their time.

Gracious Living and the Cultural Scene

From Ramesses II himself in his glittering palaces down to his humblest subject farming the fields from a mudbrick room in some tiny rural hamlet, the Egyptian's ideal was centred on the family, on home and household — "If you would be a worthy man, set up home, take as a wife a sensible woman, that a son may be born to you", said the ancient sage Hardjedef when the pyramids were new, thirteen centuries before Ramesses was born. And in Ramesses' own time, that same advice was repeated by the sage Aniy:

'Take a wife while you are young, that she may bear you your son. . .
teach him to be a man. Happy is the man whose people are many — he is
honoured because of his children.'

These and other homely precepts were well heeded by all levels of society, rich and poor, viziers or field-labourers. Life for the great officials of state — such as Vizier Paser, or Viceroy Setau, for example — and their families was 'gracious' indeed. In the great capital-cities of Memphis, Thebes or Pi-Ramesse, a notable would have at least a town house, probably in a district close to the palace precincts and the departments of state. He might also (or instead) have a villa in its own garden and walled grounds, with a chariot-garage, stabling, and so on. Such a villa, in a 'garden-suburb', was a rambling bungalow; its garden, trees and flowers around a pool with lotus and fish. A few steps up, through the front door and a lobby, and one entered the main living-room — a light-walled hall, supported by two or four brown-red wooden columns. There, the master of the house and his wife, clad in fine, pleated linen robes, heavy wig and bright floral collar, might rise from elegant wooden chairs or cushioned brick divan, to greet the visitor. The children wore much less (if very young, nothing). Beyond the main hall, the bedrooms might have low wooden beds with 'webbing' of interlaced cordage, using plentiful linen sheets and a 'head-rest' in place of pillow. The master kept his papyrus documents in wooden boxes (his 'files'), and likewise the wife her stores of linen. Folding stools, an occasional small table, some light stands, completed the main furniture. At the rear, was a bathroom, with slab, splash-back, and water-pitcher for 'self-shower', and toilet. Back in the main room, tableware of pottery was usual. Well-to-do households might boast 'services' of superb, creamy alabaster, brilliant blue faience glaze-ware, and multicoloured glass vessels; perhaps, a gold or silver piece (otherwise, the preserve of royalty). Similar items adorned milady's dressing-table (or, rather, chest), for ointments, eye-salves and other cosmetics, plus elegantly-mounted silver or bronze mirrors.

Probably lacking a garden, sited in more crowded streets, the town house contained much the same appointments as the villa — but went upwards. From the main living-room and annexes on a ground (or upper-ground) floor, a staircase led up to first and second floors for bedrooms and inner rooms, and to the flat roof with grain-bins and ventilator-cowls. Both town-house and villa had their main rooms lit only by small window-gratings high up the walls just under the ceiling-level. Thereby, the hot, blinding sunlight outside was transmuted to a cool, subdued glow, easier on the eyes and fresher for the family. In winter, indoor heating consisted simply of portable pan and braziers for burning charcoal.

Outdoor entertainments included fishing with rod and line, but much less of the fish-spearing and wildfowling in the marshes so common in earlier times. On days of high festival, the great officials might share in the ceremonial, and be presented with special bouquets; the ordinary populace cheered the great river-processions of the gods. Indoor pleasures included banquets or parties — the family and guests of the great man would assemble for a splendid meal (roast duck, beef or mutton; bread and cakes; grapes, pomegranates, dates, figs; honey), and wines and beer flowed freely. Hosts and guests might sit on well-cushioned chairs and stools, or on rush mats. Ointment-cones upon the ladies' heads melted in the warm room, running down their wigs and garments, and exhaling perfume throughout the room. To the chitter-chatter and gossip, an 'orchestra' of harp, lute, double-pipe and rhythmic clapping (usually by young ladies) provided background music, while girl dancers might entertain the company by their graceful convolutions, or a vocalist sing the favourite song of the day. New instruments and songs from abroad might enrich the repertoire. Floral garlands and attractive bracelets set off the brilliant white robes, warm complexions and heavy black wigs. Servants handed round bouquets, perfume, and drinks. But not every day was feast-day. Ordinary meals were usually much simpler, of bread, vegetables, cakes, with milk, water and beer. Likewise, the ordinary pastimes, were board-games superficially resembling draughts or chess.

Thus, life could be very comfortable, even luxurious for the great. But in an age of considerable prosperity such as that of Ramesses II, many of the lesser officials, artists and craftsmen, middle-grade priests, and military officers, these too could maintain comfortable households, much more simply appointed, but enough to live well. And in an age of prosperity, good Niles, even the toiling peasantry could keep enough back, after tax-gatherers and landlords had had their shares, to keep themselves and their families alive and well, eking out the basic bread, vegetables, water and beer with what they grew in their garden-plots, or could manage to exchange for other goods.

48. *Egyptian town house, from an ancient model. It had facilities and workplace in the basement, then front hall and living room, and above these the family bedrooms, and 'summer house' and storage on the roof.*

Tales and Tourism in Ramesside Egypt

Educated Egyptians of the thirteenth century B.C. had a considerable sense of their country's long history. The storytellers regaled young and old, rich and poor, with tales of the *Wonders of the Magicians* set at the courts of the pyramid-builders from Djoser to Kheops; of *General Sisenet*, a detective-story based on the time of Pepi II who concluded the Pyramid Age proper; of field-sports under Middle-Kingdom monarchs; of the expulsion of the Hyksos; of brave deeds of warriors under Tuthmosis III, reminiscent of Ali Baba (*Capture of Joppa*); and even of notables of the period, such as Har-Min, Chief of the Harim at Memphis under Sethos I.

Learned scribes prided themselves on their expert knowledge of the great authors of the past — "Is there one here like Hardjedef, is there another like Imhotep? There are no more among our people like Neferty, or Khety foremost of them all. I recall for you the names of Ptah-em-Djed-Thuty and Kha-kheperre-sonb. Is there another like Ptah-hotep, or Kairos, also?" The satirist of the schools quipped his rival, "You quote me a saying of Hardjedef, you know not whether it is right or wrong, or what chapter comes before or [after] it". Scholars like Tjunuroy even incorporated a list of kings into their tomb-chapels, or a gallery of famous men from Imhotep down to Ramesses II's time.

Moreover, long before and after the archaeological visits of Prince Khaemwaset to the Pyramids at Saqqara and Giza, Egyptian scribes (even, teachers with their students) paid visits to the tombs and temples of the ancient kings — the world's first tourists. Their motives were complex — 'to see the beauty' of the ancient monuments, to pay their respects to the ancient kings who ranked among the august company of the gods, and to invoke their blessings as mediators with the great gods. Thus, at the Late-Middle-Kingdom pyramid of king Khendjer (about 1740 B.C.), under Ramesses II in July 1246 B.C.:

> 'The scribe Nashuyu came to the district of the Pyramid of Teti-beloved-of-Mut and the Pyramid of Djoser-Discoverer-of-Stoneworking. He says: 'Be gracious, O King . . . ', to all the gods of the West of Memphis, and: 'May I be near you, for I am your servant!'. Year 34, 4th month of Summer, Day 24, day of the festival of Ptah . . . , Lord of Memphis, when he appears outside the Temple (?) in the evening. (Written) by the scribe Nashuyu.'

Already in Ramesses II's day, king Djoser (about 2700 B.C.) enjoyed the same repute (as first major builder in stone) that he still enjoys in Egyptology today. And within Djoser's own great precinct, one may read:

> 'Year 47, 2nd month of Winter, Day 25 (January, 1232 B.C.), the Treasury-Scribe Hednakht, son of Tjenro and Tewosret, came to take a stroll and enjoy himself in the West of Memphis, along with his brother Panakht, Scribe of the Vizier. He said: 'O all you Gods of the West of Memphis, . . . and glorified dead, . . . , grant a full lifetime in serving your good pleasure, a goodly burial after a happy old age, like yourself!' Written by the King's Treasury-Scribe, Hednakht, and the Scribe Panakht.'

As in Memphis, so in Thebes. Our old acquaintance the vizier Paser visited the ancient Eleventh-Dynasty tomb-chapel of Khety, high official of the great Mentuhotep II (2040 B.C.) of 700 years before his own time, to see the monument of "his ancestor", in Year 17 of Ramesses II. Upon another occasion, he admired the charming scene of girl musicians in the splendid tomb-chapel of Qenamun of only 150 years previously, scribbling on it the remark, "Very beautiful"!

So, even as so many do today, the Egyptians of Ramesses' time admired the superb achievements of their ancestors, paid them respect, even (in Khaemwaset's case) to the point of occasional 'archaeological' investigations, forerunners of such work in our own times.

Cultural Heritage

While in the visual arts, magnificent jewellery, elegant furniture, fine statuary and painting might be the privilege of the rich, other aspects of Egypt's cultural wealth such as her literature

49. *The god Thoth, patron of scribes and of learning, here enthroned with pen in hand, and attended by 'Vision' personified. (Temple of Ramesses II, Abydos)*

your fates into your hand; he will guard you [henceforth].' So he offered to
the Sun-god, praising and glorifying his power daily."

Thereafter, the youth when out walking had to flee from his dog —
straight into the jaws of the crocodile! It carried him off, but released him
on certain conditions . . .

No doubt Ramesses II, his officials, and the storytellers in the market-places all knew how the
tale ended, right from their boyhood days . . . but, as the sole surviving papyrus breaks off at
this exciting point, we today cannot be sure how it all ended, if the boy fell to his fates or escaped them to live happily ever after! Perhaps, some day, we shall discover the ending.

But romance in Ramesside Egypt was not limited to fairy-tales. There, as ever with mankind, it was also an affair of the heart, and found expression in lyric poems as deft and light of
touch as the splendid paintings of dancers and banquets where musicians perhaps sang such ly-
rics to harp, pipe or lute. 'Brother' and 'sister' were the customary terms that the lovers used
of each other.

The girl would invoke her absent lover:

I.

"[I yearn for] your love by day and night,
        Hours long I lie, awake, until dawn!
Your form revives my heart,
        My desire is [entirely] for you!
Your voice it is, which gives my body vigour."

And in an aside, she muses:

II.

"[I'd know how to dispel] his [weariness];
        And I say, 'Where [has he gone]?
[There's none] who matches his wish, but I alone!"

She resumes:

III

"Your love, I desire it
        . . . like butter and honey.
[You belong to me],
        Like [best ointment] on the limbs of the notables,
        Like finest linen on the limbs of the gods,
        Like incense at the nose of [the Lord-of-All]."

She muses:

"He is like fine grasses in a man's hand,
        He is like a date-cake dipped in beer,
                He is like [a jar of beejr, [set] by bread."

He appears to reply:

IV

"My companionship (will) be for (all) the days,
    satisfying (even) for old age.
I shall be with you every day,
    that I may give [you . . . my love always]."

*   *   *

The young man's love inspires him to bravado:

V.

"My sister's love is on yonder bank,
    the River swirls by my legs,
        a mighty Flood in time of [Inundation]!
A crocodile lurks upon the sandbank,
    as I descend into the water,
I wade into the torrent,
    my mind intent upon the (far) bank.
I found the crocodile as (no more than) a water-vole,
    and the water like dry land to my feet!
It is her love that makes me strong,
    for she shall cast a water-spell for me.
I see the darling of my heart,
    waiting opposite for me."

*   *   *

The girl invites her lad:

VI.

"My wish is to descend into the water,
    to bathe myself before you,
That I may allow you to see my beauty,
    in finest royal linen, soaked in fragrant oil,
    [in a pool, hedged] with reeds.
I'll descend into the water with you,
I'll come forth with a red carp glistening in my fingers,
[I'll invite] my brother, 'Come, see me!'"

*   *   *

Or the young man yearns for his inaccessible beloved:

VII.

"I wish I were her negress,
    who is at her beck and call.

   . . .

She would gladden (me) with (her) plans,
    she'd willingly reveal to me the complexion of all her limbs.

*   *   *

I wish I were the washerman for my sister's linen,
    even for but one month!

I'd be so keen to take over [all the linen]
     which has (actually) touched her limbs,
While I it would be, who washed out the oils,
     which are in her garments.
I would wipe my (own) body with her cast-offs (?),
     which she had thrown aside.
[Then I'd have] joy and exultation,
     and my limbs would be young again.

* * *

I wish I were her signet-ring upon her finger,
 seeing her love every day;
     . . . . . the one who steals away her heart.

* * *

I wish I witnessed her arrival,
     [that I might] see [her beauty].
I shall make festival for (any) god who will prevent her going afar!
     May he grant me (my) lady today, without her being absent at [all]!"

So, in many a charming cadence, bold or coy (and far more in number than the few just quoted), the young gallants and the lovely lasses who "turn the head of every man" billed and cooed in sunlit garden or in moonlight tryst in the affluent Egypt of Ramesses II. Then as now, a young man's thoughts might lightly turn to love, or a girl long for the boy of her dreams; in the inner emotions and drives of heart and will, whatever the outward cultural differences, the basic humanity of all mankind across the ages (as well as the continents) is refreshingly one.

Respect this God,
A God who loves Truth,
Whose abomination is lies!

As you love your City-God . .
A God who loves men,
in lands afar.

Especially in Ramesses' day, the most impressive buildings in Egypt were neither its villages and townships, nor the villas of the great officials, nor even the splendid, rambling palaces of the pharaoh himself. Nor yet the abodes of the dead, tunnelled away into the rock, or constructed with modest chapels above (huge pyramids now being long centuries outdated). Rather, the most awesome structures of all were the temples of the gods, especially of the great gods of all Egypt, or of Empire, or of the principal cities. Even today in their picturesque ruin, these are still among the most spectacular monuments that the visitor may see along the valley of the Nile. As huge architectural undertakings, and massive evidence of the outward piety of mighty kings (not least Ramesses II), these impress us still, and have flitted through our story, a little here, a little there, whether at Karnak or Abydos, the Ramesseum or Abu Simbel.

The Homes of the Gods

In popular imagination, a great aura of mystery haunts Egyptian temples, as also ancient Egyptian religion. For radically different reasons to those of today, this was also partly true of the great temples in the expansive days of the Empire. For, for the most part, all that the common man ever saw of the huge temples of the gods of state or metropolis was a huge mud-brick curtain-wall, enclosing a vast sacred precinct, and pierced at rarest intervals by great monumental gateways built of stone. From afar, or when the great outer doors were briefly opened for some procession to pass in or out, he would glimpse the tops of great pylon-towers, the roofs of great stone halls, the gilded points of obelisks, the head of some colossal statue of a pharaoh — indeed, these same outer gateways might themselves be flanked by colossi of the King. Except, sometimes, at modest oratories by these outer gates or for the cult of the King (focussed on his statues), the ordinary citizen did not worship here at all. Within these vast, cloistered precincts, the gods were worshipped *for* Egypt and all the Egyptians, in the king's name — but not *by* the ordinary Egyptian. His more modest personal devotions were directed elsewhere, as we shall later see.

No. The temple of this or that great god was not a place of public worship, but was the home, almost the private residence, of the god to whom it belonged. In stylised fashion, the temple reflected the form and nature of a house. Those who in practice cared for him and his house, frequenting his halls and courts on duty, were his servants, namely the priests. If for a fleeting moment of time we join some priestly procession passing in through the outer portal of the great brick enclosure-walls, we may catch a vision of the heyday of a great 'state' temple of the Egyptian Empire, of the ideas it expressed, and of how, in fact, it functioned.

154

Once through that gateway, an avenue bordered on either hand by a row of sphinxes led up to the twin towers and doorway (the pylon) of the temple itself. Like the long featureless outer walls of the courts, halls and inner suites beyond, this vast façade was a dazzling sight in the glare of the warm Egyptian sun. These blinding white-plastered surfaces abounded in sculptured scenes of gods and kings, painted in brilliant colours. On the pylon-façade, Pharaoh is shown triumphing over his foes — *Egypt's* foes — while the god grants him the sword of victory. Scenes of this or that king's great battles for the empire of Egypt (like Ramesses II in Syria) adorned the outer walls of the courts and the halls beyond. Further on, along the walls come seemingly endless scenes of Pharaoh offering to the gods, scenes outwardly alike, but often drawn from series of episodes in the complex temple rituals. At war, Pharaoh was defender of Egypt for the gods and people. At worship, Pharaoh offered (on Egypt's behalf) rich gifts to the gods, so that they, in turn, might bestow their varied blessings in peace and prosperity upon Egypt, so honouring him as their regent on earth. Before the pylon might stand tall obelisks, whose gilded tips caught the first and last rays of the sun, and colossal statues of kings.

Through the pylon-gateway, one entered an open court, enclosed by colonnades affording a margin of shade. In their shadow, the inner faces of the walls, again, bore scenes of victorious campaigning or of royal worship or of festivals. Beyond the court or courts a further great doorway led on into a vast, forest-like hall of columns or 'hypostyle hall', the central alleyway being flanked by twin rows of columns higher than those upholding the rest of the hall's roof, permitting (by gratings) a cool, diffused light to fall across the shafts of the central and nearer rows of columns whose brilliantly-painted scenes of gods and kings glowed like rich jewels in the subdued sunlight filtering down between the soaring shafts, and shading off into the ever-deepening gloom of ever-receding rows on rows of columns, fading into darkness.

The esplanades, outer courts and hall of columns were the 'public rooms' of the god's house, his temple, where he (as his image) would appear in procession for his son, the King and for his servants the priests, especially on festival-days. The great men of state who sometimes acted for the King as 'festival leaders' had access thus far.

But beyond the pillared halls lay the god's inner suite, his private rooms, plunged in ever-increasing gloom, where faint shafts of light peeped through small slots in the roof, glancing here and there on painted wall or pillar or upon some fitment of glinting gold. One thus came to a long, narrow room with central pedestal on which was the portable barque — a miniature gold-covered boat — of the god, with a cabin amidships which veiled from public gaze his little portable image. It was in this form that the god travelled forth on the shoulders of his white-robed priests for processions and festivals, both inside the precincts and outside in public. Beyond this room, lay eventually the ultimate sanctuary and shrine containing the official cult-statue of the god, and nearby possibly side-shrines for his goddess-consort and their divine son, if a triad of gods was worshipped there. And all around a series of dark corridors and service-rooms, containing all the necessary apparatus of the cult (stands, vases, censers, incense, etc.), and the main valuables, possessions and heirlooms of his treasury. Here were admitted very few people — the high priest (or oftener, his deputy) and the serving priests actually on duty, to celebrate the daily cult and festival-rites at their appointed hours and dates.

50. Section through a typical New-Kingdom Egyptian temple.

Retracing his steps back through halls and courts, out to the blazing light of noonday, the visitor would find that the great temple does not stand alone in the precinct. There are often the lesser temples of other gods and goddesses associated in some way with the main deity. There would certainly be a sacred lake, source of holy water (as for ritual bathing, and libations) and setting for dramatic rites using small sacred barques on the lake. Beyond and around lay the houses of the priests, and a long series of brick-built stores and workshops. These held the revenues in grain and other goods in kind from the god's estates, while here his craftsmen and artisans provided for the material needs of the cult, the golden offering-stands, censers, jewelled collars and statuettes, sandals and linen garments, and the rest. Fowlyards and slaughterhouses for birds and cattle, and gardens, went to complete the community within the precinct walls.

The Service of the Gods

This outward blaze of splendour and inner mysterious darkness, then, enshrined the basic principle that a god's temple was his house, his earthly home. But what form of religion was en-

In this drawing the walls, roofs, and columns are coloured black where roofs and walls have been removed to show the inside of the building

SANCTUARY

INNER HALL

POSTYLE
ny-pillared)
L L.

STORE ROOMS

SACRED LAKE

Groves of trees planted in holes dug in the sand and filled with earth

IE INSIDE OF A TEMPLE AND ITS SURROUNDINGS

acted here, and by whom? In the scenes on the walls, it is Pharaoh who, on every hand, ceaseless-ly presents a variety of offerings to the gods who promise their benefits. And in fact, the religion of Egypt's great temples was indeed a religion of formal rites and ceremonies aimed (by correct performance) at ensuring the corresponding favour of the gods, rites modelled in essence on the mode of daily life.

Thus the god, like the ordinary Egyptian, awoke each day, ate, had his day's occupations, other meals, and evening rest. Early each day with the dawn, the workshops and stores were busy with people preparing the offerings for morning service; a fresh supply of bread, cakes and beer, a flagon of wine, fresh vegetables and fruit; meat (wildfowl, calf; bull on month-days and feasts), bouquets of flowers. The priests engaged in the day's service bathed for ritual purification. They, with the offerings borne by porters, then made their way across the temple courts and halls, led by a priest burning incense and another bearing a small portable image of the King shown in the pose of consecrating offerings — for he, in principle, was the one true officiant before the gods.

With the offerings set out on the tables and altars, the morning rites began with a morning hymn to awake the deity, and the priest slid back the bolt on the doors of the shrine, opened the doors to reveal the sacred image, and performed the 'toilet' of the god's statue — offering incense and a libation, changing the linen bandalettes, anointing the statue, imposing the regalia anew. Then he presented some representative food-offerings before the image,, as 'breakfast'. All was performed in the course of a long and complicated series of ceremonies and spoken rites. Alongside the main deity, other gods of the temple also received their morning rites and offerings. As a spirit-entity, the god was thought to occupy his statue, and perhaps to benefit from the 'essence' of the offerings.

Then came the second part of the service. The shrine of the god was closed again, and the priest withdrew. At a first 'Reversion of Offerings', the offerings themselves were now presented in special rites to the whole august company of previous kings of Egypt (now, also gods), and for the sake of the reigning pharaoh. Thus was Pharaoh, past and present, indissolubly linked with the enduring cult of the gods, down through the centuries. Finally, the whole panoply of offerings was taken forth from the main temple halls. After a second rite of 'Reversion of Divine Offerings', it was distributed as food to the priests on duty — as was said in another time and place, "those who serve the altar are partakers with the altar".

The morning service was the principal one in an ordinary day; a brief midday offering was 'lunch', and an evening offering (perhaps by sundown) was the god's 'supper'. Minor rites were observed in the temple at the twelve hours of the day and of the night. At the phases of the moon (especially new moon), additional offerings were prescribed, likewise on the purely religious feasts celebrated solely within the temple precincts. As the god received his offerings, so in turn his benefits were expected in Egypt at large.

Who, then, officiated day by day in this dramatisation of daily life? At the head of the hierarchy (and as Pharaoh's main representative) was the High Priest or 'First Prophet' of the god. sometimes bearing special titles (such as 'Chief of Seers' at Heliopolis). The high priest probably officiated in person at festivals and special occasions, being otherwise concerned with the running of the whole sacred establishment, its administration and estates, new buildings and repairs. Quite often, he was not by training a priest at all, but was a royal appointee — a retired vizier or relative of one, or some other distinguished personage accorded this honour as a 'golden handshake' for his retirement. Occasionally a royal prince might serve, like Khaemwaset in Memphis.

Whatever his background, the high priest was seconded by each of a 2nd, 3rd and 4th Prophet, or equivalent ecclesiastic (a Sem-priest, in Memphis), and a college of 'God's Fathers'. As full-time priests, these men saw to the fulfilment of the daily and periodic rituals and the lesser feasts. The Chief Lector-priest was the learned expert in all matters of ritual, the theological scholar who knew the right conduct of all rites as recorded in the papyri, and probably dealt with the work of scribal scholars on religious and related manuscripts in the 'House of Life' or 'university department' of the temple.

However, the main body of 'lay priests' were the 'pure ones' (*wab* or *weeb*), who served in the temple by rota three times a year, a month at a time for each group on duty. When not on duty, they worked in the god's precinct and workshops at their own particular skills, or on his domains as cultivators, or possibly also in occupations away from the temple. Coming back on duty, they had to undergo the appropriate ritual purifications, ritual bathing repeated perhaps thrice daily. Nor were the ladies left out of all this activity. In most of the great temples of Egypt, the wives of numberless officials, high and low alike, served as 'Chantress' of this or that deity. Their part was to accompany the services with music — singing the morning or evening hymn, playing their tinkling sistra (rattle with metal rods), tambourines and other instruments —

bringing bouquets of flowers, and in some cases to help in the rites of offering. The wife or daughter of the high priest often served in effect as high priestess, with a title that made her in fact chief musicienne.

Naturally, all these services and festivals, with offerings that fed not only the gods but also possibly a hundred or more officiants and servitors, plus the whole establishment of workpeople and priests off rota, could not be run on nothing. And, in fact, the pharaohs bestowed large domains of agricultural land, cattle-pastures and marshes (for fish and fowl) upon the temples and their gods, as endowments to provision the cult, its celebrants and its servants. There existed 'permanent' endowments, and also the fields that were given by a particular pharaoh for the span of his reign (thereafter returning to the crown). Fields left uncultivated might also lapse back to the Crown, for redistribution likewise. On their land-holdings, the temples appear to have paid certain dues to the state Treasury of Pharaoh, and complicated arrangements governed the leasing and renting of lands, e.g. by one temple to another. Each year at harvest-time, the grain-ships brought their vital cargoes from the various temple-domains scattered throughout Egypt back to the main temple precincts and their granaries. Thus, each temple had not only its priestly staff and the cultivators, but also a high steward, treasurer, and other administrative officers to look after the details of its temporal possessions, in conjunction with the high priest, and in liaison with the state Chief of the Treasury.

In Egypt's agricultural economy and way of life, the gods through their temples were major employers both on the land (farmers and herdsmen) and in all the arts and crafts. Theologically, the temples were (besides the god's abodes) also microcosms of Egypt and were spiritually the 'powerhouses' by which the favour of the gods was transmitted to king and nation, in return for the service of offerings.

The Gods at Home

Who were these great gods whose blessing was so massively sought by king and people? The great peace-treaty of Ramesses II with the Hittites speaks of the 'thousand gods' of Egypt as of Hatti. Formidable indeed would be the prospect of getting acquainted with anything like such a number and range of supergods, gods, godlings, numens and demons. But not surprisingly, some of the divine population of Ramesses' Egypt mattered more than others, to him and his subjects alike.

The great gods of the state stood at the head of Egypt and of the pantheon, as patrons of Pharaoh. Most renowned was *Amun*, god of the air and of the hidden powers of generation (fertility and virility), at home in Thebes. As god of Empire, he was giver of victory to the warrior-pharaohs; after Akhenaten's reaction to his overbearing claims, Sethos I and Ramesses II restored Amun to outward primacy in that role, but limited his absolute claims by honouring Re and Ptah with him. Upon the monuments, Amun cut an impressive figure — a man in form, with flat-topped helmet bearing two tall plumes. To him belonged all the greatest temples of Thebes. His consort was Mut, a goddess linked with other such goddesses both motherly (Hathor, Bast) and leonine (Sekhmet). The local Theban moon-god, Khons, was also son to Amun and Mut in their triad.

Second of the greatest gods was *Re* the sun-god, shown as a man crowned with the sun's

disc, and often falcon-headed. Revered from of old throughout Egypt, his main seat was Heliopolis, a few miles north of Memphis and across on the east bank of the Nile. His theologians were
Egypt's most renowned. Many another god took on the cosmic, universal role of Re by adding
Re's name to theirs — even Amun of Thebes appears often as Amen-re. As in other lands, the all-
seeing sun early became patron of Justice. Thus the goddess Maat was 'daughter of Re', personifying as she did the ideal norm of life — justice, right, truth, the proper order of life — to which
all the gods, the pharaoh and the people must conform or be judged by. The storm-god Seth of
the East Delta (Ramesses' homeland) became the helper of Re, repulsing the wicked serpent from
Re's boat as it crossed the sky daily. The goddess Hathor often appears with Re. He in the morning arose as Khepri ('one who becomes'), and in the evening set as Atum (an old form of the
creator and sun-god). To Re were sacred the tall, slim obelisks whose gilded points caught the
sun's rays first and last.

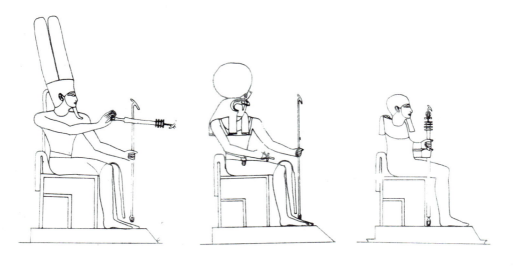

51.   A. The god Amun.   *B. The god Re.*   *C. The god Ptah.*

Third of the greatest gods was *Ptah* of Memphis, its ancient craftsman-god. He was often
shown as a clean-shaven mummiform man with skull-cap; sometimes, as a man diademed with
horns, disc and plumes when (as Ptah—Tatonen) he was creator, earth-god, and patron of royal
jubilees. His consort was the fiery lioness-goddess Sekhmet, Nefertem the lotus being their son.
Ptah's principal colleague in Memphis was the falcon-headed god Sokar, a patron of the dead
with wide powers who frequently combined with Osiris as well as Ptah ('Ptah-Sokar-Osiris'), as a
form of Osiris, lord of the hereafter.

The cycle of Osiris had in Ramesses' time the greatest, most universal appeal to the Egyptian people. Osiris was prototype of the good king, bringer of civilisation to Egypt in primeval
times. In legend he was murdered by his jealous brother Seth; his resourceful wife Isis (a great
goddess of magic) collected his dismembered body to be mummified by the jackal-headed em-
balmer-god Anubis. Magically resuscitated, Osiris reigned henceforth as King of the Netherworld

and of the after-life. On earth, his son Horus successfully contested the kingship with Seth, becoming his father's successor. In Ramesses' time, Abydos (about 100 miles north from Thebes) had been the holy city of Osiris for centuries, where both Ramesses and his father built their most beautiful temples. Osiris pictorially is a striking figure, mummiform, holding crossed sceptres, and wearing a tall white crown edged by two plumes. Isis is shown as a woman often with sun-disc and horns upon her wig. Horus (long since merged with the falcon Horus) appears as a man, often falcon-headed. The legend of Osiris became a bastion of Egyptian kingship; even as Horus, the legitimate heir, gave proper burial to his father Osiris, so at accession each pharaoh legitimised his kingship as the new Horus by giving due burial to his dead predecessor as (an) Osiris. But the appeal of Osiris went far beyond matters of kingship, for in him the Egyptians had long since placed their hopes of a happy afterlife as the netherworld subjects of Osiris. A dead Egyptian became 'the Osiris (So-and-so)'.

Important local gods had their devotees in their own provinces of Egypt; besides their own specialised roles, such local gods also served in practice as supreme god for the people in their district. Outstanding were such as the old warrior-goddess Neith at Sais (West Delta), the friendly cat-headed goddess Bast at Bubastis (East Delta), the ram-headed Herishef at Ninsu near the Fayum, and the crocodile-headed Sobek in that garden-province. Further south, going up the Nile valley, Hermopolis was the seat of Thoth, ibis-headed god of hieroglyphs, wisdom and the moon, while Siut honoured the wolf-headed Wepwawet, patroller of the desert paths. South again, the tall-plumed virility god Min reigned at Akhmim and Koptos (north and south-east of Abydos respectively). Closely akin to Amun, Min was also patron of desert explorers. Near Abydos, the provincial capital Thinis worshipped Anhur or Anhur-Shu, 'son of Re', a heroic figure like Horus. In between Abydos and Koptos, the cow-headed goddess Hathor held sway at Dendera; patron of love, motherhood, jollity, she was somewhat akin to Bast in the north. But, further south, she had a special relationship with the falcon-god, Horus of Edfu, whom she visited annually in great state for the rites of the 'sacred marriage'. The falcon-headed war-god Montu was honoured in Thebes and its 'suburb' towns as well as in his home town of Armant to the south. Then, at Nekheb, the vulture-goddess Nekhbet was patron-lady of Upper Egypt, corresponding to Udjo, cobra-goddess patron of the Delta-realm of Lower Egypt. Finally, the ram-headed god Khnum (creator of mankind on his potter's wheel) held sway in Esna near Edfu, and at Aswan at the First Cataract as lord of the cataract and the mythical 'source' of the Nile there. In Nubia, the ancient god Dedwen was recognised by the Egyptians, and a series of falcon-gods in the main centres of settlement along the Nubian Nile, all treated as local forms of Horus — 'Horus of Baki', '. . . of Miam', '. . of Buhen', and so forth. Under Ramesses II, the state gods Amun, Re and Ptah, were given greater prominence in Nubia than the local gods. Lastly, there was the 'local god' common to *all* of inhabited Egypt — Hapi, the Nile (in particular as the annual flood) who by his yearly rise over the cultivated land made life possible with his waters and silt. Throughout Egypt he received popular worship. At the narrow gorge of Silsila, Ramesses II (like his father) decreed rich official offerings to the Nile twice a year, a custom followed by his successor Merenptah and later by Ramesses III.

Foreign gods entered Egypt along with the prisoners of war, traders, diplomats and others who came in from Syria-Palestine. Some identified with Egyptian gods, as did the storm-god Baal with Seth, or (by similarity of name) Horon with Horus. Resheph, god of thunderbolts, and Anath and Astarte (Old Testament 'Ashtoreth'), lascivious goddesses of love and war, retained their own distinctive characteristics.

Sacred animals were one of the more picturesque features of Egyptian religion. Various animals and birds had become attributes of sundry gods and goddesses — the ibis and baboon for Thoth, the cat of Bast, the ram of Khnum, the crocodile of Sobek, ram and goose of Amun, the falcon of Horus, the cow of Hathor, and many more. Often, the animal concerned embodied a particular quality of the deity concerned, whether in reality or mythology. But in Ramesses' day, much more important were the successions of special sacred animals who 'reigned' one after another, such as the Apis bull of Ptah at Memphis (cared for by Prince Khaemwaset) and the Mnevis bull at nearby Heliopolis. Other special roles apart, such animals served as 'living images' that the god concerned might occupy at will, and by which even give oracles, and so were honoured accordingly.

Rites, Hymns and Theology

During the course of centuries, the elaborate religious ceremonies in the great temples gave rise to a vast 'special literature' — morning and evening hymns to awake, or take leave of, the god; long service-books with interminable 'spells' for recitation and rites for performance, by the officiating priests. Close to these works stood the great literary hymns to the gods, in some cases possibly used for special occasions. Then there were the works of mythology, stories of the gods, world origins and the like. A glimpse of some of these varied writings gives a little of the flavour of the temple-services, hymns and other 'theological' literature current by the time of Ramesses II.

Thus, daily, the deity was awakened by the early morning hymn intoned by the officiating priest, perhaps seconded by the choir of chantresses with their tinkling sistra and tambourines. In Thebes, the goddess Mut was thus serenaded in a hymn that identified her with her equals among the goddesses.

> "Awake in peace, awake *O Flame* in peace;
> > may thy awakening be peaceful!
> Awake in peace, awake *O Neith* in peace;
> > may thy awakening be peaceful!
> Awake in peace, awake *O Udjo* in peace;
> > may thy awakening be peaceful!
> Awake in peace, awake *O Menhet* in peace;
> > may thy awakening be peaceful!
>
> Restless One who traverses deserts, who courses the meadows . . . ,
> Mayest thou hear this word spoken to thee by the King . . . "

So went the stately hymn in a repetitive litany as old as the pyramids of fifteen centuries before and hallowed by age-long usage.

Over in the main Temple of Amun in Karnak, particularly on great days of festival, a more elaborate and newer morning hymn greeted the god of empire from the priest and temple-choir:

"What is sung by the Two River-banks to Amun in the morning:-

'The doors are opened at the Sanctuary,
                    the shrine is thrown open in the Mansion.
Thebes is in festivity, Heliopolis in joy, Karnak in rejoicing.
Jubilation (fills) heaven and earth . . .
Song is made for this noble god Amen-re, Lord of the Thrones of the Two Lands,
                    (and) Amun, Lord of Luxor.
His fragrance has encompassed the circuit of the Great Green (Sea),
Heaven and earth are (full of) his beauty,
                    He has bathed them in gold with his rays . . .' "

Each act of the ritual was accompanied by its proper text or 'spell', full of allusions to the rich realms of Egyptian mythology — heavy with meaning for the Egyptians (especially the learned priests), but much less so for a modern reader so many millennia later. So when, for example, the officiating priest draws back the bolt to open the doors of the innermost shrine, to see the image of the god and perform his rites, the service-book ran as follows (here, for the sun-god Re):

"Spell for withdrawing the door-bolt:-

'(So) is the finger of Seth withdrawn from the Eye of Horus; it is well!
The finger of Seth is withdrawn from the Eye of Horus; it is well!
The cord is loosed from Osiris, the sickness is absolved from the god.
O Re-Harakhte, receive your two white plumes,
                    the right one on the right side, the left one on the left side.
O naked one, be clothed; O swathed one, be swathed.
For I indeed am a prophet,
                    it is the King who has commanded me to behold the god.
I am yon great phoenix who is in Heliopolis,
                    I have pacified him who is in the Lake of the Nether-
                                        world . . .' "

For the presentation of the offerings and based on very ancient sources, the basic 'menu' in the service-book might run as follows (for Amun of Thebes on a feast-day):

"Festival-menu for Amen-re . . . to be recited:-

'Wine, two dishes: - O Amun, take to thyself the Eye of Horus, wherewith thy mouth
                                        is opened.
Shayet-cakes, 20:- O Amun, take to thyself the Eye of Horus, it shall not trickle away
                                        from thee.
Roast meat, one dish:- O Amun, take to thyself thy roast!' "

And so on, for many more items. To the acts of presenting the food before the god's image and reciting the invocations of the menu, the service-book added rubrics for the lector-priest:

"*To be recited by the Lector-priest who makes the invocation*:-

'O Sem-priest, make the royal-offering invocation (to) Amun . . . :-

"Come to this thy bread!" '

"*Carrying-in Offerings by the Lector-priest (for) this god. Recite*:-

'Come, O servants! Carry-in the offerings that are for the Presence, carry offerings
(for) Amun . . . ' "

At the appropriate point came the first 'Reversion of Offerings' from the use of the god to that of the spirits of the reigning King and those of all his deceased 'ancestors', all the former pharaohs of Egypt, the ritual-book naming here only a representative series of New Kingdom pharaohs and one or two 'ancients', going backwards through time from the reigning ruler (Ramesses II) to the early kings:

"Come, O servants! Carry-in the offerings that are for the Presence, carry offerings
for the King, Lord of the Two Lands . . . , Ramesses II;
    for Sethos I, for Ramesses I, for Haremhab, for Amenophis III; for Tuthmosis IV,
    for Tuthmosis II; for Tuthmosis I, for Amenophis I, for Ahmose, for Kamose;
    for Sesostris I, for Mentuhotep II;
— and for all the Kings of Upper and Lower Egypt . . . receiving the Crowns, . .
established on their heads . . . , that they may adore Re in life."

So, in the depth of their vast halls and sanctuaries, these elaborate and stately rituals were celebrated with the greatest magnificence for the benefit of gods and king, for Egypt's welfare.

During the Empire age, not least from Ramesses II's time onwards, splendid literary hymns were composed, extolling the creative power of the major gods, their care for mankind, and even identifying the great gods as aspects of one another as if facets of the one great god (though never reaching an effective monotheism). Thus sang the draughtsman Mery-Sekhmet, a contemporary of the last years of Ramesses II and of his successors:

"*Praise to you*, O Amun-Re-Atum-Horus-of-the-Horizons!
He who spoke with his mouth, and there appeared as beings, men and gods,
    Cattle and game, in entirety, and all that flies and alights.

You have created (both) the homelands and the distant regions,
                                    Peopled with their towns,
And verdant meadows impregnated by the Waterflood, that thereafter bring forth
    Good things innumerable, for the support of the living.

164

Valiant you are, as the Shepherd pasturing them forever, eternally.
(Their) bodies are filled with your beauty, (their) eyes see by (you),
  Awe of you is upon all, their hearts incline to you,
  Good are you at all times, all people live by beholding you.
Everyone says, 'Yours we are!'
Brave and fearful as one, rich and poor in unison, all likewise.
  Your sweetness wins them all, none are void of your beauty.

  Do the widows not say, 'You are our husband!',
and the babes, 'Our father and mother'?
  The rich boast of your beauty, the poor (adore) your countenance.
  The prisoner turns to you, the rich man invokes you."

And so for many a noble verse more; and many another poem besides this one exists in honour of both Amun and other deities.

Through the ages, the learned theologians had not only evolved the particular legends of their local gods and goddesses and local accounts of creation, but also (by Ramesses II's day) they had long since sought to interlink the various versions of myths of creation, 'adjusting' the roles of the principal gods in an overall picture of astonishing complexity; like most of Ramesses' own subjects, we must content ourselves here with just a glimpse.

Thus, in the beginning there was naught but the waters of the primeval ocean. Thence emerged the Creator who (depending on his identity) proceeded by various means to create gods and men, the inhabited world. So at Memphis, the earth rose first from the waters (as Ptah-Tatonen), giving rise to all other beings including the sun ... But across at Heliopolis, it was the sun-god who was deemed to have emerged first from the waters, thereafter creating gods and men. Later theologians 'adjusted' these competing versions by averring (for example) that the sun-god himself was immanent in the original earth that first rose — Ptah and Re were at one. At Hermopolis, they considered that a lotus rose out of the waters, from which the sun-god appeared when it opened; and so on. In his turn, Amun of Thebes also could be claimed as primeval god, by skilful adaptation of such pre-existing myths as these.

In due time, it was thought, the gods ruled Egypt in succession, as the Dynasty of the Gods — Re returned to heaven when mankind proved rebellious and he had first to send the goddess Hathor to slay them, and then (by a stratagem) to restrain her from finishing them off entirely. Osiris brought elements of civilisation, being murdered and supplanted by Seth. Young Horus then won back the rule of Egypt, while his father Osiris became ruler of the Netherworld. Then eventually came the dynasty of spirits and demi-gods, and finally the long line of historical pharaohs beginning with the union of Upper and Lower Egypt under Menes. From him to Ramesses II stretched the long line of pharaohs for nearly twenty centuries of tumultuous history.

The individual mythologies of the local gods of Ramesses' Egypt were as numerous as the gods themselves — and not always so easily recovered and understood today. Even in his time, much detail must have been the preserve of the local priests, while some favourite myths were current also among the ordinary people, notably that of Osiris.

The Gods in Festival

'All work and no play makes Jack a dull boy'. So in essence in Egypt under Ramesses II, as at other times and places. At all levels of society, regular breaks from their labours were desired and appreciated — even the humble workmen of the Royal Tomb at Thebes had their 'weekends' as we shall see. But throughout the course of a year, anywhere in Egypt, Ramesses' subjects had their annual festivals — of the great gods or of local gods. Some feasts were celebrated throughout the land, others were entirely local affairs. On a given feast-day the portable image of the god concerned sallied forth from the temple, hidden in a little shrine on the gilded portable barque borne on the shoulders of the priests, in glittering procession to music and incense, and to the acclamation of the populace in holiday mood.

Thus, at the turn of the civil year (in July under Ramesses II), the last 5 days of the old year (often) and then New Year's Day (always) with a day or so following were holidays from ordinary work. In all temples, of course, these days were all observed with the appropriate offerings. Of far greater fame were the really major festivals of such gods as Amun or Osiris, or occasions of universal interest such as harvest festivals.

52.   *The Image of Amenophis I gives an oracle on his festival-day. (Thebes, Tomb 19).*

In Ramesses' time, Abydos had already been renowned for centuries for its annual celebrations of the 'Mysteries' of Osiris, a rite observed wherever Osiris was honoured. In Memphis and Thebes its practical equivalent was the Festival of Sokar, a god often identified with Osiris. At Abydos, the mythical events of the death, resuscitation and triumph of Osiris were re-enacted with great fervour during a number of days in the 4th month of Inundation (about October/November under Ramesses II). On the first day, the insignia of Wepwawet, "opener of the ways", went out in procession before the portable Neshmet-barque of Osiris, and the ordinary people joined in the "Repelling of foes" from the barque, with rival groups impersonating the enemies and defenders of Osiris. Then came the 'Great Procession', mourning the murder of Osiris by Seth. Then, the preparation of his tomb in the District of Peqer close by Abydos, the secret temple-rites of his embalming, and his burial in Peqer. Then, finally, the "great battle" at Nedyt ('sandbank') when Osiris's foes were definitively beaten, followed by the triumphant return of the resuscitated god to his temple, as the great Neshmet barge came along the canal bearing his portable Neshmet-barque and image, so that the whole festival reached its climax amid the tumultuous rejoicing of the multitudes.

In Memphis and Thebes, the parallel feast of Sokar in the same month was largely a purely

priestly celebration within the temples, but on Days 25, 26, of the 4th month of Inundation came the high point of the festival. On the evening of the 25th, Sokar's devotees in Thebes wore garlands of onions and made offerings in their family tomb-chapels with incense, libation, and onions. Then, on the 26th with the dawn, the spectacular golden barque of Sokar was carried in a great procession of triumph, circling round the walls of the temple-precinct in Thebes, or around the old 'White Walls' in Memphis, to the plaudits of the holidaying populace encouraged by a bearer of ceremonial mace and flail.

In imperial Thebes, the two greatest festivals were the opulent Feast of Opet and the picturesque Feast of the Valley, both of Amun. Greatest of all was the Festival of Opet which, under Ramesses II, lasted from the preliminary temple-rites on the evening of 2nd month of Inundation, Day 18, to its conclusion some three weeks later on 3rd month of Inundation, Day 12, thus taking most of the month of September. From of old, the empire pharaohs had regularly journeyed up from Memphis to Thebes to attend Opet in person — as did Ramesses II in his first year as sole pharaoh, and doubtless often thereafter.

On Day 19 of 2nd month of Inundation, the portable barques of Mut and Khons (containing their images) joined that of Amun in his huge temple in Karnak — probably in the vast Hall of Columns built by Sethos I and Ramesses II. Then the procession, with its musicians and dancers before it, went forth to the temple quay, to board the great golden river-barge Userhat-Amun. The huge barge was towed out by a short canal into the river, to be met by a whole flotilla of ships — a tow-rope was passed to the King's flagship, rowed (nominally) by the great officials of the land. The real motive-power came from the tow-ropes that ran from Amun's barge and other ships to the river-bank — and over the brawny shoulders of peasants and soldiers. The whole glittering cortège sailed upriver the two miles south from Karnak to Luxor ('Southern Opet') accompanied on-shore by musicians and singers and by vast and joyous throngs of ordinary people making holiday, with bread and beer available in abundance. Songs of acclamation to god and king floated over the hubbub:

"Beautifully you shine forth, O Amen-re, while you are in the barge Userhat!
All the people give you praise, the whole land is in festivity.
For your eldest Son and Heir sails you to Luxor.
May you grant him Eternity as King of the Two Lands,
                                   Everlasting in peaceful years.
May you protect him with life, stability and dominion,
May you grant him to appear in glory as the Joyful Ruler . . . "

At Luxor, the portable barques of Amun, Mut and Khons disembarked in procession once more, to enter the Southern Opet temple of Luxor, preceded by musicians, acrobatic girl-dancers and priests burning incense, while along the way booths loaded with food and drink were held ready to regale the tired, happy participants. Thereafter, the three deities stayed in Luxor temple for nearly three weeks of inner temple-rites (perhaps in celebration of sacred marriage), while the workaday world once more went about its normal business, and Pharaoh and his dignitaries decided vital matters of state. On these occasions, Amun gave oracles — as when Ramesses II determined with Amun's oracle on the appointment of Nebwenenef in Year 1 as high priest of Amun. Finally came the day of Amun's ceremonial return. Once more, the cheerful crowds ran excitedly along the river-bank as the stately flotilla and golden barge came back home to Karnak.

Far shorter but equally impressive was the Festival of the Valley, celebrated at new moon some six months later, in the 2nd month of Summer (April). On the chosen day, Amun once more sailed in state on his great golden barge — this time, straight across the Nile to the West side of Thebes, and along the canals up to the desert edge. In former times, Amun's portable barque-image was then carried in procession up one of the causeways of the open valley of Deir el Bahri to the memorial temple of Mentuhotep II or (from her time onwards) to that of Queen Hatshepsut close by it. Later, Amun was often guest overnight in the memorial temple of the reigning king. So, under Ramesses II, the priests of Amun bore his barque-image into the ample courts and halls of *his* temple, the Ramesseum, to rest in its mighty Hall of Columns, "resting-place of the Lord of the Gods in his beautiful Feast of the Valley" as its texts say. There, splendid offerings were presented to Amun and enjoyed by the participants. Festival bouquets and fine linen were distributed to officials and priests who had helped with the festivities. Thus enthused our old friend, the vizier Paser:

> "O my Lord, my city-god, Amun Lord of Karnak! Grant that I may be like
> one of the ancestors, the blessed ones, that I may praise Your Majesty when
> you visit the Western side, that I may be foremost among those who follow you
> in your Beautiful Feast of the Valley, and that I may receive a pure garment and
> lay aside the old, like every favoured one!"

But these temple-ceremonies were only one half of the festival. That evening, the leading families of Thebes went traditionally in torchlight procession up the desert-slopes to the brilliantly-painted tomb-chapels of themselves and their forebears, with abundant provisions, there to celebrate Amun's visit to the Beautiful West (giving life to the dead) in company with those who had gone before them, to keep overnight festival. One great hymn to Amun records:

> "Beer is brewed for him (on) the day of festival, people spend the night
> awake in the beauty of the night. His Name echoes over the rooftops, his are
> the songs by night when it is dark".

Doubtless on a humbler scale, the workmen of Deir el Medina ('of the Royal Tomb') did likewise in their bright little chapels overlooking their village. On the morrow, after the final rites, Amun travelled back across the river in his barge, to the seclusion of Karnak, while (their overnight feast ended) the Thebans returned to their earthly homes and work once more.

In the temples, the provisions (and endowments) for these spectacular festivals were on the grandest scale. At the Ramesseum, the three weeks of the Feast of Opet were endowed with provisions that included over 11,400 loaves and cakes, 385 jugs of beer, and a myriad of miscellaneous offerings (oxen, fowl, wine, fruit, incense, etc.), while the Feast of Sokar for ten days had over 7,400 loaves and cakes, 1,372 jugs of beer, and up to 30 different items on one day. The festivities over at Karnak and Luxor (at least for Opet) must have been on an even more lavish scale. Needless to say, such hecatombs of offerings did not benefit solely the god and his chief clergy, but by the second 'Reversion of Offerings' these largesses reached out to the entire temple-staff and participants in the staging of the festival, both high and low — the gods played hosts to their people on a sumptuous scale.

169

Servants of the Gods

In the north, at Memphis and Heliopolis, a varied set of men served as high priests of Ptah and Re respectively. In Heliopolis, Ramesses II early on appointed one of his Chief Charioteers of the Residence, Bak, as high priest of the sun-god – perhaps as a distinguished-service reward to a veteran. After him, one Amenemopet held this post (possibly about Years 10 to 26). Amenemopet himself left no great mark, but he belonged to that ubiquitous family of Amen-em-inet, Chief of the Medjay-militia, of whom we have met not a few already. After this man, Ramesses II appointed his own sixteenth son Mery-Atum as the next 'Chief of Seers', perhaps during about Years 26 to 46 of the reign. In later years, the northern vizier Prehotep the Younger added this office to others as we shall see.

In Memphis, a closer series of men held sway as High Priests of Ptah. After others still little known, perhaps Huy officiated there in Year 16 during the burial of the first Apis bull of the reign. Then probably came Pahemneter, whose elder son Didia probably succeeded his father in office, and whose younger son was the future vizier, Prehotep the Younger. But after Didia, the latter's royal colleague the famous Sem-priest, Prince Khaemwaset, held the supreme office for a time until his death about Year 55. Then finally, the vizier Prehotep the Younger became high priest of both Re and Ptah, until in the last years of the old pharaoh's reign, the king's grandson Hori, by Khaemwaset, became high priest of Ptah, perhaps officiating also in later reigns.

In Upper Egypt, sailing resolutely upstream past many an honourable shrine in the capitals of a series of provinces, we next call at the Thinite province, first at Thinis and then Abydos once more. Thinis was seat of Anhur-Shu, 'son of Re', a warrior-hero who (in legend) brought back to Egypt the goddess 'Eye of Re' (often identified with Mut, Sekhmet, and others). The high-priest-hood here was held – with that of Hathor of Dendera – by Nebwenenef prior to Year 1 of Ramesses II, who appointed him to Thebes. Nebwenenef's son retained the benefice of Dendera (a family tradition), but a new and senior man, Hori, was appointed to Thinis. He was quickly followed there by his able son Minmose, who filled the Thinite temples with his monuments and developed friendly relations with the Ninsu family of the northern vizier Prehotep the Elder (becoming his brother-in-law), and with his successor and namesake Prehotep the Younger (from Abydos, to whom Minmose became father-in-law). But despite his long and successful career there, Minmose founded no 'dynasty'. A self-expressed 'new man', Anhurmose, was later appointed there under Ramesses II and served still under Merenptah.

In Abydos itself, site of the superb temples which Ramesses and his father had dedicated to Osiris, there held sway a remarkable 'dynasty' of no less than six high priests of Osiris, in regular succession. The earliest, To, under Haremhab and perhaps Ramesses I, left no son but passed his office briefly to his brother-in-law Hat (time of Sethos I) who in turn was followed by his own son, Mery. Mery saw out the last years of Sethos I and about the first decade of Ramesses II, witnessing the substantial completion of the two great temples of these kings. The climax came with the fourth member of the line, Mery's son Wennufer who, in a long and prosperous pontificate of probably some 35 years (about Years 15 - 50 of Ramesses II) left a mass of monuments – statues of himself, some with his parents and family, stelae, and probably a tomb-chapel in Abydos. In that chapel, he proudly listed the dates in Ramesses' reign (Years 21, 33, 33 + x; 39, 40; 47, 48 [?]) in which he had prepared statues of the King (some, of copper), perhaps with endowments. The first may have followed the signing of the Hittite Treaty, and most of the others have been made in connection with the King's many jubilees. In another inscription, the ever-loyal Wennufer prayed to Osiris, "May you maintain alive Ramesses II your son, and may you establish his glorious appearances upon the throne of Horus, may [you] distinguish [him in performing the king] ship of the Two Lands, while he lives forever! — Thus the High Priest of Osiris, Wennufer." A prayer in large measure fulfilled. Our Wennufer had exalted connections. His brother became northern vizier (Prehotep the Elder), his contemporary in the same province was his brother-in-law (Minmose, the High Priest of Anhur of Thinis), and his own wife was daughter of Qeni, Chief of the Granaries of the South and North (like a minister of food and agriculture), all of whom he commemorated on a stela at Abydos in Year 42 (1238/37) B.C. But eventually even Wennufer had to join Osiris in the afterlife, leaving his high office to his son Hori. By the next reign, Hori's son in turn inherited the high-priesthood, making him (Yuyu) the sixth holder in this tenacious family.

By-passing Dendera, and Koptos (where another Minmose was High Priest of Min and Isis, being yet another relative of Amen-em-inet!), we at last drop anchor once more in Thebes, 'city of Amun'. By about Year 40 of Ramesses' reign, the high-priesthood of Amun had changed incumbent several times. Nebwenenef had died by about Year 12, followed by the inevitable Amen-em-inet's father, the other Wennufer, during about Years 12 to 27. Then the veteran Theban vizier Paser had held the office, about Years 27 to 38 or so. For a year or so, an old man Roma (retired 2nd prophet of Amun) may have served as 'stand-in', assisting his own son Bakenkhons, currently 2nd prophet of Amun, and previously 3rd prophet, God's Father, and having served in the ranks ever since the last years of Sethos I. Now by Year 39, Ramesses II could no longer overlook the remarkably long and devoted service that Bakenkhons had rendered for more than the length of his own reign so far. So, at last, Bakenkhons became High Priest of Amun, crowning appointment in his long career. He went on to hold that office for 27 years, almost to the end of the reign of Ramesses II himself. On a statue of himself, dedicated in Karnak at the very end of his pontificate, the now aged Bakenkhons left a remarkable inscription, detailing the stages of his career from boyhood through the successive grades of the priesthood (citing years spent in each) to the exalted office of high priest, and as Amun's chief architect, building Ramesses' Eastern temple in Karnak (in the forties of the reign):

> "I was a good father to my subordinates, fostering their young people,
> giving a hand to anyone in need, maintaining alive the poverty-stricken, per-
> forming good deeds in (Amun's) temple. I built for him the Temple of
> Ramesses II-Who-Hears-Prayer, at the Upper Gateway of the Temple of Amun.
> I erected in it granite obelisks whose beauty reached the heavens, before them
> a portico opposite the town of Thebes, and basins and gardens planted with
> trees. I made two very great door-leaves (plated) with electrum that reflected
> the sky. I made two very great flag-staffs, and erected them in the forecourt
> before his temple. I constructed great river-barges for Amun, Mut and Khons."

Thus far Bakenkhons. But he did not achieve these prestigious works unaided. For none other than a son of the High Steward Yupa and grandson of old general Urhiya, the Chief of Medjay-militia Hatiay, claimed the title at this time of "one who erected great flagstaffs in the Temple of Amun". So Hatiay seconded Bakenkhons here. Even more remarkably, we also know the principal craftsman who carried out the rich decoration in gold and electrum on doors and sacred ships for Bakenkhons — the Superintendent of Carpenters, Chief of Goldsmiths, Nakht-Thuty. In his tomb-chapel (No. 189) over in Western Thebes, this man proudly had engraved pictures of many of his 'masterpieces':

> "First Door [of Gold], Second Door of Gold, Third Door of Gold, of the Forecourt of Amun; . . . Door of Khons . . . ; Double Portal of Gold, of Mut . . .",

and many more. In his biographical inscription, he lists these and other works for Amun:

> "I had understanding (as) a man of dexterity. [I wrought . . . works] of gold, great doors in Karnak, barques [to sail the River? . . .], executing the fine craftsmanship of one devoted to his skills . . . I was skilled in my craft, without anyone needing to instruct me. I directed various works . . . in gold, silver, real lapis-lazuli, and turquoise."

Such was Nakht-Thuty's renown that he was repeatedly called away from the workshops of Amun in Thebes, to be 'loaned' to other temples the length of southern Upper Egypt, from at least Abydos to Esna, during the later years of Ramesses II. His speciality was the wooden, gold-covered portable barques of the gods:

> "I obeyed the call to the portable barque of Isis . . . I obeyed the call to the barque of Khnum of Esna in Year 55 . . . I obeyed the call to the barque of Seth . . . in Upper Egypt, in Year 58",

and many more, probably totalling about 26 portable barques altogether! Nakht-Thuty's fame even reached Memphis itself, where his name was included in the 'gallery of the famous' in a great man's tomb-chapel there.

However, it was Bakenkhons' name that stuck to the temple of Ramesses II in Eastern Karnak, as in the following generation its gateway was popularly known as "the Great Portal of Baky", abbreviating the pontiff's name. In matters affecting the priesthood, and temple administration, Bakenkhons ranked with the Mayor of Thebes (Haunefer) and the king's High Steward Yupa (whose son Hatiay we saw helping at Karnak-East), as is shown by correspondence of the day. In disputes affecting temple affairs, Bakenkhons would head the bench of judges in the Theban law-court. In Year 46 of Ramesses II (late August, 1234 B.C.), such a sitting took place. It concerned a case in which one co-heir to land, the Table-Scribe Nefer-abet, challenged his co-heir Nia (agent for all the co-heirs, compare Mose of Memphis!) to yield up Nefer-abet's share instead of denying him his income from it — as he would now hand over *his* share to the Temple of Mut and obtain his allowance from *that* institution. So, we find the High Priest Bakenkhons, the 2nd prophet User-Montu, the 3rd prophet Roma(-roy), the Chief Prophet of Mut, Wenenefer, the Chief Prophet of Khons, and four other priests of Amun, besides the Secretary to the Court. In the event, Nefer-abet won his case. Others, too, perhaps frequented the Theban courts with similar disputes about that time. One such was the Theban Scribe and Accountant of Cattle, Simut called Kyky (Tomb

53. *Block statue of Bakenkhons, high priest of Amun; its inscriptions give details of his career as he rose through the ranks of Amun's priesthood to highest office (Munich, Bavarian State collection).*

173

409), a man devoted to the goddess Mut in far more than name, as he presented all his property to her estate (doubtless taking an income during his lifetime), but cutting-off his family complete-ly — perhaps in consequence of some dishonesty or quarrel?

However, Bakenkhons at length passed to his reward in the very last year or so of Ramesses II. Among the old king's last acts was the appointment of Bakenkhons's son Roma-roy to the high-priesthood in turn — a post he was to hold for two reigns and part of a third. As he himself proudly recollected later:

> "I grew up as a youth in the Temple of Amun . . . (eventually, Amun) made me known to the King, and my name was pronounced before the court-iers . . . [with] the King himself, Ramesses II, . . . who repeated his favour to me . . . and he made me chief in his temple, as High Priest of Amun."

Beyond Thebes, still others also served the gods, from Armant to Upper Nubia, but few left their mark in history as did a Bakenkhons or a Nakht-Thuty. And besides the priests proper, when Pharaoh himself could not attend some major feast in Thebes or Memphis, then one or other of the great officials was given the honour of being 'Festival Leader' of the god concerned, to play the lead in the ceremonies along with the professional clergy, as representative of the King.

Cult of the King, and the Jubilees

As Pharaoh of Egypt, Ramesses II held a unique office. Humanly, he remained in himself a mortal man, subject to life's joys and ills like all other mortals then or since, — even though as King he was in Egypt the first among all men, their official mediator with the gods. But on be-coming pharaoh, Ramesses (like any other who did so) also became *ex officio*, as it were, one of the gods of Egypt, too - not in himself, but by his office of King. From the beginning of Egypt-ian history, each ruler had been Horus the falcon-god personified, and so took a special name as the embodiment of Horus — that of Ramesses II was 'Strong Bull, Beloved of Truth'. In earliest times, the King was perhaps the very bearer of powers of deity. With changes of theology in the Pyramid Age, the sun-god Re attained pre-eminence, and the kings now became "Son of Re" — in effect, still in a measure sacred, but *subordinate* to a full deity. There came, as a result, the clearer distinction between the human being who sat on a material throne, and the 'eternal', con-tinuing office of 'King' that he for the time exercised. 'Pharaoh' as an institution was divine, in a way that a living man was not. But at death, the dual nature of the king was resolved in favour of his deity. While belief in life after death was marked in Egypt from the earliest times by the gift of appropriate provisions in the grave, and then by a special place at the tomb for offerings to be deposited (and the dead commemorated), the pyramids of the kings had *temples* for the cult of the dead king (now one of the gods), to be maintained forever after by a priestly staff with endowment, like any other temple. Man by inner nature, holding divine office in his lifetime, the king joined at death the pantheon of the gods and in particular the whole august company of pre-vious kings, the 'royal ancestors'. At death, he also became Osiris, or one with him, while his suc-cessor who buried him became the new Horus.

In the great days of the Empire, interrelations of king and gods continued to evolve. The role of Amun, giver of victory to his son, became at length too overbearing, seeming (to the kings) to jeopardise the central importance of the monarchy. Therefore, the kings of the Eighteenth Dynasty sought to redress the balance, firmly but discreetly. They thus laid more emphasis on the cults of Re and Ptah in Egypt, and in Nubia by linking the king with the gods in the temples, and by instituting worship of the reigning king – not of the human being as such, but of his kingship in some particular capacity. So, Neb-ma-re Amenophis III established two forms of such royal cults ('Emperor-worship'). In Nubia, the major temple of Soleb was in great part dedicated to the cult of *Neb-ma-re Lord of Nubia*, the divine aspect of Amenophis III as ruler of Nubia. The other form of royal cult, in Egypt itself, also deified an aspect of kingship in the name of the ruler – but embodied in the form of colossal statues before the temples, bearing the name of one or other such deified 'aspect', that could be honoured by the common people. So at Karnak, Amenophis III erected a colossus at the south entry to Amun's precinct, called *Neb-ma-re, Montu* [War-god] *of Rulers*, and elsewhere other colossi called *Neb-ma-re, Sun of Rulers*, and *Neb-ma-re, Ruler of Rulers*. Then came the cataclysm. Amenophis IV/Akhenaten had no more patience with such subtleties, swept away Amun and the rest, and made himself on earth the incarnation of Aten the sun-god – he and his queen might serve Aten, but the people should focus on Aten through *him*. But when he died, the momentum of twenty centuries of custom and tradition – held back for a split second of historical time – proceeded irresistibly to the restoration of the old gods and ways under his successors – including (with Tutankhamun), the deified aspects of the king, at least in Nubia.

Sethos I and Ramesses II deliberately resumed where Amenophis III (and, fleetingly, Tutankhamun) had left off. And Ramesses went still further, while avoiding Akhenaten's excesses. In the first place, they followed Theban tradition, in having tombs in the Valley of the Kings and their memorial-temples – now Qurneh and the Ramesseum – along the desert-edge. Such memorial-temples were called each "the Mansion of Millions of Years" of the king concerned "in the Domain of Amun", to whose cult and estates theirs were affiliated. Like the temples at the pyramids, these too were intended for the cult of the dead god-king ever after. In Thebes, they were also temples of Amun, with whose Karnak cult they were linked. In Thebes, Amun rather than Osiris ruled the West. So each of these temples had its own local form of Amun – in the Ramesseum, called "United-with-Thebes", he was "Amun dweller in 'United-with-Thebes' ". But, in fact, the sacred portable barque in whose cabin this local Amun rode forth in processions was actually that of Ramesses II himself! Just as, for centuries, the dead kings had become Osiris at death, so in Thebes they (as gods) became local forms of Amun. Although intended for perpetuity, the cult of the 'Amun-king' was, of course, instituted by himself as soon as his temple was able to function.

Among Theban memorial-temples, the Ramesseum was a remarkable blend of traditional and novel features. All previous temples of the kind had had a series of broad open courts in front of the stone-built temple proper. The latter usually consisted of an open-air colonnaded court, two or three roofed halls-of-columns (hypostyles) and a sanctuary with surrounding service-rooms. The Qurna temple of Sethos I was of this general type.

But Ramesses II did away with the great open spaces, and began his temple with a mighty pylon the full width of his building, with two successive open-air colonnaded courts. More traditional was the inclusion of a small palace (for periodic royal visits) fronting on the south of the first court. But the massive seated colossus of the king which towered up out of this court (Shelley's Ozymandias) had no counterpart elsewhere. The second court was followed by a full-sized

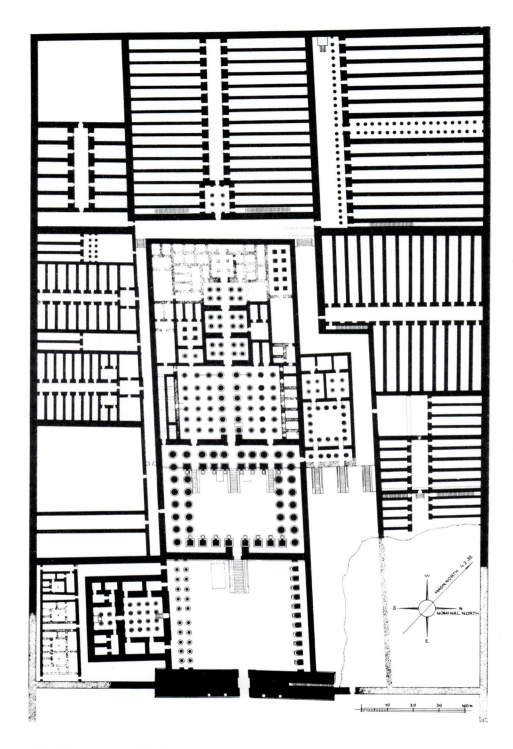

54. *Ground-plan of the Ramesseum within its precinct.*

hypostyle hall, inferior in its dimensions only to that across at Karnak. The decoration of this hall and the second court included the novelty of matching processions of the king's sons and daughters on their rear walls. Beyond the hypostyle, one reached more traditional ground with successive lesser columned halls, sanctuary, and service-rooms.

Along the middle of the north wall there stood the adjoining twin temple probably dedicated to queens Tuya and Nefertari, Ramesses' mother and principal consort respectively. All around the temples were rows of brick storage-galleries, houses of the priests and so on — and the entire complex was enclosed within a great mud-brick wall, shutting-off the richly-decorated temples and grey brick satellite-buildings from the outer world.

While possessing the chief memorial-temples of the empire kings, Thebes had no monopoly. Smaller such memorial-temples and chapels were built and endowed by such kings as Ramesses II in Memphis and Heliopolis, affiliated to the cults of Ptah and Re. And small chapels of this nature were also attached to principal temples of provincial towns like Ninsu. At Abydos, a similar function was fulfilled there by the splendid temples of Ramesses and Sethos, where they each were even more clearly identified with Osiris. Finally, in distant Nubia, the great temple at Abu Simbel was, in Asha-hebsed's words, a "Mansion of Millions of Years, excavated in the Mountain". Under the patronage of Amun and Re, the temple as executed became increasingly a temple of Re more than of Amun, and finally of Ramesses II himself as a form of Re, as the portable barque of Ramesses II was probably set in the sanctuary in front of the rock-carved gods of Empire — Ptah, Amun, Re, and Ramesses II, Re being entitled "residing in the Estate of Ramesses II, the Settlement". So, Abu Simbel became the king's greatest memorial temple in Nubia, with Ramesses II as a form of the sun-god Re.

Other forms of royal cult came back more fully into play. Like Amenophis III, Ramesses II also dedicated a Nubian temple to a statue of his own kingship — at Aksha, to "Ramesses II, Great God, Lord of Nubia". At the other end of the empire, in Pi-Ramesse in the Delta, he instituted a whole series of statues of himself as foci of worship of the divine kingship — Ramesses II as "Montu in the Two Lands", "the God", "Appearing among the Gods", "Beloved of Atum", and (like Amenophis III) "Sun of Rulers" and "Ruler of Rulers". Another series was for "Ramesses II Effective for" Amun, Atum, Seth, and Re. These colossi were erected before major temples in Pi-Ramesse, in public view; others in Thebes and elsewhere (such as Abu Simbel) were given some of the same names, as 'local manifestations' of these divine aspects of the kingship of Ramesses II. Certainly in Pi-Ramesse they became objects of popular cult, especially for the garrison-troops there. In Nubia, some time after the completion of Abu Simbel, the "Temple of Ramesses II in the Domain of Re" was cut in the rock at Derr, further downstream on an important bend in the Nile. Later still, the Viceroy Setau had to construct two other temples to match it — one similarly related to Amun (at Wady es-Sebua) and one to Ptah (Gerf Hussein). In these three, therefore, Amun, Re, and Ptah, the gods of Empire were ostensibly worshipped — but (as at Abu Simbel) the actual barque-image in the sanctuary was in fact that of the deified Ramesses II, as a form of Re, as "Amun of Ramesses", and as "Ptah of Ramesses". Such temples, therefore, were almost additional 'memorial-temples' of the king. Not only Amun, Re and Ptah, but also other gods (Seth, Herishef, etc.) were gods "of Ramesses", — and even goddesses: Udjo, Hathor, Nephthys, and Anath from Canaan. Finally, in his later years, Ramesses II took the epithet 'Great Soul of Re-Harakhte', appending that epithet to Pi-Ramesse; this seemingly made of him a manifestation of the sun-god on earth. Thus, in temple-cults, through great statues as foci in popular devotion, and by theological construction binding the gods and the monarchy in close mutual support, Ramesses II sought to anchor the restored monarchy firmly in the centre of Egyptian religious faith and practice, at all levels, in interaction with the gods, not in conflict as Akhenaten had done.

'Lord of Jubilees like his Father Ptah-Tatonen'

From of old, there had always been an unexpressed tension between the brute fact of a mortal King who ages and dies and the exalted concept of the perpetual office of the kingship. From the earliest dynasties, a special magical ritual had been elaborated to renew the powers of the reigning king: the *heb-sed* or 'Sed-festival' of so many inscriptions, often referred to as the 'Jubilee-festival' in modern parlance. In the Empire period (possibly following Twelfth-Dynasty example), a king would generally celebrate his 'First Jubilee' at the 30th anniversary of his accession to the throne ªIn a multitude of stereotyped formal inscriptions, many kings are wished or promised "millions of Jubilees" in the name of the gods — but very few Empire pharaohs either reigned 30 years or therefore celebrated 'jubilees'. However, both Tuthmosis III and Amenophis III reigned well beyond their 30th year, and so each celebrated a First (Year 30), Second (Year 34), and Third (Year 37) Jubilee.

But after Amenophis III (and leaving aside the 'non-canonical' celebrations of Akhenaten), probably no other pharaoh reigned long enough to celebrate a jubilee until Ramesses II reached his Year 30 in 1250 B.C. But then, after due preparation, Prince Khaemwaset proclaimed the First Jubilee from Memphis (traditional centre for such rites), and carried the tidings throughout Egypt, as far south as the First Cataract. But the actual celebration was in Pi-Ramesse, where Ramesses had erected a superb Festival Hall with giant columns 35 feet high, to be adorned over the years with additional statues and obelisks, all under the joint patronage of Ptah-Tatonen and the sun-god Re-Atum. The ceremonial itself was highly traditional and formal, going back in many details to the time of the earliest kings. It could last over two months with rites both preceding and following the anniversary of the king's accession. In the first month, there was the setting-up of the Djed-Pillar, emblem of stability and of renewal of kingship; the rites of illuminating the Dais; presentation of high officials to the king. Then, on the accession-day, first day of Year 30, the king appeared in the temple for the full series of complex rites, including crowning ceremonies for Upper and Lower Egypt, in the presence of the images of the gods of Egypt, brought specially from all over the land, and accompanied by their leading priests. Permanent existence was given to this concept, when Ramesses II installed in the jubilee-halls a series of dyads, or twin statues of himself with a whole series of deities. The personnel of the festival included king, royal family, priests, officials, and all manner of other actors (musicians, dancers, etc.). And for all, ample provision was laid on..

Thereafter, following hallowed precedent, Ramesses II repeated these jubilees or renewals of kingship at intervals, just as Amenophis III had done. So Prince Khaemwaset and the vizier Khay proclaimed the Second Jubilee in Year 33 (celebrated, Year 33/34), and the Third in Year 36 (celebrated, Year 36/37). And then, Ramesses II went on to celebrate a long series of jubilees unequalled by any Egyptian king in the whole of pharaonic history. The 4th came in Year 40,

55. Head of the southern colossus of Ramesses II, Great Temple at Abu Simbel.

179

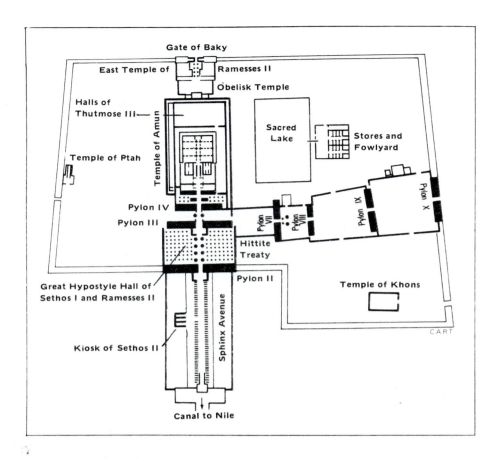

56.A.   The Karnak Temple of Amun in the Nineteenth Dynasty.

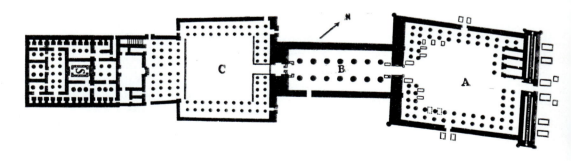

56. B.   Ground plan of the temple of Luxor.

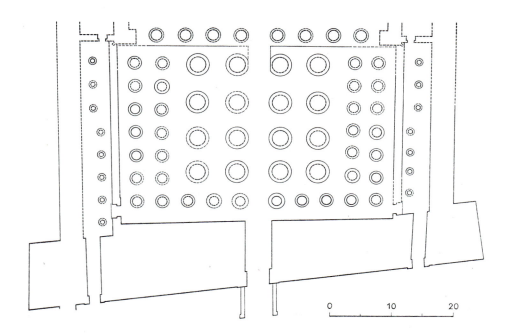

56C. *Ground-plan of the Great West Hall of Ramesses II in the Temple of Ptah at Memphis.*

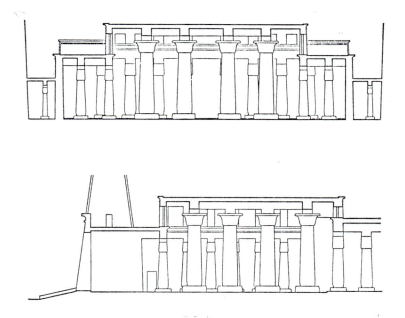

56D. *Cross-section of the West Hall of Ramesses II at Memphis.*

181

and 5th in Year 42/43 (both, proclaimed by Khaemwaset and Khay), the 6th in Year 45/46 (Khay). No details are known of the 7th jubilee (probably Year 48/49) or of the 8th (probably Year 51/52), but the High Steward Yupa proclaimed the 9th in Year 54 (celebrated, Year 54/55). Thereafter, the new Theban vizier Neferronpet proclaimed the 10th in Year 57 (for Year 57/58) and the 11th in Year 60 (for Year 60/61), if not also others. The aged king went on to celebrate a 12th jubilee (Year 61/62, or 62/63) and a 13th (Year 63/64, or 66/67), and possibly a final, 14th jubilee (Year 65/66?), shortly before his death in Year 67, by which time the strain of undergoing these repeated rites may have sapped the old king's failing strength more than he gained in inner comfort from them.

While the main rites were enacted in Pi-Ramesse at the wish of the king, parallel commemorations were held in other great temples, especially in Memphis where the splendid West Hall may have been a second great Festival Hall of Jubilee, a reassurance to the priesthood of Ptah that their special link with jubilees was not forgotten.

Moreover, the royal jubilees were occasions of great significance on a wider plane; traditionally, they were considered to be good omens for high Niles and prosperity; as one poet sang in Year 30 of Ramesses II:

> "[Behold], a great inundation for the First Jubilee of Ramesses II! (The River) brings the cubit, no dyke can stand against it, the very mountains are possessors of fish and alive with wildfowl . . . !"

Not everyone, however, had their mind on high Niles and renewed kingship that year; as we saw earlier, the 'fraud squad' had to act in Western Thebes then. But lesser people as well as the grandees were affected in some measure by these special events. Among the workmen of the Royal Tomb in Thebes, one man, Amek wrote a note to his mother, complaining of being left with an unwanted pair of leather sandals to look after, belonging to a soldier suddenly called north for the Jubilee:

> "He handed the sandals to me, saying, 'Keep them for me'; and, by Ptah, he's flitted north by night! . . . What's the meaning of *his* travelling north to the Jubilee ?"

At the head of Egypt stood one man - the Pharaoh. Immediately below him came the two viziers of South and North, then the other high officials of state. Then, department by department, province by province, the supporting cohorts of middle-rank scribes, local dignitaries, personnel of minor temples, all the way down to the village clerk. Alongside the middle and lower ranges of functionaries came the practical specialists of all kinds — artists, sculptors, jewellers, glaze-makers, metal-workers, carpenters, leatherworkers, weavers and potters, and many more whose efforts contributed to the life of all. Plus the armed forces from general to simple recruit, for defence or foreign adventures.

But the whole of this imposing social pyramid required a broad, strong, ample base to function at all — in a word, it had to *eat*. Real wealth in early Egypt consisted of land, but more especially of land flooded annually by the Nile and then cultivated by human effort, whether for crops or livestock. And, in fact, by far the greater part of Egypt's population under Ramesses II (as at other periods) worked as peasant farmers on the land, providing the physical basis of life for the whole community.

Life on the Land

Work on the land was always hard and often thankless. A good inundation meant plenty for all, farmers included; but a bad year could mean the same taxes to pay, and no grain to meet tax-demands or hungry stomachs. The scribes never tired of rehearsing the ills of the farmer to their pupils to keep them at their studies, bidding them remember:

> "the state of the peasant farmer faced with registry of the harvest-tax,
> when the snake has taken one half (of the crop), and the hippo has devoured
> the other half. The mice overrun the field, the locust descends, and the cattle
> eat up. The sparrows bring poverty upon the farmer. The remnants (of harvest)
> upon the threshing-floor (fall) to the thieves . . . The tax-official has landed on
> the river-bank to register the harvest-tax, with the janitors carrying staves, and
> the Nubians palm-rods. They (say), 'Give up the grain!', although there is none.
> They beat him up . . . he is thrown headlong down a well . . . So the grain disappears . . . "

During the flood-season (July-September) with no farm-work on hand, the peasantry could be recruited for corvée or forced labour on other projects — as manpower for quarrying stone, manhandling it on temple sites, or in brickyards, and so on. But as the Nile waters receded from the land, the land had to be ploughed, the lumps of fertile mud broken up, the seed sown and then trodden in (sometimes by pigs). Then, month by month, the care of the growing crops, and ceaseless irrigation through channels from basins of retained water and by simple water-lifts ('shaduf') from river or canal into channels and fields. Then in spring (March-April), the assessors measured-off the standing crops to determine the amounts of tax payable by the cultivators (and their employing institutions) to the state treasury, before the golden grain was cut. Then, after work on the threshing-floors, the grain could be shipped away to the granaries and stores of the land-holding institutions, and treasury, leaving the farmer with his balance. He, of course, had also his vegetable plot for lettuce, cucumbers, melons and the like, besides the grain, flax and cattle-fodder that was his from the fields. And very large quantities of fish were regularly landed by the Nile fishermen.

But if hard, the farming life was by no means all misery, and the shrewd peasant-farmers learned how to maintain themselves through most difficulties. In contrast to the propaganda by bookish scribes, the paintings in the tomb-chapels show the rosy side of the farming life: good Niles, abundant crops, fine cattle, an aura of prosperous contentment with landworker and supervisor alike. More significantly, Egyptians in other walks of life (like Sennudjem, a workman of the Royal Tomb) happily showed themselves as raising the wondrous crops of the Afterlife, an activity hallowed in Spell 110 of the Book of the Dead (and in the 'Coffin Texts' still earlier); thus, farming was widely recognised as the real basis of the community's life. The *Tale of the Two Brothers* also reflects the modest but satisfying life of the successful peasant-farmer, and in picturesque ways the feeling of the ancient farmer for his beasts:

"Now once upon a time, there were two brothers . . . Anup was the name of the elder, and Bata of the younger. Anup had a house and a wife, and his younger brother was with him like a son. He it was who made clothes for him, while he (Bata) followed his cattle to the fields as he had to do the ploughing. And he (Bata) it was who reaped (the harvest) for him and did all the work in the fields . . . Every evening, he left work to return home, loaded with all the vegetables of the field, with milk, with wood, and every good field-product; and he would place them before his elder brother as the latter sat with his wife. And so he (Bata) ate and drank, and [went off to sleep] in the byre, among his cattle . . .

Now . . . (day by day) . . . , he would drive his cattle, to pasture in the fields . . . And they would tell him, 'The grazing is good in this (or that) place!' And he heeded all that they said, and took them to the spot with good grazing that they wanted. The cattle in his care thus flourished marvellously, and they calved ever so often.

So, at the season for ploughing, his elder brother said to him, 'Get ready for us the [ox]-team for ploughing, for the fields have emerged (from the flood-waters) and they're fine for ploughing now! And also, bring the seed to the field, for we'll start ploughing in the morning.' "

The Egyptians were very fond of their cows, and often gave them names — the 'Buttercup' and 'Daisy' of those times. In the Deir el Medina tomb-chapel (No. 212) of the Scribe Ramose, in a ploughing scene, his servant Ptah-seankh says to him, "The fields are in really top condition; their grain will flourish, you being with us — you being well, along with me and 'Right-hander' and 'Good-Flood-Comes'! " At another time and place, stalled cows being given their fodder are cheerfully enjoined, "Lovely grass! Eat it up!"

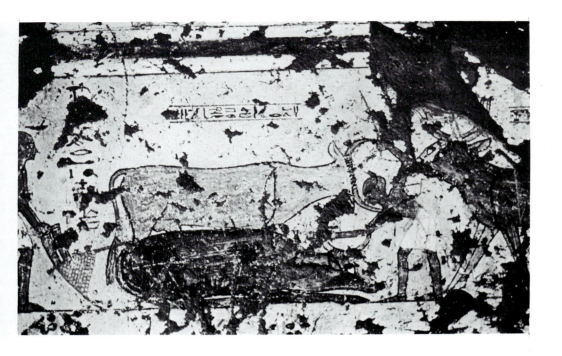

57. Trouble on the farm. The ploughman stands helpless, while an irate cowman threatens a cow that has gone on strike ! (Tomb 16)

Not all was idyllic, even in the rosy world of the tomb-paintings. In the chapel (No. 16) of the Theban priest Panehsy, we suddenly find a 'wild-cow strike'. Of a team of two animals, one has suddenly tired of the whole weary job of walking up and down, up and down, endlessly ploughing, and so had flopped flat on the ground, refusing to budge! One man belabours it with a stick, while with one large, reproachful eye, the bored beast coyly steals a glance at the ploughman, Prehotep, who hollers "Get up, get moving, stop shamming dead, you [brute] !''

The Workmen of Pharaoh : Life at Deir el Medina

While the vast majority of their brethren spent sunlit days labouring modestly and obscurely in the black mud and vivid green growth of the broad, level fields, a small group of men and their families lived apart, as a closed community, in their special village behind a sandy hill in Western Thebes, a mile or so from the nearest green cultivation. In striking contrast to the peasant-farmers out on the plain, these men crossed the dry, sun-scorched cliffs behind this village to work deep underground in a valley utterly barren of any sign of natural life — the Valley of the Kings.

185

58. *Work in the Treasury of Amun. At right, Neferronpet keeps account of the craftsmen, while, at left, servants carry off goods into the treasury vaults. (Theban Tomb 178)*

The Village

These men were the 'Workmen of the Royal Tomb' (also, 'Servants in the Place of Truth'), a community founded in the 16th century B.C. by Amenophis I, still their patron saint 300 years later. His successor Tuthmosis I had built the village that nestled close behind Gurnet Murrai hill near the south end of Western Thebes — the settlement simply called 'the Village' by its inhabitants and known today as Deir el Medina. Already in the later Eighteenth Dynasty, an extension had been built along the west side of the village. Then, probably in the first years of Sethos I, a further 'block' of 12 or 14 houses was added at the south end — the entire village being enclosed as within a long rectangle by its outer wall. The close-set 'high-density' housing for these workpeople was a tradition in Egypt going back centuries.

The main gate of the village — its only 'official' entry and exit — was at the north end, whence a single narrow street or alley ran south through the middle, with the 'terrace' houses opening off it on either side all the way along. A side-alley led round to the late-Eighteenth-Dynasty houses along the west side, and a double bend in the central 'street' led on into the south extension built under Sethos I. The houses in the village, all of mud-brick on rough masonry foundations, followed one basic layout with only minor variations. Being crowded into the minimum space, they were long and narrow from front to rear, in the terraces or rows — somewhat reminiscent of European 'industrial housing' of the last century. Each house fronted onto the street or an alley. Through the front door, the visitor stepped down into the 'front parlour' past the water-pots. Beyond the front parlour was the main living-room whose higher roof (supported by a column) allowed subdued light to filter in through a skylight between the roof-levels of parlour and living-room. From one of these two rooms descended a stairway to an underground cellar, sometimes from under (or close to) the low brick bench or 'divan' where the master of the house might sleep on mats, when at home — he thus guarded the family valuables in the vault! From the living-room also, we gain access to a workroom-cum-bedroom, and to a back-kitchen open to the sky with mortar and pestle for grinding flour and oven for baking bread. A short steep stairway led up to the roof — a useful additional living-space in the dry, sunny climate of Upper Egypt.

In the whitewashed walls of the main room, niches were cut for images of the local gods of hearth and home. A special enclosed chamber in the front parlour was particularly dedicated to (and decorated for) Bes and the household deities of womanhood; it may have been a confinement room, where children might be born under the domestic protection of Bes, Taweret, Isis and Hathor. Furnishings throughout were simple: low stools, rush mats, an abundance of pottery (which the house-wives of the village seemed to break in large quantities!), sometimes low, wooden beds with rope 'springing', and occasionally a wooden chair. Besides pottery, the family had the use of attractive basketware of woven rushwork. The family's possessions would include the workman's personal tools (like Sennudjem's plumb-line and set-square) as opposed to state-supplied tools, the family store of linen garments, perhaps a copper or bronze vessel or two, and minor jewellery of coloured glazeware. The niches for household gods or formal busts of dear departed relatives could be framed with strips of limestone, engraved with hieroglyphic inscriptions invoking the favour of the gods on the householder, and his wife and children. The main entrance to the house could have stone doorjambs and lintel with the figures, names and titles of the householder and family.

In its little valley, the village did not stand alone. Opposite its long western wall there rose up along the steepening hill-slope terrace upon terrace of the tomb-chapels of the workmen and their families — courts with low walls, whitewashed brick chapels with small pyramids upon them, rising up in impressive array, while deep below (hidden from sight) was a maze of passages and burial-chambers. Outside the north approach to the village, past the great water-cistern, there clustered a whole series of little mud-brick temples and chapels for the gods. These had open courts, outer halls, inner sanctuaries; benches for the worshipping workmen, and a clutter of votive objects presented to the gods, especially small stone stelae, often inscribed with thanksgiving for help or healing as we shall see. Finally, outside the north and south approaches to the whole area, a 'police-post' stood at either end to check on visitors — after all, this community was set aside for the service of the royal valley and the secret tombs of the pharaohs; casual contacts and gossip on these matters were probably not encouraged.

Meet the Villagers!

But not all at once. Of the nearly 70 houses inside the village, almost a dozen are known today (33 centuries afterwards) to have belonged to particular men and their families. Thus sauntering south along the main street or alley, past a dozen doors on our right and seven equally ordinary doors on the left (east), we reach on our left a distinctive doorway set back a little and having a red-painted stone frame. This is the entrance to a house (now 'N/E, VIII') more spacious than most — within, it has not only a front parlour with closet, two columned sitting-rooms and three bedrooms/workrooms with stairway-vault beyond, but also two side-rooms — kitchen (two ovens) and passage-room. The red-painted hieroglyphs on the front doorframe proudly announce this to be the residence of the Chief Workman, Qaha and his wife Tuy. The ample rooms were certainly needful, as they had eight children, including Anhur-khaw whom Qaha hoped would eventually succed to his own job.

About three doors further down, over to the right (west), probably lived Qaha's contemporary the draughtsman-painter Maai-nakhtef, son of Pashed whose house ('N/O, XV') it was in Sethos I's time. A few doors along, back on the left side, we meet Khawy, 'Guardian of the Royal Tomb' with a modest three-room abode (N/E, XV'). A few more doors down on the right is the roomier residence ('C, II') of the sculptor Neferronpet, from whose extra-broad parlour open two little suites of two rooms each. His tastes are unknown to us, but his sculptor-colleague Ipuy was perhaps an animal-lover — tomcat and kitten fawn on him in his tomb-chapel (No. 217), and on a statuette of his, both a cat and a monkey appear!

Next, the main village-alley bends sharply right then left, into the newest, southern quarter. Off to the left down a common corridor, there opened off two small three-roomed houses (now 'S/E, II, III'), one belonging to the ordinary workman Harnufer. Round the bend three doors along, lived Neb-amentet and his son Neb-amun in adjacent dwellings of five rooms each ('S/E, VII, VIII'). Opposite them lived more modestly the draughtsman-painter Prehotep (at 'S/O, IV'), in the same profession as his father Pay and brother Nebre. Finally the last two houses ('S/O, V, VI') next to his belonged to the workman Kha-bekhnet and probably his brother Khons (inheriting from their father Sennudjem of Sethos I's time).

These are only a few of the village characters, and already they include several workmen, a security-guard, a sculptor, two draughtsmen-painters, and above all a Chief Workman, all in the direct employ of "Pharaoh, their good lord" (Ramesses II) through the vizier, for the cutting and decorating of the royal tombs in the Valleys of the Kings and Queens. The organisation of the work-force was in two halves, 'port' and 'starboard' or right and left sides, corresponding perhaps to the right and left sides of the long corridor-tombs in which they worked. Containing perhaps up to 30 ordinary workmen under Ramesses II, each side was headed by a Chief Workman or Foreman; these two men each had a Deputy. Alongside these two bosses and deputies, there stood correspondingly two Scribes of the Royal Tomb — responsible directly to the Vizier for all the administration concerning the village and royal tombs, just as the foremen were for all the progress of actual work. To the two sets of workmen, chiefs, deputies and scribes, one must add the specialists: draughtsman-painters who drew the first outlines of scenes and inscriptions in the tombs, and later coloured-in the reliefs carved from their outlines by the sculptors. Then there were the guardians (like Khawy) who kept the stores of copper tools, lighting-equipment, clothing. etc. There were also 'outside services' represented by water-carriers, a staff of 'serfs' (bringing supplies of fish, vegetables, firewood, gypsum, etc,), launderers, slave-women to mill flour, and three doorkeepers used as messengers and bailiffs and to check on supplies as delivered. A small squad of police under an officer, and a physician and scorpion-curer complete the picture.

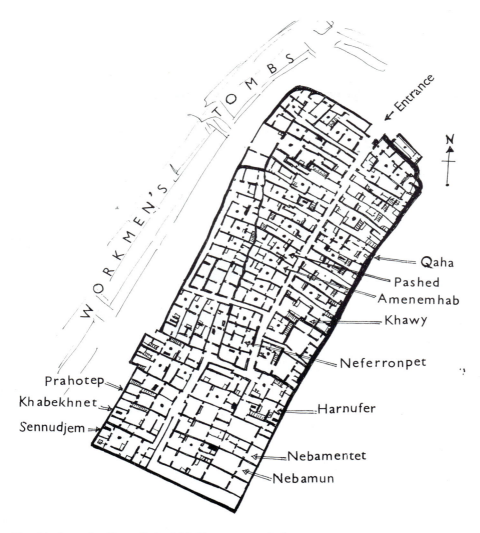

59. Workmen's village, Deir el-Medina — ground plan.

For a village thus secluded in a desert setting, all supplies had to come from outside, and efficient delivery was vital. Thus, all the water, food, etc., was brought in relays by the 'outside staff'. The water-carriers were constantly borrowing or hiring donkeys to save themselves carrying volumes of water over the mile or two between the river and canals and the village — a practice that often led to disputes. The working 'week' lasted 10 days (three 'weeks' or decades in each month). Each 10th day was a rest-day or 'weekend', when the new supplies of food were paid out to the workmen; foremen got double the pay of ordinary workmen. In Ramesses II's day, the custom·of the 'long weekend' had already begun — the 9th and 10th days of each decade or 'week' were not worked.

60. *Workmen's village, Deir el-Medina — reconstruction of typical houses.*

Work in the Valley of the Kings

Even today, the huge sepulchres of the Theban kings compel admiration – vast, brilliantly-decorated halls and corridors that run deep into the mountain. How *were* they done? And by whom, precisely? The second question is already answered. For Ramesses II, it was on the right side the Foremen Neferhotep the Elder, Nebnufer, and Neferhotep the Younger, all father-to-son, and on the left side Qaha and his son Anhur-khaw, and the sixty men under their joint command who hewed out Ramesses' vast tomb. The sculptors and draughtsmen we met in the village; such scribes as Ramose and Qen-hir-khopshef, Amenemope and Huy, kept the accounts and records of this work. The same people also produced the superb tombs in the Queens' Valley for Nefertari, Bint-Anath and the others.

So much, then, for the 'credits' – what of the methods? Once the high-powered committee of the Theban vizier Paser and other notables had finally decided (doubtless with royal approval) on the appropriate spot for the tomb, then the royal workmen took over. At the beginning of the 'week', the shift for duty was issued with its tools. To prevent any of the metal being quietly filched, these were meticulously weighed out to the men. As was the grease or fat used for lamp-wicks – it was an edible fat much appreciated by the workmen, but candle-fat was not for eating! Duly supplied, the party wended its way down the west side of the village. Then they climbed steeply up to their right (the west) by a narrow path onto the flank of the mountain. Then they turned back north, leaving the village well below, and went on along a rocky path flanked on the west by the towering Peak, their goddess Meresger, while off to their east (and right) there opened a view right across the hills of the Tombs of the Nobles, the memorial-temples of the kings, and the green-clad plain as far as the Nile, with Eastern Thebes, its temples and plain, and the Arabian hill-chain on the horizon.

Directly below the sacred Peak was a stopping-point, the 'col', with rough stone huts built by the workmen and little shrines to Meresger and the gods. From here, the workmen's path dropped swiftly down the barren slopes into the Valley of the Kings. During their eight or nine days' stint, the workmen did not return daily to the village, but slept overnight in the few small stone huts in the Valley itself, or in those up at the 'col'. Only at the 'weekend' did the party return home.

Under their chiefs, the workmen hewed their way downward into the limestone rock with copper and bronze picks, the broken stone being carted out in basketloads by their mates. But, as corridor succeeded corridor, receding ever further from the strong sunlight outside, artificial lighting became necessary. For this, long greased wicks (twisted-up from old clothing) were used, set to burn in bowls filled with salted oil. From a 'battery' of these simple lamps, a clear, non-smoky light was obtained, enough by which to quarry, plaster, draw, carve and paint in halls deep within the mountain. Thus, from the strict account kept of grease and wicks, one document of Ramesses II's time summarises thus:

"[Account of] wicks issued from the storehouse in the 3rd month of
　　Summer, [Day . .] :- 528 wicks.
　Account of consumption rendered this day:- 118 wicks.
　　Balance:- 410 (wicks)."

Thus, in the cooler depths of the royal tomb that hot summer day, at perhaps two or three wicks per lamp, over a hundred wicks (perhaps for forty lamps) were used up completely, while four hundred others (enough for some 150 'lamps') could be used again. With this prodigious quantity in use, ample light could be obtained, dimly along the access-corridors, and fully in rooms actually being hewn out or decorated.

So soon as the first corridor or so was quarried out 'in the rough', and while the quarrying-party pressed steadily onward, the newly created room was smoothed-down by chisellers and sculptors, the walls surfaced with gypsum-plaster and again smoothed-off. Upon these fine surfaces, draughtsmen such as Nebre and Prehotep could get to work squaring-off the wall and laying out in fine red line the complex scenes and hieroglyphic inscriptions of the royal 'guidebooks' to the Nether-world, the master-draughtsman touching up their work here and there in black. Then it was the turn of the sculptors — Qen, Neferronpet, Ipuy, and others — to carve down these master-sketches and texts into scenes in delicate low relief, of exquisite quality. Then finally, the draughtsmen-painters returned to add vivid colour to the finished texts and scenes. So the work progressed, each group following another, hall by hall, day by day, decade by decade, month by month, year by year. The same processes obtained in the Valley of the Queens, reached by another path that struck out south then west from the village.

Work and Play at Deir el Medina

From the site of the village, its tombs, and especially a nearby pit, there has been recovered an enormous mass of several thousands of 'scrap jottings' on slips of limestone and potsherds — 'ostraca' (singular, 'ostracon'), as today's scholars call them. These are the off-the-cuff record of every conceivable aspect of the life and work of the villagers — letters, receipts, journals of work done, lawsuits, oracles, laundry-lists, hymns, magical spells against illness, extracts from literature (classics and contemporary), artists' sketches, in fact documents of every kind, from most of the four centuries' history (1500 - 1100 B.C.) of the village, particularly the second half, from the reign of Ramesses II onwards, and with the greatest concentration of surviving material in the last years of Ramesses III and under his immediate successors. Quite a remarkable selection of documents can be attributed to the denizens of Deir el Medina of Ramesses II's time, as vivid as any of the more copious later records.

Work

While the current shift of workmen was away on their eight or nine days' stint in the royal valley, some of its members would send messages back home over the hill to the village with their requests for this or that — usually more food! Thus, one young workman to his mother, back in the village:

> "Nebneteru to his mother Henut-nofret:-
> Have brought to me some bread, also whatever (else) you have by you, urgently,
> urgently! And may Amun grant (it) to you, that you be in (his) favour. May
> you enjoy (his) favour and be given peace!"

Another request went out from one draughtsman to his uncle (called 'brother' in friendly fashion):

> "The draughtsman Khay to his brother the draughtsman Pre-em-hab:-
> Bring me a little bird and a few sycamore-figs!"

This plea is written upon a scrap of papyrus so tiny (4 cm. by 8 cm.; only 2 cm. by ½ cm., when rolled up) that it may even have been sent by 'pigeon post' back to the village. If so, one hopes the bird used was not carrying its own death-warrant!

Sometimes the people recruited to help the workmen turned out to be 'duds', as one draughtsman had to report to his father:

> "The scribe Pabaki to his father, the draughtsman Maani-nakhtef. thus:
> I have heeded what you told me, (namely), 'Let Ib work with you'. And now
> see, he's spent the whole day (supposedly) fetching the waterpot, and no other
> job laid on him the whole day long. He has not heeded your advice which I
> told to him. (Now), what'll you do today? . . . See now, the sun's gone down,
> and he's (still) away (with) the waterpot!"

That oaf Ib never reappears in the records of Deir el Medina, and doubtless his one long day of lazy malingering by the Nile bank with the waterpot (so needed by the draughtsmen up at the desert) speedily got him the sack.

However, other 'additions to staff' were in a different class entirely. It was in Year 5, 3rd month of Inundation, Day 10 (late September, 1275 B.C.), only a few months before Ramesses II set out on the fateful campaign that ended at Qadesh, that a new Scribe was appointed to Deir el Medina: Ramose. Son of a messenger or 'postman', he had been a promising young scribe attached to the treasury of the memorial-temple of the long-dead Eighteenth-Dynasty king Tuthmosis IV, down on the desert edge near the Ramesseum. Rising quickly in the administration of the older temple, he had caught the eye of the Theban vizier Paser, and so (when a new scribe was needed) Ramose joined the staff of the Royal Tomb, resident in Deir el Medina.

Perhaps retaining some of his old charges as well as sharing the Tomb administration with his colleague Huy, Ramose has been called "the richest man who ever lived in . . . Deir el Medina". No-one in all the four centuries of the village's existence left there so many memorials as Ramose did — stelae inscribed for the gods, in profusion in their chapels; not one, but *three* tombs and chapels (Nos. 7, 212, 250) and a whole series of miscellaneous mementos that still bear his name — statues, offering-tables, his own seat up at the 'col', and various bric-à-brac. Nor was Ramose any less successful in his personal relationships. He eagerly associated his name with that of his benefactor and immediate boss, the vizier Paser, on many a monument, just as doubtless the two men got on well together on Paser's periodic visits of inspection to look over the village, check through the accounts, and to see how work was progressing in the royal valleys on tombs. In turn, both men were well liked and respected by the foremen and the main body of workmen, several of whom included one or both of the pair in the painted scenes that adorned their own tombs and tomb-chapels — a warm mark of respect shown to few others of their rank. The sculptor Qen and the workmen Penbuy and Kasa did this, while Ramose himself included a scene of the King, Paser, and himself in his chapel (No. 7). He got on well with his colleague Huy whom he is shown honouring in Huy's own chapel (No. 336). The guardian Khawy showed the King and Paser on one of his own stelae.

In fact, Ramose's life and career were darkened by just one shadow: he had no son of his own to succeed him as Scribe some day, despite all his devotion to Hathor — he and Paser had built her a new temple in the name of Ramesses II, and in Year 9 had established an endowment for the king's statue there. He had also addressed fervent prayers to her, Min, and Taweret, but all in vain. Faced with no answer to his problem in the course of nature, Ramose sought another solution. He and his wife Mutemwia adopted a lad Qen-hir-khopshef son of Panakht, and he schooled him in the scribal art. Thus, on his own later monuments, Qen-hir-khopshef as often names Ramose his 'father' as Panakht. By Year 40 of Ramesses' long reign, young Qen-hir-khopshef was deemed able to follow Ramose in office, and was duly appointed Scribe of the Tomb. He was an able enough scribe, but (as time passed) his ever more cursive handwriting is *not* the favourite reading of Egyptologists at a later day! He continued in service quite some time after Ramesses' death. But he did not have the clear, attractive and upright character of his kindly teacher. He got into the habit of unduly diverting workmen to spend time on his own private projects (his own tomb, etc.), from their time on the royal tombs. Some of this was always permitted quietly 'on the side' — but not to the extent of gross abuse. He had literary interests, copying out for himself parts of the Battle of Qadesh poem, owning a manual for interpreting dreams, and writing out magical charms. He was probably a rather pushful person (even to the vizier Khay, he is barely polite), and was not too well liked in the village community. The draughts-man Prehotep, having been slighted by this Scribe, wrote him the following angry note:

> "The draughtsman-painter Prehotep greets his chief, the Scribe of the
> Place of Truth, Qen-hir-khopshef:-
> Greetings. What's the meaning of this rotten way you've treated me?
> I am to you just like the donkey:-
> When there's work (to do), they fetch a donkey, when there's eating
> (to be had), they fetch an ox.
> When there's beer, you're not wanting (me),
> when there's work, you are seeking (me)!
> If concerning us, I am (considered as) a man of bad character because of beer,
> then seek (me) out no (more). Hear it well, in the Domain of Amen-re King
> of Gods (bless him!).
> (PS): I am a man in whose house is *no* beer; I seek to fill my belly only with
> my letter to you!"

Perhaps Qen-hir-khopshef had been cutting Prehotep out of his 'party list' and loudly re-marking as excuse that Prehotep couldn't carry his drink — but was still very glad to avail him-self of Prehotep's skills as outline-draughtsman and painter of reliefs. Prehotep would not stand for that. His beerless house, of course, we have visited already (now 'S/O, IV' at Deir el Medina).

But beer (like everything else) depended on the regularity of supplies reaching the desert village, a fact that applied also to the 'dues' or special payments that the workmen looked for at

61. Damaged stela, showing Ramesses II (at left) greeted by the vizier Paser (centre) and his close associate the scribe Ramose of Deir el-Medina (at right).

certain times in the year when festivities might be afoot. Most times under Paser's crisply efficient regime, all had gone well. His successor the vizier Khay perhaps had greater difficulty here — during Years 29 to 46, he was much occupied with the proclamation and organising of the first six jubilees of Ramesses II in rapid succession, on top of all the usual duties of his office. So, from time to time, the harrassed Khay got polite reminders from the workpeople of Deir el Medina that their allowances were due, and he impatiently reassured them that they *were* coming! So do we find the draughtsman Siamun tactfully addressing many fulsome compliments to the vizier, before at last venturing to blurt out:

> " . . . a further greeting to my lord — may my lord attend to the gang and give them their rations!"

Again, the foreman Qaha's son Anhur-khaw also writes in similarly polite vein, and then makes his request for mineral colours for making paints:

" . . . a further greeting to my lord: we are working on the places of which my lord had said, 'Let (these) be really well executed!' . . . And let a dispatch be sent to the (High) Steward of Thebes, to the High Priest of Amun, to the 2nd Prophet of Amun, to the Mayor of Thebes, and to the controllers in charge of the treasury of Pharaoh, to request of them all that we need — for my lord's information, yellow ochre, gum, (yellow) orpiment, (red) realgar, red ochre, (dark blue) lapis-lazuli, green frit, fresh grease for lighting, old clothes for wicks. And then (we) can perform every task of which my lord has spoken."

The vizier Khay once replied (perhaps a little testily) to similar requests thus:

"The Fanbearer on the King's Right Hand, Royal Scribe, City-Governor and Vizier, Khay, speaks (to) the Chief Workman Nebnufer as follows:-
This letter is brought to you to the following effect. You shall be extremely vigilant in performing to full satisfaction all the tasks of the Great Place of Pharaoh wherein you are. Allow no-one to hinder you. But enquire also for the dues of the gang which are (to come) from the Treasury of Pharaoh. Let nothing of it be held back, because the controllers of the Royal Tomb had sent to me concerning your dues from Pharaoh's Treasury, saying, 'Let it be brought for them (the gang)!' Now, I shall be going north to where Pharaoh is, and I shall inform Pharaoh of your requirements. See now, I am about to send (my) Chief Scribe Pesiur on business into Thebes. When he returns to you, at the Fort of [the Royal Tomb?], you can meet him there, and you can then send him on to us, (to tell us) how you are."

Meantime, out on the job in the Valley of the Kings, the team worked day by day — but not always at full strength; one or another member of the gang might be absent from work for any of a multitude of reasons. Careful check of presence and absence was kept on 'worksheets' by the scribes, almost like a factory 'attendance sheet' or clocking-on. One great document of Year 40 of Ramesses II illustrates this side of life vividly; to each workman's name it appends dates of absence and reasons:

"Pendua: 1st month of Inundation, Day 14 — (out) drinking with Khons . . .
Haremwia: 3rd of Inundation, Days 21, 22 — with his boss (foreman); 2nd
    of Winter, Day 8 — brewing beer; 3rd of Summer, Days 17, 18, 21 — ill.
Wennufer: 1st of Winter, Day 14, 4th of Summer, Day 4 — making offering
    to his god.
Huynefer: 2nd of Winter, Days 7, 8 — ill; 3rd of Summer, Days 3, 5 — eye-
    trouble; Days 7, 8 — ill.
Amenemwia: 1st of Winter, Day 15 — mummifying Harmose; 2nd of Winter,
    Day 7 - absent; Day 8 — brewing beer; Day 16 — strengthening the door . . .

Seba: 4th of Inundation, Day 17 — a scorpion bit him; 1st of Winter, Day 25 — ill.
Khons: 4th of Inundation, Day 7, 3rd of Winter, Days 25 - 28 — ill; 4th of Winter
    Day 8 — attending his god; . . . 1st of Inundation, Day 14 — his feast; Day 15,
    — his feast [= a birthday hangover?].
Anuy: 1st of Winter, Day 24 — fetching stone for Qen-hir-khopshef; 2nd of Winter,
    Day 7 — *ditto*; Day 17 - absent; Day 24 — absent with the Scribe . . .

Still other entries record someone 'preparing medicaments' with Khons or Haremwia, also the illnesses of mothers, wives or daughters, and sundry religious observances (libations; 'burial' of a god). But the entries already quoted show the variety of incidents. Time off was allowed for brewing-up for festivals or 'weekends'; and for illness, needless to say. Especially piquant is poor Seba's being bitten by a scorpion — nearly 50 years later, there was almost a plague of these incidents in the first years of king Siptah. Specially noteworthy is the reference to mummifying Harmose — his death is actually recorded on another document, as we shall see. Likewise, Huy-nefer's eye-trouble (probably shared by Nakhtamun, not cited), as 'seeing darkness by day' was considered a punishment from the gods, as will be seen presently. Making offering to a patron-god was allowable — and apparently, both one's birthday and a hangover! Noticeable, too, are many days spent absent 'with his boss', when a workman was off helping a foreman with other tasks — including work on the boss's own tomb and chapel; the Scribe Qen-hir-khopshef is seen here, freely availing himself of this 'perk'.

While all this was going on, in and out of the royal Valleys, more domestic affairs concerned the 'outside services' and the housewives of the community. There was a 'laundry service', doing so many households per day — oddly reminiscent of the towel and linen suppliers to our own offices and hotels of today. But then, as today, outside laundering sometimes had its problems. Thus, one rather irritated Scribe of the Tomb (Ramose ?) wrote a curt note to Amenemope, his opposite number attached to these outside services, to the following effect:

> "To the Scribe Amenemope:-
> As to the 8 (households) you've done, (saying), 'Assign 4 houses per washerman
> to the washerman', and not the [6] (households per man) that Pharaoh assigned
> to him.
>
>   Now see (here), he has been assigned 6 households as work for 2 days,
> making 3 households per day . . . A (right) good thing you've done! As for
> Nakht-Sobki, I found no natron (i.e., 'soap') in his possession — you (shall)
> give him [. . some . .] . . . When you know the [amount] that's short, they can
> seek out natron for the clothes, and you shall not (further) [allow] this failure
> to supply natron. For Pharaoh has assigned natron to you — it (just) cannot be
> that he has not allotted it! And they'll high(light) your deceit. Now you know
> one side (of the matter)!"

Back in the village, the housewives sometimes sent notes to each other, or to and from their husbands out at work, and to and from other women living outside the village altogether. So, one lady sends a short, sharp missive to some 'junior miss' in her employ:

62. *Launderers hard at work, restoring the community's dirty linen to snow-fresh whiteness by the Nile. (Tomb 217)*

> "Nub-hir-maat, sister of Nebt-Iunu says:-
> Greetings. Furthermore:- Please attend to giving me the garment. Run along, gather in the vegetables that are due from you!"

Much more effusive is the lady Wernuro, seeking a second chance for Huynefer's brother Khay:

> "Wernuro to the scribe Huynefer:-
> Greetings. (Yours) be the favour of Amen-re, King of the Gods, thus — see, I ask of every god and goddess in the district of the West, that you may be hale, hearty, and (enjoying) the favour of Pharaoh your good lord every day."

Then she gets around to her request:

> "Further. Please consider your brother - don't abandon him! And (my) other message is to (your sister) Nefert-khay, too: consider Khay your brother, don't desert him!"

198

Perhaps at a date a few decades after Ramesses II's reign, a very sad little document was penned by a man less fortunate than Khay (and less deserving?). He writes:

> "Now I have no wife at all. Is she indeed my wife? — she finished saying her piece, and went out, flinging open the door . . . (Her father said): 'I am not (usually) one who'd have you seized, saying, "Look what you've done to your wife", and saying, "You are blind to the extent of your upsetting me, and to the extent of your being deaf to this crime (before) Horus! It's an abomination to Montu". (Her mother said): "I'll make you see these adulteries that your [. . .] has done to you!"

Recreation, Law, and Religion

Not all of life was work in the tombs and domestic ups and downs. Each 'weekend' was time off, when the community received the new decade's supplies, worked for themselves or each other ('odd-jobbing' on their houses, and their own tombs and chapels, or on furnishings for both) — or celebrated the festivals of their gods and patron saint, besides settling their lawsuits in their own tribunal or before the oracle of one form or another of 'Saint Amenophis I' their patron. Of those various forms (based on statue-cults of aspects of the king), their favourite was understandably 'Amenophis I, Lord of the Village', *their* Amenophis, of *their* village. Several feasts a year were celebrated for Amenophis I, when the workmen themselves served as his priests, as 'Servants in the Place of Truth", and those chosen carried his image in joyful procession. On those days, food and drink flowed freely, offerings were made in the god's chapel, and all made merry. On his "Great Feast" in 3rd month of Winter, Day 29 (February), a later ostracon records that:

> " . . . the gang made merry before him for 4 full days, drinking with their wives and children — 60 people from inside (the village) and 60 people from outside."

On a column-base from his shrine, a dozen of our villagers recorded their names in the role of priests of 'their' Amenophis I — the draughtsman Nebre served as Lector-priest, leading the rites; Apehty was fan-bearer; the sculptor Qen was 'servant'; others were *wab*, simple priest.

On other great festivals, too, the workmen had their holidays, as on the opening day of the Feast of Opet and on the Feast of the Valley (over at Deir el Bahri and the Ramesseum, nearby), both of Amun, besides others. On these joyful days, people sometimes sent presents to each other, in appreciation of kindnesses for example. One man writes to another:

> "What I'm forwarding to you by the hand of the policeman Pasaro (is) 12 cakes, two lots of incense at 5 measures each, on the day of the offering which you've made for Amun at the Festival of the Valley. They are not given from the things you sent me."

By his last remark, the writer seems to be covering himself against any charge of meanness in the source of his present!

Moreover, the workmen of Deir el Medina were by no means the only ones to appeal to the oracles of Amenophis I in Western Thebes. In his tomb-chapel (No. 19) at the north end of that area, Amenmose, a priest of Amenophis I, proudly records in word and picture such a case of his own acquaintance, in which he was one of the officiants. It was a feast-day, with booths set up, full of tempting food and drink — bread, cakes, grapes, vegetables, etc. — offerings for the saint, food to regale his worshippers. Two men, Heqanakht and the servant Ramesses-nakht, were locked in dispute, and so appeared before Amenophis I as his priests carried his glittering image in procession from his temple, attended by great feather-fans and Amenmose censing. A previous divine judgement had already found for Ramesses-nakht, but perhaps Amenophis I might judge differently? So, Amenmose, chief priest of Amenophis I, put the matter to his god: " . . . 'My good Lord, — the god actually did say that Ramesses-nakht is right and that Heqanakht is wrong.' This god (Amenophis I) approved heartily, saying, 'Ramesses-nakht is (indeed) right!' " Cheered by this second decision in his favour, Ramesses-nakht cried out exultedly, "Ah, my Lord who has seen into the hearts of his [subjects] !" Nearby stand the ladies, tinkling their sistra and with castanets and flutes, plus a trumpeter, for the music of the festival. How did Amenophis's image say 'Yes' (or, 'No')? For 'Yes', his bearers felt a movement forward; for 'No', a movement backward, — indicating the god's agreement to, or rejection of, the question or proposition set before him, whether spoken or in writing.

Back at Deir el Medina, many a little stone stela was deposited in the village shrines of Amun, Amenophis I, Hathor, Thoth, Meresger, and the other gods, little inscriptions that touchingly witness to the devotion that these Egyptian workmen and scribes felt for their gods, praising them for their benefits and imploring their aid. Fearful respect also — this or that misfortune was often intepreted as divine punishment for some misdeed, which the miscreant confessed, begging for mercy and healing from the offended deity. On one of his many stelae, the Scribe Ramose sings the praises of the goddess Mut, consort of Amun:

"Praise to Mut, Lady of Heaven, Mistress of Amun's House,
    Beautiful of hands, carrying the (tinkling) sistra, Sweet of voice.
O singers, be content with all that she says, pleasant to the heart."

The draughtsman-painter Nebre had several sons. One, Nakhtamun, fell ill, and was thought to have offended Amun. So, his father Nebre and brother Khay interceded with Amun for healing. Their plea was heard, so they set up a remarkable stela as thank-offering, to the glory of Amun:

"Giving praise to Amun:-
    I shall make hymns in his Name,
    I shall sing his praises as high as heaven, as wide as earth,
    I shall declare his might to whoever sails by, to north or south.

Beware of him!
    Mention him to son and daughter, to great and small.
    Tell of him to generation upon generation, not yet born.
    Tell of him to the fishes in the stream, to the birds in the sky.
    Mention him to those who know him, and those who do not.

63. *Deir el-Medina, above the village — tombs of the workmen's community. Each has an open court, portico, and small brick pyramid over an inner chapel. A concealed pit leads to underground burial-chambers.*

Beware of Him!
> You are Amun, Lord of the silent man,
> One who comes at the voice of the poor man.
> I called out to you when I was in distress,
> When you came, you delivered me.

Made by the Draughtsman-painter in the Place of Truth, Nebre.

Before the whole land, he made pleas before him,
> for the Draughtsman Nakhtamun, as he lay sick at death's door.
He was (under) Amun's wrath because of his misdeed.

He (Nebre) said:-
> Although the servant is inclined to do evil,
> Yet the Lord is disposed to be gracious.

He said:-
> I will make this stela in your Name,
> > And set this hymn in writing upon it,
> For you delivered the Draughtsman Nakhtamun for me
> > — so I promised you, and you heard me.
> And so now, see, I have performed what I promised."

Many another besides Nebre shared his respect for the Theban gods. The workman Nefer-abu sang of their local goddess Meresger (the Peak, guarding village and royal Valleys alike). Chastised for his errors and also healed, he enjoins:

"Giving praise to the Peak of the West:-
> (I was) an ignorant and foolish man,
> > who knew not good from bad.
> I committed a fault against the Peak,
> > and she taught me a lesson.

Beware of the Peak!
> For a lion is within the Peak,
> She strikes with the blow of a raging lion.

I called out to my Lady,
> I found she came to me with sweet breezes

She turned to me again in mercy . . . "

On one occasion, Nefer-abu frankly avowed his fault.

202

"He said:-
> I am a man who swore falsely by Ptah, Lord of Truth.
> He caused me to see darkness by day . . . "

Was this an attack of blindness, or some eye-complaint like that attested for Huynefer and Nakhtamun on the great 'work-sheet' of absences of the Year 40 of Ramesses II, quoted earlier? Or was it some darkness of the mind? We cannot now be quite sure.

Stelae and statues were by no means the only gifts that the workmen offered to their gods, besides the oblations on feast-days. But, in their little desert-valley, such people of limited means and time could not serve their gods on the lavish scale of the great state temples with rich offerings and bouquets of fresh flowers daily. The latter problem, at least, they overcame by presenting fine model bouquets, well carved in wood or thin limestone and painted to look like fresh flowers and greenery — these, on the gods' offering-stands would last indefinitely in the dry desert atmosphere, just like the use of artificial and plastic flowers today!

The lively, personal devotion to their gods was by no means restricted to the workpeople of Deir el Medina. The same breath animates the little songs of praise to Amun as like, or as being, a Vizier who renders justice to the poor, penned not only by Thebans but also by scribes far north in Memphis:

> "Amen-re, first of kings, primeval god,
> Vizier of the poor, who takes no bribe from the guilty . . ."

To the Beautiful West

The workmen of the Royal Tomb in Western Thebes had, of course, to think of their own eventual burial, besides preparing for that of the pharaoh. On the hill-flank rising up to the west of the village, they tunnelled their tomb-chambers below ground, and over these vaults built whitewashed chapels with bright paintings within, fronted by open courts and the chapels often surmounted by small pyramids with stelae. Tomb-sites were assigned to families by the vizier in the King's name. Ownership of a tomb (as of a house) was a vital matter, record of assignment of such properties being jealously remembered or preserved.

Sooner or later, like their royal patron, the workmen came to occupy their eternal abodes. Here, their beliefs were at one with other Egyptians of the day of all ranks. The mummified body provided a material 'housing' for the soul (as did statuary), as did the tomb for both body and soul (the latter, overnight). Tomb-decoration included, besides worship of appropriate funerary gods, scenes of the family (as at banquet), that all the family might be united together and be provided-for, in the afterlife. Spells from the Book of the Dead would give safety and provision in that afterlife. Magically, goods placed in the tomb would be of service then also.

In one fleeting document, we actually witness the passing of one of our workmen, and arrangements for his funeral:

64.   *Ipuy's incredible cats ! (Tomb 217)*

"The scribe Piay, and the youth of the Tomb, Mahuhy, to:-
The Chief Workman Neferhotep and the workman Pennub.
Greetings. And further.
Now, what was it that you said? — 'If anyone dies here, will you go and make enquiry about them?' Does it exclude your man?
This man died in the house of Haremhab who sent word to me, saying, 'Harmose's dead!' I went with Mahuhy, and [we] saw (it was so). And we made arrangements for him, and we had the [undertaker] fetched, saying, 'Take care of him really well — we are looking after [his affairs].' [We shall?] make shrill the cries, when you make [mourning . . .] . . . "

Doubtless the embalmers did their best for Harmose, allowing for his (and his colleagues') modest means. That his death occurred in Year 40 of Ramesses II (winter of 1240/39 B.C.), we already know from the great 'work-sheet' of absences cited above, in which Amenemwia was entrusted with the final wrapping of Harmose's mummy. We know little of Harmose's life except that he was perhaps grandfather of the workman Pennub mentioned in the letter from Piay.

Beyond any doubt, it was in the time of Ramesses II that the community at Deir el Medina enjoyed its heyday of greatest prosperity. Never again were its members able to afford new tombs and chapels such as were built in this reign. Later generations were content to be buried in the same tombs, used as family vaults, and merely to adapt the houses and chapels; fewer, too, were the stone stelae and statues. So, with the eventual failure of the Ramesside empire, Deir el Medina also fell on leaner days until, finally, under Ramesses XI, the village was abandoned, and the remaining work-force was based on the precinct of Ramesses III's great memorial-temple at Medinet Habu, still the centre of West-Theban administration at the end of the Empire. Then, during the following century and half of decline, the little group eventually shrank to *nil* with the end of all major works in Western Thebes by about 950 B.C.

10: DEATH AND AFTERLIFE OF RAMESSES II

The Closing Years

Ramesses II had been a dynamic man still, in his forties, when the Hittite peace was signed in Year 21 in 1259 B.C. In the glittering decade or so of the two Hittite royal marriages (Years 34 - 44, 1246 - 1236 B.C.), he had remained active through his fifties and on into his late sixties. By Year 46 (1234 B.C.), he had probably passed his 70th birthday. By now, there were probably very few people still alive who could clearly remember the closing years of Sethos I and the then Prince-Regent's accession to sole power, or even able to recall personally the reigning king's great exploit at Qadesh in Year 5 — two whole generations had come and gone since those days.

During the last three decades of his reign, the ageing Ramesses reigned on in godlike splendour. By the fifties of his reign, he had identified or linked himself ever more closely with the sun-god Re. He added the epithets "God, Ruler of Heliopolis" (Re's city) to his official titles and took the role of "Great Soul of Re-Harakhte", which epithet he added to the name of the Delta-Residence Pi-Ramesses (instead of "Great of Victories"). Thus, reigning on and on like the sun, he in some measure claimed more specifically the role of being a particular form or manifestation of the sun-god.

Meanwhile, with no evident foes or wars abroad to drain her resources, and blessed with good Nile-floods and sufficient food-crops most years, Egypt bathed in a relaxed, general prosperity, well able to sustain the breathtakingly vast building-programmes of the King that changed the religious landscape of the Nile Valley throughout Egypt and Nubia. The administration still had men of ability, such as the last Theban vizier, Neferronpet, and the four successive northern viziers, Pramessu, Sethy, and Prehotep the Elder and the Younger. Egypt was no lotus-eating dreamland, but hummed with busy activity in field, quarry, workshop, state office and temple precinct alike.

From Year 30 onwards, as we have seen, Ramesses sought magical renewal of his kingly powers in successive jubilee-rites at three-year intervals, perhaps more frequently later. Doubtless on the first six or seven occasions, the pharaoh had coped easily and confidently with the long, complex rituals, but during later celebrations his advancing age must have become increasingly apparent, while in his closing years (the 60's of the reign), the 10th to 14th jubilees must have become a biennial 'weary miracle' as the now very aged Ramesses went on doggedly, if stiffly, through the rites, no doubt assisted by devoted helpers such as the prince-regent Merenptah.

The Death of Ramesses II

During Year 66 of his reign, after perhaps the fourteenth pageant of jubilee in the summer of 1214 B.C., Ramesses probably remained confined to his great palaces, initially at Pi-Ramesse, then (as winter came on) to Memphis, or the Fayum resort and harim at Mi-wer. Thebes may have been too far now for the old man to travel, even for its warm winter sunshine. The Pharaoh who as a youth was impetuous enough to take on a Hittite army seemingly singlehanded at Qadesh was now, after his 90th birthday, still a tall, dignified old man of commanding presence, if of less certain step than of yore.

With the spring of 1213 B.C. and warmer weather, the king and court probably returned to Pi-Ramesses — the old king's very own creation, vast and splendid, in the heart of his family's extensive, prosperous homeland of his childhood memories in the East Delta by the "Waters of Re". If soon he was to exchange the role of Horus, king of the living upon earth, for that of Osiris, king in the hereafter, he would be happier to do so in the land of his boyhood, amid the scenes of his triumphs, and in the capable care of his appointed heir, the faithful Prince Merenptah.

During spring and summer, the aged Ramesses kept to his great palace; in June 1213 B.C., Year 67 began — should they, perhaps, plan for a fifteenth jubilee next year? Perhaps next winter one might be proclaimed? It was not to be. As the sticky summer heat built up from June into July and from July into August of 1213 B.C., Ramesses' strength at last sank rapidly, and the end came — no document survives to tell us about it from the depths of that rambling palace. So after 66 years and 2 months as sole Pharaoh on the Egyptian throne, and in fact some 75 years altogether from the early beginnings of his prince-regency, Usi-ma-re, Chosen-of-Re, Ramesses II Beloved of Amun, was no more. His spirit had travelled already the paths to the beautiful West and the realm of Osiris. 'The King is dead: long live the King!' In his place, now, there stood up as the new king, Ramesses' eldest-surviving (thirteenth!) son and official heir, a portly man already in his sixties, the prince-regent Merenptah. After official pronouncement that his father was indeed dead, the prince was perhaps conducted to the great Throne-room of the palace, and there appeared with the crowns and sceptres as Pharaoh — King of Upper and Lower Egypt, *Bai-en-Re* ('Manifestation of Re'), Beloved of Amun; Son of Re, *Merenptah*, Satisfied by Truth. For the first time in almost three-quarters of a century, a new man occupied the throne of the pharaohs.

Departure for the Afterlife

The death of the old king and the accession of the new were promptly announced throughout Egypt — within a fortnight or so, probably, swift messengers had ascended the Nile in flood, to reach Thebes with the news. On the West bank, up at Deir el Medina, the workmen mourned the old, and acclaimed the new, king. Immediately, preparations were set in hand for Ramesses II's great tomb in the Kings' Valley to be ready to receive him in two months' time. And soon, a high-powered 'selection-committee' would arrive to choose the site for the new king's tomb; the cycle of work would then resume its course once more.

Back in the north, the body of Ramesses II was submitted to the 70 days' rites of embalming and mummification. The perishable inner organs were removed, to be separately preserved in a set of four containers ('canopic jars', in today's terminology), while the body was desiccated by packing it in and with natron and salt. Duly drained and dried, it could then be treated with spices and resins, have packing stuffed under the skin to restore a lifelike appearance to the old king — to fit him for eternity — and be wrapped in miles of linen bandaging. Within these endless folds would be included a whole series of amulets (of gold, inlaid with coloured glass or semi-precious stones) to provide magical protection for the body of the king. Thus was Ramesses II made ready for interment in a set of coffins — of gold and gilded wood, perhaps, — to reside in his great

207

tomb forever. And so at last, by mid or late October of 1213 B.C., a great flotilla of ships headed by the royal barge of Pharaoh Merenptah hoisted sail for the south, to convey Ramesses II up to Thebes for the last time.

From distant prehistoric times, the Egyptians had steadily developed a series of very definite views about life after death — perhaps initially stimulated by the state of preservation seen in bodies buried in shallow, early graves and desiccated naturally by the heat of the sun. They had very early concluded that the essential personality did survive the death of the body, and that it might still inhabit the body's 'shell' as an abode. They conceived of the next life in terms of this one (the only one they knew) — a bigger and better Egypt, with grainfields and a Nile. The needs of the dead were considered to be analogous with those of the living — so, they too should have their pots, food, tools, weapons and clothing. By magic means, they would have use and enjoyment of all these things in the afterlife — and of the essence of the offerings left for them by survivors. As tombs grew in size, making natural desiccation by the sun impossible, the body was dried out artificially and bandaged up, to preserve it still. The wealth of funerary gifts grew, and the ritual of offerings likewise. The use of painting and sculpture, and of hieroglyphic writing, meant that a person could be depicted on the walls of his tomb-chapel, together with all the things he might desire or need; and by writing, his name could be recorded for ever and long lists of offerings set out in tabular form to sustain him magically, even when real offerings were presented at the tomb-chapel no more.

The lead in all this was taken by the kings, culminating first in the pyramids thirteen centuries before Ramesses. These expressed materially the hereafter of the king, more exalted than that of his subjects. He was destined to mount a stairway (step-pyramid) or else a ramp of the sun's rays (smooth pyramid), or even by ladder, to the sky to become chief in heaven, or to sail the skies in the heavenly barque of the sun-god Re. His subjects were still his subjects, whose afterlife by contrast was located on and in the earth. The cult of the god Osiris — in myth, murdered but resuscitated to become king of the afterlife in the Netherworld — offered an attractive hereafter to ordinary people by the end of the Pyramid Age, then throughout the Middle Kingdom, and on into the New Kingdom for the rest of Egyptian history. Ordinary people became 'Osiris' at death, could identify with him, and thereby gain access to his 'new life'. They had, of course, to pass the judgement of the Tribunal of Osiris (the 42 Assessors), denying guilt of various kinds. Failure meant annihilation, but to pass meant entry into the blessed realms, that otherwordly Egypt of richer harvests and abundant provisions with Osiris and the gods.

In the New Kingdom, the nobility, officials and all who could afford to do so built (or excavated) tomb-chapels over their burial-pits — rock-cut at Thebes, built chapels at Memphis. The deceased person expected his 'soul' to have freedom of movement in the sunlit land of the living by day, and to return down the tomb-shaft to the body at night. There, in the Netherworld, when the Night Sun sailed through in his barque, he would also receive light and sustenance as the Sun-god passed by. For all this range of celestial and terrestrial hereafters, and the necessary magical spells and offerings, a special 'literature' grew up. In the pyramids of later kings of the Pyramid Age, there was inscribed a great series of spells ('Pyramid Texts'), reflecting the burial-rites of the king, and intended to confer magical protection on him and his pyramid, plus spells for him to join the sun-god in his barque, or to identify him with Osiris, or for sustenance, etc. In the middle Kingdom, some of these spells were taken over for use by ordinary people, and had many more added to them. The new series were inscribed in the coffins themselves, and so today are

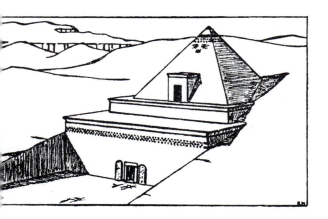
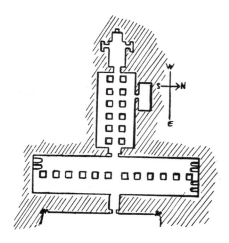

Reconstructed view and plan of a typical Theban rock-cut tomb of a noble or high official. Below a brick pyramid, a door flanked by stelae in the open court leads into a pillared cross hall, then a long hall and inner shrine. A separate pit leads down to the burial-chambers.

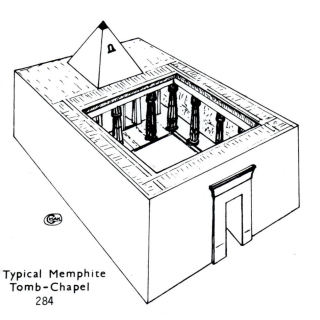

Typical Memphite
Tomb-Chapel
284

16. Quibell, IV, pl.80:10

Reconstructed view of a typical Memphite free-standing tomb-chapel of a high dignitary. An open court (often with colonnade) leads through a portico to an inner shrine capped by a light brick mini-pyramid. At right, part of an ancient picture of one of these tomb-chapels.

209

known as the 'Coffin Texts'. Then in the New Kingdom, a new selection of spells for well-being in the afterlife grew up, some old (as before) but many, new. The new anthologies were commonly written out on papyrus-scrolls to be buried with the dead owner; but extracts also came to be inscribed on the walls of tomb-chapels and burial-chambers — 'Spells for Coming Forth by Day' was their Egyptian title, but they are best known by their modern (and rather misleading) title of the 'Book of the Dead'.

The Tomb and Eternal Destiny of Ramesses II

By the beginning of the New Kingdom or Empire, pyramids could be seen to have failed in their purpose of protecting the royal dead — so many had been looted by tomb robbers in the dark days between the Old and Middle, and the Middle and New Kingdoms. Hence, Amenophis I decided on a rock-tomb, hidden away in the West-Theban cliffs, well separated from his memorial-temple on the desert edge. His successor Tuthmosis I not only housed the new special workforce of the Royal Tomb in the village at Deir el Medina, but took the final drastic step of having his tomb cut in the (then) utterly untouched, unfrequented desert valley behind the Theban cliffs — the Valley of the Kings as it became, by every monarch following his example for the next four centuries! He and each succeeding king continued (like Amenophis I) to build their memorial-temples along the desert edge; in all this — valley tomb, and great, separate temple — Ramesses II simply followed the practice of his age, but on a more lavish scale.

Parallel with the new style in secret royal tunnel-tombs there came also changes in decoration, based on the work of vigorous new theologians who sought to assure the pharaoh of maximum and harmonious benefit from life in the hereafter in terms both of the sun-god Re and of the netherworld realm of Osiris. Boldly, they asserted that, by night, Re *was* Osiris, and Osiris, Re — the two were at one. Each sunset, the sun-god sank below the western horizon, and then sailed for the 12 hours of the night in his night-barque throughout the 12 divisions of the Netherworld, bringing light and sustenance to its inhabitants, the blessed dead. During that journey, the sun-god himself became Osiris until at last, at the dawn, in the act of 'new creation', the sun was reborn to open the new day and sail in the day-barque across the heavens in triumph once more. In this exalted destiny, the regular cycle of a daily miracle, each dead pharaoh was to share eternally — *his* body safely swathed within its coffins in the underground tomb was to be as that of Osiris and of the night Sun. He, too, in spirit, travelled with (even as) Osiris-Re through those 12 hours and divisions of the netherwordly night, there enjoying the homage of his former subjects. Then, for eternity of days, he too was to be reborn daily at the dawn, along with the sun-god, to sail the heavens daily with him. The earthly cult of the dead king as a god was maintained in his memorial-temple "of millions of years" (the Ramesseum, in Ramesses II's case), while his body slumbered in gold in the valley tomb and his spirit circled through day and night, night and day, as Osiris and Re, through netherworld and heavens for ever. Such was the imagined destiny of a New Kingdom pharaoh such as Ramesses II.

All of this body of exalted concepts needed, of course, practical expression and provision. So the great tunnel-tombs in the Valley became a model of the path of the sun-god through the 12 nocturnal hours, as well as being the eternal home of the king's body. Accordingly, the walls

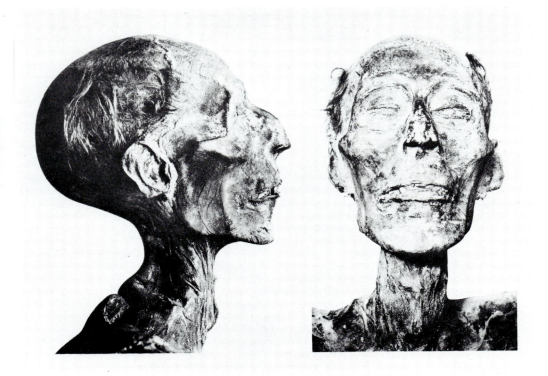

66. *Head of the mummy of Ramesses II, full-face and profile, in Cairo Museum. The features show a proud and dignified old man.*

of these great tombs were decorated with a series of special 'books' — new theological composi-tions in word and picture to set forth the nightly journey and dawn rebirth of Osiris-Re and the king. One of these books was *"the Writing of the Hidden Room"*, better known today as Am-Duat, *"What is in the Netherworld"*, strictly a general term for all the compositions of this class. Here was shown the Netherworld journey of the sun-god through the 12 hour-divisions, greeted by worshipping baboons, issuing provisions to the dead, passing as a serpent-ship by the domain of Sokar, then repulsing the wicked serpent Apophis, and giving light and instruction in the Neth-erworld, before finally being reborn at the dawn. This book was inscribed like a huge yellowed papyrus-scroll in the burial-chambers of Tuthmosis III and Amenophis II and down to Tutankh-amun (Chapter I only). Equally old was the *Litany of Re*, praise of the sun-god in his 74 forms, linking him, Osiris, and the king. Later in the Eighteenth Dynasty came the *Book of Gates*, which like Am-Duat, showed the sun traversing the Netherworld, this time through the 12 portals of its divisions. The *Book of the Heavenly Cow* told the legend of man's rebellion against the sun-god, his punishment upon mankind and his withdrawal to heaven, with various magic spells based upon the narrative and considered as of value to the deceased. All these great compositions in text and picture found their way onto the walls of royal tombs from Sethos I and Ramesses II onwards, to-gether with scenes of the king welcomed by the gods, and further ritual books.

211

Out in the Valley of the Kings, the great tomb (No. 7) of Ramesses II exemplified in full this scheme of his eternal destiny in its decoration and design. First came a short, steep descent cut down into the rock, to the main door — "the first god's-passageway of Re, which is upon the Sun's path", as the Egyptians termed it. Then, two corridors went on down, "the 2nd and 3rd god's-passageways", tracing still the sun-god's path into the Netherworld. Here, Ramesses II was shown worshipping Re, and both walls of these passages were sculptured in long columns of superb hieroglyphs with the "Litany of Re", welcoming him. In the next corridor ("4th god's-passageway") the 4th and 5th hours of the sun's Netherworld journey were shown, from Am-Duat — the serpent-barque crossing the sandy realm of Sokar, god of the dead. Then, a square room — "the Hall of Waiting" — with scenes of the King and the gods. Here, perhaps, the king's mummy had to await special rites before proceeding on to the burial-chamber. Immediately behind came a larger, four-pillared room with ramp down to the rest of the tomb, and two side-rooms

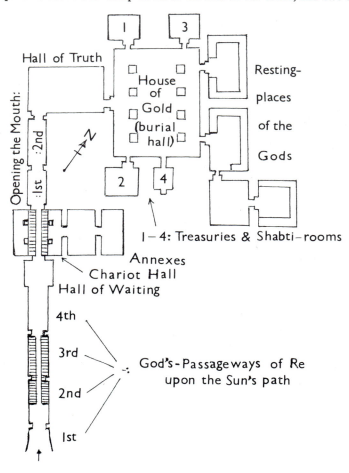

67. Ground-plan of the Tomb (No. 7) of Ramesses II in the Valley of Kings.

off to the right. This larger hall was "the Chariot Hall", or "Hall of repulsing Rebels". Here would be placed the king's chariots - perhaps that he might help Re to repulse their foes in the hereafter? The two annexes offered ample room for chariots and other royal equipment, and once perhaps bore as decoration the 9th, 10th and 11th hours of Am-Duat: the Sun-god giving out directions and provisions in the Netherworld, and Horus presiding over the destruction of the wicked foes of Re, Osiris and the king.

Beyond the Chariot Hall, two more corridors slanted ever downwards into the heart of the mountain, being termed "the 1st and 2nd god's-passageways of Opening" (?) — a name possibly referring to the great ceremonials of the *Opening of the Mouth* that adorned their walls. This elaborate ritual was usually performed on the statues and mummy of the dead person, magically to restore to them all their faculties of sight, hearing, eating, movement, etc., for activity in the afterlife; it included the putting-on of clothes and adornments, and offering-lists assured ample provisions. These corridors opened into a large room, "The Hall of Truth" (where the king was accepted as 'justified'?), extending out to the right. Finally, a door at its far right end led into the huge "House of Gold" — the great pillared burial-hall of the king himself, where in his golden coffins he was to lie in state within a massive stone outer coffin or sarcophagus. This was the focus of the entire, vast subterranean palace into which we have ventured thus far. The front walls of the Hall bore the first two portals of the Book of Gates, with the third in a side-room at the left, and the Book of the Heavenly Cow in another side-room opposite. The other walls of the great Hall had the initial title and 1st and 2nd hours of Am-Duat: the sun-god welcomed into the Netherworld and sharing-out fruitful otherworldly fields to sustain the dead, independently of offerings made upon earth. A second side-room at the right bore the 8th hour, in which the sun-god illumined the caverns of the Netherworld's inhabitants as he sailed by; while, in the second left-hand side-room, the vital 12th hour of Am-Duat recorded the triumphant rebirth of the sun-god at dawn, and so of the King with him — climax to the whole. Then, behind the Hall, two doors led to the last suites of side-rooms. The rear left one opened on a room with benches all around, and decorated above with the 6th and 7th hours — the one, the sun-god reuniting with his body for the rebirth of the 12th hour, and the other, the victory over the wicked serpent Apophis who sought to stop the sun. The rear right door led first into a similar room with Am-Duat (3rd hour, probably) and the 5th portal of the Book of Gates. From here, two last rooms led off, the final one again furnished with solid stone benches.

These suites of four small side-rooms and four rear rooms around the great burial-hall were "the Right-hand and Left-hand Treasuries", and "the Place of the Servant-figures" (*shabtis*, in Egyptian), and "the Resting-place of (the Images of) the Gods". They thus held much of the very special funerary outfit of magical, protective images for the king's benefit in the hereafter. All of this lavish equipment — in gold, gilded wood, often of superb artistry (witness Tutankhamun's equipment) — had to be finished-off and readied, or drawn from store and installed in the tomb as the day of the dead king's burial at last drew near.

The Final Farewell

So, at last, after a fortnight or three weeks' steady sail south from Pi-Ramesse and Memphis, the great royal flotilla anchored at Thebes, and Pharaoh Merenptah set all the final arrangements in motion for the days that followed. In due course the great cortège formed up — the priests and high officials, the mummy of Ramesses II in its coffins on a bier drawn by oxen, the royal family headed by Merenptah, and a veritable baggage-train of attendants carrying all the more portable items of funerary and personal belongings for the burial. On the West bank, first port-of-call was probably the Ranesseum where, from now on, Ramesses was a god like all the gods. After the fitting rites there, perhaps a day or so later, came Ramesses' last journey as the long procession went north along the desert edge, turned west along the winding, lonely desert ravine and so reached at last the Valley of the Kings.

There, as the new Horus burying his father Osiris-Ramesses, Merenptah conducted and supervised the very last rites, including doubtless 'Opening the Mouth' of the mummy at the tomb-entrance. So at last, corridor by corridor, hall by hall, by flickering torchlight past painted walls with gods and guardian demons and the mysterious texts of the Netherworld, and into the House of Gold, came the golden-coffined mummy of Ramesses II to rest in secret splendour while his glorified spirit made eternally its cycle with Osiris and the Sun.

The officiants and mourners withdrew, back up to the surface and the glaring light of day; the door-passage of the tomb was blocked with masonry, sealed, and covered over with rubble, as it was hoped, forever. From now on, Ramesses II was a member of the august company of the Royal Ancestors, one of the conclave of the great gods.

68. *Shabti-figure of Ramesses II, Brooklyn Museum, New York. In the after-life, such figures were intended to replace the deceased in doing any work, and bore an appropriate spell.*

11: AFTERMATH: EGYPT AFTER RAMESSES II

Decline and Fall of the Ramesside Empire

Merenptah and the End of the Dynasty

Although already an old man (perhaps nearer seventy than sixty?), Merenptah did not lack energy. In his Year 2 (1212 B.C.), he was back in Thebes and charged the dignitary Ioti to conduct "a great inspection of all the gods and goddesses of the South and North" — probably a census of the property and furnishings of the temples. A statue of the king was set up in Karnak at the king's visit; in Year 1, he had renewed the offerings to the Nile at Silsila.

But now, for the first time in generations, external crises began visibly to shadow Egypt's wider horizons. Between Years 2 and 5, Merenptah mobilised his army for a brief campaign, or show of force, in Canaan and South Syria. It was the first for half a century, since his father's Year 21. Incipient revolt in Canaan was quickly crushed — Gezer and Ascalon in the south, Yenoam in the north of Canaan, and a brief 'brush' with a new people — Israel — probably on the western edges of the central Palestinian hill-country. But far to the north, peace still obtained with the Hittites, ruled now by Tudkhalia IV or Arnuwandas III. Egypt's northern possessions thus remained largely intact. A 'postal register' of Year 3 records the regular comings and goings of envoys between Egypt and Canaan, carrying dispatches that probably originated from (or arrived at) the files of the Foreign Office in Pi-Ramesse, now run by Merenptah's former personal secretary, Tjay, who showed his workplace in his Theban tomb-chapel. Meantime, the Hittite Empire was increasingly embroiled in multiple crises — disloyal vassals, conflicts to east and west, crop-failures — while Egypt's inner prosperity continued. In fact, faithful to 'the auld alliance', Merenptah "sent grain in ships, to sustain that land of Hatti". For Egypt, the real threat lay west of the Delta. In Libya, migrants from the troubled Aegean and East Mediterranean had added to the growing unrest and land-hunger among the Libyan tribes. So in Merenptah's Year 5, the Libyans and their allies decided upon an invasion of Egypt to satisfy their needs and ambitions, having already penetrated south into the more northerly oases like Farafra, outflanking the Nile Valley on the west. Moreover, they had earlier sent secret emissaries (via the oases) far south into Nubia, to encourage a revolt there against Egypt, to divert Merenptah's attention on the eve of their own attack on the Delta. But late in Year 5 (summer, 1209 B.C.) Merenptah got wind of the Libyan mobilisation, readied his own troops in 14 days, and sent them out to meet the foe. From a six-hour battle, Egypt emerged victorious, and captives and booty were paraded in triumph before the aged pharaoh. But even as Merenptah's forces had marched out to battle, the news came of a revolt in Nubia — the Nubians had kept their pact with the Libyans, but acted too late to affect the pharaoh's plans. With the Libyans routed, Merenptah ordered the ruthless suppression of the Nubian rebels — after 70 years of peace in Lower Nubia (Wawat), he would make an example of them to ensure peace throughout the southern dominions.

215

So by Year 6, Merenptah had energetically reaffirmed Egypt's hold on her vast empire — there would be no diminution in *his* day, even if the great Ramesses was no more. As it turned out, his measures did afford Egypt external peace for over a generation. At home, the administration remained effective. The old king realised, however, that he could not expect a long spacious reign like his father's. So, for his own major buildings, haste and expediency were paramount if anything substantial were to be completed in his lifetime. His tomb was excavated rapidly on a large scale, and its decoration steadily pushed ahead, the vizier Panehsy inspecting progress in Years 7 and 8 (1207/06 B.C.). Merenptah planned his memorial-temple on an impressive scale — but hardly more than half the length of its vast predecessor, the Ramesseum. To speed erection of this building, his contractors got most of their stone from those parts of the great temple of Amenophis III that had already fallen into disuse or decay. Elsewhere in Egypt, Merenptah's works were on a more modest scale, but he added his name or dedications frequently to standing statues and buildings, so that ultimately he would be seen to have been active for the gods and so for Egypt.

However, when Merenptah died (in 1204 B.C.) after a decade's rule, Egypt experienced a new and unexpected crisis — over the royal succession. During his reign, Merenptah had had by his side a son Sethy-Merenptah as Crown Prince: "Heir of the Two Lands, Generalissimo, and Senior Prince", probably a man in his fifties, marked out for the throne. But the next pharaoh was not Sethy . . . but instead a completely unknown person appears as king: Amenmesses. Significantly the new ruler's mother (Takhat I) was entitled simply Queen-Mother — she had not been a princess or chief queen in Merenptah's reign. Nor was Amenmesses' queen Bekenwerel a princess. What had happened? The matter is still rather a mystery. Most probably Merenptah had died in the absence of Crown Prince Sethy (away on official business affairs?), and so a lesser son by an inmate of the harim had quickly seized his opportunity to become king by arranging and conducting the burial of Merenptah — Amenmesses thus reigned. Prince Sethy could only vow silent vengeance and await events. Amenmesses' reign was brief and undistinguished; a tomb was cut in the Kings' Valley, a few formal inscriptions were engraved at Karnak and as far away as Amara West in Nubia. The reign was marked by irregularities at Deir el Medina (and fewer holidays).

Then at last Amenmesses died (about his 4th year, 1200 B.C.). The next king, this time, was Sethos II, very probably the same Prince Sethy son of Merenptah. The legitimising formalities of Amenmesses' burial once completed, Sethos II lost no time in expunging Amenmesses' name from monuments the length of Egypt. His six-year reign saw no great events; his pompous inscriptions added to others' monuments reflected little or no reality. Sethos II probably had three queens, besides the lesser ladies of the harim. The first, Takhat II, was a royal princess, appearing only on her husband's statues. The second, Tewosret, perhaps bore him an eldest son, another Sethy-Merenptah, considered as Heir-apparent. A third, Tio, bore the king a son called Ramesses-Siptah in honour of Sethos II's mighty grandfather, perhaps in the latter's last years. Once more the succession faltered. The heir (Sethy-merenptah junior) died before his father and, at Sethos II's death, young Ramesses-Siptah was made pharaoh under the joint tutelage of the dowager-queen Tewosret and the powerful Chancellor Bay, 'kingmaker' and Syrian courtier. In Year 3, the young king changed his style to Merenptah-Siptah; but by Year 6 he was dead, leaving no heir. So Queen Tewosret herself took the throne with full titles as a female pharaoh — only the fourth woman ever to do so, in a thousand years — and with her death two years later (about 1187 B.C.), the direct line of Ramesses II ceased to rule Egypt.

69. Statue of Merenptah, son and successor of Ramesses II. From Merenptah's memorial temple in Western Thebes. (Cairo Museum)

The Last Ramessides : the 20th Dynasty

The throne of the pharaohs was now taken over by one Setnakht, who professed to set Egypt to rights after years of decline and growing corruption — a reflection on the weak rulers after Merenptah — and to have supplanted the "self-made" Syrian, probably the Chancellor Bay. But of Setnakht's origins, we know nothing — was he in any way related to the descendants of Ramesses II? At his early death, he left the throne to his vigorous son, Ramesses III (about 1185 - 1154 B.C.). This king set out to model himself on Ramesses II, to emulate his achievements in war and peace. But times had changed. Egypt was now on the defensive. The East-Mediterranean world was in political confusion, with the Hittite Empire under its last and heroic king (Suppiluliuma II) crumbling under blows from both west and east. In Canaan and Syria, incursions of

217

new groups helped disrupt the Late Bronze Age states. Ramesses III rapidly mobilised and strengthened his forces. In three epic conflicts — Year 5 in Libya, Year 8 a land and sea battle on the coasts of the north-east Delta and Canaan, and Year 11 in Libya again — Ramesses III beat back Libyans and 'Sea Peoples' alike, perhaps retaining a tenuous hold on coastal Canaan and its routes.

Thus did Ramesses III wrest victories out of international chaos, as great as those of Ramesses II but far more vital. These, he celebrated in several series of reliefs and poetical texts on the walls of his huge memorial-temple in Western Thebes (now, Medinet Habu), of the same size as the Ramesseum and directly modelled on that temple in layout and many details of decoration. Likewise, in lesser temples at Karnak. But, significantly, these Theban buildings were the *only* great works of Ramesses III. He carried out works extensively throughout Egypt, but no more Abu Simbels, no huge additions to Memphis, Heliopolis or Pi-Ramesse, and so on. Moreover, Egypt now no longer had men of comparable or adequate calibre in her administration. Certain great officials now increasingly obtained undue power in the state, and intrigues at court even led to an attempt on the king's life. Failures in administration at Thebes left the royal workmen at Deir el Medina weeks behind without pay — their rations! — driving them in starving desperation to stage strikes and sit-ins in Western Thebes. So, the reign ended in shadows undreamed of in Ramesses II's day.

Thereafter, a long line of kings reigned — but hardly ruled — in swift succession, all inevitably called 'Ramesses', from IV to XI. Ramesses IV prayed for a reign of 66 or 67 years like Ramesses II, claiming to have benefited the gods more in *his* first four years! His claim was over-bold (to say the least!), and his prayer rejected, as he died in his Year 7. The reigns of Ramesses V, VI, VII, VIII progressively saw low Niles, scarcity of food, rocketing inflation and, under Ramesses IX, famine. The administration now creaked so badly that, when a pharaoh wanted something particular done, he 'short-circuited' regular channels frequently (instead of occasionally) by dispatching a royal cup-bearer. Corruption was now rife. One scandal of embezzlement of temple grain ran for ten years before being unmasked. In Thebes, control of the estates and wealth of Amun had passed into the hands of a new high-priestly family. Tomb-robbery on a blatant scale did not spare the Valleys of the Kings and Queens (an 'inside job' by some of the later Deir el Medina workforce!), and even the great memorial-temples suffered — gold was stripped from the Ramesseum. So events moved on, under Ramesses IX, X and XI.

By now the Syrian dominions were long since totally lost. Nubia was soon to follow, leaving Egypt within her natural bounds, from Aswan to the Mediterranean Sea. Under Ramesses XI, a political 'Renaissance' was proclaimed, with organization of a triumvirate: one man (Smendes) was ruler of Lower Egypt, one man (Herihor) was ruler of Upper Egypt *with Nubia* (an unheard of combination), and the pharaoh was their sole chief. Herihor and his son-in-law Piankh easily assumed power in Thebes, but in Nubia the previous viceroy, Panehsi, refused to be deposed, and held the country against all attempts by the new men to dislodge him; so was Nubia lost to Egypt. Back in Western Thebes, Herihor had to repair the ravages of tomb-robbers — even the vast tombs of Sethos I and Ramesses II were looted, and he had to renew their burials even while Ramesses XI yet lived. Finally, as ruler of the Two Lands — Upper and Lower Egypt, pure and simple — Ramesses XI died about 1070/69 B.C., perhaps the last pharaoh to be laid to rest in the now increasingly unsafe Valley of Kings. And with him there died the New Kingdom, and the Ramesside Empire was no more.

Tanite Stagnation (c. 1070 - 945 B.C.)

The end of the Ramessides, but not of Egypt. The northern ruler Smendes as king founded a new Dynasty (the 21st), based on Memphis and on its family seat of Tanis, just a few miles north from the now decaying and moribund Pi-Ramesse. He speedily reached an accomodation with his southern contemporary, Pinudjem I, new High Priest of Amun of Thebes and Governor of the South: each recognised the other's status, as pharaoh and ruler of the south respectively, and agreed mutual respect of rights of succession in those spheres. Under this loose confederation, no great ventures could be expected, at home or abroad. Egypt slumbered as the estate of Amun, ruled by his representatives in Tanis and Thebes. Meanwhile tomb-robbery in Thebes became so uncontrollable that, finally, a bold plan was decided on, to rescue the plundered pharaohs. In Year 10 of Siamun (about 970 B.C.), the high priest of Amun and his officials collected together the bodies of all the great pharaohs of the bygone Empire — Ramesses II among them — to hide them away in group-burials, much more easily guarded than thirty scattered tombs. Some were hidden in the Valley itself, in the tomb of Amenophis II. But the main group, of some forty royal and related bodies — including our Ramesses II, again — was hidden away in a secret pit-and-corridor tomb in a rock bay south from the Deir el Bahri temples, with only the merest wreckage of their once-proud funerary treasures. Meantime, new powers were arising in Egypt — in particular, a family of Libyan-origin chiefs at Bubastis, halfway between the two capitals of Memphis and Tanis. This family developed close ties with the royal line and the high priests of Memphis, and at the death of Psusennes II in 945 B.C., his throne passed to the new family, personified in the strong man of the day — Shoshenq.

Libyan Storms (c.945 - 715 B.C.)

Founder of the 22nd, Libyan, Dynasty, Shoshenq I was perhaps the ablest man to ascend the throne since at least Ramesses III, if not since Ramesses II himself. He swiftly took measures to reunify and strengthen Egypt, bringing Thebes firmly under his control — his second son being appointed high priest there. In his early years, the old Theban priestly families finally closed the south-Deir-el-Bahri collective vault, containing Ramesses II and the rest, for the last time in antiquity. This time, Ramesses and his companions were left to slumber for some 28 centuries, until our modern times . . . However, the interests of Shoshenq I were directed not south, but north. At the death of Solomon, he encouraged the disruption of the large Hebrew realm into two rump-kingdoms, Israel and Judah in 930 B.C., and five years later, pounced (925 B.C.), raiding Palestine and returning to Egypt in triumph with his loot (1 Kings 14:25-26; 2 Chronicles 12:2-9). For a split second of time, Egypt scented the breath of long-bygone Empire, especially when Shoshenq ordered the building of a vast court in Amun's Karnak temple at Thebes, biggest thing of its kind since the works of Sethos I and Ramesses II himself. But only for a split second . . . next year, 924 B.C., Shoshenq was dead, and his grandiose schemes died with him.

70. *Surrender of the fortress of Ascalon in Canaan to Egyptian forces,
those of Merenptah rather than of Ramesses II. Karnak, Temple of
Amun.*

His successors had neither his firmness nor his sagacity, until it was too late. His successor
Osorkon I was a pale imitator of his father, and (with the death of his own heir, Shoshenq II)
was succeeded by a witless nonentity, Takeloth I, who allowed all real power to slip through his
fumbling fingers; hereditary high priests were tolerated in Thebes once more, sowing the seeds of
national disunity. Osorkon II tried to stop the rot, by appointing his own family to the pontifi-
cates in Memphis and Thebes. In adorning Tanis and Bubastis Osorkon II sought to build with
Ramesside magnificence – by re-using the stones of Ramesses II's great structures from Pi-Ramesse, now largely (but not wholly) abandoned. Under Takeloth II came the cataclysm. His son
Prince Osorkon tried to enforce his claim to be High Priest of Amun in Thebes, but local opposition led to the outbreak of civil war which raged intermittently for the rest of that reign (850 -
825 B.C.), shaking the kingdom to its foundations. Meantime, abroad, a new shadow darkened
the Syrian horizon — Assyria. Osorkon II, at least, encouraged the Palestinian states to fend off
this devourer.

Then came dissolution. Not Prince Osorkon, but one Shoshenq III took the throne, leaving
the Prince to his disputed pontificate. But in 818 B.C., Shoshenq in turn had to divide his throne

with a fellow-dynast, Pedubast I, who settled himself as co-pharaoh in nearby Leontopolis, founding the 23rd Dynasty. The dissident Thebans immediately recognised this new line, instead of the old. If two pharaohs, why not more? Sure enough, by 730 B.C., Egypt had then two senior lines of pharaohs in Tanis and Leontopolis, two lesser pharaohs in Upper Egypt (at Ninsu and Hermopolis), a Prince-regent and four Great Chiefs of the Ma in the Delta, a series of local notables everywhere — and a Prince of the West in Sais, then Tefnakht. When the latter tried to expand south, he stirred up a further power — the local kings of Nubia now laid claim to Thebes, and their prince Piye ("Piankhy") swept north to subdue Egypt and Tefnakht — and then as quickly retreated to Nubia again, leaving Egypt to her motley crew of local rulers and the line of Tefnakht (24th Dynasty). And Ramesses? Even in Thebes, the last priests of his great temple, the Ramesseum, steadily dwindled — virtually to nothing by 700 B.C.; from then on, the Ramesseum was left forlorn, and even Medinet Habu was a local administrative centre, with worship concentrated more in the little temple of Amun there.

Nubian and Saite Revival (715 - 525 B.C.)

In 715 B.C., Piye's successor Shabako swept back through Egypt, supplanting Tefnakht's successor Bakenranef. The Assyrian Empire now controlled virtually all the Levant to the gates of Egypt. Shabako wisely remained neutral, but his successors foolishly intrigued with Philistia and Judah against Assyria — bringing the annoyed Assyrians into Egypt itself: the first really foreign invaders since the Hyksos of a millennium before. At the sack of Thebes in 663 B.C., the loot must have been prodigious. Under the impact of that shattering blow, the 25th or Nubian Dynasty withdrew south, not to be seen in Egypt again. Egypt now lay under the Assyrian heel, divided among local princelings, seemingly helpless.

But new life came now from the West-Delta city of Sais. Ultimate successor to Tefnakht Prince of the West, Psammetichus I of Sais submitted to Assyria (663 B.C.), and as their vassal steadily gained full control of the Delta, then (by alliance) of Middle Egypt. Finally in his Year 9 (656 B.C.), he gained recognition in Thebes, thus restoring once more the outward unity of the country. During the decades that followed, he gradually transformed that outward unity into a real and lasting unity that survived all the shocks of the centuries that followed. Thus opened the 26th or Saite Dynasty that lasted until 525 B.C. The next of its kings, Necho II, witnessed the fall of Assyria to the Medes and Babylon, culminating first in the empire of Nebuchadrezzar II of Babylon, with whom he clashed over the possession of Judah (losing it to Babylon). Thereafter, he and Psammetichus II prudently kept clear of this entanglement, but not so Apries who got embroiled in the Judean rebellion against Babylon in 588 B.C., ending in the sack of Jerusalem in 587/586 B.C. After further failures in Libya and Cyrenaica, Apries was replaced by a new man, Ahmose II or Amasis (570 - 526 B.C.), who made peace with the would-be invader, Nebuchadrezzar. But in the Near East, events moved on. Soon the Median power became the Persian Empire of Cyrus who conquered Babylon (539 B.C.). And soon after, Amasis's successor, Psammetichus III, was overthrown by Cambyses who annexed Egypt to Persia in 525 B.C. The Saite kings had restored Egypt's political unity; in spirit, they looked back, far past the Ramessides, to the older glories of the Pyramid Age and the Middle Kingdom, breaking with the Tanite and Libyan imitation of imperial traditions.

The Closing Perspectives

Persian Empire and Independence Pharaohs

At first, with Persian emperors as 'pharaohs', Egypt was just one more satrapy of their vast empire. But Persian defeats in Greece and Egyptian priestly resentment at restrictions on their privileges combined to impel the Egyptians to try for independence, allying themselves with whichever Greek state — Athens or Sparta — happened to be opposed to Persia at any given moment: 'Persia's enemies are our friends', and *vice-versa*. Under the Saite kings, the Greeks had already got to know Egypt — Greek mercenaries stiffened the Egyptian (as other) armies, as elite troops; Greek merchants set up shop in Egypt, and Naucratis became their particular emporium. It was under Persian rule, about 450 B.C., that Herodotus toured Egypt, and many other inquiring Greeks did so then or later.

At length, during 400 - 343 B.C., the Egyptians threw off the Persian yoke (28th to 30th Dynasties). Hakor was the first strong ruler, but greatest were the kings Nectanebo I and II. Apart from keeping the Persians at bay, they undertook splendid buildings in the temple-precincts of Egypt, freely employing the hardest stones (price of ardent priestly support). They and the Saites were Egypt's greatest builder-kings since Ramesses II and III, far outclassing the Libyan dynasts. But finally, Artaxerxes III defeated Nectanebo II in 343 B.C., and pharaonic Egypt's independence was ended. A decade later, Alexander the Great was hailed as liberator, and posed as successors to the pharaohs (332 - 323 B.C.), a thousand years after the great days of Sethos I and Ramesses II.

Greece, Rome and Eclipse of Egyptian Civilisation

The death of Alexander and his heirs left Egypt in the possession of his Macedonian general Ptolemy (I). He at length declared himself king first of a long line culminating in the notorious Cleopatra, until Egypt fell under the heel of Rome in 30 B.C., to become merely a corn-producing province. Under both the Ptolemies and Romans, as price of their loyalty (and focus of national sentiment), the priesthoods obtained the building or rebuilding of great temples in the pharaonic style, upon whose walls the immemorial rites are carried out by 'pharaohs' Ptolemy, Claudius or Nero — all in Egyptian guise. But under the impact of Hellenistic civilisation, Roman rule, and then the new world religion of Christianity, the old ways gradually lost their appeal and then their meaning — and 'Pharaoh', now as a mere abstract of 'Kingship' upon secluded temple-walls, no longer a real, earthly ruler, shepherd of his people as of old. Memories of Ramesses II had survived in cults of his dynasty at Memphis and in his temple at Abydos in the Ptolemaic period, but by Roman times he was merely a curio on temple-walls, shown to visiting tourists like the visit to the Ramesseum excerpted by Diodorus Siculus. But with the eclipse in turn of pagan culture, Ramesses II and his age passed into the dimmer shadows of human memory, and when Islam took over Byzantine and Coptic Egypt in 641 A.D., even this faint tradition lapsed utterly into oblivion in Egypt itself within a short span of time. Thereafter, not until the explorations of the early nineteenth century A.D., with the decipherment of the hieroglyphs by Champollion, did both the monuments and name of Ramesses II return fully to human knowledge. And then, in the 1860's, the eternal tomb-robbers stumbled on the *cache* of royal bodies south of Deir el Bahri . . . And in 1881, at last, Brugsch and Ahmed Kamal uncovered the secret 'valhalla' — and, with his companions, Ramesses II returned to the light of day and in person to an utterly-transformed world of the living, of the nineteenth and twentieth centuries A.D.

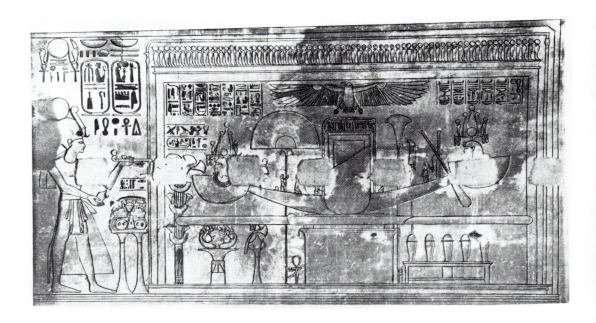

71. *Ramesses III offers before the barque-shrine of his revered predecessor Ramesses II, to whom he dedicated a special chapel in his own great Theban memorial temple at Medinet Habu.*

223

12: RETROSPECT

Ramesses II in his own time

In Egyptian history, the giant figure of Ramesses II dominates the thirteenth century B.C. In the overall history of the Ancient Near East of that day — which in effect was nearly synonymous with world history — Ramesses II was one of the major figures, with a more enduring and stable realm than any of his contemporaries. The kings of Hatti and Assyria were equally redoubtable warriors and administrators (better generals, perhaps), but the fortunes of their kingdoms waxed and waned reign by reign, of which even the longest barely exceeded half that of Ramesses II in mere length. In a word, the 66-year reign of Ramesses II in the thirteenth century B.C. in Egypt was, once in a way, analogous to the reign of Queen Victoria in Great Britain in the nineteenth century A.D. — a reign that marked an epoch, known for its great events and characteristic monumental style (after a more elegant age), and the name (be it 'Ramesside' or 'Victorian') stamped indelibly upon a nation's history in each case.

But what more specific role did Ramesses II fulfil in Egyptian history? Under Tuthmosis III and Amenophis III in the preceding two centuries, Egypt had first reached a peak, of political world-rank power and then, a climax of brilliant cultural achievement, outwardly as great as the overall Egyptian achievement in any earlier age, and certainly the equal of any other civilisation of that age or many another.. Then came Akhenaten. His virtual disregard for foreign affairs until too late, entailing major losses in Syria and Hittite defeat of his Mitannian ally, ended the international prestige of Egypt's imperial dream. His rejection of the mainstream national religious traditions and his narrowly personal adaptation of just one (sun-worship), plus failure to put anything equally satisfying in their stead, badly shook Egypt's inner self-confidence in her own traditions as a way of life, and probably bewildered many of the ordinary people. Tutankhamun and Haremhab restored Egypt to her traditional ways in outward fulness; Amen-re was again King of the Gods, and Osiris, of the Netherworld. Haremhab put the country to rights, eliminating graft and abuses that had flourished more than ordinarily while Akhenaten's attention had been on other things. Thus were most of the pieces put back together again, — but whither from here?

The answer came from Haremhab's political heirs — Ramesses I, then Sethos I, seconded by Ramesses II. They abominated both the loss of imperial possessions and prestige (being of military background) and the repudiation of national ways (as Egyptians) that came with Akhenaten. For them, he was no true pharaoh, he was "that criminal of Akhet-Aten". Their own wars, buildings, even titularies as kings, all proclaimed their solution for Egypt's future after the Aten episode.

Negatively, the Ramesside kings were content simply to destroy the names and memory of the Aten kings wherever possible (restoring the names of Amun and the gods), but nothing more. Positively, they sought alike to restore and even surpass the greatest glories of the Eighteenth Dynasty in both war and peace. By his titles, Ramesses I was a new Ahmose I, as though beginning a 'second' Eighteenth Dynasty. Sethos I from his very first year campaigned with the utmost vigour in Canaan and Syria, and (since Tuthmosis III) was the first — and only — pharaoh to recapture Qadesh (however briefly). But then he pretty certainly had to compromise and reach peace with Hatti — times had changed, this other 'great power' could not just be wished away, and Sethos I was wise enough and realist enough to face this fact and accept it. In works of peace, his success was perhaps visibly greater. For sheer size, the buildings he undertook (great hall, Karnak; memorial-temple, west bank; Abydos, his great temple) eclipsed those of Tuthmosis III and rivalled most of those of Amenophis III. In quality of decoration, at their best (as at Abydos), they came very close to the best work of the earlier Dynasty, if less tautly vigorous (except in the war-reliefs). Thus, in large measure, the aims of the new Dynasty were well established and clearly exemplified by its founders. These, in turn, Ramesses II inherited, to fulfil even more completely if he would.

In war, the young king showed himself all too facile and impetuous at first, leading to the *débacle* at Qadesh. And then stubbornly persistent in endeavouring (where his father had stopped) to recover the Tuthmosid claims in Syria for most of 20 years. Here were Ramesses' weaknesses as well as his strengths. His verve and enthusiasm were precious qualitites, if rightly applied. But twenty years of armed conflict ending in a treaty that gave no desired gain at the end meant twenty years of wasted effort, wasted lives, wasted resources, in a theatre of war where his father had had the good sense to perceive realities and cut his losses promptly after six or seven years at most. Like Sethos, Ramesses simply could not reverse the course of history. But, eventually, when progress in war could be seen to be *nil*, and the Hittite power also found advantage in peace, Ramesses II then did have the sense to conclude that 'enough was enough', and to agree on peace.

In the activities of peace, Ramesses II initially maintained the excellence of his father's works — witness his own temple at Abydos, his once superb tomb in the Kings' Valley, the famous statue now in Turin, and others (fragmentary) in Cairo. But the impatient Ramesses preferred to see more done in a given time, preferring the quicker technique of incised relief to the more laborious low relief. He desired to work not merely on the grand scale — witness the Ramesseum, Luxor, Abu Simbel, and the now vanished splendours of Pi- Ramesse — but also on the widest possible front as the years passed. Much of the work (despite its size and quantity) shows good, formal standards, but much is poor and hasty, particularly in later years and in areas of poor stone and restricted to local craftsmen (as in Nubia). But certainly in his building-works for the gods the entire length of Egypt and Nubia, Ramesses II surpassed not only the Eighteenth Dynasty but every other period in Egyptian history. In that realm, he certainly fulfilled the dynasty's aims to satiety. In the great centres Ptah or Amun celebrated their spectacular festivals in settings of the very greatest splendour, perhaps to be unequalled for over a millennium to come until the Ptolemies raised their grand new temples. In the innumerable lesser cities and towns, few did not boast a smaller temple, or addition to one, or statuary, or even just a few bright new inscriptions, in the name of the omnipresent Ramesses II.

But what of the national spirit and the kingship? In the latter case, both Sethos I and Ramesses II recognised that, however great, Amun should not overshadow the kingship, key office in the land. Hence, they resumed and developed trends where Amenophis III had left off — setting Re and Ptah alongside Amun, reaffirming the popular cult of Osiris, and setting up the worship of divinised aspects of their personal kingship (so, especially Ramesses II), in Nubia in temples, and in Egypt focussed on great statues. Ramesses II went further, claiming a special relationship with the 'gods of Ramesses', especially the sun-god. Thereby, he probably attained Akhenaten's end of binding the gods to a centrally-important monarchy, and by subtler means than that monarch.

Egyptian national life, also, seemed in large measure restored. Trained from their adolescence to handle and size-up men and their characters, Ramesses I, Sethos I and Ramesses II had (and used) the ability to select, and surround themselves with, able and devoted men to fill leading positions in the realm. Some of these, like Paser, even entered into the perpetuation of ancient traditions. The Ramesside kings also drew on a wider circle of people for high office than just from the families of metropolitan Thebes and Memphis (as the Eighteenth Dynasty had largely done), promoting men from important provincial centres the length of Egypt; foreigners (Canaanites, Hurrians) also had opportunities for advancement in royal service. Egypt thus was a more cosmopolitan society than ever before, with increased stimuli, while yet maintaining her basic cultural traditions.

However, by the end of the thirteenth century B.C., all was changed. Ramesses II's line had ended, and a new (20th) dynasty enjoyed only transient successes abroad or at home, before Egypt sank into social, economic and political decline. What happened? Probably very little that can be blamed on Ramesses II. His able sons Khaemwaset and Merenptah probably maintained a relatively effective regime during their father's later years. And Merenptah himself reigned vigorously during his brief decade — only his buildings are marked by haste, as he could not expect a long reign. The troubles seem to have come with his death — an irregular succession, intrigues, less-conscientious officials. Without an adequate hand at the helm, integrity and efficiency tailed off, with Chancellor Bay having undue power in the realm. Under the next dynasty (once Ramesses III's more vigorous years were past), venality and corruption grew; bad harvests for some years, and a line of personally-ineffective kings incapable of controlling the over-powerful officials whose families now dominated key positions in the kingdom — under such conditions did the Ramesside state rapidly decline and founder in the century and a half following Ramesses II's death. The sweeping changes in the outside world also removed Egypt's Syrian possessions and contributed to her impoverishment.

In short, Ramesses II did in large measure complete the programme of his father and grandfather, to restore Egypt's power (so far as practicable) and glory. But by the end of his vastly long reign, this active sense of mission had itself faded away into history, and Egypt was content to bask in the general prosperity of the age. No harm, so long as the key values continued to be granted their validity. Merenptah maintained this state of affairs, energetically repelling external threats to Egypt's security. But thereafter, both vision and integrity progressively failed, and decline was halted only for a time by Ramesses III while fighting for Egypt's self-preservation — and his vision was limited to being, in turn, another Ramesses II, hardly more.

Ramesses II in Later Tradition

Ideal of the Later Ramesside Kings

In the eyes of many a later pharaoh, Ramesses II bestrode their history like one of his own mighty colossi. Ramesses III in particular consciously modelled himself, his titles, his family names, his wars and buildings, and thus his reign, on the example of Ramesses II. His sons, for example, were called Amen-hir-khopshef, Pre-hir-wonmef, Ramesses, Khaemwaset, and so on, like those of Ramesses II. He founded a new district at the Delta Residence of Pi-Ramesse; his memorial-temple is so closely-based (Medinet Habu) on the Ramesseum, that one can use each temple to restore in one's mind missing portions of the other. In that temple, Ramesses III included a chapel for the cult of a barque-image of Ramesses II as his personal hero.

Thereafter, the Twentieth Dynasty consisted entirely of kings who chose to bear the name 'Ramesses' (IV to XI), often prefixing it to their own personal name (Amen-hir-khopshef, Set-hir-khopshef, Khaemwaset and Iot-Amun), even as all Roman emperors had to be each a Caesar. Even after the Empire was finished, Smendes' successor Psusennes I still occasionally called himself 'Ramesses-Psusennes' and his own son 'Ramesses-Ankhefenmut'. Ramesses IV had prayed for 66 and 67 years like Ramesses II. None, however, had the force of personality, the vision, the means or a like body of able supporters even remotely to approach their 'ideal'.

Post-Imperial Renown

Psusennes I was not alone among Late-Period kings in apeing the imperial style of Ramesses II. Besides his successor Amenemope, many of the Libyan pharaohs of the 22nd/23rd Dynasties adopted the throne-name of *Usi-ma-re* with varying epithets; Shoshenq III in particular used titles based on those of Ramesses II — and at 52 years' reign nearly rivalled his model's span of years, but his power was the merest shadow compared with the great Ramesses. During the 11th to 8th centuries B.C., minor priesthoods of the cults of Ramesses II, III and IV were jealously retained by Theban priestly families — less from piety than on economic grounds, one suspects. In the 11th century B.C., the 'blurb' attached to a magical papyrus as 'evidence' for its high pedigree was worded:

> "The writing which was found on the neck (of the mummy) of King
> Usi-ma-re Chosen-of-Re [Ramesses II], in the Necropolis".

And both the Tanite and Libyan royal courts included princes and dignitaries who boasted the high title of "King's Son of Ramesses", centuries after the Ramessides were no more. From about 730 B.C. onwards, the imperial style was abandoned by the kings, but some at least were tempted to adventure in Western Asia like the New Kingdom kings. And Psammetichus II celebrated his Nubian campaign with all the panache of a triumphant Ramesses. His army-force, moreover, left their scribbles on the legs of Ramesses' colossi at Abu Simbel, already over ankle-deep in drifted sand.

Later Egyptian Traditions of Ramesses II and Prince Khaemwaset

A thousand years after Ramesses II, he and his remarkable son Prince Khaemwaset still lived

72. *The so-called 'Bentresh' Stela of c.300 B.C., with priestly legend glorifying the god Khons as one-time healer of a foreign princess in distant parts, inspired by Egypto-Hittite relations under Ramesses II of a thousand years earlier. (Louvre Museum)*

on in priestly and popular tradition. The cult of Ramesses II's temple continued at Abydos, and he and Merenptah were still honoured in Memphis. More picturesque were the popular tales atta - ched to the king and the prince. In Thebes about 300 B.C., the priests of Khons the Planmaker (a lesser form of the Theban moon-god Khons) sought to enhance the repute of their deity by coup - ling his name with great events of a thousand years before — the Hittite marriage and Syrian wars of Ramesses II, seen through a golden haze of tradition, perhaps enriched with traditions from the time of Amenophis III. They set up in their god's chapel an impressive stela, recording how the king Ramesses (II) annually raided Syria, so at length the Ruler of Bakhtan sent him his eldest dau - ghter in marriage; she became queen of Egypt as Neferure (obviously abbreviated from Maat-Hor-Neferu-re). Then one day, a Bakhtan ambassador begged for an Egyptian physician to come and heal his ruler's younger daughter. He failed, and Khons the Planmaker was sent and succeeeded, eventually being returned to Thebes. Thus did his priests hope to bathe the little Khons in the glory of Ramesses II.

Even more remarkable was the repute of the learned Prince Khaemwaset. In Memphis, as Se(te)m-priest and High Priest of Ptah, Khaemwaset had made a name for himself as priest, scho - lar, administrator, patron of the cult of the Apis-bull, from which his repute as a scholar and magi - cian remained alive (as his system of Apis-burial remained in use) for the following thousand years down to the 2nd century B.C. His fame then and later was known also in Thebes whence came at least one of two remarkable papyri dating to about the last century B.C. and first century A.D., when Roman rule was replacing Ptolemaic in Egypt. These papyri contain two tales showing "Se-tne(Khamwas)" — as they call him — the 'son of Pharaoh Usi-ma-re' , as a super-magician eager to penetrate recondite secrets of ancient lore, and as protector of Pharaoh in contest with a magician of Nubia.

In the first tale, *Khaemwaset and Na-nefer-ka-Ptah*, Khaemwaset had penetrated an ancient tomb in the desert of Memphis, seeking a magic book written by the god of wisdom, Thoth him - self. The ghosts of Na-nefer-ka-Ptah and his wife and son guarded the book and begged Khaem - waset not to take it — they told him that it had cost them their lives. Unpersuaded, Khaemwaset insisted on playing a game (somewhat like draughts or chess) to win the coveted book. He lost the rubber of three games, was rescued by his own spells (brought by his brother), then simply seized the book and left to enjoy its lore. But the offended ghosts laid their spell on him, and such dis - grace befell Setne-Khaemwaset that he at last heeded his father's advice and returned the book to its owners in their tomb, making amends by completing their proper burials.

In the second tale, of *Khaemwaset and his son Si-Osiri*, Khaemwaset and his wife yearn for a son, and eventually one is born. Si-Osiri. The boy proved incredibly clever, becoming the most brilliant magician (his father's pride), and shows Khaemwaset even the judgement-halls of the Netherworld. Then, when the prince of Nubia sent his magician's challenge to Egypt, it was Kha - emwaset's 'wonder-boy' Si-Osiri that answered the call — reading unopened the sealed letter that the Nubian had brought. This missive told of a far earlier contest (under Tuthmosis III!) between the Nubian Hor son of a negress and the old pharaoh's 'expert', Hor son of Paneshe. Thus the message stood revealed — and Si-Osiri then announced that the Nubian envoy was himself Hor son of the negress who had returned, while he — Si-Osiri — was none other than Hor son of Paneshe who had likewise returned, to deliver Egypt from the challenge. The Nubian was immediately consumed by fire, — and Si-Osiri simply evaporated away! Finally, Khaemwaset was blessed with a real son, to replace the chimerical phantom Si-Osiri, whose memory he ever after honoured.

Such, in baldest summary, are the tales of the prowess of Prince Khaemwaset (the Arthurian legends of their time) as told at the beginning of the Christian era, long after all the empires of the Ancient East had passed away, when most of the civilised world was ruled by Rome at the dawn of a new era.

Ramesses II in Other Ancient Traditions

The name and fame of Ramesses II and his works radiated in diffuse fashion even beyond Egypt. In the Old Testament, the biblical books Genesis and Exodus preserved the pharaoh's name in the geographical terms "land of Ramesses" (Genesis 47:11), or simply "Ramesses" (Exodus 1:11, as store-city, and 12:37 (cf. Numbers 33:3,5) as starting-point for the Hebrew exodus). Here, in early Hebrew tradition, the great Delta-Residence of Pi-Ramesse ('Domain of Ramesses', cf. Hebrew 'land of Ramesses') lived on as a city where the enslaved Hebrews laboured on the eve of their departure from Egypt. For centuries, stiffened by the obscure references to kings Rapsakes and Ramesses in the Graeco-Egyptian king-lists of Manetho as preserved by Christian chronographers like Eusebius, these few biblical references were almost the sole, slender thread of tradition for the name of 'Ramesses' as an ancient royal name in Egypt, through the medieval period in Europe until the discoveries of modern times.

The one other line of transmission of Ramesses II's fame in later antiquity and after was through the writings of ancient Greek and Roman travellers and historians, attested from Herodotus (visiting Egypt under the Persians about 450 B.C.) into Roman times. Herodotus speaks of Rhampsinitus as remembered for his gateways at the West end of the precinct of Ptah in Memphis, and two statues facing them — perhaps the pylon of the West Hall of Ramesses II there, plus the colossi whose bases were excavated there many years ago. Of Rhampsinitus, Herodotus also retailed an entertaining tale of his great wealth, a skilful thief, and his visits to the Netherworld. Almost four centuries later, mainly excerpting from Hecataeus of Abdera and others, Diodorus Siculus wrote at length on Egypt. From Hecataeus, he gives (for such visitors) a remarkably accurate account of the "tomb of Osymandyas" — none other than the great Ramesseum temple in Western Thebes. 'Osymandyas' is simply a form of *Usi-ma-re*, from the throne-name of Ramesses II. The mighty statue in its forecourt was none other than the famous shattered colossus of Ramesses II, lying there still. Even the Battle of Qadesh with the Hittites is described, but as a war against 'Bactria' — a Greek 'rationalization' of the forgotten Hittite name, like the Bakhtan of the stela of Khons the Planmaker. Ramesses II recurs in Diodorus as Remphis (error for Rempsis), without conscious recognition of his identity with Osymandyas.

Later still, Pliny knew of Sethos I and Ramesses II, as 'Sesothes' and 'Rhamsesis'; and Tacitus also, of the campaigns of Rhamses. Thus, in the late classical traditions, the wars and buildings of Ramesses II still shimmered through a haze of older memory. The repute of the great Twelfth-Dynasty kings Sesostris (I-III) was enriched by confusion in part with the Syrian campaigns, use of chariotry, and many buildings of Ramesses II and his line. Josephus for his part reported a tale transmitted by Manetho (3rd century B.C.) of the wars of Sethos and Ramesses, he being quoted in turn by the chronographers Africanus, Eusebius and the Syncellus (3rd, 4th, 8th centuries A.D.). In the fourth century A.D., the abbess Aetheria on pilgrimage in Egypt could still pass through a vast area of ruins still called 'Ramesses', where she saw a great stone sculptured as two colossal figures. Although (to us) evidently a dyad of Ramesses II and a deity, these were explained to her as representing Moses and Aaron . . . some seventeen centuries earlier, Ramesses II had disdainfully dismissed the Hebrew prophet to the wilderness from this same locale, and now he was more than half-forgotten behind the awesome image of the lawgiver!

Ramesses II Today

The Resurrection of Lost Civilisations

For many a century, the wreckage of ancient Egypt slumbered in the silence of sand-shrouded ruins. Two civilisations after the pharaohs, the Egypt of medieval Islam (for all its brilliance) found the stones of Pharaoh a quarry for stonemasons building Cairo oftener than for scholars studying history. In Europe (Crusaders apart), the lands of Egypt and the East remained in large measure part of a distant, unreal Orient, the distant setting of the Bible story. And Ramesses II? . . . Forgotten.

Then in the 16th, 17th, 18th centuries A.D., first a trickle and then a stream of European travellers visited Egypt, eventually travelling upriver beyond 'Grand Cairo', rediscovering the ruins of Thebes and its temples. With the Renaissance, a renewed knowledge of classical authors brought back into view, their reports on Egypt; the popes recovered and set up Egyptian obelisks found in Rome; and the Reformation led to a greater emphasis on the Bible in spiritual life, with, in turn, a renewed interest in the lands of the Bible. From various sides came renewed study of the Egyptian hieroglyphs, but with neither proper method nor any success.

Finally at the beginning of the 19th century, the turning-point came in the wake of Napoleon's epic expedition to Egypt. His team of scholars explored, measured, drew the monuments with an industry hitherto unknown. Discovery of the Rosetta Stone (a bilingual decree of Ptolemy V) at last made possible the proper decipherment of the Egyptian hieroglyphs, following initial work by Akerblad and Young, brilliantly achieved by Champollion from 1822. Then at last, with the larger-scale publication of monuments and inscriptions in the vast folios of Champollion, Rosellini and Lepsius, and copies of texts by them and others, the whole outline history and literate civilisation of Ancient Egypt — 3000 years of it — began dramatically to emerge from the dark shadows of forgotten Time, like some stately ship refloated from the depths of the ocean bed. Parallel decipherment of the cuneiform scripts of Mesopotamia and excavation there likewise brought back to life the equally long-lived civilisations of Babylon and Assyria. The Bible and the classics no longer stood in lonely isolation against aeons of dark, 'prehistoric' night, but could be viewed against the breathtaking, richly-tapestried backdrop of millennially-ancient and brilliant civilisations. From the days of Napoleon, 'Egyptianizing' furniture was fashionable in Europe; its nations squabbled over the spoils of pharaonic antiquity (which the inhabitants of 19th-century Egypt blindly cared nothing about), to fill the great museums in Europe and beyond. Then, at last, in a slowly-reawakening modern Egypt, the ancient sites were not simply dug, but (from Mariette onwards) were increasingly supervised by a national Antiquities Service, and dug with greater scientific care from Petrie onwards. So, with a growing number of scholars (in both field and study), Egyptology came modestly to be established as a firmly-based and far-reaching province of historical and humanistic learning in its own right, covering millenia of the prehistory, history, monuments and entire culture of pharaonic civilisation, and therewith (in its long continuity) an almost unique 'laboratory for the study of mankind' in Breasted's words.

Ramesses II up to Today

What part had Ramesses II in all this? In 1817, heir to classical culture and a reader of Diodorus Siculus, the poet Percy Bysse Shelley penned his famous sonnet, 'Ozymandias':

"I met a traveller from an antique land
Who said: 'Two vast and trunkless legs of stone
Stand in the desert. Near them, on the sand,
Half-sunk, a shattered visage lies, whose frown,
And wrinkled lip, and sneer of cold command,
Tell that its sculptor well those passions read
Which yet survive, stamped on these lifeless things,
The hand that mocked them, and the heart that fed:
And on the pedestal these words appear:
'My name is Ozymandias, king of kings;
Look on my works, ye Mighty, and despair!'
Nothing beside remains. Round the decay
Of that colossal wreck, boundless and bare,
The lone and level sands stretch far away."

The Ramesseum colossus that he thus celebrated as symbol of a half-forgotten, fallen tyrant, Shelley never saw. Ramesses might indeed command, but he certainly did not sneer; and 'feet' would fit the case better than 'legs'! That very year, 1817, Belzoni penetrated the Great Temple of Ramesses II at Abu Simbel — entering it for the first time in eleven centuries — only four years after Burckhardt had first found it (1813), buried to the chin in sand, and lost to a wider world since late antiquity. And in the wake of his first brilliant decipherment in 1822 of the hieroglyphically-written names of the Ptolemies and Roman emperors, it was on receiving drawings of reliefs and inscriptions of Ramesses II from Abu Simbel that Champollion was able decisively to confirm that the older hieroglyphs of truly pharaonic Egypt really could be read by the same means — that he had, indeed, reached a true decipherment and the history and lore of the Egyptians was not to be lost forever. A cartouche of Tuthmosis III from elsewhere confirmed the evidence from Ramesses II's texts, and as Griffith remarked, "the variant spellings of the name of Ramesses were particularly instructive at this stage" of Champollion's work, as he moved forward into a full flow of Egyptian decipherement. Thus, one may fairly say that, in the event, Ramesses II and his Abu Simbel temple were a small but vital link in the modern decoding of the Egyptian hieroglyphs, toward the beginnings of Egyptology, and so of our subsequent wide-ranging modern knowledge of ancient Egypt.

With the publication of the great works of Champollion, Rosellini and Lepsius, and especially of such influential works as Sir J.G. Wilkinson's *The Ancient Egyptians*, the great monuments

73. *The 'Ozymandias' colossus' of Ramesses II in the forecourt of the Ramesseum. The wreckage include two vast and trunkless feet of stone and the rubble of the torso and head well behind them.*

and outward triumphs of the Ramesside kings (especially Ramesses II) became familiar to a wider educated public. From the 1850's and 1860's, Ancient Egypt was no longer a vague vision, but a civilisation with readily recognisable forms and characteristics — one of which was the archetypal Pharaoh: builder of huge temples, forested with vast columned halls, whose sculptured walls proclaimed imperial triumphs in Asia and Africa, with serried lines of prisoners bound for Egypt, trophies dedicated by Pharaoh (shown on heroic scale) to Amun of Victorious Thebes. So when in 1869 the opening of the Suez canal was to be celebrated by great pomp under the high patronage of Egypt's ruler the Khedive Ismail, one of the attractions commissioned was an opera from the famed Italian composer Verdi, to be performed in a new Opera House in Cairo — a glittering event delayed until 1871. For the opera, *Aida,* the 'story' was furnished by the French Egyptologist Mariette. His range of inspiration was twofold. The triumphant splendour of the imperial kings such as Ramesses II was echoed in the Grand March and the triumphal parade of Rhadames with his Nubian prisoners. But the rivalry of the kingdoms of Egypt and "Ethiopia" (in fact, Nubia or Kush) was that of a far later era — of Psammetichus II (590 B.C.), seven centuries after Ramesses II.

The splendour of Ramesses II's great monuments and his Epic of the Battle of Qadesh dazzled some early Egyptologists, but not all. Thus, Rosellini virtually hero-worshipped Ramesses II as having, by his conquests, not only "filled Egypt with luxuries that contributed alike to the graces of everyday life and the security of the state" but also that "universal peace even secured to him the love of the vanquished". In sharpest contrast (and equally prejudiced in the opposite direction), Bunsen dismissed Ramesses II as "an unbridled despot, who took advantage of a reign of almost unparalleled length . . . to torment his own subjects and strangers . . . and to employ them as instruments of his passion for war and buildings". The truth, in this case, was certainly in neither extreme. Later last century, that doughty traveller and writer, Miss Amelia B. Edwards, viewed Ramesses II with a kindly but judicial eye: "The interest that one takes in Ramesses II begins at Memphis and goes on increasing all the way up river . . . Other pharaohs but languidly affect the imagination . . . shadows that come and go in the distance. But with the second Ramesses we are on terms of respectful intimacy. We seem to know the man — to feel his presence — to hear his name in the air. His features are as familiar to us as Henry the Eighth or Louis the Fourteenth. His cartouches meet us at every turn. Even to those who do not read the hieroglyphic character, those well-known signs convey, by sheer force of association, the name and style of Ramesses, beloved of Ammon." After surveying his reign (as known a century ago), she summed up: "For the rest, it is safe to conclude that he was neither better nor worse than the general run of Oriental despots . . .".

And in this twentieth century? With the vast strides in our knowledge of the history of pharaonic Egypt in the century since Miss Edwards and the Victorians, the greatness of other epochs in that long pageant of history has become increasingly highlighted by new discoveries and increased understanding. All this process, most dramatically climaxed by the spectacular discovery of the tomb of Tutankhamun in 1922, led to fresh perspectives and new emphases in presenting Egyptian history. In contrast, the more rapidly executed art-works of Ramesside Egypt, the seemingly greater amount of rhetoric (as opposed to 'hard fact') in royal inscriptions, the shallow stereotyping of Ramesses II as the over-advertised hero of Qadesh and meglomaniac builder (especially when decipherment of the Hittite archives revealed their actual gains from Qadesh) — all this, in turn, inevitably pushed the Ramesside period of Egypt's history back from the forefront of attention, 'devaluing' it (and Ramesses II in particular) as being largely 'the beginning of the end' (even if a very long end . . .) of Egyptian civilisation. Decline with scarcely a redeeming feature was taken for granted. On the other hand, outside of Egyptology, Ramesses II has enjoyed varying notoriety as pharaoh of the Hebrew oppression and exodus, depending on the date in vogue for those events. And his treaty with the Hittites is a document admitted to have grown in value — as an additional example of a highly important group of international documents, and as evidence of 'translation-Egyptian', an Egyptian text translated from another language (diplomatic Babylonian).

So matters have largely stood until the present generation. But in the last few decades, the picture has changed, and is changing, on two fronts. In 1952 - 54, the new republican government of Egypt (then styled the UAR) decided to build a new dam near Aswan for the needs of modern Egypt. This led to the entire flooding of Lower Nubia up to the northern borders of the Sudan — with total loss of *all* ancient sites and monuments unless action were taken. So, in the following years (culminating in 1960), a double appeal was made to the world through UNESCO — for international aid to save, excavate and record the monuments of Nubia, and specifically to rescue the two great temples of Ramesses II at Abu Simbel. In the years that followed, down to 1968 when a rebuilt Abu Simbel was unveiled to the world, and until the present, a vast international effort was in fact deployed with remarkable results and a great measure of success, given the time-limits and problems involved. On postage stamps in Egypt and worldwide, in a growing number of illustrated books, and not least at irregular intervals through the current media of press, radio and television, the images of Ramesses II, Queen Nefertari and the Abu Simbel temples have become at least vaguely familiar to a larger number of people in this present world than was ever true before; the fame of Ramesses II has in some form (however vague) travelled "all lands and all foreign countries" to an extent of which he surely never dreamed. In the film world, Cecil B. de Mille's epic of *The Ten Commandments* once more set Ramesses in his intermittent (and very probable) role of 'Pharaoh of the Exodus'. Alongside the Pyramids (and inevitable mummies!), Ramesses II and Abu Simbel are again part of the popular image of Ancient Egypt. And even today, Ramesses II is perhaps the only ruler of antiquity who has had his very own 'comic strip' in today's newspapers, and travelled by jetplane to savour the delights of Paris!

Ramesses II Now

So much for the 'public front'. What of the other aspect, our understanding and evaluation of Ramesses II and his time? In these self-same recent decades, Egyptology has quietly become a more 'intensive' subject of study, with closer analyses than ever before of its raw material (inscriptions and archaeological data alike). Now, *no* period of pharaonic Egypt's long history can be left aside on mere whim; each requires to be thoroughly worked through and understood, so as to contribute its particular part to the whole. In this process, for Ramesses II and the whole Ramesside period (1300 - 1100 B.C.) renewed study has gradually yielded results and holds promise of more; this very book is one modest by-product of that process. The deed and attitudes of a Ramesses II cannot be just crudely measured-off against our own supposed social values, as simply boastful or megalomaniac; they must be compared with what were the norms and ideals in *his* culture, not ours. Only in broad universals that affect mankind generally is more direct judgement likely to be feasible.

But, whatever further work may yield for the epoch of Ramesses II generally, what shall we say of the man himself now, today? Was he, indeed, "Ramesses the Great" as the Victorians had once dubbed him? Or had he any claim to greatness at all? What has he to say today?

As pharaoh of Egypt, there need be little doubt that (following his father) Ramesses consciously and officially sought to fulfil the pharaonic ideal of the right-acting king, defender of Egypt, just intermediary between gods and people, shepherd of the people. As 'defender', in his wars, the young Ramesses II was both over-ambitious and indubitably proud and stubborn. Had he respected his father's agreement with the Hittites and been content to police what he inherited, he would have avoided nearly twenty years of wasted and wasteful conflict. His youthful over-optimism outran his intelligence (military and personal!) at Qadesh, while his determination kept him in the field for years after. But at Qadesh, he demonstrated immense 'cool' and physical courage in the face of acute danger, with rapid reflexes. His bravery at Tunip was of a lower, more foolhardy and boastful order. Then, when at last the Hittites had to consider peace, it is infinitely to the credit of Ramesses II that he was by then realist enough to see the sense of peace between the two great powers, a peace that mantled much of the Ancient Near East for nearly three-quarters of a century, something not yet achieved in our own time . . .

In affairs at home, in the service of the gods, Ramesses II surely (by Egyptian norms) outstripped every other pharaoh there ever was, in terms of buildings; alone, the quantity as opposed

74. *Ramesses the world conqueror? During the UNESCO campaign to save the antiquities of Nubia, the temples of Ramesses II were symbols of what might be lost, and he and they featured on the stamps of many countries.*

to lessening artistic quality would be a modern criticism here. In conduct of more mundane affairs, both he and his father Sethos had the gift of assessing and choosing able and usually honest men for the administration of Egypt and conduct of their works. On several criteria, Egypt appears as a prosperous and relatively happy land during Ramesses II's long reign. If a ruler's 'greatness' be measured by the prosperity, balance and relative contentment of a nation's society, then in that sense Ramesses II was 'great', and not so merely on his role of impetuous warrior or tireless builder. The enthusiasm of the young king and his human feelings for his own workpeople can be seen in his eager appeal and promises to them on his stela of Year 8, in contrast to his cynical and unfeeling attitude to foreign slave-labour, whether south-Libyans press-ganged to build Wady es-Sebua temple in Nubia, or the Hebrews with a higher God labouring in the brickfields of Pi-Ramesse and Pithom. If by no means Egypt's greatest king (Tuthmosis III and some Old Kingdom and Twelfth-Dynasty monarchs have claims here), Ramesses II must still rank overall as one of the leaders; and even now remains in some measure an 'archetypal' pharaoh, symbol of the proud majesty of Egypt through the ages.

Finally, it yet remains to turn the tables. It is all too easy for our 'modern' âge to sit in conceited judgement on an ancient king of far-away and long ago — but what, in turn, would Ramesses II have thought of the atomic age if (by some Wellsian time-machine) he could travel from the thirteenth century B.C. on a brief excursion-trip to the twentieth century A.D.? Initially, perhaps, he would be dazzled by the technology and sciences, wondrous new powers over space and matter, fascinated by undreamt-of medicinal advances and by new means of communication and scholarship. Food, modes of life, and transport likewise — what price a Ramesses let loose on a fast motorway! But before very long, he would see through the material façade and (in quest of Maat) perceive also the reverse of the coin in a world cursed with exactly the same basic human rivalries and failings that he knew in his own world — but with power to inflict holocausts of a barbarity unknown to the thirteenth century B.C. Visible would be the same vicious greed; not the West-Theban racketeer uncovered in his own Year 30, but that of selfish speculators and grasping unions, alike in exploiting and blackmailing their fellow-humans by means totally foreign to Ramesside times. Or a world where 'left' and 'right' no longer represent work-groups, but merely grotesque ideologies whose results in power seem always identical; rulers who are persecuting wolves, not good shepherds. Finally, he would doubtless also see the abiding positive values of love, devotion, regard for right, a certain mutual tolerance on non-essentials, in the ordinary paths of human life as in his own time; and in 'temples' of shape unknown to him, the message that God is love — loyal, caring, not mere lust — and not solely an impersonal concept or norm, — mere Maat.

In a word, the Egypt of Ramesses II is part of the immensely long perspective of human history, now becoming known as never before, and offering a perspective that helps us to put our own time in more measured terms, freer of the wild exaggerations so often current, that easily distort human judgement and obscure the good and lasting values, not a few shared by Ramesses II and his age and culture as well as by our own. Whatever the often picturesque outward variations, and cultural differences, humanity in both space and time remains at heart one.

CHART 1

Outline of Egyptian History

B.C.	
	ARCHAIC PERIOD
	(1st and 2nd Dynasties)
c. 3200-2700:	Union of Egypt under Menes; beginning of line of pharaohs of all Egypt; capital established at Memphis.
	OLD KINGDOM
	(3rd to 6th Dynasties)
c. 2700-2200:	Pyramid Age - Step Pyramid of Djoser, chief minister Imhotep; Great Pyramid of Kheops at Giza; his wise son, Hardjedef; decline with long reign of Pepi II.
	1st INTERMEDIATE PERIOD
	(7th to 10th Dynasties)
c. 2200-2040:	Rapid succession of powerless kings (Dyns. 7-8), replaced by 9th-10th Dyns. from Ninsu. Rebellion by Thebes (11th Dyn).
	MIDDLE KINGDOM
	(11th & 12th Dynasties)
2134-1991:	Theban kings (Dyn.11) reunite Egypt (*c.* 2040) under Mentuhotep II.
1991-1786:	Theban 12th Dynasty rules from Itjet-Tawy near Memphis; conquest of Nubia; prosperity; classical literature.
	2nd INTERMEDIATE PERIOD
	(13th to 17th Dynasties)
1786-1540:	The 13th Dyn. saw decline in royal power (14th, a Delta splinter group). Foreign 'Hyksos' regime took over (Dyn. 16 local; Dyn. 15 overall), restricting 13th to vassal-status in south. Theban 17th Dyn. finally repelled Hyksos to north (*c.* 1560/40).
	NEW KINGDOM (EMPIRE)
	(18th, 19th, 20th Dynasties)
1550-1295:	*Eighteenth Dynasty* - Hyksos expelled. Egyptian Empire in Syria and Nubia; primacy of Amun until Akhenaten.

1550-1525:	Ahmose I	1386-1349:	Amenophis III
1525-1504:	Amenophis I	1356-1340:	Amenophis IV, Akhenaten
1504-1492:	Tuthmosis I		(perhaps 7/8 yrs coregent)
1492-1479:	Tuthmosis II	1342-1340:	Smenkhkare (2/3 yrs *ditto*)
1479-1457:	Queen Hatshepsut	1340-1331:	Tutankhamun
1479-1425:	Tuthmosis III	1331-1327:	Ay
1427-1396:	Amenophis II	1327-1295:	Haremhab (maximum)
1396-1386:	Tuthmosis IV		

1295-1187:   *Nineteenth Dynasty* - Part-renewal of Egyptian Empire, with considerable prosperity and major monuments. Subject of this book.

1295-1294:	Ramesses I	1204-1200:	Amenmesses
1294-1279:	Sethos I	1200-1194:	Sethos II
1279-1213:	RAMESSES II	1194-1188:	Siptah
1213-1204:	Merenptah	1188-1187:	Queen Tewosret

1187-1069: *Twentieth Dynasty* - brief recovery under Ramesses III, then decay.

1187-1185:	Setnakht	1154-1148:	Ramesses IV
1185-1154:	Ramesses III	1148-1069:	Ramesses V to XI

LATE PERIOD

(21st to 30th Dynasties)

- '*3rd Intermediate*' or '*Post-Imperial*' *Period* -

1069-945: The 21st, Tanite, Dynasty; kings in Tanis, high priests of Amun in S.

945-715: Libyan Dynasties - Dyn. 22, Shoshenq I raids Palestine; weaker successors allowed co-rule by Dyn. 23 (818 *ff.*), collapse of unity. A princedom of West at Sais, briefly as Dyn. 24 (ancestor to Dyn. 26).

c. 750-656: Nubian Dyn. 25 - kings of Napata take over Theban area, and from 715 all Egypt; after Assyrian blow in 663, again only Thebes southward.

- *Saite Revival, Persian, and Independence Periods* -

664-525: The 26th Dynasty of Sais restores unity, power and prosperity of Egypt; renewed building.

525-400: Egypt incorporated into Persian Empire ('27th Dyn.').

400-332: Independence movement by last Egyptian pharaohs (Dyns. 28-30), and Persian reconquest (341-332).

GRAECO - ROMAN AGE

332-323: Alexander the Great, 'liberator' of Egypt.

323-30: Dynasty of the Ptolemies at Alexandria, ending with Cleopatra.

30ff.: Roman Empire, then Byzantine period (Coptic Egypt).

A.D. **MEDIEVAL & MODERN**

641 ff: Islamic conquest of Egypt. Arabic and Turkish periods. From 1922, and 1952, considerable, then full independence, of modern Egypt.

Special Note: Not all the dates B.C. are of the same exactitude. Before about 2100 B.C., there is a growing margin of inexactness (up to a century or more) back to 3200 B.C. Dates for the 11th and 12th Dynasties are close to exact, likewise those from 664 B.C. to modern times. In between, for the New Kingdom, the dates for Tuthmosis III and Ramesses II are either those as given, or else 11 years earlier (i.e., 1490-1436 and 1290-1224), with a matching increase on all dates from the death of Tuthmosis II to that of Ramesses IV inclusive, and a few additional years among the latter's successors. If (as possible) Sethos I reigned 19/20 years instead of minimum 15 years used in this book, Haremhab would reign less than 33 years; Akhenaten's co-regency is still controverted. Dates for the first half of the Late Period (1069-656 B.C.) follow Kitchen, *Third Intermediate Period in Egypt*, 1972, and (except at one or two isolated points) probably are about correct within 5 or 10 years at most. The old 'high date' for Ramesses II at 1304-1238 B.C. is now invalidated by new Babylonian dates and by 1069 B.C. for the end of Dyn. 20, with related genealogical evidence.

CHART 2. The Reign of Ramesses II

	HOME AFFAIRS				FOREIGN AFFAIRS				
B.C.	Year	State Events	Civil Appointments	Priestly Appointments	Syria	Hatti	Mesopotamia	Year	B.C.
1279/78	1	Ramesses II, sole pharaoh; Prince Amen-hir khopshef, Heir	Paser 'A', still S. Vizier; Iuny, still Viceroy of Nubia	Nebwenenef, High Priest of Amun; Hori, *ditto* in Thinis		Muwatallis, still Hittite King	Adad-nirari I, still King of Assyria	1	1279/78
1278/77	2	Aswan Stela; Aksha Temple in progress	Nebiot, prob. Treasury-Chief	Mery, still H.Pr., Abydos; Huy, prob. H.Pr. Memphis; Bak, in Heliopolis				2	1278/77
1277/76	3	Well for gold-miners, in Akuyata; Luxor, Forecourt	Urhiya, High Steward (son, Yupa, a youth by Year 5)					3	1277/76
1276/75	4	1st Syrian Campaign			R.II conquers Amurru; stelae, Byblos, & Nahr el Kalb			4	1276/75
1275/74	5	2nd Syrian Campaign (Qadesh)	Ramose, a Scribe of Royal Tomb		R.II, Battle of Qadesh; Benteshina of Amurru replaced by Shapili	Muwatallis takes Upi, changes kings in Amurru	Adad-nirari I subdues Hanigalbat (Hittite ally)	5	1275/74
1275/69	5/10	Two temples begun at Abu Simbel	Heqanakht, Viceroy of Nubia; Asha-hebsed, special emissary	Wennufer son of Mery, H.Pr., Abydos (Yrs. 10/15 ff.)				5/10	1275/69
1274/73	6/7	Libyan raid?			R. II, in Moab & Canaan?			6/7	1274/73
1273/72		[3rd.?] Syrian Campaign (E. & W. Palestine)							1273/72
1272/71	8/9	[4th.?] Syrian Campaign, Yr.8	Yr.9, Endowment, Deir el Medina, by Paser & Ramose		R.II, Galilee & Central Syria (Dapur)	Accession of Mursil III		8/9	1272/71
1271/70		Manshiet es-Sadr Stela (Yrs. 8-9)				(Urhi-Teshub)			1271/70

HOME AFFAIRS

FOREIGN AFFAIRS

B.C.	Year	State Events	Civil Appointments	Priestly Appointments	Syria	Hatti	Mesopotamia	Year	B.C.
1270/69	10	[5th.?] Syrian Campaign	Panehsy, Chief Treasurer (Yr. 10/15 ff)	Minmose son of Hori, H.Pr. in Thinis; Amenemope, Heliopolis	R.II, stela, N. el Kalb again at Dapur			10	1270/69
1268/67	12			Wennufer, f. of Amenem-inet: H. Pr. Amun			Kadashman-Turgu, King in Babylon	12	1268/67
1264/63	16	1st Apis Bull of Reign buried at Memphis	Civil case, W. Thebes, Irynofret vs. Nakhy	Prince Khaemwaset, Sem-priest in Memphis	Benteshina restored as king in Amurru	Hattusil III supplants Urhi-Teshub	Hattusil III allies with Kadashman-Turgu of Babylon	16	1264/63
1263/62	17	[The Exodus ? (now or slightly later)]	Paser's tourism in W. Thebes				Shalmaneser I King in Assyria	17	1263/62
1262/61	18	Urhi-Teshub flees to Egypt. Crisis with Hatti	Civil case, Memphis, Mose, in process		R.II on alert in Syria; Beth-Shan stela	Hattusil III demands Egyptian extradition of Urhi-Teshub	Shalmaneser I liquidates Hanigalbat (Hittite ally)	18	1262/61
1261/60	19/20	Prince Set-hirkhopshef, Heir Irem revolt crushed (Amara W. scenes, c. Yr. 21)		Pahemneter, H.Pr. in Memphis ?		Embarrassment with Assyria		19/20	1261/60
1260/59									
1259/58	21	Hittite Treaty				Treaty with Egypt		21	1259/58
1258/57	22	Queen-Mother Tuya dies						22	1258/57
1256/55	24	Abu Simbel temples inaugurated?	Treasurer Panehsy's report			Minor tensions with		24	1256/55
1255/54	25	Queen Nefertari dies ? Prince Ramesses, Heir; Istnofret, Chief Queen (Bint-Anath, associate)	Paser 'B' Viceroy of Nubia		Egyptian links with Ugarit (R.II vases there)	Egypt; more relaxed later		25	1255/54
1254/53	26	Mnevis Bull, buried	Pramessu, N. Vizier ?	Prince Mery-Atum, H. Pr., Heliopolis				26	1254/53
1253/52	27		Khay, S. Vizier; Suty Treasury Chief	Paser 'A', now H. Pr. of Amun				27	1253/49
1250/49	30	1st Jubilee 2nd Apis Bull buried	Sethy, N. Vizier? W. -Theban finance-scandal			Hattusil III, difficulties with Kadashman-Enlil II of Babylon	(Kadashman-Enlil II, King in Babylon)	30	1250/49
1249/48	31	Earthquake at Ab Simbel ?							

	HOME AFFAIRS				FOREIGN AFFAIRS				
B.C.	Year	State Events	Civil Appointments	Priestly Appointments	Syria	Hatti	Mesopotamia	Year	B.C.
1247/46	33/34	2nd Jubilee Negotiation for Hittite Princess Queen Istnofret dies?				Marriage-negotiations with Egypt		33/34	1247/46
1246/45									1246/45
1246/45	34	1st Hittite Marriage (Maat-Hor-Neferure)	Huy, Viceroy of Nubia (Nashuy, tourism, Saqqara)			Hittite Princess goes to Egypt		34	1246/45
1245/44	35	Blessing of Ptah		Didia, H. Pr., Memphis				35	1245/44
1244/43	36/37	3rd Jubilee	Prince Khaemwaset, archaeology at Giza & Saqqara, Yr. 36			Prince Hishmi-Sharruma (future Tudkhalia IV) visits		36/37	1244/43
1243/42									1243/42
1242/41	38		Setau, Viceroy of Nubia	Paser 'A' dies; Roma Elder as stand-in H.Pr. of Amun		Egypt at this period		38	1242/41
1241/40	39			Bakenkhons, H.Pr. of Amun				39	1241/40
1240/39	40	4th Jubilee	Prehotep Elder, N. Vizier; Qen-hir-khopshef, Tomb-Scribe; Absence-sheet, Deir el Medina		Ini-Teshub I, king of Carchemish about this period	Hattusil III visits Egypt about this time?		40	1240/39
1238/37	42/43	5th Jubilee 3rd Apis Bull buried?		Stela of Wennufer, Abydos Yr. 42				42/43	1238/37
1237/36									
1239/34	40/45	2nd Hittite Marriage, about this time	by Viceroy Setau			2nd Hittite Princess to Egypt		40/45	1239/34
1236/35	44	Raid in Nubia, men to build W. es-Sebua Temple	Thutmose, S. Vizier?				Kudur-Enlil, King in Babylon	44	1236/35
1235/34	45/46	6th Jubilee		Prince Khaemwaset, H. Pr., in Memphis				45/46	1235/34
1234/33									1234/33
1234/33	46	Works, Karnak-E. (Hatiay, s. Yupa)	Yupa, High Steward, Bakenkhons, H.Pr., Theban lawsuit			Tudkhalia IV, King in Hatti, about this time	Tukulti-Ninurta I, King in Assyria	46	1234/33

	HOME AFFAIRS				FOREIGN AFFAIRS				
B.C.	Year	State Events	Civil Appointments	Priestly Appointments	Syria	Hatti	Mesopotamia	Year	B.C.
1233/32	47		Hednakht, tourist, Saqqara					47	1233/32
c. 1231	48/49(?)	7th Jubilee						48/49 (?)	c. 1231
1230/29	50	Prince Khaemwaset, Heir	Neferronpet, S. Vizier. Prehotep Jnr., N. Vizier. Paytenemhab, Ch. Treasurer	Hori s. Wennufer, H.Pr. in Abydos	Sausgamuwa, King in Amurru	Rock-temple, Yazili-kaya		50	1230/29
c. 1228	51/52	8th Jubilee	Yr. 52, Ship's log, Pi-Ramesse-Heliopolis					51/52	c. 1228
1226/25	54	9th Jubilee					Shagarakti-Shuriash, King in Babylon	54	1226/25
1225/24	55	4th Apis Bull buried; Khaemwaset dies; Prince Merenptah, Heir		Vizier Prehotep Jnr., H. Pr., Memphis & Heliopolis				55	1225/24
1223/22 1222/21	57/58	10th Jubilee	Nudjem, High Steward of King	Yrs. 55, 58, works of Nakht-Thuty, Upper Egypt				57/58	1223/22 1222/21
1220/19 1219/18	60/61	11th Jubilee		Anhurmose, H. Pr., Thinis; Neferronpet, in Memphis	Hebrew tribes into Canaan ?			60/61	1220/19 1219/18
1219/18 1218/17	61/62 (?)	12th Jubilee						61/62 (?)	1219/18 1218/17
1217/16 1216/15	63/64 (?)	13th Jubilee						63/64)?	1217/16 1216/15
1215/14 1214/13	65/66	5th Apis buried ? A 14th Jubilee ?		Yuyu, H. Pr., Abydos Roma-roy, of Amun, Hori s. Khaemwaset, in Memphis		Amuwandas III about this time		65/66	1215/14 1214/13
1213	67/1	Death of Ramesses II, Merenptah, new king.						67/1	1213

CHART 3

Ramesses II - A Simplified Family Tree

A. Genealogy

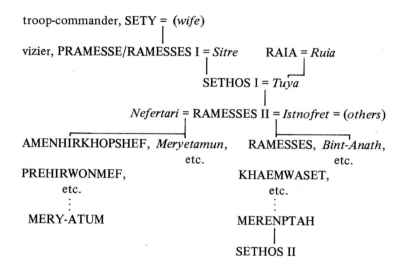

troop-commander, SETY = *(wife)*

vizier, PRAMESSE/RAMESSES I = *Sitre*   RAIA = *Ruia*

SETHOS I = *Tuya*

Nefertari = RAMESSES II = *Istnofret* = *(others)*

AMENHIRKHOPSHEF, *Meryetamun*,   RAMESSES, *Bint-Anath*,
etc.   etc.

PREHIRWONMEF,   KHAEMWASET,
etc.   etc.

MERY-ATUM   MERENPTAH

SETHOS II

Italic = female

B. Known Queens of Ramesses II

1.   Nefertari
2.   Istnofret
3.   Bint-Anath, daughter of Istnofret
4.   Meryetamun, daughter of Nefertari
5.   Nebttawy
6.   Hentmire (king's sister?)
7.   Maat-Hor-Neferure, 1st Hittite Princess
8.   (Name unknown), 2nd Hittite Princess

Special Abbreviations Used in the Notes

ANET   J.B. Pritchard (ed.), *Ancient Near Eastern Texts relating to the Old Testament*,
        Princeton, 1950 & later eds.
BAR   J.H. Breasted, *Ancient Records of Egypt*, 5 vols., Chicago, 1906-07
BIFAO   *Bulletin de l'Institut Français d'Archéologie Orientale*
BiOr   *Bibliotheca Orientalis*
BMMA   *Bulletin of the Metropolitan Museum of Art, New York*
CAH   *Cambridge Ancient History*, Cambridge, 2nd Ed. of Vols. I, II, in fascicles since 1961;
        3rd (bound) Ed., 1970-75
CdE   *Chronique d'Egypte*
END   K.A. Kitchen, *The Egyptian Nineteenth Dynasty* (forthcoming)
E.tr.   English translation(s), i.e. of Egyptian and other ancient texts
GLR   H. Gauthier, *Le Livre des Rois d'Egypte*, Tome III, Cairo, 1914
hgl.   hieroglyphic text or transcript, indicates text-editions in ancient Egyptian
Helck, W. Helck, *Zur Verwaltung des Mittleren und Neuen Reichs*, Leiden, 1958
Verwaltung
JCS   *Journal of Cuneiform Studies*
JEA   *Journal of Egyptian Archaeology*
JNES   *Journal of Near Eastern Studies*
KBo   *Keilschrifftexte aus Boghazkoi*, 27 vols., Berlin, 1923ff. (Copies of Hittite archives in
        original cuneiform script)
KRI   K.A. Kitchen, *Ramesside Inscriptions*, I-VII, Oxford, 1968ff
KUB   *Keilschrifturkunden aus Boghazkoi*, 50 vols., Berlin, 1921ff. (Cuneiform texts, as in
        KBo)
LEM   A.H. Gardiner, *Lqte-Egyptian Miscellanies*, Brussels, 1937; hgl
LEMC   R.A. Caminos, *Late-Egyptian Miscellanies*, Oxford, 1954; E.tr
MDIK   *Mitteilungen der Deutschen Archäologischen Instituts, Kairo Abteilung*
ODM   Ostracon Deir el Medina, published in *OHNL*
OHNL   *Catalogue des Ostraca Non-littéraires de Deir el Médineh*, Cairo, 1935-70, 6 parts by
        J. Černý, 1 part by S. Sauneron
pb   paperback edition
PM   B. Porter & R.L.B. Moss, *Topographical Bibliography of Ancient Egyptian Hieroglyphic
        Texts, Reliefs and Paintings*, I-VII, Oxford, 1927-1951
PM²   The same, with E.W. Burney and J. Málek, 2nd ed., I-III, 1960ff.
RdE   *Revue d'Egyptologie*
repr.   reprinted
Seele, K.C. Seele, *The Coregency of Ramses II with Seti I and the Date of the Great Hypo-
Coregency   style Hall at Karnak*, Chicago, 1940
StBoT   *Studien zu den Bogazkoy-Texten*, Wiesbaden
tr.   translation, translated in
Urk.IV K. Sethe & W. Helck, *Urkunden d. 18. Dynastie (Abt.IV)*, Leipzig & Berlin, 1906-58.
ZAS   *Zeitschrift fur Ägyptische Sprache und Altertumskunde*

NOTES

Where possible, general works are given first, as being of general background interest. Thereafter, abbreviated documentation is given for the ancient and modern sources and scholarly literature used. The special abbreviations used are given with a Key before these *Notes*. As stated in the Preface, it must be emphasised that all scholarly discussion of problems (in contrast to references for facts or views) has been deliberately excluded from this volume, being presented elsewhere (*END*) because of its bulk and unsuitability for inclusion in this volume.

Chapter 1

Geographical Background. General:- Physical background, J. Ball, *Contributions to the Geography of Egypt*, Cairo, 1939 (repr. 1952). Geography and ancient culture, H. Kees, *Ancient Egypt. A Cultural Topography*, London, 1961. Ancient Egyptian geography, including branches of Nile in antiquity, J. Ball, *Egypt in the Classical Geographers*, Cairo, 1942. Geography, monuments and background, J. Baines, J. Málek, *Atlas of Ancient Egypt*, Oxford, 1980.

Special:- Sir A.H. Gardiner, *Ancient Egyptian Onomastica*, I-III, Oxford, 1947 - Nile branches, Vol. II, pp. 153* - 158*, 168*ff. East Delta, see Ch. 6. Vineyards, cf. W. Spiegelberg, *ZAS* 58 (1923), pp. 25-36; W.C. Hayes, *JNES* 10 (1951), pp. 88-90; (cf. M.A. Leahy, *Malkata IV*, Warminster, 1978); and esp. H.W. Fairman in J.D.S. Pendlebury et alii, *The City of Akhenaten, III*, London, 1951, pp. 165ff. Numerous vineyards supplied the Ramesseum, hgl. texts, *KRI*, II/16, pp. 673-696. On Nubia, cf. T. Säve-Söderbergh, *Ägypten und Nubien*, Lund, 1941; W.B. Emery, *Egypt in Nubia*, London, 1965.

History of Egypt. General:- Sir. A.H. Gardiner, *Egypt of the Pharaohs*, Oxford, 1961 (& reprs., incl. pb.); G. Steindorff & K.C. Seele, *When Egypt Ruled the East*, Chicago, 2nd. ed., 1957 (pb., 1963); J.A. Wilson, *The Burden of Egypt*, Chicago, 1951 (pb., *The Culture of Ancient Egypt*, 1956). I.E.S. Edwards, C.J. Gadd, N.G.L. Hammond, E. Sollberger, eds., *The Cambridge Ancient History*, I-II, 3rd. ed., Cambridge, 1973-75, with rich bibliographies. W. Helck, E. Otto, W. Westendorf, eds., *Lexikon der Ägyptologie*, Iff., Wiesbaden, 1975ff., covers all aspects of Ancient Egypt (articles in German, English and French). General outline, J. Ruffle, *The Egyptians*, Oxford, 1977. Changes in Old-Kingdom Egypt, N. Kanawati, *The Egyptian Administration in the Old Kingdom*, Warminster, 1978, and *Governmental Reforms in Old Kingdom Egypt*, Warminster, 1980. Expulsion and rule of Hyksos: J. van Seters, *The Hyksos*, New Haven, 1966; L. Habachi, *The Second Stela of Kamose*, Glückstadt, 1972; C. Vandersleyen, *Les guerres d'Amosis*, Brussels, 1971.

Chapter 2

Later 18th Dynasty. General:- C. Aldred, *Akhenaten*, London, 1968 (& pb); C. Desroches-Noblecourt, *Tutankhamen*, London, 1963 (& pb.); Howard Carter, *The Tomb of Tutankhamen*,

I-III, London, 1923-33, and one-vol. ed., 1972 (& pb.). Amarna-period bibliographies, cf. E.K. Werner, *Newsletter, American Research Center in Egypt*, Nos. 95 (1976), 15-36; 97/98 (1976), 29-40; 101/102 (1977), 41-65; 106 (1978), 41-56; 110 (1979), 24-39; for the very dubious identification of Queen Nefertiti with king Smenkhkare, cf. latterly, J. Samson, *Amarna, City of Akhenaten & Nefertiti (Petrie Collection)*, 2nd ed., Warminster, 1979. Saqqara tomb-chapel of Haremhab before becoming king, cf. G.T. Martin, *JEA* 62 (1976), 5ff.; *JEA* 63 (1977), 13ff.; *JEA* 64 (1978), 5ff.: *JEA* 65 (1979), 13ff. **Special**:- Egypt & Near East, this period, K.A. Kitchen, *Suppiluiuma & the Amarna Pharaohs*, Liverpool, 1962; W. Helck, *Die Beziehungen Ägyptens zu Vorderasien*, Wiesbaden, 1962 (2nd. ed., 1971), Chapter 15. Haremhab, R. Hari, *Horemheb et la Reine Moutnedjemet*, Geneva, 1965; E. Hornung, *Das Grab des Haremhab in Tal der Könige*, Berne, 1971, pp. 11-23. Supposed Year 16 text, D.B. Redford, *Bulletin, American Schools of Oriental Research*, No. 211 (1975), pp. 36ff.); the use and content of cartouche render the genuiness of the text highly dubious, as evidence for Haremhab warring in Syria.

Career of Pramesse, his statues from Karnak - *Urk.IV*, 1958, pp. 2175f. On the Ramesside family, cf. (among others) G.A. Gaballa & K.A. Kitchen, *CdE* 43 (1968), pp. 259ff.; L. Habachi, *RdE* 21 (1969), pp. 39-47; cf. *END*. Ramesses I, monuments, *GLR*, pp. 2-9; on Haremhab's pylon at Karnak, Seele, *Coregency*, pp. 12-22. Sethos with army for Ramesses I, cited from his Abydos Dedication, *KRI*, I/4, p. 111: 10-14 (hgl.), cf. S. Schott, *Der Denkstein Sethos I für die Kapelle Ramses' I in Abydos*, Göttingen, 1964, p. 79, §§ 6, 7. Buhen stela, hgl. in *KRI*, I/1, pp. 2-3; E.tr., *BAR*, III, §§ 74-79. Medamud statue, see A.-P. Zivie, *BIFAO* 72 (1972), pp. 99-114. Tomb (No. 16), of Ramesses I, all refs. in *PM*,[2], 1/2, Oxford, 1964, pp. 534-5.

Sethos I:- Monuments & titles, *GLR*, pp. 10-33. Wars, hgl. texts in *KRI*, I/1, pp. 6-25, lists, I/1 and I/2, pp. 25-37. E.tr. (Karnak scenes), *BAR*, III, §§ 80-156; *ANET*, pp. 254-5. Beth-Shan stelae, *ANET*, pp. 253f., 255. The Tell esh Shihab and Qadesh stelae, refs. in *PM*, VII,pp. 383, 392; hgl., *KRI*, I/1, pp. 17,25. Tyre Stela, hgl., *KRI*, I/4, p. 117, cf. M. Chéhab, *Bulletin du Musée de Beyrouth 22* (1969/71), p. 32, pl. 8:3. Karnak, scenes of Great Hall, refs in *PM*[2], II, pp. 41ff.; war-scenes, W. Wreszinski, *Atlas zur altägyptischen Kulturgeschichte*, II, pls. 34-53. Year 6 Silsila stela, hgl., *KRI*, I/2, pp. 59-61; E.tr., *BAR*, III, §§ 205-8. Buildings of Sethos I:- Abydos, great temple, A.M. Calverley & M.F. Broome, *The Temple of King Sethos I at Abydos*, I-IV, London, 1933ff., in progress; older refs., *PM*, VI, pp. 1-27; hgl., dedications, *KRI*, I/5-6, pp. 129-195. Convenient survey of the temple and its cult, see A.R. David, *A Guide to Religious Ritual at Abydos*, Warminster, 1981. Osireion, *PM*, VI, pp. 29-31; chapel for Ramesses I, *ibid.*, pp. 31-33.

Chapter 3

Crowning of Prince-Regent, in great Abydos Dedication-text; hgl., *KRI*, II/6, pp. 327:15 − 328:6; E.tr., *BAR*, III, § 267. For the use of full royal titles (incl. cartouche *Usimare*) by prince Ramesses II during the reign of Sethos I, see Seele, *Coregency*, pp. 23-49; the views of J.D. Schmidt *Ramesses II*, Baltimore, 1973, pp. 154ff., are vitiated by his misreading of the evidence both of Seele's views and in the original texts (cf. Kitchen, *JEA* 61 (1975) 265-270). Breasted's views on the early career of Prince Ramesses (*ZÄS* 37 (1899) , pp. 130-9; *BAR*, III, §§ 123-131) are pure fiction, as is already clear from Seele's treatment; cf. *END*, and provisionally, W.J. Murnane, *Ancient Egyptian Coregencies*, Chicago, 1977, pp. 60-61.

Court of Sethos I. Tia, Tjia, etc., and Queen Tuya, see Ch. 6. Hori-Min, reward-scene, Louvre C. 213 - S. Gabra, *Les Conseils de Fonctionnaires dans l'Egypte pharaonique,* Cairo, 1929, pp. 41ff., pl. II. For the remarkable family of Amen-em-inet (Naples monument, hgl., Brugsch, *Thesaurus*, pp. 951-7), cf. G.A. Reisner, *JEA* 6 (1920), pp. 45-46, and his career, J. Lipińska, *ZÄS* 96 (1969), pp. 28-30, and in *Etudes et Travaux* (Warsaw), III, 1969, pp. 42-49; more fully, *END*. Bakenkhons, see Ch. 8. For Asha-hebsed in Sinai, texts, hgl., *KRI*, I/2, pp. 62-63, Nos. 247/8, 250 (cited here); E.tr., Gardiner, Peet, Černý, *Inscriptions of Sinai*, II, London, 1955, pp. 176-7. On foreigners with 'loyalist' names, cf. Helck, *Verwaltung*, pp. 272-6. On the meaning of Urhin Hurrian, cf. Gelb, Purves, Macrae, *Nuzi Personal Names*, Chicago, 1943, p. 273a. For Urhiya and Yupa, cf. Helck, *Verwaltung*, pp. 376-7, 490-1, Nos. 28-29, plus Ruffle & Kitchen, in *Glimpses of Ancient Egypt*, 1979, pp. 55-74, and in *END*.

War of Sethos I in Irem. Synoptic texts of two stelae, hgl., *KRI*, I/4, pp. 102-4; study of Sai stela, J. Vercoutter, *RdE* 24 (1972), pp. 201-8; of the Irem war and its geography, Kitchen, in *Ägypten und Kusch*, Berlin, 1975, pp. 214-8. Wells in Edfu desert, etc., for gold-miners, Kanais temple-inscriptions of Year 9, hgl., *KRI*, I/3, pp. 65-70; E.tr., *BAR*, III, §§162-198, cf. Gunn and Gardiner, *JEA* 4 (1917), pp. 241ff., esp. 244ff.; and edition, S. Schott, *Kanais, Der Tempel Sethos' I im Wadi Mia*, Gottingen, 1961. Aswan stelae, hgl., *KRI*, I/3, pp. 73-74, cf. L. Habachi, *BIFAO* 73 (1973), pp. 1-13.

Paser, chamberlain and S. vizier. Text cited for his promotion, hgl., *KRI*, I,299; other refs., *PM²*, I/1, pp. 222-3, pillar B(a). Monuments of Paser, Helck, *Verwaltung*, pp. 311-315, 447-451, No. 24, cf. Černý, *BiOr* 19 (1962), p. 142; Paser's inscriptions are included in *KRI*, I, pp. 285-301; II, p. 341:14; III, pp. 1-36. For revised date of Nebneteru (Sethos I, not Ramesses II), see *END*, and Kitchen, *Acts, 1st International Congress of Egyptology, Cairo, 1976*, Berlin, 1979, p. 386.

Abydos, gold statue, hgl. *KRI*, II/6, p. 328: 7-8; E.tr., *BAR*, III, § 268 (with misleading fnn.). Temple of Ramesses II, Abydos, *PM*, VI, pp. 33-41. For its early date, cf. Seele, *Coregency*, pp. 45-47. Qurneh temple of Sethos I, refs., *PM²*, II, pp. 407-421; Seele, *Coregency*, pp. 40-45, on dating. Tomb (No. 17) of Sethos I, *PM²*, I/2, pp. 535ff. Deir el Medina Chief Workmen, Baki and Neferhotep and colleagues, cf. J. Černý, *A Community of Workmen at Thebes in the Ramesside Period*, Cairo, 1973, esp. pp. 285ff., 291f. Paser's craftsmen, refs., *PM²*, I/1, p. 221 (6). Family of Dedia, hgl., *KRI*, I, 327-331, cf. D.A. Lowle, *Oriens Antiquus* 15 (1976), 91 ff. Ramesses' family, see Ch.6.

Minor wars. Lower Nubia, temple of Beit el Wali; *PM*, VII, pp. 21-27, to which add Ricke, Hughes, Wente, *The Beit el-Wali Temple of Ramesses II*, Chicago, 1967. Viceroy Iuny under Sethos I, refs., Reisner, *JEA* 6 (1920), 39, and hgl., *KRI*, I, pp. 303-4. Sherden pirates, cf. stelae Tanis II, 11.13ff. (*KRI*, II/6, p.290; Yoyotte, *Kemi* 10 (1949) pp. 66-69) and Aswan, Year 2, 1.8 (hgl., *KRI*, II/6, p. 345). Total reign of Sethos I, minimally 15 years (possibly 19) cf. M. L. Bierbrier, *JEA* 58 (1972), p. 303 & n.5: and *END*.

Chapter 4

Accession-day of Ramesses II, cf. W. Helck, in *Studia Biblica et Orentalia, III: Oriens Antiquus*, Rome, 1959, pp. 118-120; R. Krauss, *Das Ende der Amarnazeit*, Hildesheim, 1979 (& rpr.), 257-9. Titles and monuments, *GLR*, pp. 33-113; annotated list of year-dates, convenient but not wholly reliable, J.D. Schmidt, *Ramesses II*, Baltimore, 1973. Aksha temple, *PM*, VII, p. 127, and J. Vercoutter, *Kush* 10 (1962), pp. 109ff., *Kush* 11 (1963), pp. 131ff., and A. Rosenvasser, *Kush* 12 (1964), pp. 96ff. Amara West temple and town, *PM*, VII, pp. 157-164, refs., plus oral information courtesy H. W. Fairman. The Ramesseum, *PM²*, II, pp. 431-443; Luxor temple, forecourt, *ibid.*, pp. 302-12.

Acts of Ramesses II, Abydos, great Inscription, hgl., *KRI*, II/6, pp. 325/6, 327, 331, etc.; E. tr., *BAR*, III, §§ 261ff., *passim*. Appointment of Nebwenenef, text, tr., Sethe, *ZÄS* 44 (1901), pp. 30-35, *KRI*, III, 282-5; Tomb 157, *PM²*, I/1, pp. 266-8, esp. 267(8); to be fully published by Philadelphia.

Year 3 text, Luxor, hgl., *KRI*, II/6, pp. 345-7, and Ch. Kuentz, *La Face Sud du Massif Est du Pylone de Ramses II à Louxor*, Cairo, 1971; also, D.B. Redford, *JEA* 57 (1971), pp. 110-119, and M. Abdel-Razik, *JEA* 60 (1974), pp. 142-145, and in *JEA* 61 (1975), 125-136. Year 3, Quban and Aksha stelae on wells for gold-mining in Akuyati, hgl., *KRI*, II/7, pp. 353-360; E.tr., *BAR* , III, §§ 282-293; other refs., *PM*, VII, p. 83.

War in Syria. First Campaign, Year 4, see *END* for detail. Middle stela, Nahr el Kalb, *PM*, VII, 385; hgl., *KRI*, II/1, p.1. Byblos stela, *PM*, VII, p. 389; hgl., *KRI*, II/4, p. 224. Tyre stela, Chéhab, *Bulletin du Musee de Beyrouth* 22 (1969/71), p. 33, pl. 8:4; KRI, II/7, p. 401: Irqata, cf. *JEA* 50 (1964), p. 68, n.8; *KRI*, II/4, p. 213. Benteshina abandons Hittite suzerainty, cf. C. Kuhne & H. Otten, *Der Sausgamuwa-Vertrag*, Wiesbaden, 1971, p.9. Muwatallis used Dattassas as his capital, rather than Hattusas, but is unlikely to have abandoned the traditional capital entirely. For the vow of Muwatallis, *KBo* IX, 96, cf. H. Klengel, *Geschichte Syriens*, II, Berlin, 1969, p. 213.

Battle of Qadesh, Second Campaign, Year 5. Hgl. sources:- Editions of monumental texts, Ch. Kuentz, *La Bataille de Qadech*, Cairo, 1928-34, and S. Hassan, *Le Poeme dit de Pentaour . . . Qadesh*, Cairo, 1929; total synoptic edition, all texts (& new fragments), *KRI*, II/1-3, pp. 2-147. E trs., *BAR*, III, §§ 306ff., Erman/Blackman, *Literature of the Ancient Egyptians*, London, 1927 (& repr.), pp. 261ff., J.A. Wilson, *American Journal of Semitic Languages & Literatures* 43 (1927), pp. 266ff., R.O. Faulkner, *Mitteilungen, Deutschen Archäol. Inst., Kairo*, 16 (1958), pp. 93ff., and most conveniently, Sir A.H. Gardiner, *The Kadesh Inscriptions of Ramesses II*, Oxford, 1960. Pioneer study of the battle, of great value, is J.H.Breasted, *The Battle of Kadesh*, Chicago, 1903; cf. also A.H. Burne, *JEA* 7 (1921), pp. 191-5, and studies cited, *JEA* 50 (1964), p. 68, n.3; A.R. Schulman, *Journal SSEA* 11 (1981), 7-19 with references; *END*. Consequences of Qadesh. Benteshina dethroned in favour of Shapili, Kuhne & Otten, *loc. cit.* (see under Year 4, above). Hittites occupy Upi, cf. E. Edel, *Zeitschrift für Assyriologie* 49 (1950), p. 212. Letter, *KUB* XXIII, 102, from Muwatallis to Adad-nirari I (sometimes attributed to later kings), cf. E. Forrer, *Reallexikon der Assyriologie*, I, p. 262f., E. Weidner, *Die Inschriften Tukulti-Ninurtas I . . .* , Graz, 1959, p. 67, and M.B. Rowton, *JCS* 13 (1959), p. 10.

On special nature of Qadesh reliefs and inscriptions as a word-and-picture composition, cf. Gardiner, *Kadesh Inscriptions*, pp. 46-54. For artistic significance, G.A. Gaballa, *Narrative in Egyptian Art*, Mainz, 1976.

Abu Simbel, the two temples, refs., *PM*, VII, pp. 95-119; lesser (Nefertari) temple, now C. Desroches-Noblecourt & Ch. Kuentz, *Le Petit Temple d'Abou Simbel*, 2 vols., Cairo, 1968. Stela of Iuny is exactly aligned with this latter temple, as noted also by *op.cit.*, pp. 119-120. Iuny's stela, *PM*, VII, p.117f., (10); *KRI*, III/3, p. 68. Asha-hebsed's stela, *PM*, VII, p. 117, (9); *KRI*, III/7, pp. 203-4.

Moabite campaign, hgl., *KRI*, II/3, pp. 179-181, cf. Kitchen, *JEA* 50 (1964), pp. 47-70; also, *END*. Year 8, reliefs at Ramesseum; hgl., *KRI*, II/3, pp. 148-9. Year 10, Nahr el Kalb stela, *PM*, VII, p. 385; hgl., *KRI*, II/3, p. 149. Ramesses' bravado on his return to Dapur and Tunip, hgl., *KRI*, II/3, pp. 174-5; cf. Sethe, *ZAS* 44 (1907), pp. 36ff. Various undated scenes of the Syrian wars of Ramesses II occur in the temples of Karnak, Luxor, etc.; hgl. texts, *KRI*, II/3, pp. 152-192; II/4, pp. 195ff. Cf. refs. in *PM²*, II, and VII. In general, cf. W. Helck, *Die Beziehungen Ägyptens zu Vorderasien*, 1962 (& 1971), and *END*.

The Exodus. For foreigners in New Kingdom Egypt, cf. Helck, *op. cit.*, and references and examples, Kitchen, in J.D. Douglas et al., *New Bible Dictionary*, London, 1962, pp. 343-4, 844-5, 846. Main and best surveys of the Apiru/Habiru question remain J. Bottero (ed.), *Le Problème des Habiru*, Paris, 1954, and M. Greenberg, *The Hab/piru*, New Haven, 1955. The citation of Apiru dragging stone is from Papyrus Leiden I, 348, *verso* 6, 6-7; hgl., *LEM*, p. 134; E.tr., *LEMC*, p. 491; they were under Amen-em-inet. For date of the Exodus, its general background, etc., see Kitchen, *Ancient Orient & Old Testament*, London, 1966, pp. 57ff., 156f., where use is made of all the main Near-Eastern evidence; cf. also, Kitchen, *Bible in its World*, Exeter, 1977, pp. 75-79. 146.

Libya. Forts of Ramesses II, *PM*, VII, pp. 368-9, and L. Habachi in A. Papadopoulo (ed.), *Les Grandes Découvertes Archeologiques de 1954*, Cairo, 1955, pp. 62-65; W. Delta sites, see *PM*, IV. 'Strategy', see *END*. The new Irem conflict, cf. for Amara West, H.W. Fairman, *JEA* 34 (1948), p. 8, pl. 6; *KRI*, II/4, p. 221-2; Abydos data, hgl., *KRI*, II/3-4, pp. 192-193; and Kitchen, *Agypten und Kusch*, 1977, pp. 220-1.

Chapter 5

Reign of Urhi-Teshub and accession of Hattusil III, see 'Apologia of Hattusil', A. Götze, *Hattusilis*, Leipzig, 1925 (& repr.), Götze, *Neue Bruchstücke zum grossen Text des Hattusilis . . .* , Leipzig, 1930 (& repr.), and E.H. Sturtevant & G. Bechtel, *A Hittite Chrestomathy*, Philadelphia, 1935, pp. 85ff. Date of Hattusil's accession, about Year 16 of Ramesses II, cf. M.B. Rowton, *JNES* 19 (1960), pp. 16-18, and *JNES* 25 (1966), pp. 244-5. On the relations of Hatti and Babylon, reflected in the letter *KBo* I, 10, cf. Rowton, *JNES* 25 (1966), pp. 244-249, with refs. For Urhi-Teshub in Egypt, cf. Helck, *JCS* 17 (1963), pp. 87-97. Beth-Shan stela of Ramesses II, hgl. in *KRI*, II/3, pp. 150-151; E.tr., J. Černý, *Eretz-Israel* 5 (1958), pp. 75* - 82*. Fall of Hanigalbat cf. D.D. Luckenbill, *Ancient Records of Assyria*, I, Chicago, 1926, pp. 39-40; Ebeling, Meissner, Weidner, *Die Inschriften der altassyrischen Könige*, Leipzig, 1926, pp. 116/7ff; A.K. Grayson, *Assyrian Royal Inscriptions, I*, Wiesbaden, 1972, p. 82, § 530.

Peace between Egypt and Hatti. Journey-time, a month, cf. E. Edel, *Geschichte und Altes Testament*, Tübingen, 1953, p. 54 (where chariot-transport, not march on foot, should be understood). The Egypto-Hittite Treaty, hgl. ed., *KRI*, II/5, pp. 225-232; cuneiform edited, E.F. Weidner, *Politische Dokumente aus Kleinasien*, Leipzig, 1923 (& repr.), pp. 112-123; E.trs., S. Langdon & A.H. Gardiner, *JEA* 6 (1920), pp. 179ff.; J.A. Wilson, A. Goetze, in *ANET*, pp. 199-203; Eg. only in E.tr., *BAR*, III, §§ 367-391; Schmidt, *Ramesses II*, 1973, pp. 111ff. Comments, cf. Schulman, *Journal SSEA* 8 (1978), 112-130. For Hittite state seals, cf. (e.g.) C.F.A. Schaeffer, E. Laroche, et al., *Ugaritica* III, Paris, 1956. On 'twin-correspondence' by Hattusil III and Queen Pudukhepa, see Edel, *Indogermanischen Forchungen* 60 (1949), pp. 72-85. Congratulatory letters by Nefertari, Tuya, Set-hir-khopshef, refs. in E. Laroche, *Catalogue des Texts Hittites*, Paris, 1971, p. 23, Nos. 167-9. For Nefertari (*KBo* I, 29 and IX, 43), cf. J.Friedrich, *Der Alte Orient* 24 (1925), p. 23; also, *JCS* 14 (1960), p. 115. Letter of Paser with the others, see E. Edel, *Der Brief des ägyptischen Wesirs Pasijara an den Hethiterkönig Hattusili und verwandte Keilschriftbriefe*, Göttingen, 1978. On Queen Puduhepa, see H. Otten, *Puduhepa*, Mainz, 1975. Trace of Egyptian presence - vases of Ramesses II — at Ugarit, cf. C. Desroches-Noblecourt in Schaeffer, *Ugaritica III*,Paris, 1956, pp. 164, 167, fig. 121. Tensions: King of Mira, refs, in Laroche, *Catalogue . . .* , p. 23, No. 166. For letter (NBC 3934) of Ramesses II reassuring Hattusil, see Goetze, *JCS* 1 (1947), pp. 241-251. Hatti and Babylon, Rowton, *JNES* 19 (1960), p. 17.

Royal Wedding. For the sequence of correspondence, see Edel, *Geschichte und Altes Testament*, 1953, pp. 52-54 (also, *Jahrbuch für Kleinasiatische Forschung* 2 (1953), pp. 262-273), plus Kitchen, *END*. For Queen Pudukhepa's reproaches to Ramesses II at unseemly greed over the dowry, see *KUB* XXI, 38, and version in Helck, *JCS* 17 (1963), pp. 87ff. For the princess's route to Egypt, cf. *KBo* I, 22; B. Meissner, *Zeitschrift der Deutschen Morgenländische Gesellschaft* 72 (1918), p. 62, Edel, *Zeitschrift für Assyriologie* 49 (1950), pp. 206-8. Stelae (in Egypt) of 1st Hittite marriage, main version, hgl., *KRI*, II/5, pp. 233-256; E.tr., *BAR*, III, §§415-424, and *ANET*, pp. 256-8; Kuentz, *ASAE* 25 (1925), pp. 181-238. Lesser version for Mut, hgl., *KRI*, II/5, pp. 256-257; edited, Lefebvre, *ASAE* 25 (1925), pp. 34-35. Name of new queen, cf. C. Desroches-Noblecourt, *Kemi* 12 (1952), pp. 34-45. Text of Blessing of Ptah, hgl., *KRI*, II/5, pp. 258-281; *BAR*, III, §§ 394-414, and (on R.III version), Edgerton & Wilson, *Historical Records of Ramses III*, Chicago, 1936, pp. 119-129.

Royal Visits. Prince Hishmi-Sharruma, *KUB* III, 34 - cf. citation, Edel, *Geschichte und Altes Testament*, 1953, pp. 54-55. Yazili-kaya and Tudkhalia IV, cf. latterly, H. Otten, *Zeitschrift für Assyriologie* 58 (1967), pp. 222-240. Documentation on Hattusil III's visit to Egypt, see Edel, *Mitteilungen, Deutschen Orient-Gesellschaft* 92 (1960), pp. 15-20; 'hot-feet', p. 20. Pudukhepa's dream and vow, cf. A.L. Oppenheim, *The Interpretation of Dreams in the Ancient Near East*, Philadelphia, 1956, p. 255, No. 32. Letter of Hattusil III, en route to Egypt, Edel, *op. cit.*, pp. 16-18. Egyptian allusions, *LEM*, pp. 12-13, *LEMC*, pp. 37-8; *KRI*, II/5, p. 233 (& *JEA* 33 (1947), p. 94).

Second Hittite marriage. For doctors, cf. refs. (e.g.) in Goetze, *JCS* 1 (1947), pp. 241-251, *passim*; new data on Hittite requests for medical aid for royal ladies has been presented by Professor Edel; see E. Edel, *Ägyptische Ärzte und ägyptische Medizin am hethitischen Königshöf*, Opladen, 1976. For the 'late' Hittite correspondence of Ramesses II, see *END*, and Edel, *op.cit.*, 18-20. Kurunta letter, *KUB* III, 67; cf. *JCS* 1, p. 248. Other doctors' visits, cf. Edel, *JNES* 7 (1948), p. 15. Second Hittite marriage, two stelae, Koptos and Abydos; hgl., *KRI*, II/5, pp. 282-4; E. tr., Kitchen and Gaballa, *ZAS* 96 (1969), pp. 14-17. Later echoes, see under Ch. 12.

Chapter 6

Royal Family. Queen-mother Tuya:- Monuments (all dating to reign of Ramesses II), cf. *GLR*, pp. 29-30, 74-75; hgl., *KRI*, II/21, pp. 844-7; temple on N. of Ramesseum, cf. refs., *PM²*, II, p. 442 ('double temple'), *KRI*, II/15, pp. 664-7; see further, L. Habachi, *RdE* 21 (1969), pp. 27ff.; Edel, *Studien zur Altägyptischen Kultur* 1(1974), pp. 105 ff. Her tomb and burial, cf. C.

Desroches-Noblecourt, *Le Courrier du CNRS* 9 (July, 1973), pp. 36, 38. Tuya's parents, cf. Gaballa and Kitchen, *CdE* 43 (1968), pp. 261-2; Habachi, *RdE* 21 (1969), pp. 39-40. Ramesses' sister Tjia, her husband Tia, his father Amen-wah-su, see Habachi, *op.cit.*, pp. 41-47, and pl. 3. Hentmire, *GLR*, pp. 33, 79, refs. 'Divine Birth of Pharaoh', treated by H. Brunner, *Die Geburt des Gottkönigs,* Wiesbaden, 1964; on the blocks of Ramesses II, cf. Gaballa, *Orientalia* 36 (1967), pp. 299-304; Habachi, *op.cit.*, pp. 33ff. (hgl., *KRI*, II/15, pp. 665-7). Tomb-chapel of Tjia and Tia, now found at Saqqara.

    Monuments of Queen Nefertari, *GLR*, pp. 75-77, her tomb, H. Goedicke and G. Thausing, *Nofretari*, Graz, 1971. Gold bead of Queen Istnofret, mentioned, *BMMA, NS*, 29 (Oct. 1970), p. 75. Inscriptions cited from Nefertari's temple, Abu Simbel, cf. Kuentz and Desroches-Noblecourt, *Le Petit Temple d'Abou Simbel*, I, Cairo, 1968, pp. 12-16. Bint-Anath as a queen inside Abu Simbel (Great Temple), cf. Champollion, *Notices Descriptives*, I, p. 68. The role of the sun at Abu Simbel has intrigued visitors and scholars for at least a century, from Miss Edwards (*A Thousand Miles Up the Nile*, London, 1877, pp. 443-4; 1891, pp. 303-4) to the present; cf. (e.g.) L.-A. Christophe, *Revue du Caire*, No. 255/Vol. 47 (1961), pp. 316-332, or his *Abou-Simbel*, Brussels, 1965, pp. 200-203, and J.K. van der Haagen, *UNESCO Courier* 15/No. 10 (Oct. 1962), pp. 10-15; cf. G. Gelinsky, *Göttinger Miszellen* 9 (1974), pp. 19-24. However, I see no evidence that Abu Simbel was a jubilee-temple; Ashahebsed's text (Ch.4, above) indicates a memorial-temple — in this case linking the cults of Ramesses and Re, and secondarily with Amun. For stela of Heqanakht, Ramesses, Nefertari and Meryetamun, cf. refs., *PM*, VII, p. 118, (17); hgl., *KRI*, III/3, p. 71.

    Monuments of Queen Istnofret, cf. *GLR*, pp. 77-78 (omitting item 3). Aswan stela, Lepsius, *Denkmaler aus Aegypten und Aethiopen*, III, pl. 175*h*, Silsila stela, *ibid.*, pl.174*e*, but date (Years 30-34 - jubilee announced by Khaemwaset) clearer from Centre de Documentation photo, as utilized by F.Gomaà, *Chaemwese, Sohn Ramses'II*, Wiesbaden, 1973, p. 129, fig. 29, No. 76. Tomb of Istnofret mentioned, cf. Černý, *Community of Workmen at Thebes*, p.82, nn. 3,4. All queens, hgl., *KRI*, II/21, pp. 844-857.

    Sons and daughters of Ramesses II (approximately ninety!), mainly listed by *GLR*, pp.80-101 (sons), 102-113 (daughters, Bint-Anath the first). For Mery-Atum as Eldest King's Son by Nefertari, cf. Brussels statue E.2459 (*CdE* 17 (1942), p. 75, fig. 3); see *END* for its interpretation. Set-hir-khopshef: cf. H. Ranke, *ZÄS* 58(1923), pp. 135-7, and J. Yoyotte, *BiOr* 26 (1969), pp. 14, 15, who would both identify him with Amen-hir-khopshef; but see *END*. Princes and princesses, lists, hgl., *KRI*, II/21-23, pp. 858 ff., 916ff.

    Prince Khaemwaset, cf. *GLR*, pp. 84-90, and a monograph, F. Gomaà, *Chaemwese, Sohn Ramses'II und Hoherpriester von Memphis*, Wiesbaden, 1973, with full discussion and list of monuments. For the cult and burials of Apis (besides Mariette's original works, cf. *PM*, III, p. 206f.), cf. E. Otto, *Beiträge zur Geschichte der Stierkulte in Aegypten*, Leipzig, 1938; pp. 11-34; J. Vercoutter, *Textes biographiques du Sérapéum de Memphis*, Paris, 1962; Malinine, Posener, Vercoutter, *Catalogue des Stèles du Sérapéum de Memphis*, I, Paris, 1968 (2 vols,), esp. Nos. 5-17. Apis-Temple inscription, hgl., *KRI*, II/22, pp. 878-879; new German translation, now Gomaà, *Chaemwese*, p.44, cf. 110-111, fig. 10-11. Egyptologist-Prince, see now Gomaà, *op.cit.*, pp. 61-69, and refs.; he publishes a statue of Prince Ka-wab, eldest son of Kheops (builder of the Great Pyramid), which resulted from Khaemwaset's 'excavations' at Giza, and which he labelled accordingly (! - erecting it in Memphis temple); hgl., *KRI*, II/22, pp. 872-873. Graffito of Year 36, cf.

D. Wildung, *Die Rolle ägyptischer Könige im Bewusstsein ihrer Nachwelt*, I, Berlin, 1969, pp. 68 (XVI, 70h), 71f. The Prince as Administrator and Family man: Year 52, log, J.J. Janssen, *Two Ancient Egyptian Ships' Logs*, Leiden, 1958, esp. p. 39; *KRI*, II/20, pp. 806-815, esp. 811. Scribe Huy, Papyrus Leiden I, 366 (*KRI*, II/23, pp. 910-911), and Sunero, Pap. Leiden, I, 368 - hgl., A. M. Bakir, *Egyptian Epistolography*, Cairo, 1970, pls. 14-15, 16-17 (and *KRI*, II/22, pp. 894-5), also (with E.trs,) J.J. Janssen, *Oudheidkundige Mededelingen (Leiden)* 41 (1960), pp. 37-8, 39, 44, 45-6. Family, cf. H. De Meulenaere, *Annuaire de l'Institut de Philologie et d'Histoire Orient-ales et Slaves* 20 (1973), pp. 191-6. Jubilees, see Ch.8. Tomb and burial of Khaemwaset, cf. S. Wenig, *Forschungen und Berichte* 14 (1972), pp. 39-44; and Gomaà, *op.cit.*, pp. 48-54, who considers the Serapeum burial of Khaemwaset to be a late reburial, after removal of his ruined tomb nearby in Late-Period alterations.

Princess-Queens. Bint-Anath's daughter, cf. C. Desroches-Noblecourt, *Le Courrier du CNRS* 9 (July 1973), p. 36c; hgl., *KRI*, II/23, p. 923. Hittite queen in Egypt, refs., *GLR*, pp. 78-79. Harims - at Mi-wer, cf. Gardiner, *JNES* 12 (1953), pp. 145-9; S. Sauneron & J. Yoyotte, *RdE* 7 (1950), pp. 67-70; hgl., Gardiner, *Ramesside Administrative Documents*, Oxford, 1948, pp. 20-26 (the cloth-account, p. 23; jewels, p. 21; cf. Gardiner, *Anc. Eg. Onomastica*, II, Oxford, 1947, pp. 222*f.). Nebttawy, on tomb, cf. M. Dewachter, *Archeologia* 53 (Dec. 1972), pp. 18-24. Princess Istnofret II, estates, cf. J.J. Janssen, *Two Ancient Egyptian Ships' Logs*, pp. 20ff., 43f.; letter to her, Pap. Leiden I, 362, hgl., Bakir, *Eg. Epistolography*, 1970, pls. 10-11, and (with E.tr.) Janssen, *Oudheidkundige Mededelingen* (Leiden) 41 (1960), pp. 35-6, (*KRI*, II/23, pp. 926-7).

Younger sons. Mery-Atum, as high priest in Heliopolis, cf. M. I. Moursi, *Die Hohenpriester des Sonnengottes...*, Berlin, 1972, pp. 64-67. Mnevis-bull, Year 26, see stela, M. El-Alfi, *JEA* 58 (1972), pp. 176-8; *KRI*, II/7, 363. For Prince Si-Montu, Ostracon Louvre 2262, W. Spiegelberg, *Recueil de Travaux* 16 (1894), p. 64; *KRI*, II/23, p. 907. Prince Maat-Ptah, Pap. Leiden I, 367: hgl., Bakir, *Eg. Epistolography*, 1970, pls. 15-16 (*KRI*, II/23, pp. 911-912), and (with E.tr.) Janssen. *Oudheidkundige Mededelingen...* 41 (1960), pp. 38-9, 44-5. Coffins of Prince Neb-weben, published (with mistaken interpretations) in Brunton & Engelbach, *Gurob*, London, 1927, pp. 19-25, pls. front. & 32, and by Brunton, *ASAE* 43 (1943), pp. 135-148, pls. 7-11; *KRI*, II/23, pp. 912-914; see *END*. Prince Merenptah, *GLR*, pp. 94-96; *KRI*, II/23, pp. 902-5; career, cf. Christophe, *ASAE* 51 (1951), pp. 335-351.

Three cities. Memphis:- Remains, *PM*, III, pp. 217-227, plus R. Anthes et al., *Mitrahineh* 1955, 1956, Philadelphia, 1959, 1965 (2 vols,); M.T.Dimick, *Memphis,* Philadelphia, 1956 (popular outline). Temples, Helck, *Materialien zur Wirschaftsgeschichte des Neuen Reiches*, I, Wiesbaden, 1961, pp. 130-144, cf. Petrie, *Memphis I*, 1908, pp. 1ff., and statute of Amenhotep, Gardiner in Petrie, *Memphis V*, 1913, pp. 33-6, pls. 79-80. Role of Memphis, A. Badawy, *Memphis als zweite Landeshauptstadt im Neuen Reich*, Cairo, 1948. West Hall, its form, cf. G. Haeny, *Basilikale Anlagen in der Ägyptischen Baukunst des Neuen Reiches,* Wiesbaden, 1970, pp. 68-70; jubilee-function, cf. *END*. Arsenal, S. Sauneron, *BIFAO* 54 (1954), pp. 7-12. Holdiay in Memphis, Pap. Sallier IV, hgl., *LEM*, pp. 88-92, E.tr., *LEMC*, pp. 333-5. Lyric poem, Pap. Harris, 500, other E.trs., (e.g.) Erman & Blackman, *Literature of the Ancient Egyptians*, London, 1927 (& reprs.), p. 245; Faulkner, Wente, Simpson, *The Literature of Ancient Egypt*, 1972/73, pp. 299-300.

Thebes:- Remains, *PM²*, I & II. In general, C.F. Nims, *Thebes*, London, 1965. Poem is cited from Pap. Leiden I, 350, I:13ff. ('Ch.7'), hgl. J. Zandee, *Oudheidkundige Mededelingen ..* 28 (1947), pp. 9-10 & Bijlage I; E.tr., Erman & Blackman, *op.cit.*, p. 294.

Pi-Ramesse.:- Remains, cf. *PM*, IV, Ramesside material under Tanis, Qantir, Khataana. Excavations, M. Hamza, *ASAE* 30 (1930), pp. 31-68; S. Adam, *ASAE* 55 (1958), pp. 316-324, and 56 (1959), pp. 207-226. Study, area and remains, L. Habachi, *ASAE* 52 (1954), pp. 443-562. Geography, identification, cf. J. van Seters, *The Hyksos*, Yale, 1966, pp. 127ff., E.P. Uphill, *JNES* 27 (1968), pp. 299-316, and 28 (1969), pp. 15-39, and M. Bietak, *Tell Dab'a II*, Vienna, 1975; Bietak, *MDIK* 37 (1981), 68-71, and Eggebrecht, *ibid.*, pp. 139-142; M. Bietak, *Avaris and Pi-ramesse*, London 1981; cf. *END*. Lit. refs., Gardiner, *JEA* 5 (1918), pp. 127ff., 179ff., 242ff. Praise of Pi-Ramesse, *LEM*, pp. 12f., *LEMC*, pp. 37f. Year 8 stela (Manshiyet es-Sadr), A. Hamada, *ASAE* 38 (1938), pp. 217-230; *KRI*, II/7, pp. 360-2. Glazed decor, see W.C. Hayes, *Glazed Tiles from a Palace of Ramesses II at Kantir*, New York, 1937 (& repr.); H.W. Muller, *MDIK* 37 (1981), pp. 339-367, pls. 92-94. City layout, cf. *END*. Paser, Habachi, *op.cit.*, pp. 479f., pl.20. Lit. citations, *LEM*, 21ff., 49ff.; *LEMC*, 73ff., 198ff.

Chapter 7

Vizier Paser, career and monuments, Helck, *Verwaltung*, pp. 311-15, 447-51, No. 24, plus Cerny, *BiOr* 19 (1962), p. 142. Cf. *END*, while most of the inscriptions of Paser and other contempories of Ramesses II are collected in *KRI*, Vol. III. Letter of Mayor Ramose, Ostracon Berlin P. 11238, text in *Hieratische Papyrus, Königl. Museen zu Berlin*, III, Leipzig, 1911, pl. 32, and *KRI*, III/6, p.161; no modern tr. except that given here. Address to the vizier, in Tomb 106, R. Anthes, *Mélanges Maspero*, I, Cairo, 1935, pp. 155-163. Traditional Dyn. 18 text, E.tr., *BAR*, II, §§616-715. Tomb 106, *PM²*, I, 219ff.

Amen-em-inet, see above, under Ch.3. Dates, years 12, 27, see *END* Lawsuit, Irynofret *vs.* Nakhy, Gardiner, *JEA* 21 (1935), pp. 140ff; hgl., *KRI*, II/19-20, pp. 800-02. Hundred years' lawsuit of Mose, see Gardiner, 'Inscription of Mes', in K. Sethe (ed.), *Untersuchungen . . .*, IV, Leipzig, 1905 (& repr.), pp. 89-140, more fully republished by G.A. Gaballa, *The Tomb-Chapel of Mose*, Warminster, 1977, text, also *KRI*, III/14, pp 424-434. For Neshi under Kamose, cf. Posener, *RdE* 16 (1964), pp. 213-4. Mose's triumph, Anthes, *MDIK* 9 (1940), pl. 17; Gaballa, *op. cit.*

Land and domains, economic basis in Egypt: Sir A.H. Gardiner, *The Wilbour Papyrus*, I-IV, Oxford, 1940-52; W. Helck, *Materialien zur Wirtschaftsgeschichte des Neuen Reiches*, I, Wiesbaden, 1961, pp. 7ff.; Bernadette Menu, *Le régime juridique des terres et du personnel attaché à la terre dans le Papyrus Wilbour*, Lille, 1970, and in *Revue Historique de Droit français et étranger*, 1971 (No. 4), pp. 555-585.

Treasurers, cf. Helck, *Verwaltung*, pp. 408-9, 515-7, and *END*. Report by Panehsy, hgl. in Gardiner & Cerny, *Hieratic Ostraca*, I, Oxford, 1957, pls. 81-82, and *KRI*, III/5, pp. 138-140; tr., Helck, *Materialen zur Wirtschaftsgeschichte*, III, pp. 467-8. Suty's report on tomb-workmen's costs, Ostracon Berlin P. 12337, hgl., *Hieratische Papyrus, Museen zu Berlin*, III, pl. 31, and hgl., *KRI*, III/5, pp. 145-6. Irate taxpayer, cited from Papyrus Anastasi V, 27:3ff. (hgl., *LEM*, pp.71-2; E.tr., *LEMC*, pp. 273f.). Scandal, in Year 30, from Gardiner & Cerny, *Hieratic Ostraca*, I, pls. 74-75, and *KRI*, II/7, pp. 380-3; German tr., S. Allam, *Hieratische Ostraka und Papyri aus der Ramessidenzeit*, Tübingen, 1973, pp. 20-24. Papyri filed in boxes, Cerny, *Paper & Books in Ancient Egypt*, London, 1952, p. 30.

Viceroys, G. Reisner, *JEA* 6 (1920), pp. 38ff., 74ff.; *END*. The earthquake at Abu Simbel, cf. L.-A. Christophe, *Abou-Simbel*, Brussels, 1965, pp. 206-9. Viceroy Huy, former envoy, cf. L. Habachi, *Kush* 9 (1965), p. 220 and fig. 5. Autobiographical stela (VII) of Setau, see Kitchen, *Orientalia Lovaniensia Periodica* 6 (1975), pp. 295-302; hgl, *KRI*, III/3, pp.91-94. Stela IX of the officer Ramose, see J. Yoyotte, *Bulletin de la Société Française d'Egyptologie* 6 (1951), pp. 9-14; hgl, *KRI*, III/3, p. 95. Urhiya and Yupa, see under Ch.3 above. For Tjunuroy's king-list, cf. Wildung, *Die Rolle ägyptischer Könige*, I, 1969, p. 34f., pl.I. Simut's family, cf. Gardiner, *JEA* 24 (1938), p. 161:9,10. Letter concerning Iuny, Papyrus Cairo J. 58053, hgl., A.M. Bakir, *Egyptian Epistolography*, 1970, pl.1: *KRI*, I, p. 322. Egyptian army, see R.O. Faulkner, *JEA* 39 (1953), pp. 32-47; A.R. Schulman, *Egyptian Military Rank, Title & Organisation in the New Kingdom*, Berlin, 1964.

Schooling and students. Comprehensive study, H. Brunner, *Altägyptische Erziehung*, Wiesbaden, 1957. 'Satirical Letter' (Papyrus Anastasi I), cf. *ANET*, pp. 475-9. Word-lists or "onomastica", dealt with by Sir A. H.Gardiner, *Ancient Egyptian Onomastica*, I-III, Oxford, 1947 (& repr.). Miscellaneous documents for teaching, see (hgl) *LEM* and (E.tr.) *LEMC*. Citations ('be a scribe', etc.), cf. hgl., *LEM*, pp. 16, 27, 44, 47, 103, 107f., and E.tr., *LEMC*, pp. 50, 95ff., 168f., 182ff., 384ff. 400ff. Scope of opportunity, cf. Brunner, *Altäg. Erziehung*, pp. 40-42; Anhurmose, cf. H. Kees, *ZÄS* 73 (1938), pp. 79-81, and Brunner, *op.cit.*, p. 42.

Gracious living, cultural scene. Citations from Hardjedef and Aniy, cf. *ANET*, pp. 419-420. General information on life in ancient Egypt, cf. Posener, Sauneron and Yoyotte, *A Dictionary of Egyptian Civilization*, London, 1962; P. Montet, *Everyday Life in Egypt*, London, 1958; Montet, *Eternal Egypt*, London, 1964; H. & R. Leacroft, *The Buildings of Ancient Egypt*, Leicester, 1963; *BMMA* 31/3 (Spring, 1973), special issue, Nora Scott, *The Daily Life of the Ancient Egyptians*.

Tales and Tourism. Egyptian stories, see Simpson, Faulkner, and Wente, *The Literature of Ancient Egypt*, 1973/74, and M. Lichtheim, *Ancient Egyptian Literature*, I-III, California, 1973-80. Citations of the 'ancient authors', cf. *ANET*, pp. 432,476. Gallery of famous men, pictured in Simpson, Wente, Faulkner, *op.cit.*, fig.6 at end; hgl., *KRI*, III/16, pp. 492-4. Tourism around the pyramids, etc., cf. Helck, *Zeitschrift d. Deutschen Morgenländische Gesellschaft* 102 (1952), pp. 39-46; Wildung, *Die Rolle des Königs*, I, pp. 61ff. (Nashuyu, p. 72f.; Hednakht, p. 68); *KRI* III/5, p. 148, and III/14, p. 436. Paser in Thebes, cf. Herrmann, *Altägyptische Liebesdichtung*, p. 160 & n. Stories, see above. Love-poems, the §§ I to IV are newly-translated from the re-stored Cairo text now given by G. Posener, *Catalogue des Ostraca Hiératiques Littéraires de Deir el Medineh*, II, Fasc. 3, Cairo, 1972, pls. 74-79a; in §§V-VII, an improved text is newly translated from the same source. (Older versions, even down to 1973/74, are outdated by the new publication).

Chapter 8

Initial citations, stela from Abydos (Gaballa, *BIFAO* 71 (1972), pp. 135-7), and combinations of many Middle-Kingdom stelae with a passage in 'The Shipwrecked Sailor' (cf. Simpson, Wente, Faulkner, *op.cit.*, p. 55).

Temples and worship in them. H.W. Fairman, 'Worship and Festivals in an Egyptian Temple', *Bulletin, John Rylands Library* 37 (1954), pp. 165-203. Daily ritual, based on Abydos-temple of Sethos I, see A.R. David, *A Guide to Religious Ritual at Abydos*, Warminster, 1981. Citation of 'partakers of the altar', St. Paul's 1st Letter to the Corinthians 9:13. Priests, cf. S. Sauneron, *The Priests of Ancient Egypt*, New York & London, 1960; H. Kees, *Das Priestertum im ägyptischen Staat*, Leiden, 1953/58. Role of ladies in the cult, cf. A.M. Blackman, *JEA* 9 (1921), pp. 9-30. Domains, cf. Papyrus Wilbour, etc., cited under Chapter 7. For the great papyrus Harris (Ramesses III-IV), hgl., W. Erichsen, *Papyrus Harris I*, Brussels, 1933; note and refs. for its interpretation, Gardiner, *JEA* 27 (1941), p. 72f.

The gods of Egypt. For them and Egyptian religion, cf. such works as J. Černý, *Ancient Egyptian Religion*, London, 1952; S. Morenz, *Egyptian Religion*, London, 1973; H. Bonnet, *Reallexikon der Ägyptischen Religionsgeschichte*, Berlin, 1952.

Rites, hymns, theology. Mut's morning-hymn is cited from (hgl) in Benson and Gourlay, *The Temple of Mut in Asher*, London, 1899, p. 314. That for Amun comes from the Chester Beatty papyri, cf. Gardiner, *British Museum Hieratic Papyri, 3rd Series*, London, 1935, Vol. I, p. 96, Vol. II, pl. 55. Spell for door-bolt, hgl., Calverley, *Temple of King Sethos I, Abydos*, II, pl. 14, top right; E.tr., cf. A.R. David, *Religious Ritual at Abydos*, p. 96, Scene 4. Festival-offerings, food, rite of Ancestors, for Amun, cf. Gardiner, *op. cit.*, I. pp. 92, 94, 95. Hymn to Amun-Re-Atum-Horus, cf. *ibid.*, pp. 32-34; other such hymns, cf. *ANET*, pp. 365-372. Creation-accounts, etc., see general works on Eg. religion already cited, and J. Yoyotte in *Sources Orientales*, I, Paris, 1959.

Festivals. Survey-lists, S. Schott, *Altägyptische Festdaten*, Wiesbaden, 1950; days of holiday, cf. Helck, *Journal of Economic & Social History of the Orient* 7 (1964), pp. 136-166. Osiris-'mysteries', cf. H. Schäfer, in Sethe (ed.), *Untersuchungen . . .* , IV, 1904, pp. 47-86; Festival of Sokar, see Gaballa and Kitchen, *Orientalia* 38 (1969), pp. 1-76. Ritual drama of Horus at Edfu, see H.W. Fairman, *The Triumph of Horus*, London, 1974. Song of Festival of Opet, hgl., *Urk IV*, p. 2038:13ff.; German tr., Helck, *Urkunden, 18. Dyn., Deutsch*, Berlin, 1961, p. 370. Festival of the Valley, see S. Schott, *Das schöne Fest vom Wustentale*, Wiesbaden, 1952, with citation of Paser, pp. 95-6, No. 10 (*KRI*, III/1, p.6). Hymn to Amun, cf. *ibid.*, p. 92. Endowments (in 'calendars') for festivals, cf. most conveniently H.H. Nelson, U. Hölscher, S. Schott, *Work in Western Thebes 1931-33*, Chicago, 1934; the Ramesseum calendar of feasts was copied at Medinet Habu (hgl., Epigraphic Survey, *Medinet Habu III*, Chicago, 1934; *KRI*, V/2-3, 1972, pp. 115-184).

Servants of the Gods: outstanding high priests, and others. For Heliopolis, cf. M.I. Moursi, *Die Hohenpriester des Sonnengottes . . .* , Berlin, 1972, pp. 56-72. For sequences of high priests, in Abydos, etc., see *END*. Year-dates of Wennufer at Abydos, cf. (hgl.) Maciver and Mace, *El Amrah and Abydos*, London, 1902, pl. 34; his prayer for Ramesses II, Petrie, *Abydos II*, 1903, p. 45f., pl. 38; hgls., *KRI*, III pp. 447-460. On Wennufer's family, cf. G.A. Gaballa in J. Ruffle, G.A. Gaballa, K.A. Kitchen (eds.), *Glimpses of Ancient Egypt* (*Studies . . . Fairman*), Warminster, 1979. p. 46. Sequence and date of high priests of Amun, see *END*. High Priest Bakenkhons, from Year 39, cf. M.L. Bierbrier, *JEA* 58 (1972), p. 303 (basic dates of his career); Munich statue, most recent edition, M. Plantikow-Münster, *ZAS* 95 (1969), pp. 117-135; E.tr., *BAR*, III §§ 563-8; hgls., *KRI*, III pp. 293-300. For Hatiay, see refs. for Urhiya and Yupa, Ch.3. For Nakht-Thuty, see Kitchen, *JEA* 60(1974), pp. 168-174; hgl., *KRI*, III, pp.348-353. Portal of Baky, cf. (hgl.) *LEM*, p. 10, (E.tr.) *LEMC*, pp. 28, 29-30; Year 46 case, Helck, *Journal of American Research Center in Egypt* 2 (1963), pp. 65-73; hgl, *KRI*, II, pp. 803-6. For Simut-Kyky, cf. latterly, J.A. Wilson, *JNES* 29 (1970), pp. 187-192; hgl., *KRI*, III 331-345. Citation from Roma-roy, cf. G. Lefebvre, *Inscriptions concernant . . . Romê-röy et Amenhotep*, Paris, 1929, pp. 23-24; hgl., *KRI*, IV/7, p. 209.

On 'deity' of kings, cf. G. Posener, *De la Divinité du Pharaon*, Paris, 1960; kingship and important rites, H.W.Fairman in S.H. Hooke (ed.), *Myth, Ritual & Kingship*, Oxford, 1958, pp. 74-104. Ramesses II, see L. Habachi, *Features of the Deification of Ramesses II*, Glückstadt, 1969, and cf. D. Wildung, *Orientalistische Literaturzeitung* 68 (1973), 549-565. Refs. for statue-cults, cf. also M. El-Alfi, *JEA* 58 (1972), pp. 179-180. The deity of West-Theban memorial-temples, cf. H.H. Nelson, *JNES* 1 (1942), pp. 127ff., esp. 151-5 (on Ramesses III, but valid also for Ramesses II). Royal chapels elsewhere are noted in the lists of Helck, *Materialien zur Wirtschaftsgeschichte des Neuen Reiches*, I, II.

Jubilees. Relation of jubilee to regnal years under Amenophis III, see C. van Siclen, *JNES* 32 (1973), pp 290-300. Jubilees of Ramesses II, see L. Habachi, *ZAS* 97 (1971), pp. 64ff. High Nile, Gardiner & Černý, *Hieratic Ostraca*, I, pl. 9 (hgl.); the abandoned sandals, ODM 446 in Černý, *OHNL*, V, pl. 27 (hgl.). Jubilees, all texts, *KRI*, II, pp. 377-398, 428-431. General study, E. Hornung, E. Staehelin, *Studien zum Sedfest*, Geneva, 1974.

Chapter 9

Citation on peasant and taxmen, Papyrus Anastasi V, *LEM*, p. 64f., E.tr., *LEMC*, p. 247. Tale of the Two Brothers, cf. (e.g.) Simpson, Wente, Falkner, *Literature of Ancient Egypt*, pp. 92-107. Cow-names and grass, W. Guglielmi, *Reden, Rufe und Lieder auf altägyptischen Darstellungen der Landwirtschaft, Viehsucht (etc.) . . .*, Bonn, 1973, pp. 23, No. 16, 99, n. 303. Wild-cow strike, *ibid.*, p. 24; Baud & Drioton, *Le Tombeau de Panehsy*, pp. 44, 49, fig. 23.

The Workmen of Pharaoh : Deir el Medina. Simple outline, J. Černý, *CAH*³, II/2, 1975, Chapter 35, § III, pp. 620-6. Fuller account, J. Černý, *A Community of Workmen at Thebes in the Ramesside Period*, Cairo, 1973, and *The Valley of the Kings*, Cairo, 1973. Economy of Deir el-Medina, see J.J. Janssen, *Commodity Prices from the Ramessid Period*, Leiden, 1975; new overall survey of life at Deir el-Medina, M.L. Bierbrier, *Tomb Builders of Pharaoh*, London, 1982. Excavations at Deir el Medina, B. Bruyère, *Rapport sur les Fouilles de Deir el Médineh*, Cairo, 17 volumes in 19, 1924-53; scattered monuments, also *PM*², I/2. Ostraca, Černý, *OHNL*, 6 parts, Sauneron, 1 part, plus Posener, *Catalogue des Ostraca Hiératiques Littéraires . . .*, 2 vols., all Cairo, 1935-73; Černý, *Ostraca Hiératiques (Musée du Caire)*, 2 vols.; Daressy, *Ostraca*; Gardiner & Černý, *Hieratic Ostraca*, I, 1957, and many scattered studies. Graffiti of workmen, W. Spiegelberg, *Ägyptische . . . Graffiti aus der Thebanischen Nekropolis*, 2 vols., Heidelberg, 1921; J. Černý, *Graffiti de la Nécropole Thébaine*, Cairo, 1956; J. Černý, A.A. Sadek, et alii, *Graffiti de la Montagne Thébaine*, Sections I to IV, Cairo, 1968ff., in progress. Classified hgl. data, *KRI*, III, pp. 508-844.

The village, cf. Bruyère, *Rapport . . . 1934-35, III, Le Village*, Cairo, 1939; 'the village' in Egyptian, Černý, *Community*, p. 92, n.1. Its personnel, cf. Černý, *CAH* and *Community, passim*. Candle-grease, not to be eaten, Černý, *Valley of Kings*, p. 46. Use of lamp-wicks in tombs, *ibid.*, pp. 43ff.; account cited, hgl., Černý, *Ostraca Hieratiques*, under C. 25813, and *KRI*, III/18, p. 569.

Work. Nebneteru's letter, *ODM* 119 in *OHNL* (hgl.) and *KRI*, III/17, p. 538. Khay's letter, cf. Grdseloff, *ASAE* 40 (1940), p. 534, hgl., *KRI*, III/17, p. 542. Pabaki on Ib the oaf, *ODM* 328 in *OHNL*, and *KRI*, III/17, p. 535. On the scribe Ramose, see Černý, *Community*, pp. 317 ff.; 'richest man', cited from Černý, *Egyptian Stelae in the Bankes Collection*, Oxford, 1958, under No. 4; hgl., *KRI*, III/20, p. 620. Link with vizier Paser, cf. Černý, *Community*, p. 319, n.2. Scribe Qen-hir-khopshef, see *ibid.*, pp. 329ff. Letter of Prehotep, *ODM* 303 in *OHNL* (hgl. and *KRI*, III/17, p. 534); E.tr., also Černý, *Community*, p.337. Letters of Siamun and Anhur-khaw, hgl., Gardiner et al., *Theban Ostraca*, London, 1913, Ostr. Toronto A.11, Letters I & III; *KRI*, III/2, pp. 40-41, 43-44; on minerals, cf. J.R. Harris, *Lexicographical Studies in Ancient Eg. Minerals*, Berlin, 1961. Khay's reply: *ODM* 114 in *OHNL*, and *KRI*, III/2, pp. 45-46. The 'work-sheet' of Year 40, hgl., Gardiner & Černý, *Hieratic Ostraca*, I, 1957, pls. 83-84, and *KRI*, III/17, pp. 515-525. Laundry dispute, *ODM* 314 in *OHNL*, IV, pl. 21 (hgl.), and *KRI*, III/17, p. 537. Letters of Nub-hir-maat and Wernuro, *ODM* 117 and 560 (Černý, *OHNL*, II, pl.3; Sauneron, *OHNL*, pl. 7; *KRI*, III/17, p.539). Man without wife, *ODM* 439, *OHNL*, V,Pl 26.

Recreation, Law, Religion. Four days' feasting, from Ostracon Cairo 25234, cf. Černý, *BIFAO* 27 (1927), p. 183f.; column-base, *ibid.*, 194f, and *KRI*, III/22, p. 682. Gift by Pasaro, *ODM* 127 (hgl., *OHNL*, II, pl.8; *KRI* III/18, p. 557; German tr., Allam, *Hieratische Ostraka und Papyri, Ramessidenzeit,* 1973, pp. 97-8). Oracle with Amenmose, cf. latterly, Černý in R.A. Parker, *A Saite Oracle Papyrus*, Providence, 1962, p. 42; hgl., *KRI*, III/13, pp. 395-6. Ramose's praise of Mut, Černý, *Egyptian Stelae, Bankes Collection*, 1958, under No. 3; *KRI*, III/20, pp. 619-620. Thank-offering of Nebre, cf. Gunn, *JEA* 3(1916), pp. 83ff.; hgl., *KRI*, III/21, pp. 635-55. Nefer-abu, Gunn, p. 88f; *KRI*, III/25, pp. 771-2. Artificial bouquets of flowers, cf. Bruyère, *Rapport . . . Fouilles . . . 1934-35, Le Village,* 1939, p. 323, fig. 193. Amun as vizier of the poor, see now G. Posener, 'Amon, Juge du Pauvre', in *Beiträge zur Ägyptischen Bauforschung und Altertumskunde, Heft 12 (Festschrift für H. Ricke)*, Wiesbaden, 1971, pp. 59-63. Funeral of Harmose, *ODM* 126 in *OHNL*, and *KRI*, III/17, p. 532; see M.A. Green, *Orientalia* 45 (1976), 395-409.

Chapter 10

The closing years. The titles 'God, Ruler of Heliopolis', are attested from Years 42, 53, 56 of the reign, cf. Yoyotte and Anthes in Anthes (ed.), *Mitrahineh 1956*, Philadelphia, 1965, pp. 66-70. The epithet 'Great Soul of Re-Harakhte' for the Delta Residence appears from Year 52, on ostraca from there, cf. Hamza, *ASAE* 30 (1930), p. 44, and Helck, *Verwaltung*, p. 27.

Death of Ramesses II. His reign is given as 66 years and 2 months by Josephus (*Contra Apionem*. I, 15/16 § 97), citing Manetho (W.G. Waddell, *Manetho*, Loeb Ed., 1948, pp. 102/3, cf. other sources, *ibid.*, pp. 108/9, § 16). Two months after 3rd Shomu 27 (June) would fall well into 1st Akhet (Inundation), August, agreeing with evidence for the accession of Merenptah within the period 1st Akhet, 18 to 2nd Akhet, 13 (cf. Helck, in *Studia Biblica et Orientalia III: Oriens Antiquus,* Rome, 1959, pp. 120-1. Other references, cf. Ch. 4, above)

On mummification, cf. R. Engelbach (ed.), *Introduction to Egyptian Archaeology*, Cairo, 1946 (& repr., 1962), Chapter-section by D.E. Derry. For the funerary wealth of a pharaoh such as Ramesses II, the sumptuous burial of young Tutankhamun remains our only detailed indication. On Egyptian funerary beliefs, cf. standard handbooks, e.g. S. Morenz, *Egyptian Religion*.

1973. Pyramid Texts, convenient E. tr., R.O. Faulkner, *The Ancient Egyptian Pyramid Texts*, Oxford, 1969. Coffin Texts, likewise, by R.O. Faulkner, *The Ancient Egyptian Coffin Texts*, I - III, Warminster, 1974-78. Book of the Dead, E.trs., T.G. Allen, *The Egyptian Book of the Dead*, Chicago, 1960, and R.O. Faulkner, *The Book of the Dead*, New York, 1972. French, P. Barguet, *Le Livre des Morts*, Paris, 1967.

Tomb and destiny of Ramesses II. Overall survey of the great royal funerary compositions, E. Hornung, *Ägyptische Unterweltsbücher*, Zurich, 1972. Am Duat, E. Hornung, *Das Amduat*, I - III, Wiesbaden, 1963-67. Litany of Re (E.tr.), A. Piankoff, *The Litany of Re*, New York, 1964. Book of the Heavenly Cow, cf. in Piankoff, *The Shrines of Tut-ankh-amun*, New York, 1955 (pb. 1962). The Book of Gates, cf. J. Zandee, 'The Book of Gates' in *Liber Amicorum (Studies . . . C.J. Bleeker)*, Leiden, 1969, pp. 282-324. Plan of Tomb 7 (R.II), in *PM²*, I/2. Terminology in royal tombs, cf. Černý, *Valley of the Kings*, pp. 23-24. Tombs in Valley of Kings, see. J. Romer, *Valley of the Kings*, London 1981.

Chapter 11

Late 19th Dynasty, monuments, cf. *GLR*, pp. 113-148. Succession after Merenptah, cf. Gardiner, *JEA* 44 (1958), pp. 12-22; J. Vandier, *RdE* 23 (1971), pp. 165-191, which does not account for the data in Helck, *Studia Biblica et Orientalia III*, 1959, pp. 121-4, while adding other valuable data; cf. *END*. That Amenmesses' reign may have been a short rival regime in the South within the reign of Sethos II (directly following Merenptah) has been argued by R. Krauss, *Studien zur Altägyptischen Kultur* 4 (1976), pp. 161-199, and 5 (1977), pp. 131-174. Libyan and Nubian wars, Merenptah, cf. Kitchen, *Ägypten und Kusch,* 1977, pp. 221-4. Inscriptions of Merenptah, *KRI*, IV, 1968 & ff. (hgl.), and *BAR* §§ 569-617 (E.trs.). Hgl. texts, Merenptah to Tewosret, see *KRI*, IV.

Twentieth Dynasty. Setnakht, cf. Papyrus Harris, historical section, e.g. E. tr., *ANET*, p. 260; new stela, *MDIK* 28 (1972), pp. 193-200, pl. 49. Cf. R. Drenkhahn, *Die Elephantine-Stele des Sethnacht und ihr historischer Hintergrund*, Wiesbaden, 1980. Outlines for Ramesses III and his successors, cf. Černý, *CAH³*, II/2, 1974, and Faulkner, *ibid,* Chapters 23 and 35; royal family, Kitchen, *JEA* 68 (1982), 116-125.

Late-Period Egypt, c. 1100 to 650 B.C. (beginning of Saite Revival), see K.A. Kitchen, *The Third Intermediate Period in Egypt (1100-650 B.C.)*, Warminster, 1972, which establishes the basic chronology of the entire epoch, and includes (Part IV, pp. 243-408) a concise but comprehensive historical narrative survey; cf. also M.L.Bierbrier, *The Late New Kingdom in Egypt*, Warminster, 1975, and (on art) B.V. Bothmer, *Egyptian Sculpture of the Late Period*, Brooklyn, 1973. The Saite kings and Egypt versus Persia, cf. F.K. Kienitz, *Die politische Geschichte Ägyptens vom 7. bis zum 4. Jahrhundert vor der Zeitwende*, Berlin, 1953, and standard histories, e.g. Sir A.H. Gardiner, *Egypt of the Pharaohs*, Oxford, 1962 (& reprs.). For Ptolemaic, Roman and Byzantine Egypt, cf. later volumes of *CAH*. Re-discovery of the royal mummies, a story often told; e.g. L. Cottrell, *The Lost Pharaohs*, London, 1950 (& reprs.), Ch. 10, or J.A. Wilson, *Signs and Wonders upon Pharaoh*, Chicago, 1964, pp. 81-85.

Chapter 12

Ramesses II in his own Time. Sources, cf. Ch. 1-11 above. In Later Tradition. Prayer of Ramesses IV, E.tr., *BAR*, IV, § 471; hgl., *KRI*, VI/1, 1969, p. 19; cf. Karnak fragment, Helck, *CdE* 38 (1963), pp. 39-40, and *KRI*, VI/2, p. 42. Ramesses-Psusennes, Kitchen, *Third Interm. Period*, p. 263, refs. 'Blurb' of magical papyrus, cf. W. Erichsen, *Neue Demotische Erzählung*, Mainz, 1956, p. 51. Late graffiti at colossi, Abu Simbel, cf. Christophe, *Abou-Simbel*, 1965, pp. 67-72. Stela of Khons the Plan-maker ('Bentresh Stela'), cf. E.tr. & refs., *ANET*, pp. 29-30; hgl., *KRI*, II/5, 1971, pp. 284-7. The Demotic tales of Setne-Khaemwaset, F. Ll. Griffith, *Stories of the High Priests of Memphis*, Oxford, 1900, 2 vols.

Biblical tradition, cf. Ch.4, under the Exodus. For the chronographers (using Manetho), cf. W.G. Waddell, *Manetho*, Loeb Ed., 1948. Herodotus deals with Egypt in his Book II (many editions available). For Diodorus Siculus and the Ramesseum with 'Osymandyas', cf. C.H. Oldfather, *Diodorus of Sicily, I*, Loeb Ed., 1946, and Anne Burton, *Diodorus Siculus, Book I, A Commentary*, Leiden, 1972, (weak on Ramesseum); interesting is Ph. Derchain, in S. Schott (ed.), *Göttinger Vorträge*, Göttingen, 1965, pp. 165-171, and best for Ramesseum is W. Helck, in P. Zazoff (ed.), *Opus Nobile (Festschrift . . . Ulf Jantzen)*, Wiesbaden, 1969, pp. 68-76. For Sesostris being basically the 12th-Dynasty kings (rather than Ramesses II), see the excellent monograph long since, by K. Sethe, 'Sesotris' in his *Untersuchungen*, II, Leipzig, 1900 (& repr.). Pliny and Tacitus, cf. Sethe, *op,cit.*, p. 5. Abbess Aetheria, quoted (e.g.) by E. Naville, *The Shrine of Saft el Henneh & the Land of Goshen*, London, 1888, pp. 17, 19.

Ramesses Today. Early travellers, cf. the entertaining outline of L. Greener, *The Discovery of Egypt*, London 1966; a full series is now being edited by the Institut Français d'Archéologie Orientale, Cairo, Egypt. On the whole subject of interaction between Western Europe and its civilization (old and new) and Ancient Egypt, see S. Morenz, *Die Begegnung Europas mit Ägypten*, Berlin, 1968, which contains useful background and further references for this wide subject. For Champollion, his decipherment, and the role of Ramesses II's cartouches, cf. F.Ll. Griffith, *JEA* 37 (1951), pp. 42-43; Sir A.H. Gardiner, *Egyptian Grammar*[3], 1957, p. 15. Aida, cf. Morenz, *op. cit.*, pp. 178-9. The translated quotations from Rosellini and Bunsen may be found in Miss A.B. Edwards, *A Thousand Miles Up the Nile*, London, 1877 ed., 411-412 & n.; citation of her own view, *ibid.*, pp. 385,413. Initial appeal over saving Abu Simbel, etc., cf. Christophe, *Abou-Simbel*, 1965, Ch. VII. For the research-background to the *Ten Commandments* (in which Ramesses II was played by Yul Brynner), see H.S. Noerdlinger, *Moses and Egypt*, Los Angeles, 1956. The comic strip 'Ramesses', formerly in the *Bournemouth Evening Echo*, then in the *Southern Evening Echo*, Southampton; data, courtesy Mr. C.J. Bridger. Ramesses II, medically conserved in Paris, cf. Z.L. Balout, *Le Courrier du CNRS 28* (April 1978), pp. 36-42. General survey of Ramesses II and his time (special exhibition), cf. CH. Desroches-Noblecourt, et alii, *Ramses le Grand*, Paris, 1976.

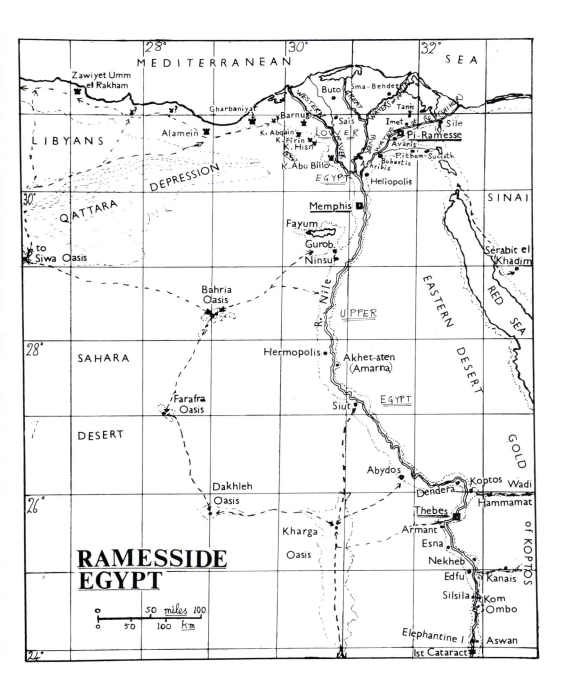

MEDITERRANEAN   SEA

28°   30°   32°

Zawiyet Umm
el Rakham
                                    Buto   Sma-Behdet
                                                    Tanis
          Gharbaniyat   Sais   Imet
LIBYANS   Barnug   Buto   Sile
          Alamein   K.Abqain   Pi-Ramesse
                     K.Firin   Avaris
                     K.Hisn   P.thom-Succoth
                                    Bubastis
                     K.Abu Billo   Athribis
                     EGYPT   Heliopolis

DEPRESSION   SINAI

30°
QATTARA   Memphis

to   Fayum
Siwa Oasis   Gurob   Serabit el
                        Ninsu   Khadim

                                              EASTERN

           Bahria
           Oasis   R. Nile

                                    UPPER

28°
SAHARA   Hermopolis   Akhet-aten   DESERT
                                 (Amarna)

           Farafra   Siut   EGYPT
           Oasis   GOLD
DESERT

                                    Abydos   Koptos Wadi
           Dakhleh   Dendera   Hammamat
26°   Oasis
                                    Thebes

                    Kharga   Armant   OF
                    Oasis   Esna
                                   Nekheb
RAMESSIDE   Edfu   Kanais
EGYPT   Silsila Kom
                                           Ombo
      0   50 miles 100
      0 50 100 km   Elephantine I Aswan
24°   1st Cataract

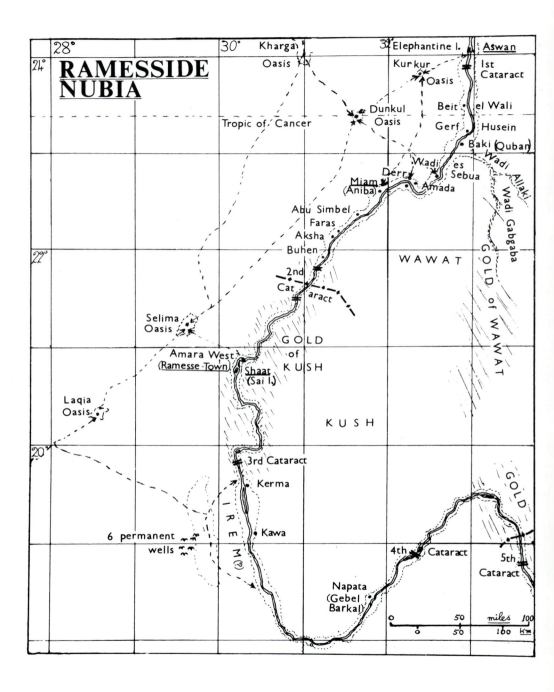

RAMESSIDE NUBIA

28°
30°
32°

24°

Kharga
Oasis

Elephantine I.
Aswan

Kurkur
Oasis

Ist
Cataract

Tropic of Cancer

Dunkul
Oasis

Beit el Wali

Gerf Husein

Baki (Quban)

Wadi es Sebua

Derr

Amada

Wadi Allaki

Wadi Gabgaba

Miam
(Aniba)

Abu Simbel

Faras

Aksha

Buhen

WAWAT

GOLD of WAWAT

22°

2nd
Cataract

Selima
Oasis

GOLD
of
KUSH

Amara West
(Ramesse-Town)

Shaat
(Sai I.)

Laqia
Oasis

KUSH

20°

3rd Cataract

Kerma

IREM (?)

6 permanent
wells

Kawa

4th Cataract

5th
Cataract

GOLD

Napata
(Gebel
Barkal)

0   50   miles   100
0   50   160   km

262

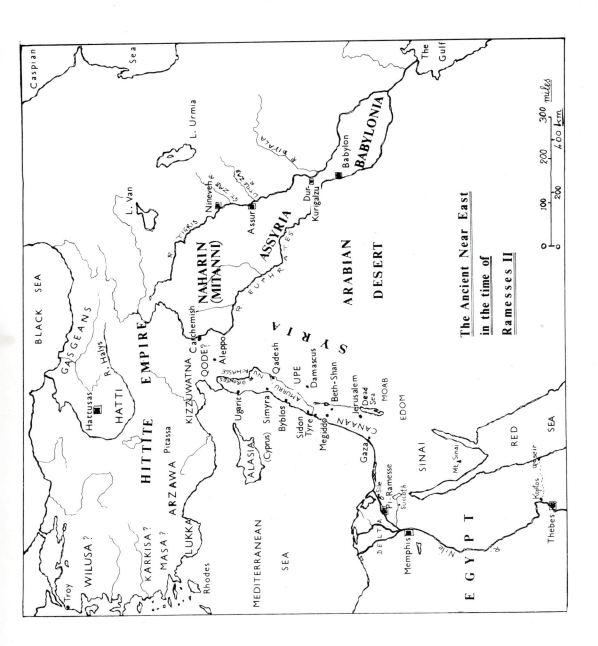

The Ancient Near East
in the time of
Ramesses II

263

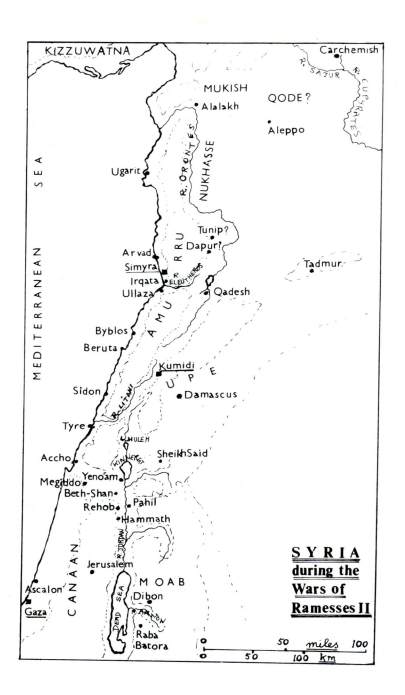

KIZZUWATNA

Carchemish

MUKISH

QODE?

• Alalakh

• Aleppo

MEDITERRANEAN SEA

Ugarit

Tunip?

Dapur?

Arvad

Simyra

Irqata

Ullaza

Byblos

Beruta

Sidon

Tyre

Accho

Megiddo

Yenoam

Beth-Shan

Rehob

Jerusalem

Ascalon

Gaza

Qadesh

Tadmur

Kumidi

Damascus

SheikhSaid

Pahil

Hammath

M O A B

Dibon

Raba

Batora

SYRIA
during the
Wars of
Ramesses II

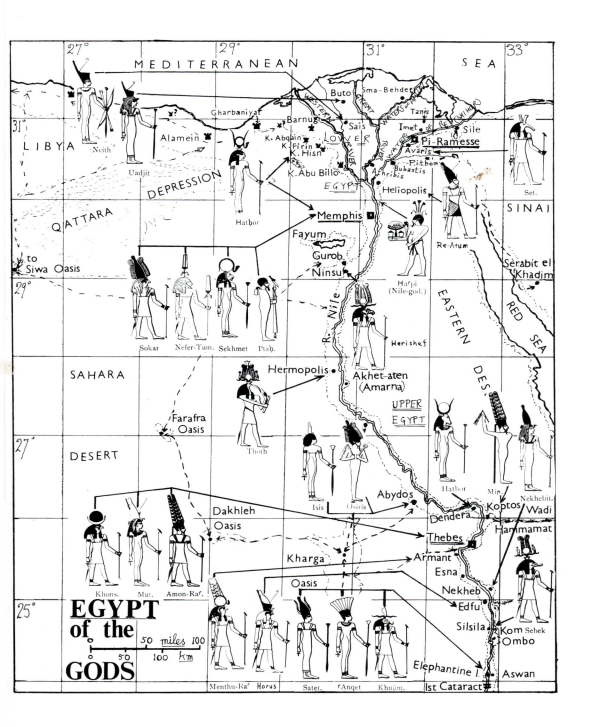

MEDITERRANEAN SEA

27° 29° 31° 33°

LIBYA

Neith

Uadjit

Gharbaniyat

Alamein

K. Abqain
K. Firin
K. Hisn
K. Abu Billo

Buto
Sma-Behdet
Sais
Barnugi
Imet
Tanis
Sile
Pi-Ramesse
Avaris
Pithom
Bubastis
Athribis
Heliopolis

Set.

QATTARA DEPRESSION

Hathor

LOWER EGYPT

SINAI

to
Siwa Oasis

29°

Sokar   Nefer-Tum. Sekhmet Ptah.

Memphis

Fayum

Gurob
Ninsu

Re-Atum

Harpi
(Nile-god.)

Herishef

Serabit el
Khadim

RED SEA

SAHARA

Farafra
Oasis

Thoth

Hermopolis

Akhet-aten
(Amarna)

UPPER
EGYPT

EASTERN DESERT

27°

DESERT

Isis   Osiris

Abydos

Hathor   Min.   Nekhebit.

Khons.   Mut.   Amon-Raʿ.

Dakhleh
Oasis

Kharga

Oasis

Dendera
Koptos
Wadi
Thebes
Armant
Esna
Nekheb
Edfu
Silsila
Hammamat

Kom
Ombo
Sebek

25°

EGYPT
of the
GODS

50 miles 100
0   50
100 km

Menthu-Raʿ Horus   Satet.   ʿAnqet   Khnum.

Elephantine I.   Aswan

1st Cataract

265

INDEX

The following simple abbreviations will be used in the body of the Index: ch - chief; drtsm - draughtsman-painter; gdss - goddess; HP - high priest of . . . ; kg - king; pr - prince; prss - princess; qu - queen; R. - Ramesses; S. - Sethos; VNb - Viceroy of Nubia; Vzr - Vizier; wkm - workman.

Aaron, 231
Abqain, (Kom el), 71
Abshek, rock of, 65
Abu Billo, 71
Abu Hamed, 5
Abu Simbel, site, 65; twin temples, 65f; inauguration, 99f.; sunrise at, 99f.; earthquake at, 135 f.; cults, 177; Late Period, 227; Great Temple rediscovered, 232; rescued from high dam, 234f.
Abydos, 3, 7, 161; Temple of Sethos I, 25, 35, 36-37, 45f.; T. of Ramesses II, 37; visit by R.II, 45-47; Qadesh scenes, 65; Nubian war, 72; 161
Accho, 68
Adad-nirari I, kg, 63
Aetheria, 230
Africanus, 230
agriculture, 183-5
Ahmed Kamal, 223
Ahmose I, kg, 9; titles & R.I, 188, 224f.
Ahmose II, kg, 221
Aïda, 233
Akhenaten, kg, 3, 11-13, 15f, 18, 25, 51, 128, 175, 178; cf. Amenophis IV
Akhet-Aten, 11, 51
Akhmim, 161
Aksha, area, 65; temple & cult, R.II, 44, 177
Akuyati, 49-50
Alamein, 72
Aleppo, 51, 54, 56, 68; prince of, emptied, 60, 61, 64
Alexander the Great, 222
Alexandria, 1
Ali Baba, 147
Amanus, mountains, 63
Amara West, ('R. the Town'), 5, 31, 44, 72
Amasis, kg, 221
Am-Duat, book, 211-13
Amenemhat I, kg, 8
Amenemhat III, kg, 8
Amen-em-inet, official, 28, 44, 65; later career, 126, 141; family, 135, 170, 171

Amenemope, VNb, 28, 31, 40, 44
Amenemopet, HP of Re, 170
Amenemope, Tomb scribe, 191
Amenemope, satirised, 142
Amenemwia, wkm, 196
Amen-hir-khopshef, pr, 67, 71, 102; later pr, 227; cf. Amen-hir-wonmef
Amen-hir-wonmef, pr, 39, 40, 67, 102; cf. Amen-hir-khopshef
Amenhotep, scholar, 140
Amenmesses, kg, 216
Amenmose, ch of harim, 105
Amenmose, priest, 200
Amenophis I, kg, reign, 9; patron at D. el Medina, 186, 199-200; tomb, 210
Amenophis II, kg, 10, 11, 211
Amenophis III, kg, 10-11, 15, 16, 19, 97; statue-cults, 11, 44, 175, 177; model for S.I, 20, 25, 39; for R. II, 44; & harim, 84; jubilees, 178; temple ruined, 216
Amenophis IV, kg, 11, 175; see also Akhenaten
Amen-re, god, see Amun
Amen-wah-su, rel. to S.I, 28
Amen-wah-su, drtsm, 139
Ammon, 67
Amun, Amen-re, god, 4, 9, 10; tensions in state, 11; priests (Dyn. 18), 11; restored, 14f, 16f; with R.I.S.I, 19; oracle, 44; Abu Simbel, 66; at Memphis, 115; wealth, 131f.; nature, 159; W.Thebes, 175f; army-div., 22, 53, 54, 56, 60; barge, 24, 25; animals, 162; feasts, 8, 10, 168-9; D. el Medina, 210f., 203
Amurru, province, 10, 16; kingdom, 13, 24; under S.I., 25; under R.II, 51, 60, 68
Anath, gdss, 161, 177
Anhur (-Shu), god, 46, 161, 170, 171
Anhur-khaw, ch. wkm, 188, 191, 196
Anhurmose, HP in Thinis, 145, 170
Aniba (Miam), 5
Ankhsenamun, qu, 15

Anti-Lebanon, mountains, 22, 53
Anubis, god, 160
Anuy, wkm, 197
Apehty, wkm, 199
Apiru, 22, 70
Apis bulls, cult & burial, 103-6, 162; temple, 105-6
Apopi, kg, 9
Apries, kg, 221
Archaic Period, 8
Armant, 161
army, Egyptian, 140f., 144f
Arnon, 67
Arnuwandas III, kg, 215
arsenal, at Memphis, 115
Artaxerxes III, kg, 222
artificial flowers, 203
Ascalon, 215
Asha-hebsed, official, 28, 30, 66. 111, 139
Ashteroth-Qarnaim, 24, 67f.
Ashtoreth, gdss, 161
Assyria, 10, 13, 220, 221
Astarte, gdss, 115, 161
Aswan, 3, 4, 7, 36, 48, 108, 234
Atbara, river, 7
Aten, god, 11, 15, 16, 175
Atum, god, 19, 160, 178; cf. Re
Avaris, 3, 8, 9, 15; temple of Seth, 70, 120
Ay, kg, 15, 16
Aya, 83

Baal, god, 3, 115, 161
Babylon, 10, 73, 221
'Bactria', 230
Bak, Hp of Re, 170
Bakenkhons, Hp of Amun, as boy, 28; as priest, 44, 126, 139; as HP, 171-4; cf. Baky
Bakenranef, kg, 221
Bakhtan, 229, 230
Baki, ch. wkm, 38
Baki (Quban), 5, 161
Bakmut, 127f.
Baky, Portal of, 172; cf. Bakenkhons
Bast, gdss, 2, 159, 161, 162
Bay, official, 216, 226
Beirut, 5, 68

Biblical references